TOUCHSTONES

A BREAD LOAF ANTHOLOGY

The Bread Loaf Anthology of
Contemporary American Poetry,
edited by Robert Pack, Sydney
Lea, and Jay Parini, 1985.

The Bread Loaf Anthology of
Contemporary American Short
Stories, edited by Robert Pack
and Jay Parini, 1987.

The Bread Loaf Anthology of
Contemporary American Essays,
edited by Robert Pack and
Jay Parini, 1989.

Writers on Writing, edited by
Robert Pack and Jay Parini, 1991.

Poems for a Small Planet:
Contemporary American Nature Poetry,
edited by Robert Pack and
Jay Parini, 1993.

American Identities:
Contemporary Multicultural Voices,
edited by Robert Pack and Jay Parini, 1994.

Touchstones: American Poets
on a Favorite Poem, edited by Robert Pack and
Jay Parini, 1995.

EDITED BY

Robert Pack
Jay Parini

Touchstones

American Poets on a Favorite Poem

Middlebury College Press

Published by University Press of New England

Hanover and London

821.009
TOU

MIDDLEBURY COLLEGE PRESS

Published by University Press of New England

Hanover, NH 03755

© 1996 by the President and Fellows of Middlebury College

Printed in the United States of America

5 4 3 2 1

CIP data appear at the end of the book

Indeed there can be no more useful help for discovering what poetry belongs to the class of the truly excellent, and can therefore do us most good, than to have always in one's mind lines and expressions of the great masters, and to apply them as a touchstone to other poetry. —MATTHEW ARNOLD

CONTENTS

Introduction

Paul Valéry, the French poet-critic, once remarked in an essay on Victor Hugo that "all true poets must, at heart, be true critics as well." It is demonstrably the case that, in the English language, the major poets of each generation have often been major critics of their age as well. A brief glance at the history of criticism testifies boldly to this.

The first systematic and taste-defining critic in the English language was perhaps Ben Jonson, himself a major poet and playwright of the English Renaissance. After him came Samuel Johnson, arguably the greatest critic of them all. While Johnson was not himself an influential poet, his "Vanity of Human Wishes" (1749) can hardly be dismissed as a minor work. His ground-breaking *Lives of the Poets* remains a standard in the realm of critical writing. Certainly, his two great (if somewhat younger) contemporaries, John Dryden and Alexander Pope, were equally poets and critics, and their work (together with that of Johnson) defined the Augustan era. Pope's *Essay on Criticism* has the unique distinction of being central as both poem and critical text.

The two preeminent poet-critics of the Romantic era were Wordsworth and Coleridge, who set the tone for literary discourse in their time with the publication of *Lyrical Ballads* in 1798. T. S. Eliot later observed that major poets seek to establish the taste by which their work can be judged, and that was demonstrably true for these Romantics. Coleridge in particular set the parameters for the age in a variety of books and essays, including his *Biographia Literaria*, which might be called a grammar of the literary imagination. Coleridge, more than anyone before him, established the importance of psychology, aesthetics, and philosophy for critical work, and his influence has remained profound. Coleridge might well be considered the founder of what today would be called "modern criticism."

Wordsworth and Coleridge cleared a path for themselves with astonishing thoroughness, changing the taste of a generation brought up on poets such as Pope, Thomas Gray, William Collins, and George Crabbe. While Shelley and Keats, who belong to the second major wave of Romantic poets, did not spend as much time in the pursuit of critical writing as their Romantic predecessors did, they nevertheless left behind important work: Shelley in his famous defense of poetry, and Keats in his deeply thoughtful letters. In retrospect, the legacy of Romantic criticism, as embodied by the major poets of the era, has been astonishingly influential.

The two most powerful poets of the Victorian era, Tennyson and Browning, were not especially interesting as critics. The age, rather, was dominated by Matthew Arnold, a poet-critic whose influence reached far beyond his own time and whose concept of poetic "touchstones" has provided us with the title for this collection. His example was crucial to T. S. Eliot, who was certainly the most provocative and formative critic of this century. Only Ezra Pound, who was Eliot's close friend in the early days of the Modernist movement in poetry, exerted a comparable influence on the art of poetry, though Pound's influence was more practical and Eliot's more theoretical. W. B. Yeats, who wrote essays in defense of traditional forms and meters and placed himself in the visionary tradition of such poets as Blake, was equally powerful in helping to create the modern dialectic of debate about the function of literary art.

The line of mid-twentieth-century poets who also did important critical work is a long and distinguished one, and it includes writers as different in style and approach as John Crowe Ransom, W. H. Auden, Robert Penn Warren, Robert Graves, Yvor Winters, Louise Bogan, and Randall Jarrell. More recently, in America, many diverse voices and positions have emerged, proclaiming aesthetic or political stances.

Our basic assumption in *Touchstones* is that poets write criticism with a sensitivity to language that is intimately connected to their work as poets. Their critical writing is, for the most part, a by-product of their own private workshop. They write, as it were, from the inside, aware of the countless internal adjustments involved in wresting a poem from the virtual chaos of linguistic signs. They understand—perhaps more vividly than critics who do not themselves write poems—how poets necessarily feed on earlier poets, and how they inevitably attempt to redefine the tradition to make room for poems of the kind they would like to write. It could well be argued that poets are more "subjective" than critics who are purely scholars, but this would not be pejorative, since every reading is an attempt to marry one mind and linguistic sense with another to produce "meaning." The meanings thus "produced" will be necessarily various, even contradictory. Yet a counterargument can equally be defended: that poets, out of a generous respect for past achievement, can give themselves over to an appreciation of another poet's work that is free of any need to rationalize or protect their own poetic stance.

In the postwar era, the criticism written by poets has veered rather sharply from that written by scholars, forming what might be considered a separate tradition. This has something to do with the rise of criticism in the universities; indeed, a vast army of scholars graduated into the world of letters in the educational boom era that followed World War II. The professionalism of literary studies, which had once been ruled by critics in the old style of belle lettres, led inevitably to the development of an academic and highly technical language. The New Critics ushered in a new era when they began to write about "verbal icons" and "intentionality" with a passionate desire to sound scientific, if not schematic. Northrop Frye's famous *Anatomy of Criticism* became a handbook for future scholars, such as Harold Bloom, Geoffrey Hartman, Paul de Man, J. Hillis Miller, and others, who (perhaps unconsciously at first) wanted to make critical writing as central as the literature they supposedly sought to anatomize. With the rise of post-structuralism, critical writing became increasingly "professional" and, alas, technical. In the hands of many, it became jargon-ridden and woefully opaque. Criticism lost sight of the beloved Common Reader that Virginia Woolf once celebrated.

Contemporary American poets, however, have continued to write critical essays, even whole books of critical prose, that attempt to achieve a direct engagement with the texts that has been lost in the academy as theorizing about literature has taken precedence over the immediate response to the work of art itself. The poets whose essays appear here, we hope the reader will agree, are refreshingly free of jargon, "unprofessional," engaging, and often idiosyncratic in the best sense that the personality and sometimes the history of the poet-critic comes through without usurping the attention of the reader from the poem at hand.

For *Touchstones*, we invited sixty-five contemporary poets—some of them extremely well known, others less so—to choose a favorite poem written in the English language and to write a short essay in response to the text. As editors, we made some effort to ensure that our poet-critics chose a range of poets, from Chaucer through Seamus Heaney, both to allow for some historical sweep and to avoid repetition. We hope that the results will be as remarkably pleasing and informative to our readers as they are to us.

From Julia Alvarez's shrewd reading of Elizabeth Bishop's dazzling villanelle "One Art," to Paul Zimmer's delicate and personally historical response to John Clare, these essays are singularly unpredictable, witty, moving, and—almost always—celebratory. In most cases, the poets chose from the standard canon; Richard Wilbur, for example, chose to write on Tennyson's well-known "Ulysses," while Sydney Lea chose Keats's classic ode "To Autumn." Paul Mariani picks a central if often neglected poem by Hart Crane for reconsideration, while Carol Frost pushes to the heart of a classic poem by Dickinson, "Because I Could Not Stop for Death." J. D. McClatchy writes fetchingly about Alexander Pope, whom he considers one of the two or three greatest poets in the language, and Miller Williams daringly tackles Milton's famous sonnet on his blindness, bringing it to life in a way that will surprise readers who thought they understood everything about "When I Consider How My Light Is Spent." Erica Jong revisits a classic sonnet by Shakespeare with equal passion: "Each time I go back to the sonnets," she says, "I find something that seemed not to be there before." Her essay ends with a riveting question: "What is great poetry, after all, but the continuation of the human voice after death?"

Other poets have chosen to write about less familiar poets, but they do so with a passion that makes their choice appear central to the enterprise of writing. This is true of Marvin Bell's inventive and amusing piece on Henry Reed's "The Naming of Parts" and of Anthony Hecht's brilliant analysis of "Gaze Not on Swans," an obscure yet powerful poem of the Renaissance era that may have been written by Henry Noel (it is attributed elsewhere to William Strode, although Hecht argues against this provenance). Maxine Kumin writes about the allure of Housman's metrical music from a bodily perspective that will surprise and delight the reader.

Lesser-known poets whose work is brought forward with all the enthusiasm of the connoisseur are an Anglo-Saxon ballad (John Balaban), Fulke Greville (Steven Cramer), John Skelton (Thomas Swiss), and Frederick Goddard Tuckerman (Stephen Tapscott). In each of these cases, one comes away from the essay eager to dig out the *Collected Poems* of the poet in question and to search for other poems to peruse and treasure.

One unifying aspect of these essays is their tendency to frame an argument within the bounds of autobiography. These are, in the last analysis, pieces written by people about experiences in reading that have mattered to them, so it makes sense that literature and life will be seen to mesh closely. Linda Pastan, for example, is writing about Wallace Stevens's "The World as Meditation" when she says: "From the time in fourth grade when the *Odyssey* was narrated to us in weekly installments by a teacher who seemed to be making the story up as he went along, I have been half in love with Penelope." Nancy Willard begins her essay on a song from *The Tempest* like this: "I grew up near the thumb of a lost mitten floating on the big waters of Lake Michigan and Lake Erie—lost, because only a single mitten remained, the left one. Until I was fifteen I lived my entire life between these two lakes." Eventually, Willard arrives at the magical point in her life where, as a child, she decided to memorize the song that begins: "Full Fathom five thy father lies," and the poem is, as might be expected, associated with her own father in the essay. "I loved that song," she concludes, "because it reminded me of water in a place where water was precious and of change in a time when I did not yet know what time would make of me."

Though they turn their attention to the qualities of image, sound, or structure, of the poem itself, these readings are deeply personal; for the poet, reading is itself an existential act, a self-defining act; it is part of that larger exploration of the self in language without which there can be no poetry. As all poets know, previous poetry—as well as one's own historical experience—is the source of poetry: all poets must kneel at the sacred stream, Helicon, which is always sweet, deep, and nourishing.

Readers browsing through this collection will also see that poets-as-critics often venture into areas normally off-limits to more academic critics, areas of bold acknowledgment and of uncomfortable recognitions. Consider this closing paragraph by Donald Justice about Philip Larkin's "Coming." Justice writes:

It has been claimed for Larkin that he was never sentimental, never brutal. But the truth is that I find him both sentimental and brutal, though in different poems or at least in different parts of the same poem. The brutal side comes out in the later poems; the sentimental throughout his career, but most straightforwardly in some of the earlier poems, as in the one we have been considering. Irony, diffidence, skepticism, wit: not all of these together are enough to keep out a certain *unreasonableness of feeling*—the sentiment, the sentimentality—that keeps rising up out of Larkin's poems. Actually, it is what saves them. Doesn't everybody really know this?

Well, not everybody knows this, but there are lots of things that people ought to know that can be found in these pages. Matthew Arnold wrote: "Indeed, there can be no more useful help for discovering what poetry belongs to the class of the truly excellent, and can therefore do us most good, than to have always in one's mind lines and expressions of the great masters, and to apply them as a touchstone to other poetry." The poems chosen by our sixty-five poets, we hope, may serve as touchstones for an increasingly discerning reader. They have, in each case, become touchstones to the poets who write about them, an intimate part of their poetic enterprises, and something they were eager to share with the Common Reader, the more the merrier.

We have tried to include as many of the poems discussed by the poets in the volume as we could. Most of the poems published in the last fifty or so years remain in copyright, so we were not able to include them.

TOUCHSTONES

Elizabeth Bishop's "One Art"

The villanelle seems to me a nearly impossible form: at worst, a mother's nag that keeps coming back every time: *did you remember to wash your hands, did you put the milk back in the refrigerator, don't forget to turn off the lights and to wash your hands and put the milk back in the refrigerator;* at best, an incantory obsessive form. The villanelle is good for reviving the dead or dying, for casting spells, a form for chanting to ourselves as we journey through the baffling mysteriousness of our lives. ("Of those so close beside me, which are you?") As we read Dylan Thomas's villanelle, "Do Not Go Gentle into that Good Night," we find ourselves engaged in a ritualistic life chant for a dying man: "Rage, rage against the dying of the light." And reading Theodore Roethke's "The Waking," we put ourselves in a hypnotic iambic state, our breaths and heartbeats doing exactly what the poem tells them to do, "I wake to sleep and take my waking slow. / I learn by going where I have to go." Maybe part of the reason I consider this form so hard to master is that the masters whose villanelles exemplify the form used it in its high church style, and what my ear wants is something more informal, more conversational, more in the style of the mother's nag than of the high priest shaking his fist from his sad height.

What I love about Elizabeth Bishop's "One Art" is that it does just that. With its strong enjambments, heavy caesuras, and softer feminine rhymes, this villanelle has an offhand, conversational rhythm that contrasts sharply with the incantory, endstopped lines, strong and straight masculine rhymes of the Thomas and Roethke villanelles. If the voice isn't quite a mother's nagging one trying to teach her forgetful daughters the art of mastering losing things, it is definitely a schoolmarm's voice (at least at the start) uttering its little schoolroom maxim. Repeat after me, please, "The art of losing isn't hard to master."

The poem then proceeds to give the writer-teacher and the reader-learner a run for their money. We are about to get a lesson on how it is done, the art of mastering losses, that is, and the villanelle form will serve as the example. This is a form that refuses to lose things: the two A lines of the first stanza are supposed to be repeated throughout intact; the two rhyming sounds echo back at the ends of all nineteen lines, and if the poet wants to indulge the obsessive repetitiveness of the form, he or she can—as Thomas does in his villanelle—repeat with some variation even the beginnings of lines: *wise men, good men, wild men, grave men.*

Against this constraint, this mastery of loss embedded in the villanelle form, Bishop pits the disasters and messiness of the human voice. Its spoken rhythms—complete with asides, corrections of itself: "my last, or next-to-last"; parenthetical phrases: "(*Write* it!)"—threaten to overturn the neat metric and rubric of the form. She begins with obvious control in her first stanza as the full breathy iambic lines unfold with only a slight enjambment in the second line. But by the second stanza and onward, all but the refrain lines have heavy caesuras and strong enjambments so that the usually incantory, controlled meter of a villanelle line is fractured: we feel the voice becoming increasingly harried, on the edge of mastering the losses she speaks of, on the edge of keeping control of the form she is writing in.

The refrain lines, too, demonstrate the struggle to keep control over the losses. Her A1 refrain line stays fiercely intact throughout the poem ("the art of losing isn't hard to master") with one minor alteration in the last stanza that captures with understatement the colossal effort of mastery ("the art of losing's not too hard to master"), but the A2 refrain line is almost "lost" in each stanza: ". . . to be lost that their loss is no disaster"; ". . . to travel. None of these will bring disaster"; "I miss them, but it wasn't a disaster"; ". . . though it may look like (*Write* it!) like disaster." The rhymes are also almost lost a couple of times, but somehow Bishop pulls them off, rhyming "my last, or" with "master". I call these rhymes last-minute rhyme-rescues that bring pleasure to readers because we were sure that this time she would lose it. Also, the feminine rhymes for the A lines create a softer, less-sure rhyme sound that contrasts sharply with the assurance of the masculine rhymes of the B lines. It is almost as if Bishop wanted her readers to see the mastered, strict adherence to form (of the A1 refrain line, of the strict B-line rhymes) next to the play and possibility of loss (the almost-lost A2 refrain line, the softer feminine rhymes). After all, this is a lesson in mastery, not dominance, one that rides the edge all the way. It might be evident by the end of the poem that the art of writing this villanelle isn't *too* hard to master, but a couple of times it did look as if Bishop was headed for disaster.

There is only one art, this one of writing, and there is also only "won art," no freebies. Bishop won this villanelle (as opposed to the form having the upper hand) by writing and righting the losses she speaks of. It is her joking voice that I love, her seemingly offhand gesture of tossing off line after line. In back of this conversational, spoken voice is all the hard work of mastery, the struggle for control, losses mastered by practice.

With "One Art," Bishop provides a model of how to master a form, the villanelle. She also provides a model for writers of how to deal with our losses by writing about them.

e. e. cummings's
"Space being . . . Curved"

Nineteen ninety-four was the centennial of e. e. cummings's birth. He is surely one of the twentieth century's most variously loved and spurned American poets. Several editions of his poetry are currently in print, including George J. Firmage's invaluable centenary edition of *Complete Poems*, which adds 195 previously uncollected cummings poems to the standard 1972 *Complete Poems*. But it's a pity cummings is so unevenly represented in our textbooks and anthologies. We may more likely find a handful of his sillier or trite poems, whistling "far and wee," than the rigorously odd and passionately intelligent poems that were his metier. It's an unavoidable pity, too, that he is often regarded today, as one of my students recently wrote, as the poet with the broken typewriter—the one who dismantled the formal structure of lyric verse, who sprinkled words and letters like pepper on the page, whose liberties with syntax seem, to some, like larceny. And it's probably true: no other modern poet has so distracted young writers with the glitz and apparent chaos of his "visual prosody," as Richard D. Cureton calls it. I say "apparent," because to me, while cummings is the easiest modern poet to imitate, he is also the most difficult to imitate well. His chaos is deliberate, exacting, and formally apt. Indeed, it bears more similarities to the repetitions and formal logic of chaos theory than to the chaos of the merely random or capricious.

I think of cummings as one of our last true Romantic poets. He is more a troubadour, a lover, than a Modernist inquisitor. But this too: cummings knew more about science than most other American poets of his day or ours. He is enlivened by it, curious, occasionally exasperated, but never intimidated, drawing extensive images and tropes from mathematics and physics for his own exuberantly demanding poems. Often his application of science serves as a foil to his persistent Romantic inclinations. In poems like "stand with your lover on the ending earth," "life is more true than reason will deceive," "pity this busy monster, manunkind," and dozens more, cummings employs images of progress, history, and science as negative counterpoints to his Romantic valorizations of self-reliance, passion, and intuition. These two sets of competing tropes give a sense of scale to cummings's dialectic. Typically in his poems, the boggling immensity of science, space, and the vastness of "time time time time time" shrivel to nothingness in the presence of love, imagination, and spirit: "love's function," he writes, "is to fabricate unknownness." Or, in another poem, the "hugest whole creation may be less / incalculable than a single kiss." In the 1920s, when cummings wrote some of his finest poems, physicists became embroiled in a similar debate, trying to correlate the mathematics of Einstein's relativity theory, on its massive scale, with the minute scale of quantum mechanics as described by Eddington. In many cases, the behaviors of one system did not jibe with the behaviors of the other. Many of cummings's poems enact a parallel, insuperable tension between matters of an enormous scale and those minuscule.

"Space being(don't forget to remember)Curved" is one of my favorite cummings poems, and it provides a fine example of his insightful application of physics. Published in book form in 1931, in *ViVa*, when only a few specialists understood Einstein's theories, this poem is almost visionary in its perception of the dimensions and operations of Einstein's space/time continuum. In 1905 Einstein's special theory of relativity combined the concepts of space and time by describing them with a single set of equations, where even time is a spatial dimension. By 1917, in his General Theory, he more fully calculated into his hypotheses the influence of matter, and therefore of gravity, and so could go far beyond the flat space/time dimension of the special theory. In other words, Einstein asserted that in four-dimensional space/time—in the "real" universe—space itself is "curved," or distorted, by the influence of massive objects; the shortest distance between two points is *not* a straight line. A simple illustration: place a bowling ball on a mattress, and then roll a marble firmly enough to insure its path from one end of the mattress to the other. The marble will complete its journey, but its trajectory will arch, curved by the weight of the heavy ball. In Einstein's four dimensions, where even distance is measured in terms of light-years, the light that travels through the universe is, if ever so slightly, bent by the gravitational pull of objects like stars and black holes.

And here is where cummings commences his poem, itself both a thematic and structural articulation of the curvature of space and time. By the merest curving of a line, the "least crooking" of a straight finger, the simplest bending back down to four legs by a standing human figure, cummings establishes, then twists, a number of poetic devices and conventional mores. Even the stance of this poem is complicated by the intrusion of strongly conflicting points of view. No single or "straight" position will suffice to represent the complex gravity of the situation. These opposing forces appear in the first stanza, even in the first line, when one assertion, that space is curved, is interrupted by a command "(don't forget to remember)." Though parenthetical, this order is conspicuous for its central position in the line, as well as for its slightly incongruous meaning and its taunting tone. Another parenthetic addition immediately follows, separating the poem's initial absolute phrase even further from its main clause. Here, after a self-interruptive, befuddled introduction in his second line, cummings paraphrases, in his third line, the first line of Robert Frost's 1914 poem "Mending Wall." This poetic allusion corroborates and illustrates cummings's initial scientific reference. In Frost's poem, the forces of gravity and of entropy (described by the second law of thermodynamics, which states that the destination of all things is decay, that, to use Yeats's phrase, "things fall apart") undermine the stability of a rock wall, a straight line, if you will, drawn across the subtle curvature of the world: the rocks keep falling off. We know even in cummings's first stanza, then, that space is curved—and also that the universe inhabited by his poem is terribly complex, in tension with itself, composed of science as well as art, seriousness as well as satire. Positions shift. Voices intrude and instruct at the same time.

The syntactic integrity of this poem shudders even more deeply in the second stanza, where cummings again employs a pair of intruding parentheses, and where the poem's apparent main clause seems now suspended, incomplete. It is as if the poem moves too quickly, its ideas too complex, for ordinary syntax. Cummings imagines here the inheritance and reconception of Newton's law by Einstein as a kind of scientific lineage, another step in the history of science; as he exhorts, "(but we read that beFore)." It is, indeed, another line that must "curve" or bend to be fully realized. One of the landmark advances in physical science between Newton's time and Einstein's was James Clerk Maxwell's unification of the laws of electricity and magnetism in the mid 1800s. His electromagnetic force became acknowledged in the twentieth century as one of the four fundamental forces of nature, along with gravity and the strong and weak nuclear forces. Light, so important to Einstein's relativity equations, is one type of electromagnetic radiation. So cummings's adjective "electromagnetic" is quite accurate in describing Einstein. Einstein extended and thereby "preserved" the "conTinuum" of physicists and their discoveries by applying the laws of electromagnetic force to Newton's laws of motion. Again, this is why light bends, why the universe is curved.

In the two-line third stanza, the very middle of this poem, cummings employs an even more punning, tongue-in-cheek discourse, deserting the previous fractured sentence. This shift indicates the crisis of the poem. Along with the ascendancy of science in the early twentieth century came serious doubts about cosmologies based on deities. As Bertrand Russell reasoned, if physicists can address and plumb the most intricate mysteries about the universe, then what use is God? If life is a physical, synaptic "Reflex," if indeed "Everything is Relative," as cummings puns on Einstein's term, then perhaps God—at least the more antique conception of God—is indeed both "Dead" and buried, deposed by those who "sum it All Up," and decapitalized by the poet. Given cummings's well-documented ambiguities about this question in dozens of other poems, it is not hard to understand his reluctance, here at the poem's center, to admit to God's demise. In fact, Richard S. Kennedy argues that this whole poem is "a bitter attack on humankind's presumptuousness in an age of new scientific theory." Certainly cummings frets about the potential erasure of the sacred, even as he understands the science involved. But if this poem is just an attack on science or vanity, I wonder why cummings so thoroughly applies—and fruitfully confirms—Einstein's curving paradigm.

If God is "Dead," cummings muses, then maybe the features historically attributed to God are really human. His lament turns into a robust, if still partly satiric, toast to "that Upwardlooking / Serene Illustrious and Beatific / Lord of Creation,MAN." In his bold and capitalized shout "LONG LIVE . . . MAN," he echoes the European salute that "the King is dead, long live the King" in his own version of continuity and lineage, the "conTinuum" along which power is passed. I think cummings's understanding of science here provides him a means by which to praise human perception and accomplishment and not, as Kennedy argues, merely to attack science as a human folly. What was Einstein's great breakthrough if not a kind of poetic vision itself, a transcendental leap from one sort of cosmos to another?

Having begun this more-than-quantum leap from the godly to the human, and from the logical and cynical to the joyous, cummings completes his poem with a strange and fascinating description of "MAN." Again he "curves" a straight line when he crooks that "compassionate digit." Now bestowed with "terrific" powers, the human being's slightest gesture becomes monumental, enlivening. The crooked finger replicates Einstein's theoretical curve, but it also suggests a welcoming signal, perhaps even an erotic come-on. After all, this (com)passionate digit elicits a "swoon." And the "quadruped" who is swooning must be another human. (We did once move on all four limbs.) Cummings has simply continued or extended Einstein's logic: if space is curved, then any projection into space must bend, spiral, even swirl rather than follow a straight trajectory, and any projection extended far enough, for long enough, may eventually arc back on itself, may meet its own prior position and condition. To look out into space is to look back in time. And so the curve begun in the poem's first line becomes longer, rounded, more extended, eventually turning back toward our own earlier selves. The curve, in fact, becomes a complete circle in the image of the "billiard-Balls." On the surface of, or within, such a sphere, a curving line can be infinite and yet contained within a finite space—an image that corresponds to physicists' estimations of the nature of our universe. By the end of the poem, cummings's tone has become playful, even exuberant, composed of a multiple capacity—to be *both* logically coherent and gladly creative, mixing science and love, reason and transcendence, relativity and billiards.

Einstein fused inexorably the concepts of space and time. In a similar way, a poet of cummings's skill can fuse content and form. Cummings is brilliant with technical matters, so it should not surprise to see how his "curving" of poetic form complements his notions of space/time curvature. A cursory glance at the poem on the page reveals his strategy. The poem seems to decay, at least to loosen, as it moves from its tight two first triplets, downward, into shorter stanzas, broken lines, and an increasing chaos of letters, punctuation, and voices. It is as if cummings escalates the pressure on his lines as the poem proceeds, bending them more and more. If we recombine the poem, however, we can see that it is an example of cummings's favorite form: the sonnet. I do not use the term "favorite" lightly here. Cummings is often labeled a free-verse poet, and given his radical maneuvers with visual form, it is not hard to see why. But it is also reductive to call him that. Indeed, by my count, of the 775 poems in his 1972 *Complete Poems*, about 225 of them are sonnets. That's a third of all his poems, and many more are composed in other set forms and regularities. Even among the 195 uncollected poems that Firmage adds in the new *Complete Poems*, I found fifty-five more sonnets, some dating back to his earliest attempts at poetry.

Cummings matches his technique to his theme. What he does, of course, is to bend, or curve, the rules of the sonnet. Reconnected, there are fourteen complete lines in this poem, and while these lines are not metrical, they clearly echo their iambic lineage and are all within a step or two of being ten syllables long. Cummings also maintains the structural rhetoric of the sonnet. The critical, and isolated, ninth line with its central assertion (and fear) "god being Dead" completes the traditional rhetorical shift of the sonnet's first eight lines. This formal turn, or bend, moves the poem from its problem toward its solution, and is reinforced by the poem's conspicuous change of both attitude and subject in the final five lines, where cummings sings his complicated praise of humanity. He also maintains the rhetoric of a sonnet's final couplet—to summarize, to deploy the poem's lesson—here in the two-and-a-half lines after the colon, where he converts the turn into a complete "ball" or circle. Seriousness evolves into joy, history arcs back around, and the early doubt of the poem transforms into acceptance of the poem's earned truth. As I pointed out, the poem seems to loosen in shape as it proceeds, but the syntax itself actually becomes less fractured in the poem's second half, as if this ultimate realization—of human beatitude and vision—provides for the salvation of syntax and of meaning.

Cummings applies the convention of rhyme as delicately and as masterfully as he uses form. The severe enjambment of his line breaks (he uses six different parts of speech at the ends of these lines), his fondness for internal alliteration, and the ongoing challenge of his syntax and clarity, all deflect our attention from these constant, if irregular, rhymes. A reader may not even notice the rhymes at first, but they are reliable echoes; and the most thrilling of his rhymes is certainly the final "billiardBalls," which must be traced all the way back to the third line's straight "walls." Somehow, this long reach, this last sonic memory, suggests that even as it curves and expands, stretching each line, the universe of this poem still, and at last, coheres. Cummings shows us that science and poetry both depend on formal reasoning and faithful intuition; both are human creations, after all, two of our best attempts to understand the universe and our place in it. Abundance, contradiction, reason, joy, praise, despair, chaos, and form—cummings contains all of these in the bending, relative space of the sonnet.

JOHN BALABAN

"Wulf and Eadwacer"

One of the limitations of the modern mind—whether modern in 1995 or in 995—is the almost-reflexive assumption that it knows more than its predecessors—i.e., that the past has less to tell us than the present because the present offers a truer perspective on human affairs than could possibly have been provided a generation earlier, much less one or two hundred years ago.

Poets are just as susceptible to this modernist prejudice as, say, pharmacologists or historians. Contemporary poets and their readers are often happy to assume that today's poems are far more revealing of the full complexity of the human condition than earlier poetry with its limitations of belief and style. Surely we have gone beyond the dull traditionalism of the Victorians, the effusions of the Romantics, the clockwork contraptions of the Neoclassicals, the religious constraints of the Metaphysicals. Surely we have gone beyond the restrictions of traditional formal poetry, the "sequence of the metronome" as Ezra Pound described it. Every age of poets seems to have a need to tell itself: we alone are charting new ground.

This is both a necessary belief and a limiting misconception. As soon as poets fall into it, they become stuck in a quotidian now. Indeed, a main strength of the modern mind lies in its ever-enlarging sense of the human past. For poets this is a sense not only of earlier beliefs and insights, but also of the very tools of prosody. The makers of the free-verse movement understood this, ranging across continents and centuries in poetic explorations; their contemporary successors mostly do not, satisfying themselves with a colloquial, free-verse style like an orchestra of one-string guitarists. If artistic prejudice—like Dantean sin—has its appropriate punishment, theirs is to sound alike, to have lost their poetic voices, or perhaps never to have gained them, strumming away at their single strings, mute with so much to say.

I have chosen "Wulf and Eadwacer" as my case in point. It is an Anglo-Saxon poem—an *Old* English poem in the West Saxon dialect, found in the Exeter Book, ca. 1000 A.D. "Wulf and Eadwacer," as scholars have called it from its named characters, seems to be a short lyric poem, although it may have been part of something longer. No one really knows. Yet, it reads as complete in itself and says things that we might find surprisingly modern.

It seems to be a dramatic monologue, something we were not expecting to find in English literature until several centuries later. To challenge our contemporary prejudices further, a woman is speaking in defiant, passionate, and personal terms to two men, one whom she despises, but who is perhaps her husband; the other, her lover and an outlaw to her people. "Eadwacer," used to be a common name, like Edmund or Edward. Is Eadwacer also the "bold man" (*beaducafa*) who embraced the unnamed speaker, causing her both pleasure and disgust? They seem to have had a son, the whelp whom Wulf has taken away.

But who is Wulf? Scholars have speculated that he may be a Viking marauder. It was common practice for a Viking raiding party to sail up English estuaries to set up a base camp on an island that could also serve as a natural fortress, "surrounded by fens," from which they could attack towns and monasteries. Wulf is clearly some kind of outlaw. The speaker, whose love for Wulf has made her sick, nonetheless belongs to a people who would "thank" Wulf for his gift if he were to show up in force. The irony—something else we are not prepared for at this point in English literary history—is intended. *Athecgan* gives us our modern word "thank," although "receive" is probably a more accurate translation here.

The woman speaker is the powerful center of the poem. Whoever fashioned the poem created in these nineteen lines a real voice filled with passion, conflict, and longing. In the artifice of the interior monologue, we seem to overhear her speaking honestly to herself. She has no illusions about her circumstances, yet she waits for Wulf's return. When she calls out to Eadwacer, she is sneering and direct. When she calls out to Wulf, the tone is pained and halting, the syntax of the Old English breaking apart grammatically, like someone talking to herself in thoughtful fragments. Her narrative point-of-view—so much a concern in contemporary fiction—never lapses.

The music of the Old English prosody—and the way in which this poem plays against the hypothetical standard form—is a central force in the success of the poem. Ideally, an Old English poem followed certain conventions: unlike later Continental poetry that influences English habits, syllables were not counted and poems did not rhyme. Instead, lines had four strong stresses, two on each side of a medial pause. In each line, three of the four stresses fell on syllables that held either alliteration or assonance—words that began with the same sound:

> Wulf is on iege   ic on otherre
> Wulf is on an island   I am on another.

Throughout "Wulf and Eadwacer" these rules are relaxed, perhaps because this is a meditative voice, not requiring the strong declamations of narrative poems like "The Battle of Maldon" or "Beowulf" where content drives the rhythms more loudly.

Across the centuries—muffled by the vagaries of English spelling, by great shifts in English pronunciation, by changes in English vocabulary, and by our modern hesitation at old poetry—the poem speaks to us in familiar ways. One reason is the surprisingly modern treatment of a love triangle, but another, equally important, is that although the poem *looks* foreign, its *sound* is familiar, even in the faint echoes provided by my translation. English, after all, is a Germanic language with something like 75 percent of its wordstock derived from Anglo-Saxon origins.

This is something contemporary poets might want to investigate: if the modern rebellion against tradition led by Pound and *les Imagistes* was against the Continental tradition, might there not be something in the pre-Continental, Anglo-Saxon style that is still alive in the way we speak? Old English poetry ignored rhyme and favored other kinds of sound echoes: alliteration, assonance, and an ablaut, slant rhyme on the order of ring, rang, rung (or, to use an example from one of my students: "a *roan* mare *running* in the *rain* / *mad*, she gallops through the *mud* . . .). In terms of rhythm (perhaps the most important aspect of poetry whatever the culture), Anglo-Saxon poets did not count poetic feet; they required only that the line hold four stresses. Weak syllables were not counted, and this allowed for great variation in delivery, from the ringing heroic battle poetry to the *sotto voce* searchings of "Wulf and Eadwacer."

Clever poets will make use of whatever in the language might work on the unconsciousness of the reader. This is far different from imitating the English poetic past. It is making use of it (as well as the poetry of other cultures) for contemporary ends. Only weak practitioners believe they work independent of tradition. Indeed, as T. S. Eliot tells us in "Tradition and the Individual Talent," "Someone said: 'The dead writers are remote from us because we *know* so much more than they did.' Precisely, and they are that which we know." Ezra Pound, perhaps the most programmatic in his explorations, translated from Chinese, Provencal, and Old English. Before him, Gerard Manley Hopkins experimented in native measures he called "sprung rhythm" and which he heard in Welsh *cynhanedd* and in Milton's *Samson Agonistes*. Closer to us, Robert Lowell's poetry, in the earliest poems and in the whale-killing *canzone* of "Quaker Graveyard in Nantucket," is filled with the alliterative echoes and strong stresses of Anglo-Saxon verse. Wilfred Owen, Emily Dickinson, and, perhaps most brilliantly, Theodore Roethke rediscovered the possibilities in native slant rhyming. And, Sylvia Plath, with her gift for finding the appropriate rhythms for extraordinary mental states, uses Anglo-Saxon alliterative stresses to convince us of the inevitability of the protagonist's self-destruction in "Suicide at Egg Rock."

So I value this old poem for reminding me that the past is always full of surprises. And that one of the pleasures of pursuing the exotic is the discovery of the familiar. And, finally, that the truly new and original always holds in it some echo of the past.

And I love the poem's stunning last lines:

> A man can easily cut to pieces   what never was joined:
> our song together.

Wulf and Eadwacer

Leodum is minum   swylce him mon lac gife;
willað hy hine aþecgan,   gif he on þreat cymeð.
　Ungelic is us.
Wulf is on iege,   ic on oþerre.
Fæst is þæt eglond,   fenne biworpen.
Sindon wælreowe   weras þær on ige;
willað hy hine aþecgan,   gif he on þreat cymeð.
　Ungelice is us.
Wulfes ic mines widlastum   wenum dogode;
þonne hit wæs renig weder   ond ic reotugu sæt,
þonne mec se beaducafa   bogum bilegde,
wæs me wyn to þon,   wæs me hwæþre eac lað.
Wulf, min Wulf,   wena me þine
seoce gedydon,   þine seldcymas,
murnende mod,   nales meteliste.
Gehyrest þu, Eadwacer?   Uncerne earne hwelp

bireð wulf to wuda.
Þæt mon eaþe tosliteð þætte næfre gesomnad wæs,
uncer giedd geador.
It is to my people   as if someon gave them a gift.
They will thank him   if he comes in force.
It is otherwise with us.

Wulf is on an island   I am on another.
Fast is that island   surrounded by fens.
There are fierce men   on that island.
They will thank him   if he comes in force.
It is otherwise with us.

Wulf's long wanderings   I suffered with hope.
When it was rainy weather   and I sat forlorn,
the bold man came   and held me in his arms.
That was pleasant for me   and also it was loathsome.
Wulf, my Wulf   my ache for you
has made me sick   your seldom visits
a mourning mind   hunger for nothing.
Do you hear that, Eadwacer?   The wolf has taken
our cowardly whelp to the woods.
A man can easily cut to pieces   what never was joined:
our song together.

ANN BARKER

Principles of Exclusion:

Erotic and Spiritual Visions

in Spenser's *Faerie Queene*

A climactic, enthralling vision rewards each of the heroes of *The Faerie Queene*'s Books I and VI. Each vision is perfect in its own kind: the sacred, mystical vision of Book I, and the romantic, erotic vision of Book VI. In the similarities and contrasts between these two enchanted moments, Spenser suggests the beauty and fulfillment unique to each kind of aspiration, as well as the crucial differences in their respective dangers and limitations.

Until this highest vision, the Redcrosse knight, hero of Book I, does not fully know himself, being ignorant of both his name and his heritage. He keeps stumbling onto projections of unknown portions of himself, which appear in a field of allegorical figures. These projections include the false Una/Duessa, the Geant of sexual pride, guilty Despayre, and many other figures, whose nature as projection, as aspects of the self, cannot be grasped by a mind unwilling to acknowledge its own darker side. The nature of allegory in this phase of the quest of the Redcrosse knight is largely that of personification of inward states that are not recognized as such.

After the knight "hits bottom," wanting only to kill himself, he is ready to begin leaving behind the corpse of his ego-centered and projecting selfhood, to begin opening himself to an instruction and discipline that will free him from the trap of unconscious narcissism and open him to the possibilities of seeing beyond himself.

When our passage opens, the Redcrosse knight has been imprisoned by pride and then nearly overcome by the dark side of his own character. His gracious guide Una has led him to a house of spiritual instruction, where he is taught by such figures as Dame Caelia, "Whose onlie ioy was to relieue the needes / Of wretched soules, and helpe the helplesse pore"

(I, x, 3). This instruction to look beyond the self to the needs of others is exactly what the self-imprisoned knight lacks most painfully. He has been swamped by the particular sufferings brought on by his own self-entrapment; he needs the specific freeing from his own troubles, which he can learn through discipline and repentance. Only then is he ready for a new kind of vision expressed in an allegory different from that which has come before.

No longer do the allegorical figures find their origin primarily in ego projection. Instead, the descriptions and analogies of the mount and vision of the hill of Contemplation arise primarily from what Spenser's Christianity would have regarded as scriptural or ecclesiastical Truth, existing independently of the individual's mind. Such truth is capable of being perceived by that mind after it has been purified of self-absorption, when it no longer sees the world as a mass of fragmented mirrors, or rejected parts of the self.

In other words, the Redcrosse knight becomes able to see his holy vision when he has accepted and transcended his own dark side, when he no longer banishes it from his consciousness. This process is the antithesis of the process of "purification" that will give rise to Sir Calidore's vision of Mount Acidale.

Charissa, that divine love who accepts others with neither demands nor possessiveness, leads the Redcrosse knight by a "painful way" up "an hill, that was both steepe and hy" to the hermitage of Contemplation, who often saw God

> ... from heauens hight,
> All were his earthly eyen both blunt and bad,
> And through great age had lost their kindly sight,
> Yet wondrous quick and persant was his spright,
> As Eagles eye, that can behold the Sunne.
>
> (I, x, 46–47)

Paradoxically, the blunting of external sight through contemplation reveals an inner sight that alone can see outside of the self. This is the sight that can see God, who, in Spenser's world, has an absolute existence, rather than the world of projections that Redcrosse, internally blind, imagined he saw around him. Further fasting and praying release Redcrosse's "spright" from its "bands," its bondage to the self, as our passage from the text begins.

At that moment, the mountain before him is introduced with a rapid trinity of epic similes, evoking both the sufferings and the mystical triumphs of Moses and of Jesus as well as the classical, Parnassian source of that particular inspiration needed for "heauenly notes" (I, x, 52–54).

These passages do not blink at the pain both Moses and Jesus faced on Sinai and Olivet. The parting of the sea is described as "blood-red billows," and the triumph itself is that Moses received

> . . . writ in stone
> With bloody letters by the hand of God,
> The bitter doome of death and balefull mone.
>
> (I, x, 53)

This reception of God's truths about damnation and the agonies of the passion of Jesus are significantly not excluded from the heavenly vision of Redcrosse. On the contrary, the knowledge and experience of suffering seem to be at the heart of this vision. Excluded instead are sin and self-entrapment.

This vision of the heavenly city is beyond the power of language to express. In a sense, then, the poet himself, whose inspiration comes from the classical muses, fails here:

> . . . earthly tong
> Cannot describe, nor wit of man can tell;
> Too high a ditty for my simple song.
>
> (I, x, 55)

Nevertheless, in a kind of *occupatio*, the poet goes on to describe the indescribable. Contemplation himself describes this new *Hierusalem* in terms of the purgation of the sin and guilt, the pain that was needed to transform evils like those that are simply banned on Mount Acidale. The redeemed in the holy city are God's

> . . . chosen people purg'd from sinful guilt
> With pretious bloud, which cruelly was spilt
> On cursed tree, of that vnspotted lam,
> That for the sinnes of all the world was kilt.
>
> (I, x, 57)

The cleansing here takes place in an agonizing purification of spirit, which necessarily precedes the approach to vision by the saved and by the visionary. By the time Redcrosse approaches the mountain, there is no need to go in and clean up the grounds, ejecting undesirables, as there is on Mount Acidale.

Explicit preparation for Calidore's vision on Mount Acidale (VI, x) begins with Calidore throwing over duty. "Who now does follow the foule *Blatant Beast*," the narrator asks,

> Whilest *Calidore* does follow that faire Mayd,
> Vnmyndfull of his vow and high beheast?

Rather than obey his vow to the divinely ordained Faerie Queene, Calidore is now "entrapt of loue, which him betrayd." He rejects his "former quest, so full of toyle and paine" (VI, x, 1–2). From the beginning of the canto, then, Calidore's path toward vision involves explicitly rejecting difficulty, including the difficulty of obeying his vow, or keeping his language truthful.

As our passage begins, the sense of abandoning or abolishing the unpleasant—and of pilfering the sense beauties of other places—intensifies. Increasingly, Calidore leaves the path in which truth can be recognized and enters a place of seeming, where fantasy seems to replace reality. This is a place "whose pleasures did *appere* / To passe all others" (my italics). Even nature works by artifice here; her "skill" was "Deuis'd to worke delight," as if to adorn Acidale "she all the rest did pill" (VI, x, 5).

Much as in the Redcrosse knight's early work of repression or suppression, here the unpleasant is rejected, excluded, or banished by Acidale. To replace them in this erotic fantasy, pleasant aspects are gathered from whatever fragments of life they may inhabit.

For this courtly pastoral, distinctions are made according to a kind of class-consciousness; the superiority of the "soring hauke" and the "King of fowles in maiesty" are admitted whereas the "ruder clowne" is excluded. This antithesis of pleasant and unpleasant is intensified when the wood "of matchlesse hight . . . seem[s] th'earth to disdaine." Earth is rejected by "maiesty and powre" (VI, x, 6–7), a perspective from which earth is too dirty to suit the artificial perfectionism.

Acidalian water is "a gentle flud" whose

> . . . siluer waues did softly tumble down,
> Vnmard with ragged mosse or filthy mud,
> Ne mote wilde beastes, ne mote the ruder clowne
> Thereto approch, ne filth mote therein drowne.

Nymphs and Fairies keep "all noysome things away from it" (VI, x, 7), suppressing them from awareness. Everything is provided "which for pleasure might / Desired be, or thence to banish bale" until it "seems" possible to "ouerlooke the lowly vale," both to condescend to and to ignore that which seems base (VI, x, 8).

As is characteristic of a condition in which the unpleasant is suppressed, a reflection of the rejected material reappears repeatedly, here in many forms of repetition, such as the rebounding "Eccho" of rhythmically thumping feet on "hollow ground" (VI, x, 10). Far from being an insight into deepest truth, as is the Redcrosse knight's vision, this is a vision of artfully formed but empty and evanescent projection.

In the following stanzas, Calidore's Peeping-Tom erotic excitement and shame, added to the intensity of his having separated the pleasant from the unpleasant in his vision, divide and alienate him from himself, so that "euen he him selfe his eyes enuyde" (VI, x, 11). His sense of self and other are deeply confused.

Calidore himself is not sure about what he is seeing; his curiosity and overmastering erotic desire spring him from his hiding place, and he barges into the dance uninvited. The scene itself disappears as soon as he appears, in contrast to the Redcrosse knight's own turning away from his vision back to his now-inspired duty. This disappearance heightens the sense of unreality and unreliability in the love song of Colin Clout, the piping shepherd, who elsewhere embodies the pastoral aspect of Spenser himself. This sort of imaginative vision can exist only in the absence or concealment of the imperfect self. By contrast, Calidore's vision brings him into unity with his own true identity by revealing to him his name and mission.

Colin breaks his pipe in irritation and grief, the disruption and loss of the pastorally evoked vision contrasting vividly with the Redcrosse's eyes "dazed . . . through passing brightnesse . . . / So darke are earthly things compard to things diuine" (I, x, 67). The Redcrosse knight, now known as Saint George, departs with dazzled sight and with grave and loving gratitude. He has discovered who he is and has found out what it takes to see beyond the self. Colin (and his alter ego Calidore) have created a lovely piece of pastoral art. Both visions represent kinds of perfection; both are arguably the climaxes of very different quests. From the poem's perspective, the moral and divine values of the two visions and of the two genres nevertheless differ radically.

Henry Reed's "Naming of Parts"

Henry Reed's "Naming of Parts" is a golden oldie, a classic, a point of reference, a seminal text, a beacon in a sea of fog, and a shining star in an increasingly muddied heaven. Why do I give it such a buildup? Because it welcomes us with confident, lucid sentences. Because it is clearheaded and organized. Because it contains subject matter that matters. Why is it as good the tenth time as the first? Because it is greater than the sum of its parts.

Reed's poem expresses how it feels to be in class while wanting to be elsewhere. It feels the difference between the mechanical and the human. It contrasts the cold and sometimes oppressive artificial order of civilization with the free sensuality of nature.

The person speaking in "Naming of Parts" is a soldier in training. Like military instruction, whether in the classroom or in the field, the poem repeats and repeats itself. Yet underneath all that insistence lies a subversive element: the recruit is not paying attention only to the weapons instructor. He listens to some instruction, but then his mind wanders. His attention returns to the class, but then it goes away again. His mind wanders to the gardens nearby, to the change of seasons, and to the bees among the flowers. All the while, wherever his attention may be, the lesson continues. Classroom, outdoors, classroom, outdoors: which is in the foreground and which in the background? The more rifle instruction, the more his mind wanders from the military matter at hand. Yet even as his mind seeks relief from the mechanical instruction and the instrument of killing, even while he thinks of the bees pollinating the flowers in the early life-giving spring, the instruction drones on. The poem begins and ends with it.

Reed's poem has particular meaning for me because I trained at Fort Bragg, North Carolina, in 1957 and served in the U.S. Army in 1964–

1965. Like all military service, my time included weapons instruction and "close-order drill." The U.S. Army at that time issued its soldiers M-1 rifles. The speaker of this poem, being in the British Army, would have been issued an Enfield: a bolt-action rifle very similar to the M-1. The close-at-hand things in this poem—components of my M-1—helped furnish a world of parts and specifications, manuals and marching.

The admonition in the poem to move the safety-catch with one's thumb, not one's finger, reminds me of the most awkward, difficult part of rifle drill: the part that produced subversive laughter, swollen thumbs, and frustrated sergeants. It involved raising the rifle diagonally across one's chest, forcing back the bolt with one's left hand against the "operating rod handle" (or "cocking-piece") to open the chamber (or "breech") so that one could check it for bullets, then with the right hand releasing the bolt from its lock while still holding it back until commanded to let it slam closed before pulling the trigger.

These actions followed a series of three commands: "Port arms" (we brought the rifle up across our chests), "Inspection arms" (we locked back the bolt and checked the chamber), and lastly a two-part command: "Ready" (followed by a pause while we tried to set free the bolt but still restrain it), and finally "Port arms" again.

Why so awkward and difficult? Why swollen thumbs and sputtering sergeants? First, everything about the M-1 rifle is heavy. It is not easy to push back the bolt of an M-1 with the knife edge of one's left hand while holding it in the air. Next, one switches hands and holds back the bolt with the knife edge of the right hand while with the thumb of the same hand pressing slightly in the chamber to release the "bullet follower" and bolt. But the bolt is driven forward by a very powerful spring, and the position in which one tries to restrain it affords little leverage, so that it is tempting to hold back the bolt by sticking one's thumb farther into the chamber—or, if doing this at a classroom table rather than in formation on the drill field, finding a way to use other fingers!

This is forbidden, perhaps not so much because the action of the bolt can break fingers, but because it isn't a crisp, military way to do it. It was amusing to us and enraging to the sergeant to hear the strung-out sounds of bolts slamming shut and triggers being clicked as those who had "cheated" had trouble releasing their thumbs from the painful pressure of the bolt.

It's a truism for everyone but career soldiers that, while in the Army, one wishes to be almost anywhere else. When one is in formation, the sight of civilians walking any way they wish across the post grounds is heartbreaking. Yet there is also a seductive pleasure to the constant organization, the unambiguous nature of one's studies ("This is the upper sling swivel"), and the sense of achievement in learning new tasks such as stripping and reassembling a rifle. The rifle, properly cleaned, oiled, and reassembled, works with a snappy precision in wholesome contrast to the mixed emotions of the conscripted. And the use of weapons is, after all, basic to the military. Discharged from the army in October 1965, I drove off the post by a back road, past the rifle range, a route that made my new freedom all the more immediate to me.

Now to the poem, which is composed of connecting parts (like a rifle) and at the same time expresses contrasting feelings. The language of the soldier who speaks is conversational but controlled. It isn't just the soldier's language, but also the instructor's. The student mimics his teacher. (Remember that the speaker is British.)

The first three lines sound to me like a tightly organized teacher at the start of a class. If you accent the first word of line two ("we"), you will hear the unmistakable tone of a teacher treating his students as if they were children. Later, I hear a controlling tone of voice in such a phrase as "whose use you will see." We can imagine the student being told at some point "not to get ahead" of the lesson plan. This is not the public school but the army: the lesson will be taught, to use a phrase often heard in military classes, "by the numbers."

We can't help but hear how often words and phrases are repeated. The poem doesn't employ rhyme words at the ends of lines, but still it has the sound of rhyming. The first stanza alone contains the word "today" four times, plus "yesterday," "daily," and "morning."

The speaker sounds as he does because he speaks in overlapping sentences and repeated words. The second stanza repeats the little turns-of-phrase "this is" and "have not got" (which will turn up again in stanza five) as well as "sling" and "swivel." "In your case" turns into "in our case," to be repeated three stanzas later. "Finger" and "thumb" occur twice each in stanza three. "If you have any strength in your thumb" appears in stanza three and will reappear in the last stanza. In stanza four, the phrases "you can see" and "as you see" echo "you will see" from stanza two. The phrase "easing the spring," first seen in stanza four, quickly appears twice more, but with "Spring" capitalized. Like the phrase "easing the spring," "backwards and forwards" shows up in two different contexts, and the title phrase "naming of parts" reappears three times. These repeated words and phrases make us feel the repetitiousness and insistence of the instruction. If we think of marching, we may remember how teachers sometimes try to "drum the information" into students. It is the sort of teaching in which we sense that we are being "talked down to," a class from which we too might let our minds wander.

Enduring such a class, we might come to believe that we could put the teacher's language to better use, and indeed some of the repetitions in the poem reveal how a word or phrase can mean one thing, then another. In stanza four, speaking of releasing the rifle bolt, the speaker says, "We call this easing the spring." One sentence later, the bees are said to call their pollinating of the flowers "easing the Spring." The same sounds mean different things. The first use of the phrase is factual, objective, impersonal. The slightly altered second version of it is poetic, subjective, and personal. In the same way, "which we have not got" first is part of a factual sentence telling us that the rifle lacks a piling swivel, but later what "we have not got" is "the point of balance." By then, "point of balance" seems to be not just a location on a rifle but a place somewhere inside us where normally we feel emotional and psychological equilibrium.

"Naming of Parts," as its title suggests, is also, by implication, about what we call things. But we simply do not have words for everything. Compare the wordy exactitude of the lesson on rifle parts to the description of the japonica, which "glistens like coral," the branches ("silent, eloquent"), and the blossoms ("fragile and motionless"). We know what to call the sling and the swivel, the breech and the bolt, but what are the words for our feelings? No single word can describe one's feelings in early spring, just as no one word can define either physical or spiritual love. The look of nature—tree branches, bees, and flowers—can trigger in us definite emotions. When it does, we often locate these emotions outside ourselves, seeing them in nature.

In "Naming of Parts," phrases change their meanings right before our eyes. Like the speaker, we understand that the same phrase can be applied to a piece of cold equipment or to sensuous nature. Perhaps, like the speaker, we cast an ironic eye on the whole business of the rifle instruction because we have come to know more than the language says. Like him, we know that the world has many parts, including classrooms and gardens, fields of fire and fields of poppies. We know, too, that a man or woman plays many parts, including, for some, soldier or lover, obedient apprentice or distracted student. We may remember the line in Shakespeare that tells us, "All the world's a stage." We may know that a military assault is said to be "staged." We may notice that the bees in the poem are said to be "assaulting" the flowers. They are also said to be "fumbling" those same flowers. Language, it seems, can go anywhere.

Also, we can research an author's history, motives, and obsessions. We can look into this writer's youth and life-style. If we did, we would find out that Henry Reed was born February 22, 1914, and died December 8, 1986, and that in 1941 he was drafted into the Royal Army Ordnance Corps. We could read the letter he wrote to his sister during basic training, in which he complains that it seems as if his group is expected to learn nearly everything but "the management of a tank." We would learn that at college he acted in plays and was known for his gift of mimicry.

But the poem by itself does not demand that we go outside it. Reading Reed in the classrooms of America is in one respect like reading portions of Walt Whitman or many other authors. Although one is free to interpret the poem in terms of the author's life, one need not: the drama is in the dichotomy of macho, mechanical army weapons training and the sensitive recruit who speaks about it. Nor is this all he has to say about his time as a soldier. "Naming of Parts," written in 1942, is the first part of a five-poem series published together as "Lessons of the War." The other four are titled "Judging Distances" (1943), "Movement of Bodies" (1950), "Unarmed Combat" (1945), and "Returning of Issue" (1970).

The language in "Naming of Parts" could be called "straightforward." It is the language of the kind of poetry to which we can apply one of the simplest and most convenient definitions of poetry: "heightened prose." Now, there are as many definitions of poetry as there are writers and critics who wish to establish their turf. Some definitions are particular and restrictive, while others are deliberately general so as to include as many kinds of poetry as possible.

Many people believe that a poem must rhyme—absolutely. Many also feel that it must establish a rhythmic pattern—called "meter." Others will settle for some form of counting from line to line—usually of syllables. These and others argue that poetry must appear in lines, never in paragraphs. To some, the defining characteristic of poetry is compressed language. To others, it is imagery or figures of speech. To still others, poetry depends on a special quality of vocabulary or syntax. There are some to whom no poem is poetic without an elevated tone of voice. To others, good poems must speak partly by implication: they argue that such indirection creates the alert reading we associate with poetry. Some say that poetry depends on what is left out, and that the "poetry" occurs in the reader as much as in the writer. However they define poetry, readers agree that good poems cannot be easily or quickly summed up in prose. They agree that how a thing is said affects what is said.

But the definitions continue to come and go. Some say that poetry has an intimate quality: its tone of voice is personal. Others insist, "I know it when I see it." Finally, there is a kind of "behavioral" definition: if the publisher says it's poetry, it's poetry.

Among such a crowd of definitions, "heightened prose" may seem banal. But it touches the heart of the verbal condition, in which the language of poetry and the language of prose overlap. The border between prose and poetry remains invisible, and moreover it is constantly shifting according to the latest poetic experiments. It has proven impossible to fix the boundary for very long. Artists being artists, rules about art are made to be broken. In that sense, art is the truest kind of freedom.

This may be more true for poets than for prose writers, since the writer of prose often has a practical purpose in mind.

Henry Reed made a living writing good prose, especially radio plays. Could it be characteristic of poets who also write stories and scripts that the style of their poems will generally be direct and efficient? They might be assumed to favor Samuel Taylor Coleridge's often quoted distinction between prose and poetry: prose, he said, is "words in their best order," while poetry is "the best words in the best order." Although coming up with the best words and the best order often cannot be accomplished step-by-step, but is sufficiently complex to be largely intuitive, poets who live by writing prose do seem generally also to write their poems in a language close to prose. That is, their poetic language usually stays close to the language of clear conversation.

If, as the French poet Paul Valéry said, prose is like walking and poetry is like dancing, such a style doesn't exactly boogie. It's too hands-on for that. On the other hand, nearly any reader can follow the steps. Its "readability" can be a powerful advantage. When this way of writing succeeds, it works with precision, insistence, and inevitability. None may deny it. Such a poem may appear to be a kind of "found object," a mix of sound and meaning that seemed to exist out there in the ether, waiting for the right mindset to come by, absorb it, and then express it.

"Naming of Parts" is just such a poem.

ROSELLEN BROWN

On Marianne Moore's "Silence"

I am not going to make a brief for "Silence" as the best poem by Marianne Moore. My favorite might be her extraordinary "Marriage" or "The Octopus" or "A Grave," if I really pushed myself to choose (and I wouldn't want to; I never quite get the point of making hierarchies like that). The bizarre yet illuminating juxtapositions and leaps without warning; the observations scientific in their precision; the unique playfulness of the shapes of her stanzas and their cool conversational wit make those poems rewarding in the best possible way: by offering up new and different pleasures at every approach.

But I want to talk about "Silence" anyway, because it marked for me a way into Moore's poetry, a rather less demanding, more gradual means of access, after which the richer, more ambitious poems seemed less daunting. Nothing in the poetry of my early reading years (I was not precocious; I'm talking about college) prepared me for the originality and obliqueness of Marianne Moore. I came of age in the four-square fifties, when, in spite of Pound and Williams, among others, received forms were still a routine expectation—my first published poem was a sonnet, my second a sestina. The hardest task we had was to parse out as many of the seven kinds of ambiguity as we could find in any poem as if we were peering into one of those faces-hidden-in-the-trees puzzles, assiduously tracking every plausible turn of irony, every darkening shade. Very little in Frost, Yeats, Williams, or even Stevens (difficult though he was) prepared me for Moore, and "The Wasteland" which, in spite of its scrupulous pages of notes, seemed to contain enough overt narrative to keep me happily engaged. (I can't forget my humiliation the first time I read that Eliot considered narrative the red meat a burglar throws to keep the dogs at bay. Guiltily I accepted the judgment that I was enough of a Yahoo to—yes—need it.) I had been instructed to unpack a poem by applying prosaically most if not all of the 5 W's usually associated with journalism: Who's speaking? To whom? Why—under what circumstances? About what? And so on. In that rather limiting litany, About what? loomed especially large.

Marianne Moore, though—she of the superordinary love of baseball and Brooklyn, which certainly sat queerly with the sharp-cornered hat and what appeared to be (but was actually much more complicated) the old-fashioned-lady's demeanor; she of the curiosity-about-the-world that Digesteth Harde Yron—I didn't know what to make of her and so I searched her poems for all the wrong paths. Lost in the thickets, chasing down the literal amid the figurative (or was it the figurative amid the literal?) I shrugged her off as a balmy maiden aunt, so eccentric that I didn't expect, ever, to penetrate (let alone like) her work.

But then I came upon "Silence" and—perhaps because it is only mildly eccentric and because it is so brief that one needn't put on high-water boots to walk into it—I discovered what I hadn't heard right before: the tonality of a profound (and anti-"poetic") reserve that alternated almost wantonly with a voracious love of the things (chiefly living things) of this world. The formality of this code was wholly unfamiliar to me as a stance; this withholding, or, less pejoratively, this reticence, was deeply at odds with anything in my own life and anything I'd heard in poetry before. It recommended, it firmly insisted upon, a high WASP dignity and control that extended to behavior, and finally, inevitably, to speech and thence to prosody. There may have been Christian rigor in Eliot, but it was angst-ridden and passionate, so hot that it was cool to the touch, a different temperature entirely. Moore, as it happened, daughter of a midwestern Presbyterian minister, believed not so much in dampened passions as in the enlivening effects of their chastening.

Suddenly, how perfectly in character was the austere epigraph to the complete poems, "*Omissions are not accidents*," which, like the closing line of "Silence," makes its assertion in the negative. It can be read as a warning, a map of her intentions and method, a challenge to plumb the absences as well as the presences in the poems: a figure-ground conundrum. At the very least it announced a rather forbidding control: somewhere, I couldn't resist wondering, did all those promised excisions—those judicious erasures—live together like lost socks, jostling, depressed by having been cast away with a clear purpose? It is a peculiar way to beckon a reader in; as a welcome to the major book of one's life, it hardly promises a warm hearth and a glass of foamy brew.

Then too, how interesting it is that what looks like a straightforward report of the real speech of a real father in "Silence" is in fact a fiction, a construction of the "feel" or the essence of reality by means of her habitual collage. Virtually all of Moore's poems presume no other narrator than the poet, and few are about a single individual who thinks or speaks. When people surface—Adam, Moliere, Handel, Dürer, Gieseking, a translator of Hippocrates named Littré—most frequently they perform some function in the poem and then vanish; they are metaphors, not subjects. As for the construction of her fictitious father's speech, her notes are, as usual, quite open about it: Two contributors to his (quite convincing) speech are credited: Miss A. M. Homans (unidentified) and Edmund Burke, as reported in an 1872 biography.

Thus the apparently genuine father seems to be the poet's own creation, and the expression of an ideal. This purported father, eager to recommend an exemplary decorum, does not flinch at invoking the elitism of "superior people." Class is not invoked, however, or not explicitly, though just who might be interested in the glass flowers at Harvard or Longfellow's grave? He is speaking of a natural nobility, superiority earned, not conferred by privilege. He chooses as heroic example the cat, that least sloppily demonstrative of domestic animals, superior as well; he lauds its hunger for privacy, for solitude (person now conflated with cat), and finally calls forth the opposite of speech as the ultimate response to speech. He turns silence into the ultimate compliment, literally beyond words. Words, in this context, seem easy, even vulgar. For a poet this is a paradoxical ideal, yet control and restraint seem more valuable here than any common display of enthusiasm.

I would rather not pursue the ultimate implications of this style whose celebration of glacial northern inhibition over Mediterranean volubility has a long history of political and economic snobbery behind it. I'd rather search out its happy result in Moore's work, where it leads her to aesthetic subtlety and understatement. Her preoccupation with the precise or minimal gesture is everywhere evident: In "The Past Is Present," she enunciates a corollary that is itself a fine definition of poetry: "Ecstasy affords the occasion and expediency determines the form." Ecstasy here is (safely) past. Recollected in tranquillity, it is subject to the expediency—the control—that will shape it. "There is a great amount of poetry in unconscious / fastidiousness" (*Critics and Connoisseurs*). In "To a Snail," she is quoting Demetrius when she prescribes that "compression is the first grace of style." The "contractability" of the snail becomes, then, like modesty, a virtue. She looks to the unlikely little slug for the human qualities she most values—principle and method. A riffle through the poems shows her returning to a purposeful omission again and again ("To a Steam Roller", "The Monkey Puzzle," whose "complicated starkness" is beautiful, perfectly proportioned; "The Hero" who, seeing an El Greco, "covets nothing that it has let go," and of course the jerboa who lives without water but has happiness: "one would not be he / who has nothing but plenty.")

Odd, odd, yet there is a certain sense in it, that amid the sensually voluptuous and assertive creatures of this world that the poet piles exuberantly one on top of another, there is a counterbalancing passion for the ascetic, for control, for paring away, the quiet eye of a hurricane of reference. Or, to change metaphors in mid thought, as she might, in the middle of the prop shop the delighted collector nonetheless (therefore?) lauds the punctilious, the straitened, the stringent: "the power of relinquishing / what one would keep; that is freedom" ("His Shield"). I seem to remember Alice B. Toklas announcing that the only objects worth owning were the breakable ones.

But these strictures are more refined than mere renunciation, as it happens: what pleases Moore best, in the end, is a natural tendency toward restraint by the powerful or the beautiful; the denial of abundance only by those who could easily possess it proves that, like her omissions, it is a choice. The old insult comes to mind that "prudence is a rich, ugly old maid courted by incapacity." Moore, though, awards moral points only to the capable; she enjoys the spectacle of the powerful flinging off of their power, the abundantly blessed opting for a kind of willed poverty. Poem after poem depicts—is full of wonder at—a world in which the fit and the fine elect modesty or finesse, a quiet gesture rather than a flamboyant display. These are her spiritual heroes; they are enlarged by their refusals.

I suppose a case could be made for this cribbing and constraint as the superego's stifling of the id. Or it could be called an eighteenth-century love of decorum over a nineteenth-century spontaneity, a Tory reserve over a populist inclusiveness.

But the uses to which Moore puts her stringencies and denials are humane and, like the "superior" person whose profound emotion demands respectful silence, all her invocations of constraint channel and deepen feeling, which, like a flood, would (she seems to believe) become diffuse were it not curbed.

The "dark energy of life" is found, instead, in contrasts of scale, in pianissimo alternating with fortissimo: " 'Like happy souls in Hell,' enjoying mutual difficulties the Greeks / amused themselves with delicate behavior / because it was 'so noble and so fair' ("An Octopus"). Metaphors tumble out energetically in this magnificent, funny, earnest, and playful poem, and wild analogies leap forth: a flower "like Henry James 'damned by the public for decorum'; / not decorum but restraint; / it is the love of doing hard things / that rebuffed and wore them out—a public out of sympathy with neatness. / Neatness of finish! Neatness of finish!" And back, then, to the octopus of ice "with its capacity for fact."

What a strange rude hectoring, a brief fit of fury by the poet who loves silence. She sounds for a moment like nothing so much as the British

Parliament. This scolding comes in the middle of a dizzying, though never haphazard, compilation of sources both ordinary and rarefied. In the end, the contradictory impulses toward buoyancy and inclusiveness on the one hand and restraint and exclusion on the other, not to mention that moment of fishwifelike irritation, constitute the slightly mad and wholly original charm of a pastiche like "An Octopus," which is a fairly typical Moore poem. Her method resembles what she says, in "A Grave," of the sea: "repression . . . is not the most obvious characteristic of the sea; / the sea is a collector, quick to return a rapacious look." Without their elastic quality—the subject pulled open to an implausible size, gaping like a snake that swallows mice much wider than its own body but quick to snap taut again—these poems might not have discovered their discipline or their form.

All this, I've discovered, looks far easier than it is. Everyone should try to write a Moore imitation to discover how easily flatness takes over, and wordiness, and a tendency toward the aphoristic that's slightly too explicit, not quite cool enough (yet cool without chill) to feel like the dry touch of this masterly hand.

"Silence" is one of the most straightforward and uncomplicated of her exhortations to moral and aesthetic virtue. If "by darkness a star is perfected," ("By Disposition of Angels") then by constraint is plenty amplified. If this is a paradox, it is the paradox that separates poetry from mere words on a page. It is the way, for Marianne Moore, silence speaks.

TERESA D. CADER

Geoffrey Chaucer: Where Colloquial Speech Meets Prosody

Six hundred years ago, Geoffrey Chaucer began his famous *Canterbury Tales* with a brief evocation of the coming of spring. That evocations of spring were standard conventions in the Middle Ages, and that the modern ear has been saturated with clichéd and dim-witted lyrics about daffodils and crocuses, does nothing to diminish the magnificent accomplishment of these opening eighteen lines. The appeal of this verse, the reason it is so loved and so often memorized, lies primarily in its sound, rather than its sense. Geoffrey Chaucer was the original sculptor of our poetry: out of the chaos of regional dialects, irregular syntax, and loose grammar of medieval England, and in opposition to the bad imitations of French and Italian masters that postured as native English verse, he hammered out the nation's first sophisticated poetry rooted in the authentic speech patterns and daily life of England. With Chaucer, English poetry entered the ranks of great world literature, much as Latin and Italian had some time before through the accomplishments of poets such as Ovid, Virgil, Dante, and Boccaccio. Like his Latin and Italian predecessors, though, Chaucer was not just a master versifier: his was a great literary imagination, fueled by vast learning in philosophy, science, and the arts, nurtured by his extraordinary insight into human nature, and animated by his idiosyncratic, unmistakable voice.

The first thing a reader new to Chaucer notices is the strange spelling and vocabulary of *The Canterbury Tales*: this London dialect, now known as Middle English, became the standard form of the language (because London was the mercantile center of England) that preceded our own usage. While an earlier form of the language had been used in poetry and prose for at least six centuries before Chaucer, the Norman Conquest, with its political and cultural turmoil, put an end to a unified form of the language and to the cultivation of writing. Chaucer was uniquely positioned to observe the chaos of the language and to become *the* innovator whose genius would prove that elegant poetry could be written in the English of London. In "Troilus and Criseyde," he writes:

> . . . ther is so gret diversite
> In Englissh and in writyng of oure tonge
> (T&C V, 1793–94)

He understood, too, that he stood at a historical apex: in the midst of flux, he could become the shaper of a new English poetry or he could disappear among a flood of competing forms of speech:

> Ye knowe ek that in forme of speche is
>   chaunge
> Withinne a thousand yeer, and wordes tho
> That hadden pris, now wonder nyce and
>   straunge
> Us thinketh hem
> (T&C II, 22–25)

It seems clear that Chaucer was not enamored by much of the English poetry he was familiar with. The Host in *The Canterbury Tales* rants and raves about a contemporary poem, but one suspects the viewpoint is really Chaucer's:

> "By God", quod he, "for pleynly, at a word,
> Thy drasty rymyng is nat worth a toord!"
> (CT VII, 926–27)

For Chaucer, the inferior craftsmanship of many fellow English poets left him with few models in his native tongue. (There were other fine medieval poets, such as the Gawain poet, but they wrote in regional dialects that became arcane.) He deeply admired the French and Italian poets of the Continent—and apparently had met Boccaccio and others on royal diplomatic missions—but found that their metrical intricacy was inimitable in English. In Chaucer's time English verse was composed in two different traditions: one type evolved from Old English and the general Germanic tradition and used alliteration instead of rhyme and a pattern of stressed syllables, rather than regular meter; the other, derived from French and Latin models, depended on the number of syllables in each line and the linking of lines in couplets or groups by their final sounds. Before the fourteenth century, the most prominent form of the latter type was a four-stress line. The number of unstressed syllables was less restricted than in French. Although Chaucer began his early work in this four-stress beat, by *The Canterbury Tales* he had begun to perfect the five-stress line. His greatest contribution to the prosodic evolution of English poetry was his arrangement of five-stress lines into formally rhyming couplets. The great stylistic innovation of Chaucer was his marriage of native London speech to these formal patterns of rhyme and meter, thereby creating a natural but elegant verse in his native tongue and preparing the way for the great English poets, like Shakespeare, who would follow him.

To see what Chaucer was up to, it is important to look at the text itself, in this case the opening eighteen lines of the General Prologue to *The Canterbury Tales*. The setting is, of course, a pilgrimage to Canterbury, which begins at the Tabard Inn in London in April. These lines comprise one long sentence: its nine rhyming couplets in iambic pentameter and its symphony of sounds pull one from beginning to end so smoothly that it is easy to miss the fact that this is all happening within one sentence. The sentence has two thematic centers. The first eleven lines consist of a series of subordinate clauses describing the renewal of life in the plant and animal kingdoms. These subordinate clauses culminate in a boldly stressed main clause in the twelfth line: the awakening of spring in the physical world causes a longing for spiritual renewal in man. The lines read as follows:

> Whan that Aprill with his shoures soote
> The droghte of March hath perced to the
> roote,
> And bathed every veyne in swich licour
> Of which vertu engendred is the flour;
> Whan Zephirus eek with his sweete breeth
> Inspired hath in every holt and heeth
> The tendre croppes, and the yonge sonne
> Hath in the Ram his half cours yronne,
> And smale foweles maken melodye,
> That slepen al the nyght with open ye
> (So priketh hem nature in hir corages),
> Thanne longen folk to goon on pilgrimages.

This thematic movement is rhetorically orchestrated by the repetitive device of "Whan," "Whan," "Thanne." But the turn in the twelfth line is not simply the introduction of the main clause in which the real subject—the pilgrims' longing for spiritual birth—is introduced. The twelfth line involves a change of diction: the elevated, melodious language, the complex syntax is suddenly simplified. The elevated style is reserved for flowers and crops and small birds that sleep all night with their eyes open. The spiritual longing of the pilgrims, which is at the apex of this medieval sense of hierarchy, is, by contrast, described in a plain, or "low" style. This reversal of our expectations gives us a glimpse into the kinds of games, paradoxes, and puzzles Chaucer will introduce in *The Canterbury Tales*: the elevated, sensuous description of spring begins to sound like a parody of the medieval literary convention itself.

In contrast, the pilgrims are not very elevated, and their longings, as we discover in the *Tales* themselves, are very often not spiritual. Chaucer's birds are so excited by spring that they sleep with their eyes open all night: while this image might seem tender, even sentimental, in my view it is associatively linked with the pilgrims by virtue of its placement in the lines directly introducing them. The birds sleep little because it is the mating season. Several of the pilgrims, we later learn, suffer from similar kinds of sleep deprivation. The Squire is described as loving so hotly that he slept no more "than dooth a nyghtngale." The longing to go on a pilgrimage turns out to have as much natural, as spiritual, impetus. The medieval pilgrimage was also a good party at the end of a hard winter. Part of Chaucer's genius is that he never makes such a scandalous assertion: he embeds his meaning in his language, through skillful manipulation of association, nuance, and sound.

Chaucer, the master versifier, is evident in these opening lines. The rhyming couplets ("soote" / "roote," "licour" / "flour," "breeth" / "heeth," "sonne" / "yronne," "melodye" / "ye," "corages" / "pilgrimages") are skillfully orchestrated with enjambed lines that keep the reader from landing like a cat on a keyboard. Chaucer also uses alliteration and assonance in phrases that use the rhyme words: "shoures soote," "every veyne," "yonge sonne," "straunge strondes," and "sondry londes." In line 5 the sound of the wind Zephirus is invoked in the repetition of long vowel sounds in "eek" and "sweete breeth." To appreciate Chaucer fully, one must read him aloud. Three rules guide Middle English pronunciation: pronounce all written consonants as we do those in modern English; pronounce all final syllables (even those with a final e); and give all written vowels, both long and short, their so-called Continental sounds. Thus, 'dame' is pronounced *dah-meh*. "Doute" has the *ou* sound of *soup*, not the *ow* sound of *doubt*. The phonetic transcription of the first line would thus look as follows:

> Whan that Ăhprĭl with hĭs shōurĕs sōhtĕ

The meter of the first and fourth lines is accordingly:

> Whán that Áprill wíth his shóures sóote
> Of whích vertú engéndred is the flóur

That Chaucer's meter was not rigid is noticeable immediately in the opening trochee of the first line. His irregularities were conscious attempts to break the regularity of the iambic pentameter line and to strengthen the infusion of London speech patterns.

The final seven lines are preoccupied with pilgrims, who include among their ranks professional seekers who have been to the Holy Land

and the more ordinary variety, who are on their way to the grave of St. Thomas à Becket in Canterbury. The last couplet turns on a linguistic play between "seke" and "seeke":

> The hooly blisfil martir for to seke
> That hem hath holpen whan that they were
> seeke.

The rhyme is on two words that are identical in sound but have different meanings: seek and sick. Chaucer and the French poets were enamored of this elegant and witty form, known as "rime riche" or "rich rhyme." By yoking sickness and seeking, Chaucer is not just describing the medieval desire to go on a pilgrimage after battling or witnessing ill health: he has literally injected the notion of "sick" into "seek." Chaucer's pilgrims also are battling spiritual sickness, though in most cases the pilgrimage does little to cure them. This again is Chaucer at his best: not a moralizer or an ideologue, Chaucer makes his words resonate with a complexity of meaning and viewpoint that seems quite modern.

I first read Chaucer in a course in Middle English in college. I remember being intimidated by the language, but mastering it gave me personal access to the poet, much as four years of Latin in high school had enabled me to translate *The Aeneid* and therefore know Virgil in a way I couldn't have without the ability to hear his words. (This same fascination for original texts led me to study Old English in graduate school, in order to know *Beowulf*.) My original love of Chaucer was rooted in pleasure: he is enormous fun. But I am not in concurrence with Matthew Arnold, who found that Chaucer lacked the Aristotelian seriousness required of great poets. Chaucer was an original thinker, a poet of enormous learning and sophistication. Rather, Lionel Trilling's declaration that Arnold was confusing seriousness with solemnity seems more apt. The brilliance of Chaucer is inseparable from the kind of serious literary fun he was capable of. This, of course, we see again in Shakespeare some two hundred years later.

Today I find myself examining Chaucer's poetic techniques for things I learn from him: the sheer intoxication of his sounds; his perfect word selection; the application of sophisticated narrative and dramatic strategies to verse; the counterpoint rhythm of colloquial speech embedded in formal meter and rhyme; and the infusion of vast learning and psychological wisdom into poems that refuse didactic or judgmental postures. Despite his medieval trappings, Chaucer is timeless.

The Canterbury Tales

General Prologue

Here bygynneth the Book of the Tales of Canterbury.

   Whan that Aprill with his shoures soote
The droghte of March hath perced to the
     roote,
And bathed every veyne in swich licour
Of which vertu engendred is the flour;
Whan Zephirus eek with his sweete breeth
Inspired hath in every holt and heeth
The tendre croppes, and the yonge sonne
Hath in the Ram his half cours yronne,
And smale foweles maken melodye,
That slepen al the nyght with open ye
(So priketh hem nature in hir corages),
Thanne longen folk to goon on pilgrimages,
And palmeres for to seken straunge strondes,
To ferne halwes, kowthe in sondry londes;
And specially from every shires ende
Of Engelond to Canterbury they wende,
The hooly blisful martir for to seke,
That hem hath holpen whan that they were
     seeke.

Geoffrey Chaucer

MICHAEL COLLIER

The Truant Pen

"**L**ook in thy heart and write" is the direct and simplifying command
the muse gives Astrophil, Sir Philip Sidney's foil, at the end of sonnet
one in "Astrophil and Stella," the first sonnet sequence in English litera-
ture. Critics, more than common readers, have debated whether Sidney's
sonnet sequence, as well as much of his work, is merely the expression
of a Renaissance courtier's wit or if Sidney is writing to a real Stella
about a real love. Although both of these issues figure prominently in
"Astrophil and Stella," my interest in the sonnets has always had to do
with how Sidney struggles with the influence of the past and tries to
make something new of the old situation, "Loving in truth."

If we go back to Wyatt and Surrey and gaze at their sonnets, we find
they possess the rough beauty and uniqueness of some very early auto-
mobiles—true horseless carriages—but Sidney's sonnets are the result
of a more fully developed industry in which "the exact, regular corre-
spondence of features of language to the same features in the metrical
pattern" are brought to perfection, as John Thompson points out in *The
Founding of English Metre*. In the same way that Henry Ford's produc-
tion line created an automobile "industry," Sidney's understanding of
the relationship of abstract pattern to the supple effects of colloquial
language created a self-consciousness in him and in English poets ever
since that has made language itself the underlying subject of poetry.

For Sidney "Loving in truth" is equal to, if not indivisible from, poetry
and the act of writing. The long multiple clauses of the first sentence,
which stretch across the octet, when reduced to its essence ("Loving in
truth . . . I sought fit words") demonstrate the close connection Sidney
believed existed between the experience of love and his desire to "show"
its effects in language. The connection Sidney sees between love, truth,

seeking, and fit words is articulated as a desire to share, with his Stella, the "pleasure of my pain."

Pleasure and pain create the emotional nexus of the sonnet and sequence. It is also the source of Sidney's argument with Petrarchan convention, in whose ideal and spiritualized love he does not believe. His difficulty in writing is linked to the difficulty he has in beatifying Stella. Dante's Beatrice might represent an abstracted form of Christian beauty, but Sidney's Stella is a star—celestial matter, yes, but also resolutely a body. Astrophil, in name, as well, shares in the celestial and corporeal attributes of his love. "Loving in truth" for Sidney means not only feeling reverence and respect for Stella but also the desire to consummate the love in a tangible way.

"Loving" and writing render Sidney, as we see in the twelfth line, "helpless," caught in the "throes" of childbirth. What causes the pain is not the verity of Sidney's love matched with Stella's laudable indifference but rather the self-consciousness Sidney experiences in trying to find "fit words" to describe the particular courtly and troubled love he possesses. Sidney's initial response to this situation is to look outward "Studying inventions fine . . . / Oft turning others' leaves," hoping to discover in the tradition of the Italian sonnet "Some fresh and fruitful showers" to sooth his "sun-burn'd brain." The irony of these lines tells us how empty his search really is and prepares us for the rather comical and klutzy action in the first half of the sestet in which words halt, stay, flee, and trip over each other. Sidney transforms "Other's leaves" into "others' feet," conflating the literal leaves and feet across the octet and sestet, with their metaphorical counterparts—book pages and metrical feet. The conflation is a rhetorical compression, a flourish of wit, that shows the depth of Sidney's frustration with the Petrarchan convention. The conflict or gap Sidney discovers between the need to write about his love and the available resources of language become the underlying theme of the entire sonnet sequence. The high contrast of this conflict is between the heart and mind, the emotions and reason, and is delineated in the argumentative structure of the sonnet.

Before Sidney is saved by his imperative-giving muse, he finds himself cartoonishly paralyzed: "helpless in my throes, / Biting my truant pen, beating myself for spite," trapped in the very self-consciousness he knows he must avoid. By telling Sidney to "Look in thy heart and write," the muse makes it sound simple, but the conjunction that separates "heart" and "write" has rarely loomed as large. Isolated from the rest of the sonnet this command reminds me of how Red Barber, the late *New York Times* sportswriter, characterized the act of writing: "It's the easiest thing in the world to do. You just sit down at your desk and open a vein." The conflict Sidney finds himself in—between the conventions of the past and his desire to find an adequate form for his experience of love—is the basic condition all poets find themselves in each time they write. When the muse impatiently calls Astrophil a "Fool," she does so as a way of bringing the lover back to the present and his immediate concern: finding the words to express his love that will bring him the "grace" of his lover. When the muse tells Astrophil to look in his heart, she means it literally, yes, but also metaphorically, for Sidney has made his heart out of living language.

(from Astrophil and Stella)

I

Loving in truth, and fain in verse my love to show,
    That she, dear she, might take some pleasure of my pain,
    Pleasure might cause her read, reading might make her know,
    Knowledge might pity win, and pity grace obtain,
I sought fit words to paint the blackest face of woe:
    Studying inventions fine, her wits to entertain,
    Oft turning others' leaves, to see if thence would flow
    Some fresh and fruitful showers upon my sun-burned brain.
But words came halting forth, wanting invention's stay;
    Invention, Nature's child, fled step-dame Study's blows;
    And others' feet still seemed but strangers in my way.
Thus, great with child to speak, and helpless in my throes,
    Biting my truant pen, beating myself for spite:
    "Fool," said my Muse to me, "look in thy heart and write!"

Sir Philip Sidney

WILLIAM C. COOK

Langston Hughes's "Painting"

In "Lenox Avenue Mural" Langston Hughes turns to one of the oldest literary genres in the European tradition. His poem belongs to that group of works we label ekphrastic, works that are constructed as literary versions of graphic images. Keats's "Ode on a Grecian Urn," Ashbery's "Self-Portrait in a Convex Mirror," Stevens's "Lapis Lazuli," and Tolson's "A Gallery of Harlem Portraits" all aspire to the condition of ekphrasis. The latter text, written by an African American poet, deals however with a gallery and with paintings that exist only in the imagination of the poet. In describing such texts, John Hollander coined the phrase "notional ekphrasis." The popularity of "notional ekphrasis" with African American writers during the early part of this century may be attributed to their conception of an erased past: there are "no images," at least none they would wish to acknowledge as representative of their lives, to be found in the galleries of America. Hence the need to imagine that which is absent.

It may be argued, however, that Hughes does have in mind actual murals created by African American artists. Most prominent among these would be the works of Aaron Douglas, Jacob Lawrence, and Romare Bearden. In 1934 Douglas attempted in four murals to depict the African American experience. Mural one was set in Africa; mural two dealt with emancipation, reconstruction, and the Ku Klux Klan; mural three with Southern agriculture and the horror of lynching; and mural four, titled "Song of the Towers," with the escape from serfdom and entry into the "machinery and sterility of the industrial depression." This last mural bears a striking thematic resemblance to Hughes's "Lenox Avenue Mural." Douglas's work (like that of many others of the period) was supported by the W.P.A. and, in conformity with both the populism and primitivism of those public works, he attempted to depict not a particular individual experience, not his own response to being black in America, but the soul and the experience of a people. Jacob Lawrence in 1940–1941 created a series of sixty panels titled "The Migration of the Negro." Here the focus on the Great Migration was even sharper than in the work of Douglas.

"Lenox Avenue Mural" connects with the painters' populism and primitivism in seeking a literary equivalent of their visual representation of African Americans' unique racial experience. In his black and white illustrations for *The New Negro* (a text in which Hughes's poetry was featured) and in color in his murals, Douglas uses stylized "African" imagery, an "African" preference for design over representation and embedded recreations of African sculpture. Hughes in his literary mural foregrounds black speech and music. He attributes to his speakers of standard English an inability to understand the reality and depth of the suffering that marks the lives of his common black folk. This experience and the response of the common folk to it are not found in the scholarly record or in the high arts; the true soul of a people is preserved in the folklore, folk music, and dance of the "lowdown." This is the artistic basis of Hughes's notional ekphrasis.

The "mural" consists of an introduction ("Harlem") and a conclusion ("Island") that surround four sections dealing with the experience of the Great Migration. In "Harlem" the poet, assuming an educated and distanced persona, poses the problem of the Great Migration: will it end deferred, as have all the earlier dreams of freedom and a better life? What will be the response to yet another postponement of the promise of full participation in the American dream of success? The voice of this persona offers a counterpoint to the more clearly racially and class-specific tone of the second voice in the poem, a voice that will come to dominate the poem.

"Good Morning" begins the series of pictorials that develop Hughes's argument. Here, a speaker emerges whose opening lines mark him as different from the speaker in the introduction. In clearly black street-speech, he enumerates the host of "wondering/wide-eyed/dreaming" seekers who made up the greatest population shift in the history of the United States. Two million African Americans left the south for the north in 1915. August and Meier's *From Plantation to Ghetto* offers additional evidence of the dimensions of this migration. Between 1900 and 1910 New York City experienced a 51 percent gain in African Americans: Philadelphia and Chicago more than 30 percent. By 1913 the Harlem district of New York included 35,000 in only eighteen city blocks. Fleeing racism, and economic depression, seeking a new life, they came in response to leaflets from the north describing the opportunities possible there due to the drying up of European immigration, as well as in response to ads in African newspapers extolling the new land of Phillymeyork. Hughes's speaker describes this "dark tenth of a nation" streaming into "Harlem / dusky sash across Manhattan." He closes this description not in the standard English of the introduction but in the same register with which he began, but with a difference. "Good morning, daddy" opens the section on a note of promise. "Daddy, ain't you heard" closes it on a note of bitterness, betrayal, and wonder that anyone can be so naive as to believe any longer in the reality of the dream.

"The Same in Blues" repeats the promise-become-frustration that marks "Harlem." Here the twelve-bar blues provides a structural and thematic source. Blues stanzas, those folk recordings of dashed hopes, are juxtaposed to "translations" in standard English. The closing verse, skillfully blending that voice with the blues pattern, unites the seemingly divergent speakers just as it rejects limiting the disenchantment to one group of Harlemites:

> From river to river
> Uptown and down,
> There's liable to be confusion
> when a dream gets kicked around.

In "Comment on Curb" the blues poet rejects attempts to generalize his observations to such an extent that they are simply part of the human condition. "I'm talking about Harlem to you." It is toward such specificity that the poem has been moving as it has focused in from the wide angle of the flood of migrants to the individual (representative?) depiction found in "Letter." Here the subject is named. Joe writes to a mother still in the South about the reality of life in Harlem. This reality, recreated in his own speech register, is not softened by the contrasting standard English of the earlier sections. His letter is the record of unfulfilled dreams, of poverty and rain, and not of the wealth and sunshine of the Dream. But Joe's is not a record of complete despair or desertion of his values. He has not lost his love for his mother (he shares the few dollars he has with her) or, as his closing demonstrates, his respectability. More important, he has retained some vestige of hope.

The closing section of the poem, "Island," while returning us to the voice of the opening section, speaks in a lyrical voice darkened by the observation of the four panels of the mural. What had been posed as a question about the nature of frustration and loss is now presented as a clearly realized conclusion. Harlem is not a part of the mainland; it is an island and a place of darkness:

> Between two rivers,
> North of the Park,

Like darker rivers,
The streets are dark

This darkness and the clear possibility of explosion is firmly entrenched in the closing dialogue. To the cheery "good morning, Daddy" the response is a disgusted and incredulous "ain't you heard?" How can a viewer of the mural, its opening generalized images of the migrant crowds streaming into Penn Station and coming face to face with barred gates, the blues laments of the second section, and the single portrait of one individual in "Letter" retain any optimism or hope?

Hughes, through his skillful manipulation of multiple voices, succeeds in associating his reader with the abstract and abstracted standard English speaker of the opening section. That reader, as a result of his viewing of the mural, must become less naive. More important, however, is the obvious blues referent of "The Same in Blues," a referent that, although absent structurally, is present thematically in each section of the poem. "Lenox Avenue Mural" is a blues poem as are other poems in *Montage of a Dream Deferred*, poems like "Boogie: 1 a.m.," "Deferred," "Children's Rhymes," and "Dream Boogie." In Hughes's notional ekphrasis language and folk blues do the work of color, form, and spatial arrangement.

STEVEN CRAMER

Images of Self-Confusedness:
Fulke Greville (1554–1628)

I first read Fulke Greville's poems on the recommendation of Robert Pinsky, who was introduced to Greville's work by Yvor Winters. Friend and biographer of Philip Sidney, Greville is the quintessential word-of-mouth poet. Readers pass his work on to new devotees as if it were a precious rumor that is still in the process of becoming news.

Greville is represented in major anthologies like the *Norton Anthology of Poetry* by a handful of poems, yet his complete *Poems and Dramas*, edited by Geoffrey Bullough, comprises a hefty two volumes, and many specialists of sixteenth-century English verse rank his "sonnet" sequence *Caelica*—only 41 of its 109 poems are true sonnets—as one of the great works of the age, a complex reworking of Petrarchan and plain-style traditions that rivals and often surpasses his more famous friend's *Astrophil and Stella*.

Greville's love poetry is stark, disabused, at times sneeringly cynical, its project to scrutinize and ultimately dismantle the Neoplatonic idealizations of desire that constitute the tradition of courtly love. Although *Caelica* starts off rather conventionally, portraying the well-worn figure of the exasperated yet devoted courtly lover, the sequence turns increasingly caustic until, in Sonnet 84, the witty Petrarchan bids "farewell, sweet boy" to Cupid, foreswearing secular love for the divine adoration of Christ. This arc of development was familiar enough in Greville's time for a contemporary, George Peele, to devote a poem to the spiritual passage whereby a "lover's sonnets [turn] to holy psalms."

But if Greville is not unique in this evolution from bowing courtier to kneeling penitent, there is, I think, something special in his adopting the penitential stance to engage in rigorous self-analysis. The depth of introspection in Greville's devotional poetry speaks powerfully to our modern sensibilities.

I've taken to calling Sonnet 100 Greville's "insomnia poem" because its open-eyed sleeplessness accounts for much of its disquieting effect. For all its gaping anxiety, however, the poem contains not one specific visual image. The reader encounters evocations of "colors," "light," "distinction," and "sight"—and perhaps an implied metaphor in the eye as a "watch," or sentinel, to "inward senses placed"—but these plurals and abstractions only reinforce the absence of visual context, reducing the "power of sight" to a blocked potential. The poem wakes in the dark and stays there, not *at* night but *in* night—enveloped, swallowed up— and with nothing to look at, the eye turns inward, keeping watch on memory and imagination, and continually on the lookout for attacks of conscience.

This sensation of groping in the dark is further conveyed through the syntax of the poem's single, tortuous sentence. The reader fumbles among the first stanza's introductory clauses, anticipating cadence and grammatical resolution but unsure where to settle on a subject. Is "the eye" the subject we're counting on, or an appositive to "colors" and "distinction"? Stanza two answers that question—"the eye," it turns out, *is* the subject, giving "vain alarums" to the "inward sense." But this solution introduces a new perplexity—how might a visual organ serve as agent for auditory warnings? The question lingers as another state of suspension follows—the chain of subordinate clauses beginning with "where fear" and carrying us through to "tells," the second verb in the poem's compound predicate. Indeed, stripped of its obsessive subordination, the poem makes this unnervingly synesthetic claim: "in night the eye gives vain alarums and tells news of devils."

And yet, entangled within the poem's subordination, a paradoxical design takes shape, again primarily in the verb forms. First the objects of sight are "cast" to black and "gone down with the light," so that the faculty of sight sinks into a state of "not seeing." This descent induces a countermovement upward, whereby fear "stirs up," "forges" (a wonderfully double depiction of the imagination as both shaper and deceiver), and "raises" delusional visions of "impossibility"—the "monster under the bed," as a student of mine aptly put it. In the last stanza, this interior sense "sees" and "tells news," but that news is a false projection— "devils" that are actually "evils"—reconfirming the speaker's lost condition in a dark world of inward chaos. The way down may lead to the way up, but in Greville's lapsed condition, not to a way out.

I'm also arrested by the poem's provocative off-rhymes—"cast/ placed" and especially "devils/evils"—but a different event of language stands out after one has read other poems in *Caelica*: line six's "witty tyranny." "Tyranny of wits, exaggerated imaginings," says Bullough's note, which is helpful. But I also detect in this figure the peculiarly modern recognition that the mind lords its reflexive habits over us tyrannically. In an earlier poem in *Caelica*, Greville demonstrates how wit, through agile figure-making, can construe delayed erotic fulfillment as preferable to gratification, because "absence maintains the treasure / Of pleasure unto pleasure." But in the poem's last stanza he chides his own mental gymnastics:

> But thoughts be not so brave
> With absent joy;
> For you with that you have
> Your self destroy.
> The absence which you glory
> Is that which makes you sorry
> And burn in vain;
> For thought is not the weapon
> Wherewith thoughts-ease men cheapen.
> Absence is pain.

This poem's courtly lover can't purchase mental tranquility with thought any more than the sin-ridden insomniac of Sonnet 100 can will himself to sleep. Whether secular or sacred, Greville's introspective poems dramatize the mirroring face-offs of a mind on the outs with itself. What he calls "images of self-confusednesses," Wallace Stevens once called the "Nothing that is not there and the nothing that is," and we now call "self-consciousness." *Caelica*'s Sonnet 100 offers an especially sharp diagnosis of the mind's capacity for projecting its inward void onto external forms, rather than acknowledging that void as its own.

SONNET 100 (from Caelica)

In night, when colors all to black are cast,
Distinction lost, or gone down with the light,
The eye, a watch to inward senses placed,
Not seeing, yet still having power of sight,

Gives vain alarums to the inward sense,
Where fear, stirred up with witty tyranny,
Confounds all powers, and through self-offence
Doth forge and raise impossibility,

Such as in thick depriving darknesses
Proper reflections of the error be,
And images of self-confusednesses,
Which hurt imaginations only see:—
    And from this nothing seen, tells news of devils,
    Which but expressions be of inward evils.

THOMAS M. DISCH

Emerson's "Mithridates"

This morning, early in October, the groundhog whose burrow abuts my backyard was out there, under the apple tree, munching on windfalls in just the spirit of voracious contentment that Emerson summons in "Mithridates." At such moments the whole world is edible, a kitchen steamy with invitations.

Emerson, as a New Englander, a Transcendentalist, and an eminent Victorian, generally isn't thought of as an advocate of glorious excess, of mellow fruitfulness, *luxe*, *calme*, and *volupté*. But "Mithridates" is typically Emersonian in its celebration of unbounded and transgressive appetites. He was, after all, the man who gave Whitman his first, authenticating blurb and became by that act the godfather of the Beats. Of course, there is the other Emerson, who reneged on that blurb out of a canny sense of what the traffic would bear. He might commend the poppy; there was poetic precedent for that in Keats and Coleridge. But drug abuse, in so many words? Or sex?

Emerson's poems of voluptuary delight—and there are many—are like the poems of those Sufis who commend the wine their religion forbids them to taste and who insist (disingenuously, one always supposes) that the wine of their verse is a metaphor for Wisdom, or some such unassailable abstraction.

There is, in that very denial, a spice whose savor our tongues, schooled in the candors of a nouvelle cuisine, have difficulty savoring— the spice of hypocrisy, of disguising our meaning, even from ourselves; the tang of that hemlock in Emerson's sherbet.

But suppose that instead of Emerson the poem were ascribed to Baudelaire. Wouldn't the author of *Les Fleurs de Mal* have been delighted with such a couplet as "Swing me in the upas boughs, / Vampyre-fanned, when I carouse"? It is pure Theda Bara. Campy, certainly, but isn't any middle-class evocation of Oriental delight a camp? Fitzgerald's Omar Khayyam? Matisse's odalisques? Wallace Stevens's "green freedom of a cockatoo"? Emerson should certainly be allowed equal license.

And then there is simply the sound of it and the syntax—the man's knack for giving a freshness to the stalest words in the language: that "works" in the fourth line has the modern valence of "if it works, then use it"; his forcing "few," at the start of the last stanza, to do service as a noun signifying scarcity; and, best of all, the extraordinary catalogue in that same stanza that summons, in a single ecstatic breath, "virtues, methods, mights, / Means, appliances, delights, / Reputed wrongs and braggart rights, / Smug routine, and things allowed, / Minorities, things under cloud."

At such moments, the moralizing Emerson of the essays and the rhapsodic Emerson of the poems fuse into a single, distinctive rhetoric that entitles the man to have his own adjective: Emersonian. At its fullest stretch, as in the last four lines, the Emersonian moment sails out beyond sight of the shores of didacticism and common sense and utters the ineffable. He is then closer kin to the Sybil, Dickinson, than to Longfellow, and more likely, therefore, to satisfy contemporary appetites.

If, despite this, his books gather dust, the reason may well be political rather than aesthetic, for when one takes the trouble to puzzle out the last vatic couplet of "Mithridates," the poem can be construed not as a simple hymn of praise to large appetites but rather as one more strophe in a national anthem celebrating the course of the American empire— "from the earth-poles to the line . . . from all zones and altitudes." For what other bird would sun itself in the capitol unless it is the eagle— the same emblematic bird, both Roman and American—that appears in the finale of another of the author's Heldentenor arias, "Fate":

> One thing is forever good;
> That one thing is Success,—
> Dear to the Eumenides,
> And to all the heavenly brood.
> Who bides at home, nor looks abroad,
> Carries the eagles, and masters the sword.

We are unaccustomed to poetry celebrating nationalist or martial sentiments. Most readers of serious poetry would even find them reprehensible. Yet Emerson's popularity in his own time undoubtedly owed much to the underlying triumphal vision of an America ever expanding, assimilating along the way everything and everyone in its path, including "minorities, things under cloud," and doing so, like Mithridates, harmlessly and without indigestion. In this regard, Emerson was the first prophet of the Pax Americana. Even those who don't approve such an ambition must credit his prophetic acumen.

If one doesn't squint too closely at his patriot raptures (and they are seldom overt; more like the marches threaded through an Ives or Mahler symphony), Emerson can be read unproblematically as America's most accomplished Romantic poet, in lively dialogue with Coleridge and Shelley. And possibly with Hegel, for it may be his owl, living belatedly at the end of European civilization, that Emerson has in mind in "Mithridates": "The owl of Minerva [that] spreads its wings only with the falling of the dusk." Emerson wrote in the springtime of America. We read him in the fall, and so his sweetness seems to us to have a tang more of cider than of apple juice.

Mithridates

I cannot spare water or wine,
    Tobacco-leaf, or poppy, or rose;
From the earth-poles to the line,
    All between that works or grows,
Every thing is kin of mine.

Give me agates for my meat;
Give me cantharids to eat;
From air and ocean bring me foods,
From all zones and altitudes;—

From all natures, sharp and slimy,
    Salt and basalt, wild and tame:
Tree and lichen, ape, sea-lion,
    Bird, and reptile, be my game.

Ivy for my fillet band;
Blinding dog-wood in my hand;
Hemlock for my sherbet cull me,
And the prussic juice to lull me;
Swing me in the upas boughs,
Vampyre-fanned, when I carouse.

Too long shut in strait and few,
Thinly dieted on dew,
I will use the world and sift it,
To a thousand humors shift it,
As you spin a cherry.

O doleful ghosts, and goblins merry!
O all you virtues, methods, mights,
Means, appliances, delights,
Reputed wrongs and braggart rights,
Smug routine, and things allowed,
Minorities, things under cloud!
Hither! take me, use me, fill me,
Vein and artery, though ye kill me!
God! I will not be an owl,
But sun me in the Capitol.

                    Ralph Waldo Emerson

"Mr. Flood's Party"

"Mr. Flood's Party," one of Edwin Arlington Robinson's Tilbury Town portraits, above all shows his mastery of tone, and in this case how such mastery rescues—almost entirely—his subject matter from the bathos with which it flirts. "Almost" will be one of the concerns of this essay, though Eben Flood remains a memorable Robinson character, in the good company of Reuben Bright, Miniver Cheevy, Richard Cory, and the less-defeated Cliff Klingenhagen.

Eben Flood, his aloneness intensified by old age, may or may not be a drunk, but on this particular evening he has the regular drinker's comic sense of self-imposed propriety. He needs to give himself permission. For some, it's when the sun is below the yardarm; for Eben, the solitary that he is, it's the need for social drinking, for a companion, to have, as the title suggests, a party. It's one of the smallest and saddest parties ever registered in a poem, made so by Eben's elaborate formalities with his compliant alter ego. But the same formalities make us smile, too, which is Robinson's genius. We are regularly distracted from bathos by felicities both tonal and prosodic.

I found myself admiring Robinson's ambition to work as closely as possible to his subject while still orchestrating all of its effects. "Reuben Bright" and "Richard Cory" are also poems that display Robinson's gift for this kind of intimacy, though their famous endings (one character tears down the slaughterhouse, the other goes home and puts a bullet through his head) succeed with tones so matter-of-fact that they suggest a greater balance of distance and intimacy than Robinson was able to achieve at the end of "Mr. Flood's Party." This may be why the last stanza doesn't resonate beyond what has already been established in the poem.

The poem's first stanza situates us immediately, both physically and psychologically. Its five-line opening sentence couldn't be much better paced or orchestrated.

> Old Eben Flood, climbing alone one night
> Over the hill between the town below
> And the forsaken upland hermitage
> That held as much as he should ever know
> On earth again of home, paused warily.

Eben Flood is between a place that is forsaken and a town (we will soon learn) that no longer remembers him. And this hermitage of his "held as much as he should ever know / on earth again of home." The word that pricks us is "again," because it suggests that home was once a homier place, and no doubt also because of its consonantal resonance with the other *n* sounds, as those in "alone" and "forsaken." And how adroitly Robinson emphasizes "paused" after the long clause that establishes Eben's plight. The three iambs before it prepare us for an unstressed syllable. When instead we get a stressed syllable, we feel that a dramatic moment has been properly timed and delivered. Eben has paused, warily. He's about to begin his party, and it would be too embarrassing for him if others were about. In the lines that follow, we don't quite know how good and ironically understated "having leisure" is until we read further. And the road Eben is on is "his" in more ways than one, and more ways than one is how Robinson likes it.

> Well, Mr. Flood, we have the harvest moon
> Again, and we may not have many more

commences Eben's address to himself and, almost in passing, allows us to hear that he doesn't expect to live much longer. The poet of "the bird is on the wing" is Khayyám. Eben has his prop; the social drinker offers a toast to the only companion he has, and acceptance is guaranteed. They drink to the bird in flight. It's a toast to the departed or the departing—an excuse to indulge, perhaps even a death wish. Probably both.

The third stanza deepens what we already know, and the highly stressed "a valiant armor of scarred hopes outworn" distinguishes itself as language while complicating our attitude toward Mr. Flood. (Eben is valiant; he no longer even has *scarred* hopes.) We learn that he once had been "honored" by his friends. The allusion is either to Browning's "Childe Roland to the Dark Tower Came" or to the medieval French poem "Chanson de Roland." The former suggests a quest and the latter a kind of stubborn heroism. If it's the former, it's for purposes of comic disparity (Eben's quest is drink). If it's the latter, there's reason to receive it poignantly, since Roland, trapped by the enemy, refused to blow his horn to signal help from Charlemagne's army until the moment of his death. Just as plausibly, it is there to suggest that Eben is already like a ghost. He can hear the town's "phantom salutation of the dead" calling to him.

But in stanza four, his context firmly established now, Robinson most artfully makes his poem resonate beyond its sentimental concerns. "He set the jug down slowly at his feet / Knowing that most things break; / And only when assured that on firm earth / It stood, as the uncertain lives of men / assuredly did not" are arguably the poem's finest moments, the poet allowing himself wise asides happily mitigated—though not reduced—by the fact that he's talking about a jug. No feel of the didactic here. These editorials on the human condition are rooted in setting and circumstance. Moreover, they represent a perfect blending of two sources, Eben's thoughts and Robinson's—just the right intimacy.

Eben's handling of the jug, which carries in it a temporary surcease of loneliness, is likened to the tenderness with which a mother would handle a sleeping child. This action is both comedic and heroic. We can imagine the slowness, the delicacy, with which a drunk puts something down so as not to break it. Eben is in the middle of a journey between two equally undesirable places, home and town; his heroism is in his effort toward good humor while he steels himself with drink. The jug is another character in the poem. In modern parlance, it's his baby, and he will care for it as such.

His invocation to his second self, his drinking companion, is more convivial at this point than self-pitying, though it's an edgy conviviality: "many a change has come / to both of us, I fear, since it was / last we had a drop together." The "I fear" registers with us, as does the end of his toast, "Welcome home!" We feel the irony in that last word, emphasized by its placement and its rhyme. It should be noted that Robinson employs only two rhymes (with one exception) in each of his eight-line stanzas: at the ends of the second and fourth lines and the sixth and the eighth. Here Robinson gets maximum effect out of rhyme, even though it's more near than exact. "Home" stops us, or is stopped for us by both its exclamation point and the click of cooperative sound. We have not forgotten where he is. Home now is stupor, in the middle of nowhere.

The toast complete, Robinson mimics successfully the manners of the drunk who might also be a Puritan: "if you insist" and "Only a very little." This is an engaging burlesque within the larger, pathetic scene. Tonally, at this moment, we as readers are not asked to feel sorry for Eben. We are allowed to enjoy how well the poet, by blending tones, has been equal to the psychological and linguistic imperatives of his task. The lines that follow serve further to demonstrate Robinson's deft comic timing, which is linked to his metrical brilliance.

For auld lang syne. No more, sir; that will do.
So, for the time, apparently it did.
And Eben evidently thought so too;

Throughout, the poem has employed a mixture of blank verse and rhymed, often loose, iambic pentameter. The iambic pentameter has been regular enough to permit Robinson many variations and substitutions. The illusion of natural speech has been maintained while "the grid of meter" has served as underpinning. To my ear, the line, "For auld lang syne. No more, sir; that will do," arguably has seven stresses. Only "For" and "No" and perhaps "will" would seem to be unstressed. But the prosodic fun occurs with the semicolon after "sir." It breaks the iamb-spondee-iamb flow of the line (a string of two-syllable feet), while conforming exactly to the way that we trust Eben's elaborate formality with himself would be spoken. The ten-syllable line has been kept, but has been metrically fractured right at the point where Eben, or at least half of him, is trying to stop drinking. The narrative coyness inherent in "apparently" and "evidently" also serve the comic. Robinson would have us entertain that the narrator-observer, heretofore omniscient, is suddenly uncertain in this highly managed fiction. The uncertainty serves to underscore the narrative playfulness at this juncture, as does the placement of "did" after "do" as end words in successive lines. These are welcome balancing touches in a poem so potentially sentimental.

In the lines that follow, Robinson returns to a device that worked well for him earlier in the poem: the apparently positive word or phrase that in context suggests a harsh irony. Earlier we were told "The road was his" and that Eben had "leisure." Now Eben is "secure," a word set apart by commas, which denotatively means he's not worried about being overheard singing out loud. We wait a full line before the "until" comes, and then his entire landscape echoes back to him the song of old times, his sad anthem.

I'm not sure what "with only two moons listening" is supposed to mean. It's a curious moment, the "only" suggesting that Eben expects more than two. My guess would be that Eben's selves each have a moon, or that to Eben's drunken eye there appear to be two moons. Frost's enigmatic reading of the two moons ("Two, as on the planet Mars.") in his "Introduction to Robinson's *King Jasper*" seems only to beg the issue.

When the landscape echoes "For auld lang syne," the poem reaches its climax. Eben cannot escape the sound of his own lamentation. Afterward, his "weary throat gave out" and the poem spirals into unrelieved pathos. It is in this stanza that Robinson's compositional balance of intimacy and distance—his ability to deliver to us with multiple tones this valiant, sad, and drunken man—fails him. He can only sum up for us what we already know. One longs for some resonance comparable to what he was able to effect in stanza four, a line that would evaluate and measure Eben's condition as much as it declares it, or the sudden rightness that makes poetry poetry.

"Mr. Flood's Party" is a very good poem by a very good poet, as close to a great poet as a very good poet can be. Who knows, perhaps a great poet. I wouldn't argue. But in "Mr. Flood's Party," Robinson's language at the end neither pulls back far enough to position Eben as sufferer, nor does he stay close enough to him to participate sufficiently in his thoughts. Instead Robinson gets caught in the middle, a toneless ground that has to depend on easy (if momentarily effective) wordplay and juxtaposition: ahead/below; many doors/many friends; would have shut/had opened. Closure is accomplished, but tonal resonance is lost.

Compositional intimacy, like most intimacy, may be at its best when one keeps in reserve something peculiarly his own to, at last, give away. Robinson had said all he had to say about Eben halfway through the last stanza. But before that he gave us an exquisitely managed portrait of a man presumably without family and who had outlived his friends, struggling one evening to create his own solace.

Theodore Roethke: "Frau Baumann, Frau Schmidt, and Frau Schwartz"

The shape of Theodore Roethke's "Frau Baumann, Frau Schmidt, and Frau Schwartz," narrow at the top and gradually widening, first to the pentameter of the break line, then, after an opening pentameter, back into eight two- and three-stress lines, abruptly resolves in the expansion and powerful stabilization of the heptameter. It moves from the passive declaration of the first line, through the furious activity of the next seven and three-quarters lines to the stop of the semicolon after "chrysanthemums." Then, after a slow interval of four lines—where all the windings and climbings of the opening are undercut by "the stiff / stems, jointed like corn" which the old women "tie and tuck," flat, truncated words and actions—it hurls itself into the next sequence and builds to its grand conclusion. These old women bring life out of cold sleep, they order the very light of the day, they plan beyond their own concerns.

The old women, long dead, return in the second stanza to the object of their plotting, or, perhaps, to the one who has made himself imaginatively the object of their plotting—the poet, lying cold in his bed, the seed asleep in him. They hover over him, the poem turns back on itself to all the doubleness of meaning that is in everything, and we are required to draw parallels between the poet and the forces that manipulate him, that order his wildness, that draw out his life—that work, as he must work, beyond themselves, for more than themselves.

In other words, these old women, like poets, are *caretakers*, orderers of plenitude, who take joy in their work. They *creak*, they *wind*, they *straighten*, *tie*, and *tuck*, *dip*, *sift*, *sprinkle*, and *shake*, *straddle* and *billow* and *twinkle* and *fly*. They do these things in the world of a greenhouse crammed to overflowing with flowers whose reality is their names; *sweet-peas*, *smilax*, *nasturtiums*, *climbing roses*, *car-*

nations, chrysanthemums, and their lively extensions—*tendrils, coils, loops,* and *whorls.*

All this takes place in short, three-stress lines, strongly enjambed, ending in twenty-one nouns, six verbs, and four adjectives, breaking over to nine lines that begin with verbs, six with nouns and two with strong adjectives, including five that consist of nothing but action: "to wind, to wind," "they tied and tucked," "they trellised . . . they plotted," "pinching and poking." Further, the first nineteen lines are dense with verbs, the poem as it resolves trailing off into the relative passivity of the dream of the old women, long gone, but still in attendance on the speaker "in his first sleep" "alone and cold in his bed."

These old women, tenders of the greenhouse, are "witches" who tease out all those spiralings, inward-turnings, reachings-out, and relentless vegetable graspings that in the greenhouse poems and throughout his career signified for Roethke the obduracy of life. The old women are life-givers, who provide the same service to the "spindly kid," as to the flowers, pinching and poking him, who, like the plants, would otherwise lie forever "cold in his bed." They come to him, muses whose responsibility it is to "tease out the seed that the cold [keeps] asleep." And lest it seem that he has transformed them beyond themselves and out of real breath, Roethke at the end of the poem is emphatic that the world is their province—they have awakened from their first sleep and fallen into their last, but they still sweat and bleed, and "their snuff-laden breath blows lightly over [him] in [his] first sleep."

I've always preferred Roethke's earlier poems. The later ones seem to me often overwrought and over-wrought, while the early poems, though certainly not always understated, usually display a control beyond their obvious formalities. They play off a considerable exuberance of language and feeling against a base restraint, and exhibit a controlled wildness of voice and spirit that in some of the later work is gone at too hard and can seem manufactured.

My favorite of the greenhouse poems is "Frau Baumann, Frau Schmidt, and Frau Schwartz." I admire its massing of detail, its rapid accumulation of disparate elements until suddenly, quite unexpectedly, a critical mass occurs, and the whole edifice ignites, develops the momentum that jazz musicians call *drive,* and that force the music critic of *Time* once attributed to Helen Traubel's voice, saying it was like a steel girder abruptly flung across the auditorium. I like the effect of the long coordinate sentences run through and over short lines, that Yeatsian trick, forcing the reader at every line ending to the life-threatening little decision as to whether or not to go on, as the sentence requires, or to stop, as the line with an equal imperative insists—and in making that decision, feeling the orchestration of tiny propulsive shocks that manipulate the poem's *tempi* and rhetorical strategies.

Roethke is not addressing us expositorily in this poem. As he says elsewhere, the poet always "perceives the thing in physical terms." He is realizing the substance of an emotion. In another genre he might have been more analytical, or dealt with matters more fully, paying more attention, for example, to characterization, narrative, or setting. But here, in the especially immediate and concentrated vision of the poem, he is re-presenting and reimagining a particular experience that at the same time provides us the name for something we suddenly are required to realize we have always known.

"Frau Baumann, Frau Schmidt, and Frau Schwartz" is a poem that demonstrates particularly well this characteristic double vision of the artist, this illumination of the simultaneity of two realities. Thus the three old ladies of this poem are at the same time quite literally three old ladies with sensible Teutonic names, greenhouse workers, sweaty, smelly, "thorn-bitten," but strangely passionate about their work, at the same time that they are mysteriously transubstantiated to keepers of Creation.

A great poem is an improvisation, something both individual and collective, ending in something new and strongly punctuated by bursts of ego in the solos, during which the rest of the world riffs. But nothing is ever given up by one vision to the exclusion of the other. As Marvin Bell points out, "poetry is a quality of the imagination and language inextricably bound up with the recognizable world . . . a kind of flying, that . . . gets up and goes." In other words, a poem, though it begins and ends in time and the world, is never simply a representation of nature—for, as someone has said, "a mirror returns to us not our identity but our anonymity." We require to be brought to our identities, to the source of the common life we recognize intuitively in one another.

Thus the sense we have, in any lively work of art, of dimension, of more than one thing happening at the same time, of contingent existences, mutually energetic, none disposing of the other for its own sake, nor of itself for the other. The poet must generalize the subject, without destroying its particularity, in order to extend its significance beyond the limits of that particular experience. The result is to merge our understanding with others, to enlarge it—to emphasize community. Experience is not univocal, but orchestral, and cannot be expressed adequately in templates of experience.

Lev Loseff points out that "words are accumulations of immense practical experience. Language is a million matters of thought, and the aim in a poem is to make it untranslatable." Roethke succeeds especially well here, I think. Still, poets are devious, and this poem is interpretable, as I hope we have seen, if not paraphrasable. We come to its truths as in the real world we come to conclusions, first through the provision of our senses, the practical intellect that feeds the speculative.

We are dealing here with the issue of indirectness, the meaning of the poem as a complex interrelationship of expressive elements, a resonant matter. What happens, for example, when one tries to paraphrase "Frau Baumann, Frau Schmidt, and Frau Schwartz"? What is the poem doing, except describing an action? How does one paraphrase an action? There is no meditative process here, no interpretation of the action, no exposition, no metaphor, and, despite its allusiveness, not much in the way of symbolism. This poem seems to be doing no more than reporting what it sees and appears at first glance to be almost nothing but literal surface.

But poets are not much in favor of the self-evident; they are not only concerned, in the words of R. P. Blackmur, with "the matter in hand," but wish to add "to the stock of available reality." For poets, as for any artist, the world is not expendable. No artist wants to abandon its determinations, but always to transform the observable without destroying it, to incorporate realities into the unified vision of the work. And so in "Frau Baumann, Frau Schmidt, and Frau Schwartz," beyond the description and apart from the narrative, there occur points of transformation at each of which the literal surface, while powerfully presented and sustained, is extended to what Caesar Pavese has called the double vision "through which, from the single object of the senses vividly absorbed and possessed, there radiates a sort of halo of unexpected spirituality."

Thus the catalysis of the phrases "these nurses of nobody else" who "keep creation at ease," "teased out the seed the cold kept asleep" and "plotted for more than themselves." These inform the poem to its extension from what until that point has been—however resonant, active, and richly textured—no more (or less) than a vivid recreation of the quotidian. At such nodes in all great concatenations of language, the drive is given impulse, the voice flung out into and over the anonymities of the auditorium, and the incarnation takes place—in short, there commences the poem.

The Wife of Usher's Well

According to the *Princeton Encyclopedia of Poetry and Poetics*, the ballad is "an oral phenomenon, and, as a consequence, preserves traces of the archaic modes of preliterature." This is undeniable, but it is hard not to hear in the word "preliterature" (and in certain adjectives in the encyclopedia article like "illiterate," "semiliterate"—or even "folk" or "popular"), a faintly patronizing tone. The ballad comes out sounding a bit like some backward country cousin. Certain characteristics of the ballad derive from the fact that it wasn't originally designed to be read, but to be heard. It was produced in the context of an oral culture, which depended for its transmission on word of mouth, rather than the printed page. The ballad may predate the printed poem, but today the two forms exist side by side. Literate people continue to this day to compose all sorts of songs, including ballads. The "modes" of song aren't necessarily archaic, or the product of an illiterate culture; they are to a great degree the result of the demands of the melody to which they were intended to be sung and into which each phase of the narrative must fit.

"The Wife of Usher's Well," one of the early ballads collected by Francis Child on the border between England and Scotland, is a ghost story told in ballad form. A wealthy widow's three sons, who have perished at sea, seem to fulfill her wish by returning home, but since they are ghosts, must disappear at dawn. It is probable that the form in which this ballad comes down to us is markedly different from the form in which it first appeared. Born some time between the fourteenth and sixteenth centuries on the lips of a nameless, long-dead balladeer, passed from singer to singer, generation to generation, it was most likely altered along the way, evolving an adverb here, incorporating a stanza there, mutating for five or six centuries until ballad collectors—most prominently the American philologist Francis Child—came along in the nineteenth century with their nets and bottles.

A true enthusiast, Child had dedicated his life to the border ballads, collecting and printing over three hundred of them, some in as many as twenty-five versions—none of which purported to resemble the true original except in the most general way. Fixed to the page for over a century like some rare butterfly, "The Wife of Usher's Well" has finally achieved the status of a poem. These days it hangs out with other poems in what professors call the canon of English literature. It no longer has any reason to change. It is not quite dead; it has simply stopped evolving. After who knows how many incarnations, it is barely a ghost of its former self. Its lifeblood, the music, has long since drained away.

Though the ballad had been modified repeatedly as it passed from singer to singer, it underwent an even more extreme (though unintentional) transformation in the process of being preserved in print. Coming across such ballads in black and white, primarily between the covers of poetry anthologies, the contemporary reader often finds it difficult to keep their origin in mind. It is so easy to forget and to approach it as one would any other poem in the volume. Worse yet, were this ballad in its present form to fall into the clutches of what Robert Frost called an "eye-reader," he wouldn't hear any sound at all, merely a sort of tuneless humming in his skull while his eyes skimmed lickety-split across the lines. Like the poems that it appears to resemble, the ballad asks to be read—if it must be read—with the inner ear, with a fair degree of attention to matters of rhythm, alliteration, and assonance. But unlike the poems, it requires some further effort on the reader's part.

The encyclopedia article goes on to inform us that there are in a ballad "few arresting figures of speech and no self-conscious straining after novel turns of phrase"—the kind of thing found in a "literate" poem, where the reader has time to pause in order to relish rich or complex figures of speech. No such images can be allowed to "arrest" the progress of a ballad, which proceeds at its own fixed pace, and will not allow the listener time to appreciate them.

Cast in the form of a ballad, a story takes its own sweet time emerging, for the sounds of the words in a song are lengthened to fit the music. Moreover, in a performance, the breaks between stanzas can be considerably longer than they might appear on the printed page, as they are often filled with musical interludes. Like all music, a ballad unfolds in musical time, corresponding to, though not reflecting, the time of the story it unfolds. In the break between the first and second stanzas of this ballad, for instance, a whole week passes, whereas the last eight stanzas cover only a single night. Ballads characteristically hurry through the events leading up to the climactic episode. Though in one sense time in the ballad is fixed and inflexible as the four-line stanzas march one behind the other, from another point of view it might be said to expand and contract, alternating between passages of drawn-out suspense and moments of abrupt action.

With only the present version to go by, it's anyone's guess what its first, most distant ancestor sounded like. It may well have been missing the third stanza, which might have been borrowed somewhere along the line from another version and incorporated, perhaps for the sake of emphasis, or for the simple pleasure of repetition. The same goes for the tenth stanza. With the passage of time, the ballad has apparently cast off certain details as insignificant or irrelevant, while simultaneously taking on fresh ballast through repetition.

The simple, strictly repeated melody, into which each phase of the narrative must fit, helps to determine at the outset what is included and what dispensed with. To shift metaphors, it is as if the widow's story here has been poured into a series of identical measuring cups. Only so much can fit in each one; any excess details would slop over the rim and soon evaporate. Someone attempting to recount this same tale free of the strictures of the ballad form would perhaps dwell a while longer on the widow's motive for sending her sons on that perilous journey; surely he would say something about what caused their deaths. Further, in the present version, nothing in the words of the ballad tells us who the speaker in stanzas four and seven is; we must deduce from what she says that the speaker is the Wife of Usher's Well. The ballad has no time for embellishments like "she sighed" or "she cried."

As the Shakespearean critic G. L. Kittredge remarks of the ballad in general,

there are no comments or reflections by the narrator. He does not dissect or psychologize. He does not take sides for or against any of the dramatis personae. . . . If it were possible to conceive of a tale as telling itself, without the instrumentality of a conscious speaker, the ballad would be such a tale.

"Dramatis personae" is especially apt, because the story relies so heavily on dramatic dialogue. The impact of "The Wife of Usher's Well" depends on the stark, unmediated contrast between the mother's and her sons' speeches. Fully a third of the ballad is taken up with uninterrupted dialogue. The "stage directions," for example, in the eighth and ninth stanzas are remarkably sparse. Despite all the repetitions, there is a spareness to the ballad's narration that is rarely encountered in prose tales. What we've inherited after all these years in these twelve little measuring cups is a precious distillate. It is worth sipping slowly.

After the crisp economy of the first stanza, the next two stanzas slow things down again in order to build suspense. The folk for whom folk ballads were composed and performed were doubtless quick to grasp the significance of the birch-bark headgear and recognize that when, in response to the mother's wish, her sons returned as obediently as they'd set out, they were answering only half her prayers. Those early listeners would have realized that the widow's sons had come home all right, but not "in earthly flesh and blood." Perhaps for dramatic effect, building further suspense, the singer devoted an entire stanza to their unearthly headgear.

Now comes the most emphatic shift of narrative pace in the ballad. This version is divided evenly into three sections of four stanzas each. The first concludes with the mother's desperate prayer. The second section establishes an atmosphere of expectation—there will be feasting to celebrate the sons' return. But the third section opens with an abrupt and brutal reversal of those expectations. The repeated cockcrow and "channerin' worm" in the next two stanzas, like the birch-bark headgear in the middle section, warn that the sons have not really come home. The early listeners recognized the significance of these symbolic clues. To them the hats signified that the sons were incorporeal; the cocks and the worm reminded them that ghosts are doomed to disappear with the first intimations of daybreak.

In the fourth stanza, the mother's wish for her sons' return is clearly understandable, but it sounds more like a curse. It's one thing to wish for her sons to return from the dead; it's another to wish that the storm, which probably sank their ship and took their lives, would continue, threatening the lives of many another mother's son. The ballad, in its characteristically blunt, laconic way, neither judges nor comments nor explains. Still, the listeners get the message that death is final. Already in the third stanza the ballad tells us that "her sons she'd never see." "Never" means *never*. That's what the "channerin' worm" is saying. But the widow appears to have not understood, and she remains speechless while her sons speak to each other. Only in the final stanza does the youngest son bid farewell to his mother, but he saves his last and most poignant valediction for "the bonny lass that kindles my mother's fire."

The lass is apparently the one the youngest son is most loath to leave behind. One can't imagine a prose version having failed to describe their cruelly interrupted relationship, whereas the ballad barely implies it, and only in retrospect. It is, however, the culminating detail, which still echoes in the silence after the last chord has ceased resonating. This points to the cruellest irony of all: as the sons disappear into the chilly Scottish dawn, their mother is left with the fire she intended for them (who will never be warm again) and with the warm-blooded lass who kindles it for her. There's nothing left to be said. It's truly her fire now;

for, despite her prayers, she's the only one left to enjoy it as the curtains drop simultaneously between the widow and her sons and between the singer and his listeners.

The Wife of Usher's Well

1

There lived a wife at Usher's Well,
    And a wealthy wife was she;
She had three stout and stalwart sons,
    And sent them o'er the sea.

2

They hadna been a week from her,
    A week but barely ane,
Whan word came to the carlin wife   *peasant*
    That her three sons were gane.

3

They hadna been a week from her,
    A week but barely three,
Whan word came to the carlin wife
    That her sons she'd never see.

4

"I wish the wind may never cease,
    Nor fashes in the flood,   *troubles*
Till my three sons come hame to me,
    In earthly flesh and blood."

5

It fell about the Martinmass,   *The feast of St. Martin,*
   Nov. 11.
    Whan nights are lang and mirk,
The carlin wife's three sons came hame,
    And their hats were o' the birk.   *birch*

6

It neither grew in syke nor ditch,   *trench*
    Nor yet in any sheugh;   *furrow*
But at the gates o' Paradise,
    That birk grew fair eneugh.

7

"Blow up the fire, my maidens,
    Bring water from the well;
For a' my house shall feast this night,
    Since my three sons are well."

8

And she has made to them a bed,
    She's made it large and wide,
And she's ta'en her mantle her about,
    Sat down at the bed-side.

9

Up then crew the red, red cock,
    And up and crew the gray;
The eldest to the youngest said,
    " 'Tis time we were away."

10

The cock he hadna crawed but once,
    And clapped his wings at a',
When the youngest to the eldest said,
    "Brother, we must awa'.

11

"The cock doth craw, the day doth daw,
    The channerin' worm doth chide;   *fretting*
Gin we be missed out o' our place,   *if*
    A sair pain we maun bide.   *sore / must*

12

"Fare ye weel, my mother dear!
    Fareweel to barn and byre!   *cow house*
And fare ye weel, the bonny lass,
    That kindles my mother's fire!"

                        Anonymous

Dickinson's *"Because I could not stop for Death"* Restored

"**B**ecause I could not stop for Death" was first published in much-diminished form as "The Chariot"—changed in several important respects to take the sting out of the lines. For Emily Dickinson, death, God, and the eternities were regarded too conventionally, even lightly, by those around her, but her poetic stance and her themes—interpretations of mortal experience—were in turn too much for her first editors, her friends Thomas Higginson and Mabel Loomis Todd. The poems in the 1890 edition were trimmed down, when deemed necessary, to the Puritan dimensions that her sensibility exceeded. Sixty-five years later they were restored to the original, as written by her, and sewn into fascicles starting in 1858.

Interpreters of "The Chariot" are meant to believe that death's chariot (one that "swings low"?) comes to bring the dead one to everlasting life—that with death the immortal soul journeys to heaven. But for Dickinson the theological notion that Christ offers redemption was not a fait accompli, as her early letters prove—"give up and become a Christian. It is not now too late, so my friends tell me, so my offended conscience whispers, but is hard for me to give up the world" (letter to Abiah Root, May 1849). Her understanding remained in flux even as her girlhood friends succumbed to revival and scripture, and even as she felt strong pricks of conscience: "*I* am one of the lingering *bad* ones, and so I slink away, and pause, and ponder . . . and do work without knowing why—not surely for *this* brief world, and more sure it is not for Heaven—and I ask what this message *means* that they ask for so eagerly" (letter to Abiah Root, 1850).

Death, and what comes thereafter, is the heart of the matter for religious faith, which offers reassurances against death's impersonal and sudden power. At the heart of this heart is fear. That the fear could be washed away simply by baptism, Dickinson, it seems, couldn't entirely believe or accept. She chose instead to live with and admit death's power and to express the fear, committing herself to "My second Rank," after having "ceded": "I've stopped being Theirs— / The name They dropped upon my face / With water, in the country church / Is finished using, now, / And They can put it with my Dolls, / My childhood, and the string of spools, / I've finished threading—too—."

On the surface, the first lines of "Because I could not stop for Death" appear to invoke orthodox reassurance against the fear of death. Death is portrayed as sensitive to the ordinary busy life of mortals—too occupied with life to stop—when he "kindly" stops and invites her for a carriage ride. In reality, the lines offer the first of several ironic reversals of what Dickinson suggests might be but isn't. If the conditional phrase seems to suggest that the dead one has rights and options in the matter—a choice of when to die—the main clause is the reminder of death's absolute nature. He stops, and that's that. The sentence points to the very human capacity to fool ourselves when we are afraid. Faced with the large unknown, we pretend it is manageable. Because it is unacceptable in its brute form, we make it governable. We whistle in the dark. That death, "kindly" and civil, is really in charge is pointed out in lines 2 and 5. He is in the driver's seat, and he drives as slowly as he likes.

There is a third occupant in the carriage, Immortality–shadowy, and if not a person, a condition to be desired. Immortality is consoling and recognizable, what one hopes will come with death. With Immortality as a companion, the speaker can accede to the trip in death's carriage; it becomes a leisurely afternoon drive—a gentleman taking a lady and her friend (a chaperone?) for a ride in the country. "And Immortality," on a line by itself, helps to emphasize the importance of the presence of the other passenger. Without Immortality present, might not the speaker have been afraid? Perhaps she'd have refused to go along to the otherwise undisclosed destination.

Death by itself in Dickinson's other poems and letters is not so gentle or refined. In "He fumbles at your Soul," for instance, death (or deity) "scalps your naked soul" while "The Universe is still." If "The Maker's cordial visage" (1718) provides something hopeful for the drowning man (who drowns), death produces a "Stiff stare" (1624), a "Forehead" that "copied stone," and "congealed" eyes. In her letters death is ever present:

I can't stay any longer in a world of death. Austin is ill of fever. I buried my garden last week—our man, Dick, lost a little girl through scarlet fever. I thought perhaps you were dead, and not knowing the sexton's address, interrogate the daisies. Ah! dainty—dainty Death! Ah! democratic death—grasping the proudest zinnia from my purple garden,—then deep to his bosom calling the serf's child. Say, is he everywhere? Where shall I hide my things? Who is alive? The woods are dead. Is Mrs. H. alive? Annie and Katie—are they below, or received to nowhere? (letter to the Hollands, 1858)

Who would go along willingly with death, forgetting all terror, unless a promise were offered? Dickinson offers the reader Immortality, as the Congregational ministers once offered it to her in their sermons. Is it a ruse? The reader, like a member of the congregation, will have to wait to see.

In the second stanza Death and the speaker ride along without concern for time. Her "labor" and her "leisure" are done, and she is content to be in the carriage, as if now there were no other concern but death's luxury. The word *labor* in line 7 recalls the good works to be done for God's world by true Christians—works now no longer necessary. Dickinson means for us to regard the word ironically. In lines 9 and 10 the poem reads, "We passed the School, where Children strove / At Recess in the Ring." In the use of *strove* to indicate labor, we are meant to understand something more than, and including, "play," for isn't that what children do at recess, after their lessons and schoolwork? *Strove* emphasizes the children's energy, while the speaker, her life over, sits passively in the carriage; but it is also a reminder that as Christians children are meant to start early to labor for their salvation. Should they be allowed simply to play? In the 1890 version of the poem the lines read, "We passed the school where children played, / Their lessons scarcely done." Why did Dickinson write "strove"? Was it because she knew from experience that time pressed, even upon children, and death often came early? "How swiftly summer has fled and what report has it borne to heaven of misspent time & wasted hours. Eternity only will answer. The ceaseless flight of the seasons is to me a very solemn thought, & yet Why do we not strive to make better improvement of them?" Dickinson wrote to her friend Abiah Root when she was fifteen and a student at Amherst Academy in September 1846. As much in danger from death as adults and thus in need for early belief in the trinity, children *strove*.

The word choice seems clearly ironic, with Dickinson playing reality against the romantic view of childhood and death, where one's salvation is so little in danger that a schoolyard is solely for play ("the school where children played," "The Chariot"). The speaker enters the carriage as a believer, immortal soul intact, but the adult Dickinson was not such a one in the conventional sense. The poem is informed ironically with theology; it is the inexorable law of time's direction that the little narrative uncovers: the carriage seems to be going where God's chariots are supposed to go, but it ends up in the graveyard.

I had been perplexed by the line, "We passed the Setting Sun," turning over all its possible implications and a little in awe of Dickinson's ability to make the situation of the poem seem both commonplace and ominously strange. Perhaps the carriage had turned heavenward after all and made a celestial pass by the sun. But wasn't the sun setting, which meant that the point of perception was on earth? How could one pass the sun? Surely the line was not there only to set up the next line's reminder of nature's significant power over us, "Or rather—He passed Us." Then I remembered a ride in the country late one night in my husband's big old Buick. The moon was full and always a little ahead and to the right of us as we traveled east on Route 7; but when the road curved north, the moon seemed to fall behind. We passed it in a sense. The poet's essential task isn't to hold up a mirror to nature, but even when Dickinson is altering reality—bringing the dead to life, condensing and stretching time and space—her oblique language contains the necessary details to make her readers believe that what they've read has happened.

The third stanza takes note of the daily routine of the life the speaker is passing from, starting with children at recess and ending with the setting sun. The day seems to have gone down quickly, in part because of the dual suggestion of both a day's cycle and the cycle of the seasons. How clever the mixture of details that suggest both beginnings and decline, youth and ripeness. Time speeds, in part because of the insistent echo, in the short lines, of the verb ("passed") as the carriage travels through realms of living—human, animated nature, and nature becoming passive—the "setting sun," which seems even more passive in contrast with the striving children.

The imaginative reach in this stanza is for me most evident in the phrase "Gazing Grain," with all its implications about what it is like to be alive and dead at the same time—the condition of the speaker throughout the poem. The phrase emphasizes the speaker's passivity, assigning the human task to nature, animating the grain. By its placid and constant presence, it seems to stare. But it is the speaker, who has gone with death, who takes note of this. She watches from the carriage as mortality slips by—though with death, and passive, she still registers sensory details. She sees, and as long as she does, she still *is*. This sense of an unwillingness to relinquish the world and the self—of being— carries throughout Dickinson's work; and if death offers, as here, immortality, immortality had better provide an experience like the one life offers: it had better let her see. In a somber mood Dickinson writes this in a letter to Abiah Root: "I cannot realize that friends I have seen pass from my sight . . . will not walk the streets and act their parts in the great drama of life, nor can I realize that when I again meet them it will be in another & far different world from this." It is interesting to me that in her depictions of this "different world," the speaker is by herself, as in the poem under consideration. She is alone to experience death and the nature of posthumous grace. Is this not what frightens one likely to die?

In the same letter Dickinson asks, "Does not Eternity appear dreadful to you? I often get thinking of it and it seems so dark to me. . . . To think that we must forever live and never cease to be." As the sun sets, darkness and a chill set in in stanza four, the stanza that was entirely removed in "The Chariot," perhaps because it was too grim, or because the editors didn't understand it. Death has been kind and civil, but he drives the carriage toward the dark and cold of the grave. The speaker feels the chill, for she is flimsily dressed with a scarf not made of fur or wool but of "Tulle" (a thin, fine machine-made net), and in "Gossamer." *Gossamer* brings to mind the light gauze used for veils (Is she to be Christ's bride?) and the cobwebs I've walked through in the grass fields and scrub in September and October. The details are consistent with death: autumn and winter are death's perennial seasons. The subtle emphasis in the poem on a growing cold mimics both the process of dying, as if the dead one were dying even more, and our earthly answer to the mystery that separates the warm living from the cold dead. Cold (and dark) also represents our fear, as in "And zero at the bone," from "A Narrow Fellow in the Grass."

The supernatural journey ends in the graveyard, where the carriage pauses by a "House that seemed / A Swelling of the Ground," with its cornice "in the Ground." By rhyming *ground* with itself Dickinson emphasizes the carriage's destination and the body's disposition. For her even death is a physical experience—the dead experiencing the cool damp air after the sunset and hard on that arriving at the tomb where one imagines a similar quality of air. In the Todd/Higginson version of the poem the rhyme is altered to ground/mound, softening Dickinson's thematic intentions and nudging the verses toward conventionality, as indeed the editors tried to do throughout.

What a shock it was to first open the first edition of *Poems by Emily Dickinson* after having known the poem first in the version published in 1955. *How could you!* I heard myself think. When *ever* was Dickinson's emphasis on the peace that passeth all understanding? How could they not see that hers was no romantic sensibility but one capable of writing about death as it is? The carriage isn't a chariot, it's a hearse. How could they change the extraordinary rhyme? The ground/ground rhyme had always been a favorite of mine, unusual, I thought, in poetry, though not unheard of, and pretty unusual in Dickinson. The *Concordance to the Poems of Emily Dickinson* (S. P. Rosenbaum, Cornell University Press, 1964) shows how rarely she used a same-word rhyme. Though *death* is an important word and concept in Dickinson, the rhyme never appears. Out-of-stanza both *die* and *dead* are rhymed with each other once. Other such rhymes occur with the words *passion, noon, dark, day, green, sky, night, rose, soul, grave,* and *god* (once in-stanza and four times out-of-stanza). Excluding refrains, then, the in- and out-of-stanza same-word rhymes occur infrequently except for the words *me*, which rhymes with itself in fifty-three of her poems, and *be*, rhyming with itself sixteen times.

Having given up her identity as a conventional Christian, continuing to wonder about the nature of those things past ordinary understanding, trusting her eye and things face-to-face over the vision of the true believer, thinking death certain and God remote, by turns defiant, wry, perplexed, wouldn't she consider the question of how to "be," and doesn't she find its expression and emphasis in many of her poems? "Because I could not stop for Death" certainly addresses itself to the question of being by describing the state of being alive and dead at the same time. She doesn't explain how the dead live, except to give us glimpses of the perceptions the living have, ending with the partial, remembered image of the "Horses' Heads" facing eternity.

The speaker is in the cemetery, left to wonder at her progress from the moment of her first encounter with Death, with his promise of immortality, to her present situation. Immortality has changed into Eternity—an uncomfortable change, one would think, from everlasting life to a long time of waiting for redemption. The final stanza is written in the present tense, which emphasizes the hereness and withness (the existence) of the speaker after death and also suggests that the implied questions cannot be answered. What is Immortality like? We don't know—he has disappeared. Death and his carriage also recede. Only snatches of memory are left and a little narrative in stanza three representing life and also death. Time has elapsed quickly and been agonizingly slow, a psychological truth that is recognizably real—when people are excited, bored, fearful—but things for the speaker are much the same. Why hasn't redemption come? The questions, Dickinson implies, persist. People will always wonder what heaven is like and live with the hope that immortality will be granted. And until the unknown bliss is achieved, then, Dickinson suggests, the world of grain and carriage rides and, yes, graveyards, is all there is. "Instead of getting to Heaven, at last," Dickinson says in an earlier poem (#324), a person can be "going, all along." And in another wording of a similar sentiment, Dickinson says in a letter to Mrs. J. Holland in 1856, "If God had been here this summer, and seen the things that I had seen—I guess that He would think His Paradise superfluous."

Emily Dickinson's poems are personal and, however strange the experience she presents, inviting. If they are strange, they are no less real for that, the strangeness relating less to her oblique language (which *can* be read, even in the difficult stanzas) than to her refusal to put down the experience as if it had been experienced the same way by everyone, or as if there were conventions for feeling and knowing. Her untrammeled imagination and intellect require an individual reading and reader. The good reader intuits this and feels welcomed. Higginson and Todd, like other of her acquaintances, her family, and some of her literary heirs, felt the poems alien to what they knew, having predilections toward a style of versification and thematic locus that weren't sufficiently present in Dickinson's poems for them to understand the lines, and so they changed entire verses, radically altering the poems. They were unwilling to accept the elite place among writers she chose for herself as early as 1855 or 1856 and managed to reach a scant five or six years later, by then "Erect / With Will to Choose, or to reject" (508). Critics today, it often seems, are guilty of similar dismantlings, and for the same reasons: putting forth central meanings that they find more agreeable or more theirs, and being unable to accept the authorial ambition to write not "adequate" (508) but great poems. They are too willing to discard the individual reach toward meaning in individual poems and to replace it with what society, they think, ought to be aware of—truths they deem more significant or revealing than what the writer intended. And so with all the best intentions (one hopes) critics can do a disservice to the reading public. Any author's death, corporeal and real or greatly exaggerated, makes that possible. (Higginson would not publish Dickinson's poems in the *Atlantic Monthly* during her lifetime.) Authors of the caliber of Emily Dickinson don't stay dead when there are good readers to read the poems as they were written. In "Because I could not stop for Death," perhaps her finest poem on the theme of what lies beyond death, both in cosmic terms and in the feeling of those bound to die, she presents us with the strangeness of such a condition. There are no lectures and no overt theological speculations, though the experience is every way conditioned by the abstract: motion and stasis; everlasting life; youth; nature; time; immortality; what it is to *be*. The poem allows us to feel our own discomfort at not fully knowing, despite what we might surmise, and to experience fears and wonders about time's evanescence and the mystery of death. We yearn for immortality, so he accompanies one of us, the one invited into death's carriage. We feel the yearning and the fear as Dickinson must once have, their expression being so palpable, and while we do the poem belongs to us, common readers.

> Because I could not stop for Death—
> He kindly stopped for me—
> The Carriage held but just Ourselves—
> And Immortality.
> We slowly drove—He knew no haste
> And I had put away
> My labor and my leisure too,

For His Civility—
We passed the School, where Children strove
At Recess—in the Ring—
We passed the Fields of Gazing Grain—
We passed the Setting Sun—
Or rather—He passed Us—
The Dews drew quivering and chill—
For only Gossamer, my Gown—
My Tippet—only Tulle—
We paused before a House that seemed
A Swelling of the Ground—
The Roof was scarcely visible—
The Cornice—in the Ground—
Since then—'tis Centuries—and yet
Feels shorter than the Day
I first surmised the Horses' Heads
Were toward Eternity—

Emily Dickinson

ANTHONY HECHT

"Gaze Not on Swans"

I first came upon this lovely lyric in the five-volume anthology, *Poets of the English Language*, edited by W. H. Auden and Normal Holmes Pearson, where it is attributed unambiguously to William Strode. So much did I delight in it that I eventually found a copy of the *Poetical Works of William Strode*, edited by Bertram Dobell, who is by no means as confident as the anthologists regarding the poem's authorship. Indeed, Dobell says, "The only authority for attributing the lines . . . to Strode, is that the poem is mentioned in Dr. Grosart's list of his poems. It, however, is included in [Henry] Lawes' 'Ayres and Dialogues' where it is assigned to Henry Noel, who would seem therefore to have the best claim to it." I am persuaded by the judgment of Dobell, the opinion of Lawes, and my own instincts gained from reading the whole of Strode's poetic output, in the course of which he never rises to anything like the level of this extraordinary poem. (Neither, for that matter, do any of the poems confidently attributed to Edward De Vere, Earl of Oxford, approach the qualities of the songs, poems, or plays of Shakespeare, though obstinate Oxfordians continue to suppose the former wrote the works of the latter.)

Yet, remarkable as it is, this poem belongs to a little genre of elaborate quatrain-verse compliments to ladies that would include a number of other graceful and elegant poems: Thomas Carew's song, "Ask me no more," Sir Henry Wotton's poem in praise of Princess Elizabeth, daughter of King James, who married the Elector Palatine in 1619, "You meaner beauties of the night," and Sir Francis Kynaston's "Do not conceal thy radiant eyes." These poems, all extravagant praises of a woman's beauty in grand and hyperbolic terms, go out of their way to ring changes upon the commonplace similes, the conventional imagery, that crop up in so much Elizabethan and Jacobean poetry, and venture instead upon a more daring originality and a more arresting kind of metaphor. Three of four of them (those by Carew, Kynaston, and, as I now think, Noel) are framed rhetorically as injunctions: "Ask me no more," "Do not conceal," "Gaze not on swans," while Wotton's poem quivers with aristocratic disdain for the presumptions of the natural beauties of the universe. Beyond this point their rhetorical strategies vary, and in my view Noel's is the most imaginative, subtle, and satisfying.

In its first stanza, the "full hatcht beauty" of swans is itself nearly miraculous, suggesting, first, the purity and cleanliness of a birth that emerges unsoiled from within the solid confines of an eggshell, and the sort of birth unique to Athena, come forth full-blown and mature from the brow of Zeus. The swan's "soft breast" has all manner of feminine, erotic, maternal associations, and its whiteness does not even require mention, though it is obviously meant to chime with the whiteness of the snow mentioned in the third and fourth lines. That this snow "hovers in its virginity" betokens its lightness, its vulnerability, its purity, and its danger of imminent extinction.

It may be precisely the mutability of the snowflake's existence that suggests to the poet those twin emblems of female beauty, the rose and the lily, that trace their way back to the *Song of Songs*, and became standard symbols of feminine beauty, found in such lyrics as Campion's "There is a garden in her face, / Where roses and white lilies grow." Though conventional (the rose was regarded as the most perfect of flowers and associated with the Blessed Virgin, as well as with the royal English houses of York, Lancaster, and Tudor, while the lily was associated with the royal dynasties of France and with Christ as a descendant of Kings David and Solomon), the very word "complexion" in connection with the rose summons not only something like the epidermal beauty of a woman but "the combination of qualities in a certain proportion" that would make it the most perfect, and regal, of flowers.

The "kissing chemistry" of the bee suggests the amorous, yet pure, sexual activity of pollinization, the delicacy of the bee's address to the flower's nectar, a chemistry that will convert this precious fluid into the honey of the hive. Between humans, of course, kissing would accelerate the "chemistry" of mutual attraction, but even in the purer context of bee and flower a slight residue of the voluptuous lingers on. There remains a question about the word "rob'd," which can be (for want of certainty) construed as either "robbed" or "robed," and can be made sense of either way. The lily is robbed of its nectar by the bee, but it is also robed in its glory (Matt. 6) by the bee's chaste sexual offices. If "no subtle bee" has performed this office, the chastity of the lily remains intact, and its beauty must be attributed to more supernatural causes.

The Milky Way is described as "pure" (and in this it resembles all the preceding imagery) because the stars are the visible signs of the angelic hosts of heaven. (Looking up at a starlit night, Hopkins exclaims, "O look at all the fire-folk sitting in the air!") It is, in the words of another poet, a *via lactaea*, suggestive of heavenly nourishment and supernatural abundance, and the first two lines of the third stanza equate it with, as well as distinguish it from, the splendor of the day. As for the pearls in the following lines, they, too, are biblical in the freight and wealth they carry, recalling the pearl beyond price (Matt. 13); yet at the same time the pearl was regarded as one of the few adornments of the otherwise naked Venus in her role as goddess of profane love. The pearl is here brilliantly described as hiding its full value invisibly within its exterior walls, and in fact the nacreous luster of pearls derives from its capacity at once to absorb and to reflect light, and its interior layers of accretion are the central ingredients of its beauty and worth. It should go without saying that in Elizabethan and Stuart times the richest of gems were all thought to come from the Orient, and this is why Columbus undertook to find a new route there, and believed he had succeeded.

We have now considered three stanzas, each with a double, or mated, set of subjects: swans and snow in the first, roses and lilies in the second, stars and pearls in the third. There now follow two (not three) stanzas in which the beauty of all six emblems mentioned are disqualified when contrasted with the sudden appearance of "my emperesse." It is of no great consequence whether this woman is indeed an empress or simply the empress of the poet's heart. On what authority I do not know, Dobell, who lists the poem under "Doubtful Pieces" as regards attribution, nevertheless give it the title of "On His Mistresse." But we must recall that the word mistress had many meanings in Renaissance parlance, some of them utterly devoid of any sexual overtone; a mistress was one who could command any service from her devotee, and Wotton's poem is called "On His Mistress, the Queen of Bohemia," and was composed in a spirit of perfect propriety. In stanzas four and five all the beauties that have been listed now wilt, wither, withdraw in shame, or, finally, brilliantly, commit suicide out of envy. The bloom and health of the rose is, by juxtaposition with the woman's beauty, converted to a blush of embarrassed mortification; the lilies, by the same shaming context, are forced to withdraw into their beds as George Herbert observed: "as flowers depart / To see their mother-root, when they have blown; / Where they together / All the hard weather, / Dead to the world, keep house unknown." And the Milky Way, which earlier had vied with the splendor of the day, now hastens to veil itself. The pearls become the sacrificial, self-immolated adornments of the woman, as pearls traditionally bedecked Venus herself and certain royal ladies, prominently including Elizabeth. (The royal portraits of the queen almost invariably present her as adorned with a very firmament of pearls.) I have never ceased to admire the asymmetry in which the six admonitions of three stanzas are justified in two. This swift triumph of demonstration represents an easy and perfect confidence. But more importantly, it leaves a final stanza for the clinching, irrefutable analogue.

The last stanza seems to me a triumph. Its excellence consists in a brilliant, delicate balance and combination of ingredients, all at the service of a grand concluding fanfare of praise, as undeniable as a sunrise. The stars are "big with light" in several senses, and it is important, I think, to discover these ways gradually, by gradation, in the order they are likely to occur. First, they look big in darkness because, as Gilbert Murray reports Epicurus observing, "the Sun was probably about as big as it looked, or perhaps smaller; since fires at a distance generally look bigger than they are." The stars also look big because of the pride attributed to them in the second line of the stanza. There they dignify themselves as guides, indispensable cicerones to the Cyclopean, one-eyed, "moone-ey'd" night. The stars are proud of their torch-bearing, illuminating office and are swollen with pride. The night, being one-eyed, requires guidance, and when full the moon resembles a single ocular pupil, especially of someone made at least partially blind by cataracts. The word "sockets" in the final line is meant first of all to recall the "lanthorns" of the second line. The first three definitions of "socket" in the *Oxford English Dictionary* are all mechanical in character, and the third is: "The part of a candlestick or chandelier in which the candle is placed." If we can assimilate, as I think we are expected to do, the idea of lanterns to the sockets of candlesticks, the sudden presence of the sun in the third line both overwhelms the light of the candles and melts them by its warmth, and both powers account for the candles' sinking and decaying. But the last line seems also to convey an almost grotesque memento-mori flavor, and in this it recalls the first line of the stanza. Those stars were "big with light" as a woman is said to be "big with child." But the potentially rich pregnancies of starlight, when overpowered by the birth of a new sun at dawn, are effaced, doomed, and destroyed, as night itself becomes the skull of what had been a dazzling nocturnal beauty. The sovereignty of the newborn sun is inaugurated by the skeletal diminution of the old, inferior order.

I remember once recommending this poem to a lady who was generally skilled in reading poetry, taught it, and whose approval I thought it reasonable to count upon. She was repelled by the last stanza, and could find in it nothing but the image of a skull from which the eyes and flesh had withered away. I think this reading, while probably present in some latent way, is meant to be altogether secondary to the sense of the socket as receptacle to a candle, and we are meant chiefly to envision the melting of wax and effacing of candlelight by the superior brilliance and warmth of the sun. For me, in any case, the poem works like a charm.

Gaze Not on Swans

Gaze not on swans in whose soft breast
A full hatcht beauty seems to rest,
Nor snow which falling from the sky
Hovers in its virginity.

Gaze not on roses though new blown
Grac'd with a fresh complexion,
Nor lilly which no subtle bee
Hath rob'd by kissing chemistry.

Gaze not on that pure milky ways
Where night vies splendour with the day,
Nor pearls whose silver walls confine
The riches of an Indian mine:

For if my emperesse appears
Swans moultring dy, snow melts to tears,
Roses do blush and hang their heads
Pale lillyes shrink into their beds;

The milky way rides past to shrowd
Its baffled glory in a clowd,
And pearls to climb unto her eare
To hang themselves for envy there.

So have I seene stars big with light,
Proud lanthorns to the moone-ey'd night,
Which when Sol's rays were once display'd
Sunk in their sockets and decay'd.
(attributed to William Strode) Henry Noel (?)

The "Banked Fire" of Robert Hayden's "Those Winter Sundays"

For twenty years I've been teaching Robert Hayden's most fre-
quently anthologized poem to undergraduate poetry-writing students.
By "teach," I mean that from our textbook I read the poem aloud in the
classroom, I ask one of the students to read it aloud, I make some obser-
vations about it, I invite the students to make some observations about
it, then we talk about it a while longer. Usually to wrap up the discus-
sion, I'll read the poem through once more. Occasions for such teaching
come up about half a dozen times a year, and so let's say that during
my life I've been privileged to read this poem aloud approximately 240
times. "Those Winter Sundays" has withstood my assault upon it. It re-
mains a poem I look forward to reading and discussing in my classroom.
The poem remains alive to me, so that for hours and sometimes days
after it visits my classroom, I'm hearing its lines in my mind's ear.

Though a fourteen-liner, "Those Winter Sundays" is only loosely a
sonnet. Its stanzas are five, four, and five lines long. There are rhymes
and near-rhymes, but no rhyme scheme. The poem's lines probably aver-
age about eight syllables. There are only three strictly iambic lines: the
fourth, the eighth, and (significantly) the fourteenth. It's a poem that's
powerfully informed by the sonnet form; it's a poem that "feels like"
a sonnet—it has the density and gravity of a sonnet—which is to say
that in its appearance on the page, in its diction and syntax, in its tone,
cadence, and argumentative strategy, "Those Winter Sundays" presents
the credentials of a work of literary art in the tradition of English letters.
But it's also a poem that has gone its own way, a definite departure from
that most conventional of all the poetic forms of English and Ameri-
can verse.

The abstract issue of this poem's sonnethood is of less value to my
beginning poets than the tangible matter of the sounds the poem makes,

especially those *k*-sounding words of the first eleven lines that one comes to associate with discomfort: "clothes . . . blueback cold . . . cracked . . . ached . . . weekday . . . banked . . . thanked . . . wake . . . cold . . . breaking . . . call . . . chronic . . . cold." What's missing from the final three lines? The *k* sounds have been driven from the poem, as the father has "driven out the cold" from the house. The sounds that have replaced those *k* sounds are the *o* sounds of "good . . . shoes . . . know . . . know . . . love . . . lonely offices." The poem lets us associate the *o* sounds with love and loneliness. Sonically the poem tells the same story the poem narrates for us. The noise of this poem moves us through its emotional journey from discomfort to lonely love. If ever there was a poem that could teach a beginning poet the viability of the element of sound-crafting, it is "Those Winter Sundays."

Quote its first two words, and a great many poets and English teachers will be able to finish the first line (if not the whole poem) from memory. Somewhat remarkably, the poem's thesis—that the office of love can be relentless, thankless, and more than a little mysterious—resides in that initially odd-sounding two-word beginning, "Sundays too." The rest of the line—the rest of the independent clause—is ordinary. Nowhere else in Anglo-American literature does the word *too* carry the weight it carries in "Those Winter Sundays."

Not as immediately apparent as its opening words but very nearly as important to the poem's overall strategy is the two-sentence engineering of the first stanza. Because they will appreciate it more if they discover it for themselves, I often maneuver Socratically to have my students describe the poem's first two sentences: long and complex, followed by short and simple. It almost always seems to me worthwhile to ask, "Why didn't Hayden begin his poem this way: 'No one ever thanked my father for getting up early on Sundays, too'? Wouldn't that be a more direct and hospitable way to bring the reader into the poem?" After I've taken my students that far, they are quick to see how that ordinary five-word unit, "No one ever thanked him," gains meaning and emotion, weight, and force, from the elaborate preparation given it by the thirty-two-word "Sundays too" first sentence.

So much depends on "No one ever thanked him" that it requires the narrative enhancement of the first four and a half lines. It is the crux of the poem. What is this poem about? It is about a son's remorse over never thanking his father not only for what he did for him but also for how (he now realizes) he felt about him. And what is the poem if not an elegantly fashioned, permanent expression of gratitude?

"Those Winter Sundays" tells a story, or it describes a circumstance, of father-son conflict, and it even makes some excuses for the son's "Speaking indifferently" to the father: there was a good deal of anger between them; "chronic angers of that house" suggests that the circumstances were complicated somewhat beyond the usual and ordinary conflict between fathers and sons. Of the father, we know that he labored outdoors with his hands. Of the son, we know that he was, in the classic manner of youth, heedless of the ways in which his father served him.

Though the evidence of his "labor" is visible in every stanza of this poem, the father himself is somewhere else. We don't see him. He is in some other room of the house than the one where our speaker is. That absence suggests the emotional distance between the father and the son as well as the current absence, through death, of the father on the occasion of this utterance. It's easy enough to imagine this poem as a graveside meditation, an elegy, and a rather impassioned one at that, "What did I know, what did I know?"

The grinding of past against present gives the poem its urgency. The story is being told with such clarity, thoughtfulness, and apparent calm that we are surprised by the outburst of the repeated question of the thirteenth line. The fourteenth line returns to a tone of tranquillity. Its diction is formal, even arch, and its phrasing suggests an extremely considered conclusion; the fourteenth line is the answer to a drastic rephrasing of the original question: *What is the precise name of what as a youth I was incapable of perceiving but that as a life-examining adult, I now suddenly understand?*

I tell my students that they may someday need this poem, they may someday be walking along downtown and find themselves asking aloud, "What did I know, what did I know?" But what I mean to suggest to them is that Hayden has made them the gift of this final phrase like a package that in ten years' time they may open and find immensely valuable: "love's austere and lonely offices." Like "the banked fires" his father made, Hayden has made a poem that will be of value to readers often years after they've first read it.

"Those Winter Sundays" has articulated a treasure of an insight and preserved it for me until I was old enough to appreciate it. The poem always has the power to move me, to make me understand something so subtle that apparently I need to be reminded of it again and again. Hayden's poem is a "banked fire" that holds its warmth and allows me to rekindle my spirits whenever I come back to read it.

"Those Winter Sundays" honors a much-criticized figure in American culture of the 1990s—the withdrawn, emotionally inexpressive, and distant (and probably unhappy and angry) father. The poem makes its way toward perceiving the emotional life of such a man. The poem *realizes* love as it lived in such a man. That my own father was somewhat similar is perhaps why the poem particularly affects me, but I have witnessed its affecting so many others that I must assume either that such fathers exist in multitudes or that the poem cuts across vast differences of background in its instruction to the reader to reconsider the lives of those who helped us make our way into adulthood.

Whenever I teach "Those Winter Sundays," I face a dilemma of personal, political, and pedagogical consequence. Do I tell my students that Hayden is an African-American poet? That fact *does* make a difference in how we read the poem: the "cracked hands that ached / from labor in the weekday weather" may be seen in a context of a racial-economic circumstance, and thus "the chronic angers of that house" may also be seen as a result of racially enforced poverty. There are, however, manual laborers and poor families of all ethnic backgrounds, and so one need not necessarily read "Those Winter Sundays" as a poem that has anything to do with racial issues. It might even be argued that to read the poem as being about race is to give the poem a racist reading.

My students are almost always white, they are only beginning to learn about modern poetry, and they aren't likely to be acquainted with any African-American poets. If I tell them that Hayden was an African American, am I practicing a subtly racist bit of pedagogy? On the other hand, if I don't tell them that the man who wrote this poem is an African American, aren't I denying them a piece of knowledge that is essential not only for the understanding of this poem but for their general poetic education? (One wonders what the equivalent might be for another poet. To omit telling students of a Robert Frost poem that he lived for most of his life in New England? To say nothing about Walt Whitman's homosexuality? To leave unmentioned Emily Dickinson's reclusiveness? Is there really any equivalent?)

I'm a teacher; I almost always look for a positive approach to such dilemmas. I see an admirable ambiguity and psychological complexity in the fact that the poem can be read in both ways, as a poem that has nothing to do with race and as a poem that is somewhat informed by the circumstance of racial injustice. I do tell my students that the author was an African American, but I tell them only after we've read it a couple of times and talked about it. That piece of information is very nearly the last thing that I tell them before I read it to them the last time, the reading in which once more I journey in my own voice through the words, the lines, the stanzas, down through the cold house into the waiting warmth it always offers me, that necessary, inspiring insight it delivers to me again and again, that the duties of love (like the duties of poetry) are often scrupulously carried out in invisible and thankless ways.

RICHARD JACKSON

"Auguries of Innocence":
Blake's Poetry in Motion

"**W**hat is Liberty without Universal Toleration?" Blake asks in his annotations to Dante, and which I find myself asking a few friends in Slovenia while one war wages a little south of our comfortable bar, a few dozen others rage within a few hours by air, and countless others are marching towards us like so many rough beasts from over the horizon. For Blake, like Dante before him and Yeats in our own time, the question does not apply simply to a worldly situation but to a spiritual vision, not simply to political argument but to the life of the imagination. He writes, for example, in "Auguries of Innocence," the poem I find myself citing more and more in our conversation, "A Robin Red breast in a Cage / Puts all Heaven in a Rage." There will be proverbial hell to pay, Blake tells us, and it will lie in the destructiveness of our own hate and the blindness of our own vision. As Blake reminds us again and again in this poem, when we ignore the ethics of the imagination we lose ourselves in a spiritual and political forest as dark as that which confronted Dante's pilgrim.

So it is, then, that Blake's "Auguries of Innocence," part of the Pickering Manuscript written between 1801 and 1805, still seems to suit the times perfectly. For Blake, innocence is a perspective, a point of view in which things are not seen with any prescribed lens, any biased vantage point; innocence has allegiances to the disorganized, the loosely connected where one perception suggests myriad others. The result is to give the illusion of plenitude, to suggest a cosmos where one can "Hold Infinity in the palm of your hand / and Eternity in an hour." It is not the perspective of experience, the kind of poem Pope would write that evolves steadily and logically towards an encompassing vision. Blake's vision is more revolutionary, a collision of what he called "contraries" that are always in flux, a poem that is nonlinear and subverts our expectations of poetic order.

Blake seemed perfectly happy with our position in the midst of this free flux somewhere between the grain of sand and the infinity of the opening lines of "Auguries," an attitude he derived from Swedenborg, but which also derives from Pascal's "Pensee 199," and which Keats would later celebrate as "negative capability." I am reminded, too, of Nabokov's notion that under the microscope there is "a kind of delicate meeting place between imagination and knowledge, a point, arrived at by diminishing large things and enlarging small ones, that is intrinsically artistic." The dealers in experience want to impose a specific order to destroy this imaginative freedom of shifting perspectives. These are the very people Blake, one of the most political of poets, fought his whole life against. They insist on what Blake called "single vision," a constricted, party-line point of view that brings predictable results.

For Blake, these sorts of connections between writers such as Pascal and Nabokov, between literature and a savage war, the imposition of a single order and the imposition of a dictatorship, are not as far-fetched as many people today would think, for, as he says early in the poem, "A dog starvd at his Master's Gate / Predicts the ruin of the State." Indeed, if we could be more observant, could look with more innocent eyes, not see only what we want to see, each of us in our little bar would recognize a number of such masters lurking around the corners of the next few years. And we could have foreseen, for example, Sarajevo, south of us, a city forced to cut down its trees for firewood, shoot the animals in the zoo, terrorize the innocent—uncannily the very things Blake's poem enumerates—all in the name of preserving some rigid order or another.

For Blake, then, an essential self-questioning of the poem's order is paramount within the poem itself. That is why it is somewhat ironic to see a critic such as Harold Bloom impose his own sense of how poems move from citing social or personal injustice to a prophetic sense of the moment, or Mark Schorer's imposition of his sense that the poem must be unfinished but nevertheless shows a movement from man's cruelty to animals to man's cruelty to other men and the subsequent rise of false authority. David Erdman, in his edition of Blake, goes so far as to offer an alternate structure for the poem that he hopes tidies up all the discordant impulses. To be sure, such structures can be culled from the poem, and I don't mean to suggest that all is chaos, but these critics tend to generalize and thus oversimplify a poem whose main principle is complexity and unpredictability as the essence of innocence. As Blake himself writes in the poem, "Under every grief & pine / Runs a joy with silken twine." And as he wrote in his "Marginalia on Sir Joshua Reynolds," "To Generalize is to be an Idiot. To Particularize is Alone Distinction of Merit."

Blake's aim is to see things particularly, without the larger polemical apparatus he associated with experience, and to avoid stereotypes that dehumanize our individual selves. That is why his emphasis is equally upon the idea of "Auguries," which suggests the chaotic—that is, an emphasis on particular visions instead of on a finalized worldview. Order emerges only as possibility so that the poem must always have what we might call a provisional structure; it would take contemporary chaos theory, with its intricate fractals, to describe it fully. The emphasis on the particular also accounts for the aphoristic style: the speaker takes jabs at the world around him and interrogates it in a series of statements rather than describes it as some final structure. So one can find strands that run through the poem—things wandering or swept aside, things crying out, and sequences like the starved dog, the misused horse and lamb, things tormented, each of which is related to something larger.

This mode of relationship is Blake's peculiar brand of metaphor and it reveals the texture of his language and thinking. For example, rather than simply saying that the skylark looks like, or reminds him of, an angel, he finds a common ground: "Skylark wounded in the wing, / A Cherubim does cease to sing." There's a cause-and-effect relationship here, but it seems, especially in the context of the emphasis on vision in the opening lines (to see "Heaven in a Wild Flower," for instance), that the overriding concern is the metaphoric link that allows the physical and spiritual to be seen on the same level. For Blake, in a sense, they were—the skylark is the angel, or at least participates in its mode of being. He says in *The Marriage of Heaven and Hell*, "If the doors of perception were cleansed everything would appear to man as it is, infinite." We live, he suggests, in a spiritual world parallel to the physical one of the everyday, if only our lack of imaginative vision did not prevent us from seeing it.

We begin the journey towards such vision through the play of contraries: "Without Contraries is no progression," he says in *The Marriage of Heaven and Hell*. That's why we find so often an aphorism qualified or even undercut by another. Take, for example, this six-line sequence:

> A truth thats told with bad intent
> Beats all the Lies you can invent.
> It is right it should be so
> Man was made for Joy & Woe
> And when this we rightly know
> Thro the World we safely go

It is difficult to decipher when Blake is being ironic, when trying to provoke a reaction, when being deadly serious. In any case, the first couplet here subverts our usual categories about the absoluteness of truth, while the second two couplets suggest a kind of complacency about truth and living in the world that the rest of the poem seems to argue passionately against. A little later in the poem some lines occur that would suggest he is being fully straightforward—"The Questioner who sits so sly / Shall never know how to Reply." Yet by the end of the poem he says: "We are led to Believe a Lie / When we see not Thro the Eye." In several other poems Blake talks about seeing *with* the physical eye, as opposed to seeing *through* the physical eye toward the spiritual. In this context, he treats the idea of safety with near-sarcasm, and what we are "made for" is not the issue, but rather what we make of our world, how we see it. But then perhaps safety becomes a straightforward term in the spiritual sense, ironic in the physical. The aphoristic structure tends towards seeing the very act of questioning and adjusting our vision as far more important than arriving at a settled point of view or theme. No single perception, no single aphorism can be taken on its own, but rather in the context of the play of contraries and metaphoric relations Blake sets in motion.

The point, then, is possibility. There is an intense questioning of the world and the self, while at the same time there is an insistence upon faith. So when Blake says "If the Sun & Moon should doubt / Theyd immediately Go out," it is not to forestall questioning but to suggest that behind the poem's questionings, its aphoristic stabs at provisional order, is a faith in the self that will ultimately achieve a fuller vision.

The poem is written, finally, not from the world of innocence it augurs, but from the bleak world of our experience, a world ordered and chained by our "Lame Philosophy." It is written in a world where Sarajevos are destroyed physically and spiritually and lie in their own "winding sheet" as Blake predicted England would in a spiritual sense. This poem is especially important for our own pitiful world. And so in a sense its auguries look back in order to again look forward to a more innocent time, for past and future, those temporal terms, are informed by the spiritual terms *light* and *darkness*. The visionary is finally, for Blake, spiritual, a vision that transcends the political, the sociological, that is, in the end, human and humane:

> God Appears & God is Light
> To those poor Souls who dwell in Night
> But does a Human Form Display
> To those who Dwell in Realms of day.

I like to see Blake looking forward with some apprehension and yet some faith towards today's world. Sitting at our little bar, reading "Auguries" in this visionary light, we can begin to understand that the poem not only marks what has been already lost, our innocence, but maybe, too, what can be recovered, a vision where contraries and questions move us towards an active, always unfolding spirituality. The poem is, finally, an act of faith and of love for and through the world, and this is perhaps our best hope in such bleak times.

Auguries of Innocence

To see a World in a Grain of Sand
And a Heaven in a Wild Flower
Hold Infinity in the palm of your hand
And Eternity in an hour
A Robin Red breast in a Cage
Puts all Heaven in a Rage
A dove house filld with doves & Pigeons
Shudders Hell thro all its regions
A dog starvd at his Masters Gate
Predicts the ruin of the State
A Horse misusd upon the Road
Calls to Heaven for Human blood
Each outcry of the hunted Hare
A fibre from the Brain does tear
A Skylark wounded in the wing
A Cherubim does cease to sing
The Game Cock clipd & armd for fight
Does the Rising Sun affright
Every Wolfs & Lions howl
Raises from Hell a Human Soul
The wild deer wandring here & there
Keeps the Human Soul from Care
The Lamb misusd breeds Public strife
And yet forgives the Butchers Knife
The Bat that flits at close of Eve
Has left the Brain that wont Believe
The Owl that calls upon the Night
Speaks the Unbelievers fright
He who shall hurt the little Wren
Shall never be belovd by Men
He who the Ox to wrath has movd
Shall never be by Woman lovd
The wanton Boy that kills the Fly
Shall feel the Spiders enmity
He who torments the Chafers sprite
Weaves a Bower in endless Night

The Catterpiller on the Leaf
Repeats to thee thy Mothers grief
Kill not the Moth nor Butterfly
For the Last Judgment draweth nigh
He who shall train the Horse to War
Shall never pass the Polar Bar
The Beggers Dog & Widows Cat
Feed them & thou wilt grow fat
The Gnat that sings his Summers song
Poison gets from Slanders tongue
The poison of the Snake & Newt
Is the sweat of Envys Foot
The Poison of the Honey Bee
Is the Artists Jealousy
The Princes Robes & Beggars Rags
Are Toadstools on the Misers Bags
A truth thats told with bad intent
Beats all the Lies you can invent
It is right it should be so
Man was made for Joy & Woe
And when this we rightly know
Thro the World we safely go
Joy & Woe are woven fine
A Clothing for the Soul divine
Under every grief & pine
Runs a joy with silken twine
The Babe is more than swadling Bands
Throughout all these Human Lands
Tools were made & Born were hands
Every Farmer Understands
Every Tear from Every Eye
Becomes a Babe in Eternity
This is caught by Females bright
And returnd to its own delight
The Bleat the Bark Bellow & Roar
Are Waves that Beat on Heavens Shore
The Babe that weeps the Rod beneath
Writes Revenge in realms of death
The Beggars Rags fluttering in Air
Does to Rags the Heavens tear
The Soldier armd with Sword & Gun
Palsied strikes the Summers Sun
The poor Mans Farthing is worth more

Than all the Gold on Africs Shore
One Mite wrung from the Labrers hands
Shall buy & sell the Misers Lands
Or if protected from on high
Does that whole Nation sell & buy
He who mocks the Infants Faith
Shall be mock'd in Age & Death
He who shall teach the Child to Doubt
The rotting Grave shall neer get out
He who respects the Infants faith
Triumphs over Hell & Death
The Childs Toys & the Old Mans Reasons
Are the Fruits of the Two seasons
The Questioner who sits so sly
Shall never know how to Reply
He who replies to words of Doubt
Doth put the Light of Knowledge out
The Strongest Poison ever known
Came from Caesars Laurel Crown
Nought can deform the Human Race
Like to the Armours iron brace
When Gold & Gems adorn the Plow
To peaceful Arts shall Envy Bow
A Riddle or the Crickets Cry
Is to Doubt a fit Reply
The Emmets Inch & Eagles Mile
Make Lame Philosophy to smile
He who Doubts from what he sees
Will neer Believe do what you Please
If the Sun & Moon should doubt
Theyd immediately Go out
To be in a Passion you Good may do
But no Good if a Passion is in you
The Whore & Gambler by the State
Licencd build that Nations Fate
The Harlots cry from Street to Street
Shall weave Old Englands winding Sheet
The Winners Shout the Losers Curse
Dance before dead Englands Hearse
Every Night & every Morn
Some to Misery are Born
Every Morn & every Night
Some are Born to sweet delight

Some are Born to sweet delight
Some are Born to Endless Night
We are led to Believe a Lie
When we see not Thro the Eye
Which was Born in a Night to perish in a Night
When the Soul Slept in Beams of Light
God Appears & God is Light
To those poor Souls who dwell in Night
But does a Human Form Display
To those who Dwell in Realms of day

William Blake

"But to Our Tale": "Tam O'Shanter"
by Robert Burns

The story goes that the Scottish poet Robert Burns (1759–1798) composed this poem aloud in the spring or summer of 1790 while on a picnic with his family in Ellisland, beside the River Nith, near Dumfries in southwestern Scotland, where he spent the last years of his short life. Alan Bold in *A Burns Companion* cites Lockhart's *Life of Burns* for a description of how the poet made up the poem:

> The poem was the work of one day, and Mrs. Burns well remembers the circumstances. He spent most of the day on his favorite walk by the river. . . . Her attention was presently attracted by the strange and wild gesticulations of the bard, who, now at some distance, was *agonized* with an ungovernable access of joy. He was reciting very loud, and with tears rolling down his cheeks, those animated verses which he had just conceived.

While Burns knew "Tam O'Shanter" was his masterpiece, and may have sensed what he was on to when he began to compose it, the poem may not have been the work of one day. In November 1790 he sent an incomplete copy of the poem to his friend Mrs. Frances Anna Dunlop and commented that the poem had "a finishing polish that I despair of ever excelling." And before that strange and wild poem-making began by the river, according to Bold, Burns had promised Francis Grose "a witch tale to accompany a drawing of Kirk Alloway in the second volume of his *Antiquities of Scotland*."

It might be better to say that "Tam O'Shanter" was the work of a day and several centuries, of a genius and his tradition. The epigraph to the poem is from Gawin Douglas's fifteenth-century translation into Scots dialect of Virgil's *Aeneid*. Homeric echoes are obvious in Burns's use of simile and in Tam's comic odyssey home to his "sulky sullen" Penelope, Kate. The verse is octosyllabic couplets, a form of English poetry perfected by Andrew Marvell in the seventeenth century and used for satiric effect by Jonathan Swift in the early eighteenth. In his poems and songs, Burns had already demonstrated his gift for the dialect of his native southwestern Scotland and the Augustan English of proper late-eighteenth-century poetry. In "Tam O'Shanter" he combines both kinds of language. Thus when Tam sets about to get drunk one market day, an opportunity he rarely passes up, the narrator scolds in broad Scots,

> O Tam! had'st thou but been sae wise,
> As ta'en thy ain wife Kate's advice!
> She tauld thee weel thou was a skellum,
> A blethering, blustering, a drunken blellum,
> That frae November till October
> Ae market-day thou was noe sober

We can hear the screeching reproach that awaits Tam when he arrives home. In a more elegant vein, in similes Pope might have approved of, the poet describes the brevity of Tam's happiness while drinking.

> But pleasures are like poppies spread,
> You sieze the flow'r, its bloom is shed;
> Or like the snow falls in the river,
> A moment white—then melts for ever;
> Or like the borealis race,
> That flit ere you can point their place;
> Or like the rainbow's lovely form
> Evanishing amid the storm.—

Part of the poem's elegance has to do with its narrative structure. The demonic scene that Tam witnesses at Kirk Alloway might indeed be the inspiration of "bold John Barleycorn." But Tam's wife Kate has also "prophesied that, late or soon" because of his excesses Tam will be found drowned or "catch'd wi' warlocks in the mirk, / By Alloway's auld haunted kirk." And the latter is what almost happens, although Tam lives to tell the tale, the most elaborate and inventive excuse in English literature. Of course, he has the proof of his horse's clawed-off tail, the stump left to poor Maggie by the hag Nannie just before the mare conveys Tam safely across the Brig o' Doon. That is the evidence that makes his a "tale o' truth."

Yet the narration of this tale, its telling, gives as much pleasure as its structure, and one can imagine that Burns's joyful tears in the composition were for the telling as much as the tale. The narrator lingers for thirty-five lines setting the scene before he hurries on "to our tale." Then he lovingly creates the alehouse atmosphere. With a storyteller's finesse he builds the storm outside that foreshadows the supernatural rage that

Tam will encounter at Kirk Alloway and the wrath he will meet when he returns home. The vividness of each scene reminds us that the action we expect of cinema was at one time most effectively created by words alone. The shooting script for "Tam O'Shanter" is complete within the poem. As an extra we get the satirical commentary of the narrator when he shows us the satanic revelry at Kirk Alloway. The relics on the altar, "the haly table," are a suggestive catalogue of contemporary sins. However, Burns omitted the most controversial lines and replaced them with a sly couplet, "Wi' mair o' horrible and awefu', / Which even to name wad be unlawfu'." In his recording of the poem, the modern Scottish poet Hugh Macdiarmid restores them. Among the bodies, bones, and murder weapons on the altar, Burns originally included

> Three Lawyers' tongues, turn'd inside out,
> Wi' lies seam'd like a beggar's clout;
> Three Priests' hearts, rotten, black as muck,
> Lay stinking, vile, in every neuk.

These are not merely props for a ghost story. Finally, dialect adds both comedy and darkness to events, and it enhances the sexy play of the sacrilegious dance. "Even Satan," the narrator tells us, who in the form of a shaggy dog—a "towzie tyke"—plays the bagpipes, is excited by the dancing and "fidg'd fu fain, / And hotch'd and blew wi' might and main," wriggling with joy and arousal.

In fact, "Tam O'Shanter" is as much a satire as it is a ghost story, and in that regard it brings to mind Nathaniel Hawthorne's "Young Goodman Brown." Both tales expose a society's confusions about evil and eroticism. Tam, drunk, has a good deal more fun than the young Puritan, and puts himself in greater peril, too, though the satirical ends of both works may be the same. Hawthorne's narrator, however, remains chastely detached from Brown's anguish. As for Burns's narrator, at the idea of what the reeling hags might look like if they were nubile teenage girls, he exclaims that he would have been happy to dance naked with them.

> Thir breeks o' mine, my only pair,
> That ance were plush, o' gude blue hair,
> I wad hae gi'en them off my hurdies,
> For ae blink o' the bonie burdies!

The comic letdown to this sexual bravado is the reminder that the "bonie burdies" are "wither'd beldams." Only Nannie, the new enlistee in the witch's corps, is described as "A souple jade" and "strang." She is a fit adversary for Tam's own jade, Maggie. Drink has whirled Tam's sexual revelry, which began with his flirtation with the alehouse landlady, into a nightmare. For Young Goodman Brown the revelation of uninhibited sexuality is a nightmare in itself, from which he never wakes. Tam's ends with his escape across the River Doon. The penalty for his transgression is the mutilation not of himself but of his innocent and courageous steed. Maggie receives the wound that Tam has earned, though she is merely deprived of her tail. Yet the narrator turns Maggie's tail into a moral for those who would behave like Tam O'Shanter. If you drink late and tempt the devil, you may end up acting like a horse's ass.

But Burns has acted like a master. For him, "Tam O'Shanter" was a poem, lucky for any poet, that combined all of his considerable gifts— for storytelling ("Tam O'Shanter" is a genre unto itself, the shaggy-dog epic), for dialect and the literary language of his time, for humor, for satire (so rich he had to rein it in), and for moralizing and sympathy, an extraordinary combination found in abundance only in Shakespeare. Burns's talents made a poem that, while it cautions against drinking and womanizing, also cunningly links the hypocrisy of contemporary society with its phantom of license and taboo, the devil himself.

Tam O'Shanter

A Tale

Of Brownyis and of Bogillis full is this buke.
Gawin Douglas

When chapman billies leave the street,
And drouthy neebors, neebors meet,
As market-days are wearing late,
An' folk begin to tak the gate;
While we sit bousing at the nappy,
An' getting fou and unco happy,
We think na on the lang Scots miles,
The mosses, waters, slaps, and styles,
That lie between us and our hame,
Whare sits our sulky sullen dame,
Gathering her brows like gathering storm,
Nursing her wrath to keep it warm.

Chapman billies, peddlers; *drouthy*, thirsty; *neebors*, neighbors; *gate*, the road; *nappy*, ale; *fou*, drunk; *unco*, extra; *na*, not; *moss*, bog; *slaps*, gaps in walls.

This truth fand honest Tam o'Shanter,
As he frae Ayr ae night did canter,
(Auld Ayr, wham ne'er a town surpasses,
For honest men and bonny lasses).

O Tam! had'st thou but been sae wise,
As ta'en thy ain wife Kate's advice!
She tauld thee weel thou was a skellum,
A blethering, blustering, a drunken blellum;
That frae November till October,
Ae market-day thou was nae sober;
That ilka melder, wi' the miller,
Thou sat as lang as thou had siller;
That ev'ry naig was ca'ed a shoe on,
The smith and thee got roaring fou on;
That at the Lord's house, even on Sunday,
Thou drank wi' Kirkton Jean till Monday.
She prophesied that, late or soon,
Thou would be found deep drown'd in Doon;
Or catch'd wi' warlocks in the mirk,
By Alloway's auld haunted kirk.

Ah, gentle dames! it gars me greet,
To think how mony counsels sweet,
How mony lengthen'd sage advices,
The husband frae the wife despises!

But to our tale: Ae market-night,
Tam had got planted unco right;
Fast by an ingle, bleezing finely,
Wi' reaming swats, that drank divinely;
And at his elbow, Souter Johnny,
His ancient, trusty, drouthy crony;
Tam lo'ed him like a vera brither;
They had been fou for weeks thegither.
The night drave on wi' sangs and clatter;
And ay the ale was growing better:

Fand, found; *ta'en,* taken; *ain,* own; *skellum,* rogue; *blethering,* chattering; *blellum,*
braggart; *ilka melder,* every flour-grinding; *siller,* money; *ev'ry naig was ca'ed a*
shoe on, every time a horse was shoed; *kirk,* church; *gars,* makes; *greet,* weep; *Ae,*
one; *unco,* uncommonly; *bleezing,* blazing; *reaming swats,* foaming ale; *Souter,* shoe-
maker; *lo'ed,* loved; *thegither,* together; *drave,* drove; *clatter,* gossip.

The landlady and Tam grew gracious,
Wi' favors, secret, sweet, and precious:
The Souter tauld his queerest stories;
The landlord's laugh was ready chorus:
The storm without might rair and rustle,
Tam did na mind the storm a whistle.

Care, mad to see a man sàe happy,
E'en drown'd himsel amang the nappy:
As bees flee hame wi' lades o' treasure,
The minutes wing'd their way wi' pleasure:
Kings may be blest but Tam was glorious,
O'er a' the ills o' life victorious!

But pleasures are like poppies spread,
You sieze the flow'r, its bloom is shed;
Or like the snow falls in the river,
A moment white—then melts for ever;
Or like the borealis race,
That flit ere you can point their place;
Or like the rainbow's lovely form
Evanishing amid the storm.—
Nae man can tether time or tide;
The hour approaches Tam maun ride;
That hour, o' night's black arch the key-stane,
That dreary hour he mounts his beast in;
And sic a night he taks the road in,
As ne'er poor sinner was abroad in.

The wind blew as 'twad blawn its last;
The rattling showers rose on the blast;
The speedy gleams the darkness swallow'd;
Loud, deep, and lang, the thunder bellow'd:
That night, a child might understand,
The Deil had business on his hand.

Weel mounted on his gray mare, Meg,
A better never lifted leg,
Tam skelpit on thro' dub and mire,
Despising wind, and rain, and fire;

Rair, roar; *lades*, loads; *evanishing*, vanishing; *maun*, must; *sic*, such; *skelpit*, dashed; *dub*, puddle.

Whiles holding fast his gude blue bonnet;
Whiles crooning o'er some auld Scots sonnet;
Whiles glowring round wi' prudent cares,
Lest bogles catch him unawares:
Kirk-Alloway was drawing night,
Whare ghaists and houlets nightly cry.—

   By this time he was cross the ford,
Whare, in the snaw, the chapman smoor'd;
And past the birks and meikle stane,
Whare drunken Charlie brak's neck-bane;
And thro' the whins, and by the cairn,
Whare hunters fand the murder'd bairn;
And near the thorn, aboon the well,
Whare Mungo's mither hang'd herself.—
Before him Doon pours all his floods;
The doubling storm roars thro' the woods;
The lightnings flash from pole to pole;
Near and more near the thunders roll:
When, glimmering thro' the groaning trees,
Kirk-Alloway seem'd in a bleeze;
Thro' ilka bore the beams were glancing;
And loud resounded mirth and dancing.—
   Inspiring bold John Barleycorn!
What dangers thou can make us scorn!
Wi' tippeny, we fear nae evil;
Wi' usquabae, we'll face the devil!—
The swats sae ream'd in Tammy's noddle,
Fair play, he car'd na deils a boddle.
But Maggie stood right sair astonish'd,
She ventur'd forward on the light;
And, wow! Tam saw an unco sight!
Warlocks and witches in a dance;
Nae cotillion, brent new frae France,
But hornpipes, jigs, strathspeys, and reels,
Put life and mettle in their heels.
A winnock-bunker in the east,
There sat auld Nick, in shape o' beast;

Glowring, staring; *bogles*, bogeys; *ghaists*, ghosts; *houlets*, owls; *smoor'd*, smothered; *birks*, birches; *meikle*, great; *stane*, boulder; *whins*, gorse; *aboon*, above; *bore*, chink; *tippeny*, twopenny ale; *usquabae*, whiskey; *boddle*, farthing; *sair*, sorely; *brent*, brand; *strathspeys*, Highland dances; *winnock-bunker*, window-seat.

A towzie tyke, black, grim, and large,
To gie them music was his charge:
He screw'd the pipes and gart them skirl,
Till roof and rafters a' did dirl. —
Coffins stood round, like open presses,
That shaw'd the dead in their last dresses;
And by some devlish cantraip slight
Each in its cauld hand held a light. —
By which heroic Tam was able
To note upon the haly table,
A murderer's banes in gibbet airns;
Twa span-lang, unchristen'd bairns;
A thief, new-cutted frae a rape,
Wi' his last gasp his gab did gape;
Five tomahawks, wi' blude red-rusted;
Five scymitars, wi' murder crusted;
A garter, which a babe had strangled;
A knife, a father's throat had mangled,
Whom his ain son o' life bereft,
The grey hairs yet stack to the heft;
Wi' mair o' horrible and awefu',
Which even to name wad be unlawfu'.

As Tammie glower'd, amaz'd, and curious,
The mirth and fun grew fast and furious:
The piper loud and louder blew;
The dancers quick and quicker flew;
They reel'd, they set, they cross'd, they cleekit,
Till ilka carlin swat and reekit,
And coost her duddies to the wark,
And linket at it in her sark!

Now, Tam, O Tam! had they been queans,
A' plump and strapping in their teens,
Their sarks, instead o' creeshie flannen,
Been snaw-white seventeen hunder linnen!
Thir breeks o' mine, my only pair,

Towzie tyke, shaggy dog; *gart,* made; *skirl,* sound shrilly; *dirl,* rattle; *presses,* wardrobes; *cantraip slight,* weird trick; *cauld,* cold; *haly,* holy; *airns,* irons; *rape,* rope; *gab,* mouth; *cleekit,* joined hands; *carlin,* hag; *swat,* sweated; *reekit,* steamed; *coost,* cast off; *duddies,* rags; *linket,* danced; *sark,* slip; *queans,* girls; *creeshie,* greasy; *flannen,* flannel; *seventeen hunder linnen,* the finest linen, woven with 1700 threads per width; *breeks,* trousers.

That ance were plush, o' gude blue hair,
I wad hae gi'en them off my hurdies,
For ae blink o' the bonie burdies!

But wither'd beldams, auld and droll,
Rigwoodie hags wad spean a foal,
Lowping and flinging on a crummock,
I wonder didna turn thy stomach.

But Tam kend what was what fu' brawlie,
There was ae winsome wench and wawlie,
That night enlisted in the core,
(Lang after kend on Carrick shore;
For mony a beast to dead she shot,
And perish'd mony a bony boat,
And shook baith meikle corn and bear,
And kept the country-side in fear).
Her cutty sark, o' Paisley harn,
That while a lassie she had worn,
In longitude tho' sorely scanty,
It was her best, and she was vauntie.—
Ah! little kend thy reverend grannie,
That sark she coft for her wee Nannie,
Wi' twa pund Scots ('twas a' her riches),
Wad ever grac'd a dance of witches!

But here my Muse her wing maun cour;
Sic flights are far beyond her pow'r;
To sing how Nannie lap and flang,
(A souple jade she was, and strang),
And how Tam stood, like ane bewitch'd,
And thought his very een enrich'd;
Even Satan glowr'd, and fidg'd fu' fain,
And hotch'd and blew wi' might and main:
Till first ae caper, syne anither,
Tam tint his reason a' thegither,
And roars out, "Weel done, Cutty-sark!"

Ance, once; *hurdies*, buttocks; *ae blink*, one glimpse; *burdies*, lasses; *beldams*,
witches; *Rigwoodie*, scrawny; *spean*, wean; *Lowping*, leaping; *crummock*, staff;
brawlie, well; *wawlie*, choice; *core*, company; *baith*, both; *meikle*, much; *bear*, bar-
ley; *cutty sark*, short slip; *harn*, coarse cloth; *vauntie*, proud; *coft*, purchased; *pund*,
pounds; *cour*, stoop; *lap and flang*, leaped and kicked; *fidg'd fu' fain*, wriggled with
delight; *hotch'd*, jerked; *syne*, then; *tint*, lost.

And in an instant all was dark:
And scarcely had he Maggie rallied,
When out the hellish legion sallied.

As bees bizz out wi' angry fyke,
When plundering herds assail their byke;
As open pussie's mortal foes,
When, pop! she starts before their nose;
As eager runs the market-crowd,
When "Catch the thief!" resounds aloud;
So Maggie runs, the witches follow,
Wi' mony an eldritch skreech and hollow.

Ah, Tam! Ah, Tam! thou'll get thy fairin!
In hell they'll roast thee like a herrin!
In vain thy Kate awaits thy comin!
Kate soon will be a woefu' woman!
Now, do thy speedy utmost, Meg,
And win the key-stane of the brig;
There at them thou thy tail may toss,
A running stream thy dare na cross.
But ere the key-stane she could make,
The fient a tail she had to shake!
For Nannie, far before the rest,
Hard upon noble Maggie prest,
And flew at Tam wi' furious ettle;
But little wist she Maggie's mettle—
Ae spring brought off her master hale,
But left behind her ain grey tail:
The carlin claught her by the rump,
And left poor Maggie scarce a stump.

Now, what this tale o' truth shall read,
Ilk man and mother's son, take heed:
Whene'er to drink you are inclin'd,
Or cutty-sarks run in your mind,
Think, ye may buy the joys o'er dear,
Remember Tam o'Shanter's mare.

Robert Burns

Fyke, vexation; *herds*, shepherds; *byke*, hive; *pussie's*, hare's; *eldritch skreech and hollow*, otherworldly shrieking and hullabaloo; *fairin*, deserts; *brig*, bridge; *fient*, devil; *ettle*, intent; *hale*, whole; *claught*, clutched.

Devouring Time:
Shakespeare's Sonnets

My love affair with Shakespeare's sonnets began when I was in college. Looking back, it seems to me that at every stage of my adult life, the sonnets have meant something different to me—always deepening, always inexhaustible.

The most daunting challenge is to choose a favorite out of the 152 best poems in our language, since there are so many that move me deeply. I begin this impossible task by reading through the sonnets to myself silently, and then by listening to Sir John Gielgud's astonishing rendition of them, recorded in 1963, Shakespeare's quatercentenary. (I deliberately do not turn to my groaning bookshelves of Shakespeare criticism with their pointless, and ultimately snobbish, debates about the identity of "Mr. W. H." or whether or not our "Top Poet," as Auden called him, could really be a mere middle-class man of Stratford rather than the Earl of Oxford—or perhaps even the Virgin Queen herself. I want to return to the sonnets freshly—as a common reader, responding to them as a person first, a poet second.) As Gielgud's great actor's voice reawakens these dazzling poems for me, I hear again the toll of mortality in the sonnets, the elaboration of the themes of love and death and the stark repetition of their central word: "time."

Devouring time, the wastes of Time, Time's scythe, Wasteful time, in war with time, this bloody tyrant time, time's pencil, time's furrows, dear time's waste, Time's injurious hand, Time's spoils, Time's fool, a hell of time, Time's fickle glass. . . . It seems I cannot read or hear the sonnets without being reminded of how little time is left—which sends me to my desk to write with frenzied hand.

Time is the all-powerful, wrathful God of the sonnets. And to this awesome power, the poet opposes procreation, love, and poetry.

The first thirteen sonnets urge begetting a child to oppose death:

Th'ou art thy mother's glass, and she in thee
Calls back the lovely April of her prime.

(Sonnet 3)

Then the theme shifts, and by Sonnet 15 the poet is comparing his own craft to procreation as a way of winning the war with time:

And all in war with Time for love of you,
As he takes from you, I ingraft you new.

But poetry is fired by love, so these two forms of redemption are really the same. Children redeem us from time, poetry redeems us from time, and love is the force that drives them both. As the sonnets go on to tell their twisted tale of rival loves, rival poets, love, passion, parting, obsessional sexuality, wrath, reunion, forgiveness, self-love, self-loathing, and self-forgiveness, time never ceases to be the poet's alpha and omega, the deity he both worships and despises.

And so I find myself coming back again and again to Sonnet 19, a poet's credo if ever there were one.

Devouring Time, blunt thou the lion's paws,
And make the earth devour her own sweet brood;
Pluck the keen teeth from the fierce tiger's yaws,
And burn the long-liv'd phoenix in her blood;
Make glad and sorry seasons as thou fleet'st,
And do whate'er thou wilt, swift-footed Time,
To the wide world and all her fading sweets;
But I forbid thee one most heinous crime:
O, carve not with thy hours my love's fair brow,
Nor draw no lines there with thine antique pen;
Him in thy course untained do allow
For beauty's pattern to succeeding men.
Yet do thy worst, old Time: despite thy wrong,
My love shall in my verse ever live young.

Sonnet 19 is hardly the most complex of Shakespeare's sonnets, nor the most tortured. The sonnets that recount obsessional love, jealousy, and lust are far darker and more fretted. But Sonnet 19 calls me back again and again because it is one of the few in which the poet addresses time directly and takes him on—David against Goliath.

The simplicity of the sonnet's "statement" delights me: "Time, you big bully, you think you're so great. You can make people die and tigers lose their teeth and change the seasons so fast it makes us dizzy. But spare my love. Don't scribble on him with your antique pen. On second thought, do whatever the hell you like. You have the power to destroy, but I have an even greater power: I create. And by capturing my love in poetry, I can keep my love young forever, whatever you may do to destroy him!"

There is a fluidity to this sonnet that seems to me a triumph of this difficult form. The three quatrains flow into one another and become one exhortation. The couplet argues with them all, changing the direction swiftly and ironically. The poet is standing up to the bully. Suddenly "Devouring Time" becomes "old Time," as if in the course of fourteen lines he had withered like a vampire thrown into a raging inferno. The poem itself has subdued time, made him old before his time, vanquished him. The force of poetry alone defeats time.

This theme is elaborated often in the sonnets, but seldom with such simplicity, the simplicity of a person addressing a fearsome deity without fear: the poet speaking to the gods. Throughout the sonnets, the poet addresses his love, his siren, his lust, even himself, but only in this sonnet (and once more in Sonnet 123) does he address Time directly. He throws down the gauntlet and takes Time on as if one might defeat a powerful foe simply with the force of language.

And, of course, one *can*, as Shakespeare's sonnets prove. We go back to them again and again, discovering new depths in them as time carves new depths in our hearts.

In youth, we tend to love the love poems, the poems of obsessional lust, jealousy, and rage. "Th'expense of spirit in a waste of shame" (129) reminds us of our own struggles to master lust. "So are you to my thoughts as food to life" (75) reminds us of the yearning of first love. As we age, we increasingly see Time shadowing love and the bliss of creation as the only redemption. Shakespeare's sonnets are a fugue on the theme of time. They can be read together or separately, line by line, quatrain by quatrain, or as a narrative of the power of art against decay. They prove the poet's point by their very durability.

Each time I go back to the sonnets, I find something that seemed not to be there before. Perhaps I have changed and my vision is less clouded, or else the sonnets metamorphose on the shelf. The sonnets I love best are those with sustained voices, those that sound like a person speaking. I think I hear Shakespeare's private voice in these sonnets, as if he were whispering directly in my ear.

That Shakespeare's sonnets have defeated death comforts me—for what is great poetry, after all, but the continuation of the human voice after death?

A Certain Unreasonableness of
Feeling: Philip Larkin's "Coming"

What Betjeman was for the English reader, Larkin has come to be for the American. Betjeman may be a bit too much for us, but Larkin comes across as the quintessential Englishman, almost a caricature of the type. Nor have we been far wrong to think of him in this way, for Motion's biography has made clear how disappointingly close the poet came to living up to the type. Curmudgeonly and tory, secretive and aloof, insular, not to say xenophobic, coolly polite at best, one who, in his poems, could go rather soft over English character and English land-scape, but quietly, while pretending not to. On an American reader this ought to wear pretty badly, one would think, and yet it does not seem to have worked out that way. To those—a dwindling number, to be sure—who are still willing to read verse that has close and honorable ties to the past, verse that behaves well metrically and makes sense, without pre-tension or overreaching ambition, verse firmly grounded in the social realities of period and place, Larkin is an object of admiration, usually the American reader's favorite English poet after Auden. Certainly he is mine.

Such a reader may well prefer the sort of Larkin poem typified by "This Be the Verse" or "Annus Mirabilis," and I gather that it is for such poems that Larkin is now most famous. In the hands of a lesser master they might pass for *vers de société*, clever and very fine, but not much more than that. There is no denying the wit in these pieces, and wit of that particularly mordant strain that the term Larkinesque points to and may eventually come to be restricted to. But I would argue that to insist on this Larkin (rather than the *other* Larkin we will presently be considering) is, perhaps unconsciously, a way of putting Larkin down, or at least in his "place." Certainly it is to put limits on his work, which in consequence must come to seem not altogether "serious," not, in any case, serious in the approved American manner, all earnestness and raw emotion.

But even into such poems there normally comes a note of plangent bitterness or regret, some perhaps sudden invasion or flash of feeling, which surely must surprise any unaccustomed reader of the poet. Just such a reversal occurs at the end of "High Windows."

> And immediately
> Rather than words comes the thought of high windows:
> The sun-comprehending glass,
> And beyond it, the deep blue air, that shows
> Nothing, and is nowhere, and is endless.

The poem had begun as though aimed in a quite different direction:

> When I see a couple of kids
> And guess he's fucking her and she's
> Taking pills or wearing a diaphragm,
> I know this is paradise.

The ground between these two stanzas is not really covered: it is simply leaped over in a great chancy leap that is strictly Larkin. The effect is often found at the end of a Larkin poem, a kind of structural trick we grow to expect but can still at times be moved by.

In any case, it is the capacity to reach an ending like this that marks Larkin and sets him apart from—indeed, above—the writer of society verse, however topical and smart, which he might otherwise have been —a sort of Cole Porter (whom he admired) without the music. It is more than a capacity: it is a positive inclination and bent. That it should happen so frequently is less an indication that it is a formula the poet tends to fall back on than that it is there always as an ineradicable part of the poet's very self.

Another way of regarding these two Larkin voices is to think of them as representing, in the one case, an audience-conscious, public Larkin, and in the other, an excruciatingly private Larkin, someone who in real life would not like letting his feelings show. The poet is like one of those British character actors in the old Ealing comedies who stand around on the fringes of a scene smoking a pipe, looking awkward and embarrassed, probably envying the Lucky Jimmish hero. Do they even possess deep feelings? On this question we might have voted no, but for Larkin.

Occasionally Larkin writes a poem that starts at the end, so to speak, a poem that is tonally all of a piece throughout. "Coming" is a very beautiful early example. It stands at the beginning of his career, the fifth oldest of the poems Larkin chose to collect. The poet was twenty-seven years old; he could not yet have recognized in himself what it was to be Larkinesque, but he can hardly have doubted that *something* was.

"Coming" lacks the rich social detail of many of the later poems. It is rare, if not quite singular, in that it contains no satiric touches whatever; it is as pure a lyric as can be found in the mature Larkin. Already it features a couple of the characteristically lovely compounds that distinguish so many of his poems and that were to become a virtual Larkin signature: *laurel-surrounded* and *fresh-peeled*. The closest approach to the cynicism and weariness of later Larkin is the reference to the poet's childhood as "a forgotten boredom," but the point is not pursued. It proves to be no more than a passing note that creates a dissonance immediately resolved, for this is a poem of classical harmony.

There are relatively few verbal repetitions in Larkin. The repetition here in line 10—"It will be spring soon"—therefore probably warrants some mild speculation. A friend calls it, very handsomely, a "resurrecting, vernal force," and I could not hope to better that. In a poem written twenty years later, "The Trees," something similar does occur.

> Last year is dead, they seem to say,
> Begin afresh, afresh, afresh.

Curiously enough both repetitions have to do with spring, but I do not see much in that; it could be and very likely is coincidence. Yet the repetition itself exerts some odd slight power. To me it has always seemed both poignant and musical. I happen to be constitutionally suspicious of claims purporting to find imitative effects in poems—people can and do find them everywhere, foolishly—but once I let my guard down here I see what should have been obvious from the start and doubtless has always been so to others. The repeated line is an imitation of the thrush's song, faint perhaps, as all such imitative effects are, but true. Not that it intends, of course, to reproduce the actual sounds of the bird's song, but only to stand in for it in a poem by way of a familiar but unexpressed convention.

Already I have made too much of this. And reading what others have had so far to say about Larkin's work keeps reminding me of how easy it is to say too much out of the mere desire to find something, anything at all, to say about work that does not choose to show off, that takes no pride in being difficult. It is a point the poet himself made more than once.

Somewhere Larkin speaks of a poem he was working on as "a little unrhyming poem." This description fits "Coming" exactly. Larkin's lines are usually iambic, a standard four or five feet long. These lines, perhaps because they are shorter, seem more lyrical than usual, less sharp-tongued. They come about as close as Larkin ever comes to free verse, though they are not quite that either. I would propose that the lines be read accentually. That is, each line *can* be read as having two accents, but in practice should probably not be held strictly to that. In other poems with a similar metrical base Larkin appears to allow himself to stretch the line out occasionally to three accents, and several of the lines here could be so interpreted—"Astonishing the brickwork," for instance—but Larkin himself in his own recording of the poem keeps very close to the two-accent base. Several lines have a relatively large number of syllables to be got through in a sort of deliberate hurry ("But the unusual laughter"), while one line has almost as few syllables as possible for a line of two beats ("A thrush sings"). These extremes suggest the variety and ingenuity, the energy, in fact, and the very high delicacy, involved in Larkin's handling of this strange little line. For further variety let it be noted that what might be called a "long" or "strong" word from time to time comes into play in a "short" or "weak" position, contributing to the attractive and indeed essential rhythmical ambiguity of the whole. Take *bare*, for example, in "In the deep bare garden" or *peeled* in "Its fresh-peeled voice": these stiffen up the lines in which they appear. In each line one feels the care taken and at the same time the naturalness and ease of it all.

Until I heard Larkin's own version, I was not quite sure where to place the stronger accents in the repeated line, nor did I at all mind the controlled uncertainty: *Be, spring,* and *soon* all offered as candidates, even perhaps *It*. Larkin chooses *spring* and *soon*, surely the best reading, with a sort of half-accent on *It* to get the line going.

Overall this short line is harder to control than the more familiar iambic pentameter, which comes trailing a great deal more tradition and precedent. (I know how hard this short line can be, having tried it myself.) It too readily gives way to the jingly and singsongy, making everything in it sound light or even comic—but not in this poem. In "Tops" the same sort of line does suffer a little from this tendency, which may be why Larkin never put this poem into one of his books.

> So they run on,
> Until, with a falter,
> A flicker, soon gone—
> Their pace starts to alter.

But "Coming" manages to sound serious throughout and, for my money, more deeply felt than, say, the celebrated conclusion of "Church Going," which for all its ironic, skeptical stance nevertheless ends up sounding somewhat preachy.

It has been claimed for Larkin that he was never sentimental, never brutal. But the truth is that I find him both sentimental and brutal, though in different poems or at least in different parts of the same poem. The brutal side comes out in the later poems; the sentimental throughout his career, but most straightforwardly in some of the earlier poems, as in the one we have been considering. Irony, diffidence, skepticism, wit: not all of these together are enough to keep out a certain *unreasonableness of feeling*—the sentiment, the sentimentality—that keeps rising up out of Larkin's poems. Actually, it is what saves them. Doesn't everybody really know this?

Andrew Marvell, "To His Coy Mistress"

"Make it new," Ezra Pound advised his fellow poets. Few have taken a theme older and more familiar than Andrew Marvell does in "To His Coy Mistress," his most celebrated work, and rendered it with such lasting freshness. The idea of *carpe diem* ("Seize today!") resounds through the poetry of ancient Greece, Egypt, and Persia, and is a particularly favorite theme of Latin poets, notably Catullus and Horace. "Enjoy the present smiling hour," Horace counsels (in *Odes* III, 29, as translated by John Dryden), and many a later poet has urged the same policy.

Though he became a committed servant of the English Puritan party —toiling as Latin Secretary to Oliver Cromwell, the Puritan Lord Protector himself—Marvell cannot be called Puritanical. He did not resemble those American Puritans who burned witches, and (it is said) condemned the cruel sport of bearbaiting, in which dogs were turned loose upon a chained bear, not because it hurt the bear but because it gave pleasure to the spectators. Though Marvell switched political parties over the course of his career, his biographers have found one consistent thread informing his life: a love of liberty. Marvell continually attacked censorship, wrote pamphlets urging religious freedom, and condemned those who borrowed their opinions from others—people who displayed, he said, a "party-colour'd mind." His best poems appear to hold clashing views with nearly equal sympathy; for example, though Marvell supported Oliver Cromwell, his "Horatian Ode upon Cromwell's Return from Ireland" expresses admiration for Charles I, the Stuart king whom the Puritans had deposed. Some degree of this broad-mindedness and complexity of feeling is evident in "To His Coy Mistress."

To begin, consider the title. The lady's coyness—her hesitancy, her coquetry—sets the dramatic situation. It may be a temptation to misread the word "Mistress" to mean a kept woman, but the poem makes it clear that in Marvell's time the word referred to an unmarried woman. (Were she kept, the speaker wouldn't need to argue her into bed; she would be there already.)

The poem is divided into three parts, each clearly announced by an indented line. Let me offer a few notes on what goes on in each part. The reader who already knows this poem by heart will, I hope, forgive these remarks their simplicity.

In the introductory portion of his argument, Marvell assumes that women and men naturally differ in their attitudes toward love: women prefer to be wooed slowly, men want to forge ahead with all haste possible. The speaker pretends to consider the woman's attitude sympathetically, although (as we shall see) he is all for forging ahead. He opens his argument diplomatically, not by protesting the woman's reluctance to yield, but by suggesting that leisurely dalliance, while desirable, would be possible only in a world far larger and less hurried than the world we know. On a globe, the fact that England's River Humber is on the opposite side of the earth from the Ganges River in India throws the largest possible distance between the lovers. In imagining a vast extent of time, Marvell is equally definite. His speaker would begin the wooing back before the time of Noah, and his mistress might refuse "till the conversion of the Jews," which unlikely event, according to tradition, is to take place just before the end of the world. And so this ideal wooing would have to span human history as told in the Bible from the Old Testament book of Genesis through the New Testament book of Revelation. For "vegetable" in line 11, read "vegetative," or growing. (This line recalls one of my favorite bits of parody, author anonymous: "My vegetable love should grow / Quick as bamboo in Vigoro.") With loving playfulness, the speaker wishes that, indeed, that much world and time were available to do his lady justice. He turns a pretty compliment: "For, Lady, you deserve this state" (this slow and stately ritual). We can see his strategy. He puts the case for delay in terms so preposterous that no sensible mistress could agree to it. I find this part quietly hilarious, especially in the lines, "Two hundred, to adore each breast, / But thirty thousand to the rest." The scrupulous specificity of that number of years!

The second part begins with a magnificent "But." Then comes Marvell's awesome vision of the immense extent of death:

> But at my back I always hear
> Time's wingèd chariot hurrying near
> And yonder all before us lie
> Deserts of vast eternity.

That famous phrase "Time's wingèd chariot" may echo the classical myth of Apollo, the sun god who daily drives his fiery chariot around the sky, drawn by winged horses. How they loom large in this poem, these stressful forces—the pressure of passing time, the swift approach of eternity. This is no cheerful Christian view of eternity, but a doleful, pagan one. Foreseeing no pleasant afterlife, Marvell expects death to lead to nothing but an endless wasteland. This is a reason for lovers to leap into the sack while they still may. What's the good of keeping your maidenhead intact, he argues, just for some dumb worm in the ground to pierce (to "try," like trying a door), when (he might have added, but tactfully doesn't) you could enjoy my worm instead? Delectable is the tongue-in-cheek understatement of "The grave's a fine and private place, / But none, I think, do there embrace." Who can argue with that?

I can never read this stanza without admiring Marvell's tremendously skilled handling of meter. The rhythm of his lines has been ticking along fairly regularly in a basic iambic beat: unstressed syllables alternated with stressed ones. Then the poet hits the beginning of the line hard—"Time's wingèd." In the ensuing phrase "chariot hurrying," each word has one stressed or heavy syllable followed by two light, unstressed ones. The effect is a skipping or rippling rhythm, like a fast-moving chariot jolting over a rocky road.

In its third part the poem, with an agreeable shock, returns us to the present moment. Here we are, says the speaker, two healthy youngbloods whose vigor won't last forever. In line 34, that morning *glew* isn't Elmer's. The word, according to scholar Helge Kökeritz, is Northern English dialect for *glow*. Marvell, a Yorkshireman, may well have known it. The imagery is violent, of meat-eating. Time is a ravenous beast with slow, irresistible jaws; we must devour him or be devoured. Obviously, being mortal, we can't make the sun stand still as Joshua did, or Zeus, who in order to enjoy the mortal Alcmena made the night last a whole week. Some readers find a serious pun in the next-to-last line. Though the lovers cannot halt time, they can have a *son*, a child who can literally run, a living inheritance. However we read the ending, Marvell gives us a solution to the problem of fleeting time. In making love, we'll render the immediate moment as good as eternity itself— indeed, eternity being a desert, we'll render it far better.

Despite the brilliance of the poem, some readers have found difficulty in subscribing to what is said in it. The ending expresses a male-centered view that women may find a bit chilling. Many a sensitive young woman has felt like declining this invitation to tear pleasures with rough strife. One reaction is summed up wittily by contemporary poet Katherine McAlpine, who sarcastically paraphrases Marvell:

From His Not-So-Coy Mistress

> You think that argument's so suave and shrewd:
> "C'mon, let's screw before we're both worm food."
> Sorry to have to interrupt your song—
> here comes time's wingèd chariot. So long!

McAlpine zeroes in on the weakest point in Marvell's argument. But I shouldn't attribute the argument to Marvell himself; perhaps, just for fun, he is deliberately speaking from a typical stud male point of view. Whoever is speaking, those "iron gates of life" suggest the doors of the womb through which infants emerge and the penis enters. To call them iron, a base metal, seems harsh, but the speaker appears to mean the physical side of lovemaking, which he sees as a rough game. It is as though, after all this dilly-dallying courtship, the speaker can't wait any longer. He would fling his loved one into the sheets and jump in after her. I find the last lines, which McAlpine paraphrases so deftly, more than a little smug. In reality, the lovers may accelerate the aging process, for the young mistress, presumably a virgin, will quickly become a woman of experience and eventually, perhaps, a married mother. But Marvell doesn't go into all that. (For some of the finest observations ever penned on the paradoxically sweet sadness of girls' growing into women, see Alexander Pope's mock epic "The Rape of the Lock.") Despite these possible objections, many other readers have accepted Marvell's poem in its entirety, argument and all.

Considering the poem as a whole, I find its tone—the speaker's apparent attitude toward his subject—intriguingly complicated: the speaker banters lightly yet seems deeply serious. He addresses his loved one kiddingly (those breasts, deserving the attention of four centuries!), much as in another famous poem, "On Stella's Birthday," Jonathan Swift addresses his close friend Esther "Stella" Johnson, who had turned thirty-four:

> However, Stella, be not troubled
> Although thy size and years are doubled
> Since first I saw thee at sixteen

You have to know someone extremely well to get away with such affectionate fun-poking, and even then, it is a task easy to flub. From these two poems, I cannot think that either Stella or Marvell's mistress (if indeed she was an actual person and not just a literary convention) would have taken offense. "Poetry," said W. H. Auden, "is the clear expression of mixed feelings." "To His Coy Mistress" illustrates what Auden may have meant. The emotions in this poem are surely an odd blend: love, lust, laughter, impatience, awe, mockery. The poem, in its view of the inevitable progress of time, projects a wistful sadness. Yet it is a sadness tempered with wry humor.

I know of a small college founded on religious principles where today this poem is forbidden. I had edited a poetry textbook containing "To His Coy Mistress," and the college banned my book as a consequence. The administrators stated that Marvell's poem was immoral, and they did not wish their students to be exposed to it. This complaint is by no means obtuse. The administrators missed, perhaps, the humor and loving fun of the poem; they couldn't appreciate ironies worth a hoot, and very probably they assumed that *mistress* meant an illegal concubine. But the speaker's purpose is seduction, all right, and I give the administrators credit for reading carefully, as best they were able. Surely Marvell's poem can have the very effect that they must have feared. A college teacher, a friend of mine, once reported that one day soon after he had taught "To His Coy Mistress," a male student who had expressed no previous enthusiasm for poetry came up to him after class and boasted, "Say, you know that 'Had we but world enough and time' stuff? Well, I tried it on the girlfriend, and it worked."

To His Coy Mistress

Had we but world enough and time,
This coyness, Lady, were no crime.
We would sit down and think which way
To walk, and pass our long love's day.
Thou by the Indian Ganges' side
Should'st rubies find; I by the tide
Of Humber would complain. I would
Love you ten years before the Flood
And you should, if you please, refuse
Till the conversion of the Jews.
My vegetable love should grow
Vaster than empires, and more slow.
An hundred years should go to praise
Thine eyes, and on thy forehead gaze;
Two hundred, to adore each breast,
But thirty thousand to the rest,
An age at least to every part,
And the last age should show your heart;

For, Lady, you deserve this state,
Nor would I love at lower rate.
   But at my back I always hear
Time's wingèd chariot hurrying near
And yonder all before us lie
Deserts of vast eternity.
Thy beauty shall no more be found,
Nor, in thy marble vault, shall sound
My echoing song; then worms shall try
That long preserved virginity
And your quaint honor turn to dust
And into ashes all my lust.
The grave's a fine and private place,
But none, I think, do there embrace.
   Now therefore, while the youthful hue
Sits on thy skin like morning glew
And while thy willing soul transpires
At every pore with instant fires,
Now let us sport us while we may;
And now, like amorous birds of prey,
Rather at once our time devour
Than languish in his slow-chapped power.
Let us roll all our strength and all
Our sweetness up into one ball
And tear our pleasures with rough strife
Through the iron gates of life.
Thus, though we cannot make our sun
Stand still, yet we will make him run.

Andrew Marvell

MAXINE KUMIN

Trochee, Trimeter, and the MRI

About a year ago, while the medical profession rooted around looking for the source of lameness in my shoulders and back, I underwent an MRI. The initials stand for magnetic resonance imaging, a sophisticated method of viewing the human interior without X rays or surgery. An MRI requires the subject to lie absolutely still in a very narrow coffin for as much as an hour and a half at a time. Your head is held in a restraint that is quaintly dubbed a "birdcage." As they slide you into the dark tunnel on a slab, the roof of the coffin grazes your hairline, the sides embrace your sides. You are advised to keep your eyes closed in order to resist the claustrophobia that may otherwise overwhelm you. In some cases you are given a sort of rubber bulb to squeeze in case you panic. You are told it will convey a signal to the operators and supposedly an attendant will then extricate you (I never trusted this). All in all, an MRI is an aboveground trial burial.

Soon after you are entombed, the terrible knocking commences. A disembodied voice gives you fair warning: "*There will now be four and a half minutes of knocking,*" "*There will now be eleven minutes of knocking,*" and so on, with pauses in between while they adjust the equipment and you lie enclosed, unable to move, anticipating. The sound is as percussive as a jackhammer and it is happening not down the block or across the street, but exactly where you are pinioned. Like childbirth, or a turbulent flight through a thunderstorm in a two-seater plane, the only way out is to go through it, to endure.

What saved me during this ordeal was reciting lines of poetry. I have, in common with others of my generation, something of a memory bank acquired in an era when students were expected to commit poems to memory. Over the years, I have relied on this method with my own students, ranging from Princeton undergraduates who, initially, were superciliously disdainful of the assignment, to MIT engineers, who graciously gobbled up difficult poems by Yeats and Gerard Manley Hopkins and then disgorged twenty to forty lines on Monday mornings in front of the whole class. I tell the students who groan and the ones who do not that I am doing them a favor: I am providing them with an inner library to draw on when they are taken political prisoner.

My inner library is rather spotty and eclectic, ranging from selections from Robert Louis Stevenson's *A Child's Garden of Verses* and big patches of James Russell Lowell's "The Vision of Sir Launfall," up through chunks of Gray's "Elegy in a Country Churchyard," passages of Arnold's "Dover Beach," a dozen sonnets from Shakespeare, Milton, Wordsworth, Donne, and Millay, several Emily Dickinsons and Robert Frosts, and best remembered and most useful during my MRI ordeal, A. E. Housman.

I came upon Housman's major collection, *A Shropshire Lad*, when I was perhaps fourteen or fifteen and terribly susceptible to what Basil Davenport has called his "romantic revivalism." It is, actually, a synthesis of the severely classical—Housman was foremost a classics scholar who gave up the study of Greek, which he loved, to specialize in the later Latin poets, who were less well known—and the melancholy romantic, an appealing combination when you are at the mercy of hormones and second- or third-year Latin yourself. His themes are somewhat limited: hangings, suicides, betrayed love, an early demise. Contemporary and universal as these themes may seem, we would do well to remember that Housman's war, or antiwar, poems reflect British losses first in the Boer War of 1899–1902 and then, a scant generation later, in World War I. I think he could not have chronicled the even more searing events of World War II, for as destruction grows more impersonal the poet's personal voice is commonly forced to go under.

At any rate, the first Housman poem I remember reading and adoring was an untitled little dialogue in eight quatrains, numbered XXVII, from *A Shropshire Lad*. The two voices are those of young men, presumably chums from boyhood, farm raised and rather wholesome. The dead man addresses his living friend. Although war is not mentioned in the poem, we can perhaps assume that the dead lad—*lad* is a favorite Housman term—lost his life in battle, for many of the other poems in this collection are elegies for fallen soldiers. The plot of the poem is extremely simple: the living lad has inherited his fallen comrade's sweetheart. The fulcrum of the poem, the place where it turns and sweeps into its conclusion, comes late, with the final stanza, but there is a portentous foreshadowing from stanza to stanza in the question-and-answer format. Nothing surprises us in this poem. The drama is mild and full of pathos, riding on dramatic irony. As an adolescent female, I found it deeply gratifying.

Lying in my MRI tomb and doggedly reciting the poem against the terrible rapping, I realized what saved me were the successive stresses.

Before I define stresses, let me say something about the traditional meters English prosody depends on. While early English poems were largely alliterative, as in "Gawain and the Green Knight," stanzaic lyrics developed soon after, along with end rhymes. From the close of the medieval period, English poets began to take on French and Italian models, and with them the line of fixed syllables. But in English, unlike French, a word of two or more syllables almost always has one syllable more strongly accented than the other or others. To differentiate these, the convention of syllabic feet has grown up, the most common being the iamb, one unaccented syllable followed by an accented one. The poet and critic John Nims calls this "flub-DUB," and claims it imitates the heartbeat's diastolic and systolic pulsings, which accounts for the iamb's popularity not only in poetry but in prose cadences as well. If you reverse the iamb you get the trochee: one accented syllable followed by an unaccented one. These two syllabic feet are called disyllabics because they consist of two syllables. Easy, right?

Then we have the convention of trisyllabic feet—three syllables—the more common of which is the anapest, da-da-DUM, in which two unaccented syllables are followed by an accented one, as in "with the WIND and the RAIN in her HAIR." The dactyl, its counterpart, is an accented syllable followed by two unaccented ones, as in "THIS is the FOR-est pri-ME-val."

So much for our very quick trip through the principles of prosody, except to say a word about the terminology of end rhymes. When lines end on an accented rhyme as in "moon/June," the result is called a masculine rhyme. When, as is frequent in Housman, the lines end with unaccented syllables as in "shatters" and "tatters," the rhyme is said to have a feminine ending. I hope that eventually we can find some genderless way of expressing this difference—Italianate rhyme is one such suggestion—but for the time being these are the conventional terms. Feminine endings lie a bit longer on the ear and help to carry the verse forward; masculine rhymes achieve a stronger end-stop. You will probably already have noticed that Housman alternates these to good effect.

What is striking about number XXVII, my chosen mantra against the MRI pounding, is not that it is structured in quatrains but that the poem proceeds with a series of unusual stresses hammering the first line of alternate stanzas. I scan these lines as containing four direct stresses and one unaccented syllable. You may call this whatever you wish: two spondees and a leftover syllable, perhaps? — a spondee being a two-syllable word with supposedly equal stresses, as in "moonlight" or "daybreak" — but I think the simplest characterization is just to say four strong stresses in a row. I cannot think of any other poem in the English language that does this, but maybe you can. I cannot find any other way to scan these lines, though doubters will try to force them into iambs and trochees. I cannot call up another poet who works so successfully in trimeter — three-beat lines — alternating feminine and masculine endings, or indeed another poem in which the voice from the grave enters into dialogue with the living. Since making this rash statement, however, a fellow poet has pointed out Thomas Hardy's "Channel Firing," in which the buried soldiers engage in conversation with God and with each other.

I think you can see Housman's artful shaping hand here, in the parallel constructions "Is my team ploughing," "Is football playing," "Is my girl happy," "Is my friend hearty." But notice, too, the answering quatrains and how each one opens with an accented syllable, "Ay, the horses trample," "Ay, the ball is flying," and so on. I hurled these lines against the jackhammer over and over and prayed for deliverance.

As the MRI test continued, I found that truncated lines worked best to defend me. Arnold's "Ah, love, let us be true / To one another! for the world, which seems / To lie before us like a land of dreams, / So beautiful, so various, so new" simply did not cut the dinning. The exhortation is too lyrical, the plea too rhetorical, the language too rich with qualifications to hold up against such pounding. Frost's "There is a singer everyone has heard" also fell short, as did the Bard's "Let me not to the marriage of true minds / Admit impediment," although I lingered a little on how to scan "LET me NOT," discovering once again that the best weapon I had in my head just then was the thwack of a trochee. I ran through my available Dickinsons on death, "I died for Beauty" and "I heard a fly buzz when I died."

These served me fairly well, both in terms of mood and brevity of line and even archaism of diction: "Themself are One," "We Brethren are," "When the King be witnessed," and so on. Best of all, the lines alternate between tetrameter and trimeter and the music of four beats played against three not only makes the poem easier to memorize but reinforces the hymnal aspect, in the manner of Isaac Watts's "How doth the busy little bee / Inform each shining hour," which is probably where Dickinson acquired her sense of the quatrain.

Parenthetically, it is interesting that the poems I leaned on most heavily during my diagnostic ordeal were death centered. In my temporary tomb I said aloud these incantations that purported to be about dying but wanted to defend against it. I concede that these poems are dated, both by the formal pattern of quatrains and by their rather lovely lugubrious insistence on our mortality. I confess that the tragic mood and underlying stoicism in Housman cause me to love his poems more, rather than less. The concluding quatrain of IV, titled "Reveille," neatly encapsulates his message:

> Clay lies still, but blood's a rover;
> Breath's a ware that will not keep.
> Up, lad: when the journey's over
> There'll be time enough for sleep.

Nobody knows where the notion of rhyming comes from, but anyone who has spent any time in the company of a curious child knows that the playful possibilities of the language emerge early on. Various abracadabras and fee-fie-fo-fums suggest that rhyming was an integral part of the casting of spells. It is a short step from incantatory magic to prayer and thence to paeans of praise and celebratory lyrics of, say, undying love. It is far easier to memorize a rhymed poem than, for instance, the free verse of Walt Whitman.

In the last hundred years, free verse has become far more widespread. While many poets have abandoned the rhyming convention, they still rely on other traditional devices such as simile, metaphor, and other figurative language, and most of the time they employ stanza breaks the way we employ the paragraph in prose. A free-verse poem may certainly be rhythmic; each free-verse poem sets up and reinterprets its own prosodic rules, as it were. None of this is exactly news. Milton eschewed rhyme in the writing of his solemn Paradise epic because he thought rhyming too trivial for the events described. Whitman substituted long, flowing cadences for rhymes, and did so to majestic effect. So did Wilfred Owen, one more flower of British manhood cut down in World War I, who wrote: "I sing of war and the pity of war. The poetry is in the pity."

But for many of us contemporary poets, formalism is a way of life, a sustenance, a stout tree for the vine of our poems. We are, for better or for worse, committed to make rhymes, be they exact rhymes or slant. We are still writing sonnets, villanelles, sestinas, even pantoums and triolets, ballades and rondels, as well as inventing "nonce" forms to suit our uses. Practicing formal poetics does not in any way suggest that a poet is elitist or reactionary. Often a poet will choose to write in a historically powerful form in order to transform it.

Fifteen years ago, in an interview, I was quoted on the same subject. What I said then feels no less true to me today:

I know that I write better poems in form—within the exigencies of a rhyme scheme and a metrical pattern—than I do in the looser line of free verse. Others can argue this point, claiming that free verse is a form and as such just as formal.

But the harder—that is, the more psychically difficult—the poem is to write, the more likely I am to choose a difficult pattern to pound it into. This is true because, paradoxically, the difficulty frees me to be more honest and more direct. It is Yeats's "The fascination of what's difficult."

Death was much on my mind during the MRI—which, incidentally, turned up nothing. The correct diagnosis was made by a thoughtful general practitioner, and the right medication quickly did away with the worst symptoms. But death is much on the mind of the poet in general, which helps account for the profusion of elegies we write. We are all mortal, but it is the poet who shivers most articulately under the thin blanket of mortality.

XXVII

'Is my team ploughing,
    That I was used to drive
And hear the harness jingle
    When I was man alive?'

Ay, the horses trample,
    The harness jingles now;
No change though you lie under
    The land you used to plough.

'Is football playing
    Along the river shore,
With lads to chase the leather,
    Now I stand up no more?'

Ay, the ball is flying,
    The lads play heart and soul;
The goal stands up, the keeper
    Stands up to keep the goal.

'Is my girl happy,
    That I thought hard to leave,
And has she tired of weeping
    As she lies down at eve?'

Ay, she lies down lightly,
    She lies not down to weep:

Your girl is well contented.
 Be still, my lad, and sleep.

'Is my friend hearty,
 Now I am thin and pine,
And has he found to sleep in
 A better bed than mine?'

Yes, lad, I lie easy,
 I lie as lads would choose;
I cheer a dead man's sweetheart,
 Never ask me whose.

A. E. Housman

On Keats's "To Autumn"

At many a reading in our time, this or that author will introduce a given poem in a certain way; the words of course vary, but the gist is generally as follows: "I here notice something that one of you out there might have noticed, if only you were as sensitive as I, which you're obviously not."

The premise here, that to be a poet is automatically to possess supranormal sensitivity, has never sold well with me (especially when used to defend awful behavior). Thus, even though he does so in one of my favorite works, I wince some at Wordsworth's claim that "We poets in our youth begin in gladness; / But thereof come in the end despondency and madness," wondering why this truth—if a truth at all—applies any more to poets than to other folks.

I could refer to more egregious claims by contemporaries, but why bother? I wish simply to suggest that a good writer of poems may be more sensitive to *language* than the average Joe or Jane (though not obviously more so than a good writer of prose), and that's about as far as it goes. I mention all this only because John Keats was crucial in bringing me to such an attitude, and he remains a fine corrector of the self-vaunting that I, like anyone, am utterly capable of, as man and author.

I first read Keats when I was a college boy who hoped some day to write; but I'd beforehand gotten addicted precisely to Wordsworth, treating as shibboleth a passage from the *Recluse* fragment:

> Paradise, and groves
> Elysian, Fortunate Fields—like those of old
> Sought in the Atlantic Main—why should they be
> A history only of departed things,
> Or a mere fiction of what never was?

> For the discerning intellect of Man,
> When wedded to this goodly universe
> In love and holy passion, shall find these
> A simple produce of the common day.

At the time, I was pretty innocent even of canonical literary history, so the idea that epic or romance energies might inhere in the ordinary, that they might therefore be available to anybody, including me, felt at once like a revelation and a permission. It was also a relief: I'd been getting a lot of my poetry, as I still do, from the blues tradition in American music, and now I believed I might say, for example, that the image of sexual infidelity in Muddy Waters's "Long Distance Call," *another mule is kickin' in your stall*, rooted as it was in acute observation of the commonplace, qualified as sublime writing. If people challenged me, I'd recite to them from *The Recluse*.

Trouble was, the more I read by *The Recluse*'s creator, the more I had night thoughts: why should this proponent of the quotidian himself seem persistently so highfalutin? I mean an epic subtitled "The Growth of a Poet's Mind"? Come *on*! Needless to say, my understanding of Wordsworth's effort was imperfect at very best, yet the poet seemed to premonish the attitude I caricatured on beginning these thoughts: Watch my mind grow, and your own pathetic little mind just might grow an inch or so, too.

And now, still convinced that in most ways Wordsworth remains the greater figure, I'm far less apt to take him up than I am the author who said in a February 1818 letter to John Reynolds that

Wordsworth &c should have their due from us, but for the sake of a few fine imaginative or domestic passages, are we to be bullied into a certain Philosophy engendered in the whims of an Egotist[?]

This is the Keats who, in another letter to Reynolds, wrote that

by every germ of Spirit sucking the Sap from mould ethereal every human might become great, and Humanity instead of being a wide heath of Furse and Briars with here and there a remote Oak or Pine, would become a grand democracy of Forest Trees.

Keats, in short, would at his best decline to play that more-sensitive-than-thou game. And for my money his best showed itself in "To Autumn," whose most affecting lines were for me not the celebrated closing ones but those at the start of section II:

> Who hath not seen thee oft amid thy store?
> Sometimes whoever seeks abroad may find
> Thee sitting careless on a granary floor

The poet had seen the goddess; on the other hand, so had everyone else who made the least effort. The idea delighted me: if the great poet Keats was just another onlooker, then the other onlookers, including me, were conceivably great poets *in potentia*.

And yet, from my later perspective, the very issue of greatness seems progressively dismantled by the poem in question. Yes, "whoever seeks abroad" is prospectively an artist, an avatar of the imagination in its holiest sense, but it strikes me that "To Autumn" makes even more radical claims in pursuing its democratic mission. Not only does it dismiss individual greatness as an important aim, but it also de-emphasizes the importance of individuality itself. From the moment just cited, the author's own ego progressively cedes itself to something far broader (in this case, "To Autumn" being a so-called nature poem, the landscape), Keats thereby suggesting that the numinous really *can* inhere in the simple produce of the common day, perhaps without any great exercise of will on any single person's part.

In short, the willful and ambitious writer, the would-be prophet, of a work like *The Fall of Hyperion* seems to have recognized (and not only for "literary" reasons—recall the speed with which his health deteriorated by September of the great year) the inutility of such prophetic aspirations. Let's see how this comes about.

I am not the first to notice the absence from the opening stanza of the classical address to god or goddess. Autumn is addressed as a season, a natural phenomenon, however multifaceted. This breach of odic convention is not, admittedly, original even within Keats's own corpus: several of the other 1819 odes are similar in this way, but most do contain classical allusions or quasi-allusions at one point or another, as "To Autumn" does not. Indeed, the first stanza is a grammatical fragment (*anacoluthon* is the rhetorical term). Authorial comment on the season's presence is thus entirely elided, the only active wills within the fragment being those of the "conspiring" sun and the "thinking" bees.

Stanza two follows, a section, as I've already indicated, that asserts the omni-availability of poetic vision. And then, at the start of the final stanza, we find the one instance in which Keats, though very subtly, allows his old prophet's ego to intrude. "Where are the songs of Spring?" he asks, no doubt recalling, and a bit mournfully, the odes composed those few months earlier, "Ay, where are they?" But he quickly rallies himself: "Think not of them, thou hast thy music too." In the very act of addressing himself in the second person, the poet joins the company of *all* seekers abroad.

If that last surmise seems overwrought, note that after so minimal an egoistic intrusion, the poet becomes increasingly descriptive, even "imagist." So far from being prophecy, "To Autumn" in its closure is not even testimony. It isn't Keats, for example, who laments the fact that he is dying, as indeed he is; he notes rather that the *day* is "soft-dying." Nor is it he who mourns the demise of the day, of the year, of life itself; "small gnats" do so. The "full-grown lambs," which is to say lambs ready for slaughter, do not even mourn but simply "bleat."

We have moved quickly away from pathetic fallacy, pathos itself—largely a human construct, even in the portraiture of insects—seeming to drain from the poem entirely as it ebbs. If "bleat" struck us as a predictable verb to apply to sheep, hear how generic, almost trite, certainly colloquial, the remaining verbs in the ode become, crickets merely singing, the redbreast whistling, swallows twittering. The very vocabulary that predominates in the dramatic components—the verbs themselves—of Keats's grammar is as commonplace as any unschooled observer's might be. So much, the author implies, even for a poet's superior "sensitivity" to language.

In a song of spring like the "Ode to Psyche," Keats could write the following passage:

> So let me be thy choir, and make a moan
>   Upon the midnight hours;
> Thy voice, thy lute, thy pipe, thy incense sweet
>   From swinging censer teeming;
> Thy shrine, thy grove, thy oracle, thy heat
>   Of pale-mouth'd prophet dreaming.

Now he eschews such mighty agenda. The ego's vatic aspirations surrender themselves to something well outside the ego: in the third stanza's vision of nature, even brutes and bugs have as much right to voice themselves as does a bard.

And yet, even as he downplays the issue of the great (the "sensitive") poet, Keats leaves us "To Autumn," itself an undeniably great poem. We may be up against a paradox, though I prefer to think that the author himself would prefer to see this Septembral ode less as great than as—to choose the ubiquitous Keatsian term—beautiful.

However feckless the semantical effort to escape paradox, the power of "To Autumn" stems in the end from its modesty and from its democratic impulse. And so long as we are stuck on paradox, the ode may show our antiprophet to be prophetic after all. Ours is a poetic era often sneered at for producing so many poets but so few great ones. If, however, a progressively democratic spirit is to attend the unfolding of human history (and I for one must believe it will, so that I can remain a hopeful man), can't we conceive of our era as the excellent one forecast by Keats in his letter to Reynolds?

Can't we conceive of the world as one in which a *collective* expression of beauty will offer the vision to sustain us? Can't we take heart from the many kinds of voice that are currently chanting their way into the so-called canon? If so, then our poetry—as Keats put it in as early a poem as "Sleep and Poetry"—will "be a friend / To sooth the cares, and lift the thoughts of man." And woman, too. And all humanity.

To Autumn

I.

Season of mists and mellow fruitfulness,
    Close bosom-friend of the maturing sun;
Conspiring with him how to load and bless
    With fruit the vines that round the thatch-eves run;
To bend with apples the moss'd cottage-trees,
    And fill all fruit with ripeness to the core;
        To swell the gourd, and plump the hazel shells
With a sweet kernel; to set budding more,
    And still more, later flowers for the bees,
    Until they think warm days will never cease,
        For Summer has o'er-brimm'd their clammy cells.

II.

Who hath not seen thee oft amid thy store?
    Sometimes whoever seeks abroad may find
Thee sitting careless on a granary floor,
    Thy hair soft-lifted by the winnowing wind;
Or on a half-reap'd furrow sound asleep,
    Drows'd with the fume of poppies, while thy hook
        Spares the next swath and all its twined flowers:
And sometimes like a gleaner thou dost keep
    Steady thy laden head across a brook;
    Or by a cyder-press, with patient look,
        Thou watchest the last oozings hours by hours.

III.

Where are the songs of Spring? Ay, where are they?
    Think not of them, thou hast thy music too,—

While barred clouds bloom the soft-dying day,
   And touch the stubble-plains with rosy hue;
Then in a wailful choir the small gnats mourn
   Among the river sallows, borne aloft
      Or sinking as the light wind lives or dies;
And full-grown lambs loud bleat from hilly bourn;
   Hedge-crickets sing; and now with treble soft
The red-breast whistles from a garden-croft;
   And gathering swallows twitter in the skies
                                          John Keats

GARY MARGOLIS

"Shall We Return to Beatings of
Great Bells In Wild Trainloads?"

In all my dreams, before my helpless sight,
He plunges at me, guttering, choking, drowning.

Dulce Et Decorum
Wilfred Owen

I

In 1963, I entered a college that required its freshmen and sophomore men to participate in the R.O.T.C.—Reserve Office Training Corps. There were a few exemptions, each acquired with difficulty. We took two courses a year on military tactics and officer leadership, marched on Thursdays for an hour in our green, woolen uniforms, and anticipated an eight-week summer orientation—basic training—at Fort Devens, Massachusetts, where, it was rumored, we would be captured and held in a mock Viet Cong village by regular Army vets back from Vietnam. Most of us believed and were told that, as we had to go into the service anyway, we might as well "go as officers," as if that rank were a shield from a bullet or a bungi stick in the jungle.

Nights we studied, drank, and danced. We watched the CBS news with Walter Cronkite. We saw the demonstrations at Berkeley, the body bags loaded onto planes in Saigon. We heard of our fraternity brothers who were already there, some safe after a year, a few wounded, and one, a marine platoon leader, our All-American lacrosse goalie, dead. A few years ago I touched Bayard Russ's name on the memorial wall in Washington. Incredibly, we called him Bye-Bye on the athletic field.

I graduated with gold, second lieutenant's bars on my shoulders and a temporary graduate-school deferment that allowed me one more degree, which gave me four years in Buffalo, New York—drawn by antiwar marches, shoved up against buildings by police, and surrounded, saturated in poetry. I had courses with James Wright and Irving Feldman. I went to readings by Bly, Merwin, Levertov, Corso, and Snyder. I shared poems on Wednesday nights around Mac Hammond's kitchen table with Charlie Baxter, Carl Dennis, John Logan, and Alan Feldman. I went back to Vermont in August to serve Bloody Marys at the Bread Loaf Writers' Conference. I graduated, again, and was called, finally, to duty.

I was ordered to Fort Sam Houston in San Antonio, Texas, for basic medical-service training, a base rich in retired officers and bandaged with the burned—hundreds of wounded American and Vietnamese soldiers who were treated and convalescing at Brooke Army Hospital. My barracks were next to a medevac helicopter pad. I heard the whirring chopper blades and looked out my window to the men and women on crutches, the colonels driving their golf carts. I imagined myself, ten thousand miles away, over there.

But I only had to imagine this. I was assigned a three-month active-duty tour, because the war, they said, was winding down, because there were too many career officers who wanted to go back to Vietnam to increase rank, to fight in the war. I went home never having been sent off, with Wilfred Owen's poem "The Send-Off" in my head.

II

In war, we say, a soldier *sees action*. He is in the firefight doing the bloody work, while at the same time seeing its effects, sight here meaning all of the senses which, when he is wounded, become distinct and overwhelmed—seeing, hearing, smelling, touching, all feeling combined and numbed. At the same time, the action sees, encompasses, the soldier, the squad, the armies, the fields of jungle and trenches. Death surrounds and invades the action with shrapnel, with gas, with fear, with its disembodied voice and eye.

It is the voice of Death I hear in "The Send-Off," a poem Owen originally entitled "The Draft" and completed in May 1918, writing enthusiastically to his mother—"I have long 'waited' for a final stanza to 'the Draft.' When I think of men, and now women, going to war, I see them being sent off by their families, their lovers, their neighbors. I remember the embraces I saw on newsreels, the last waves more recently held on videotape. Often I hear a military band, the echo of notes in a bus station, on a wharf.

Owen sends off his soldiers and himself in a first, hard line of sound, a string of *d*'s sounding the death march. "Down the close, darkening lanes they sang their way / To the siding shed, / and lined the train with faces grimly gay." They seem to be singing their own dirge. No song is named, no face particularly identified. From here, now, our generation in that image sees Eastern European Jews, too, twenty years later herded onto their trains. The *g*'s—"grimly gay"—close the broken stanza in a combination of celebration and grief, a celebrated grief.

After its spacing, its breath on the page, the stanza continues in its fierce ambivalence, its doubled meanings. "Their breasts were stuck all white with wreath and spray / As men's are, dead." The soldiers are already pierced, wounded with the flowers that will mark and mourn their deaths, with the softening of language in w's and th's.

Stanza two tightens into its *abaab* form, but in a voice and narrative that keeps its voice distant, defended in a gauze that tries and purposively fails to keep us separated from feeling. "Dull porters watched them, and a casual tramp / Stood staring hard, / Sorry to miss them from the upland camp. / Then, unmoved, signals nodded, and a lamp / Winked to the guard." Death's *d*'s are continued in these lines. Family is absent; the stranger in "porter" and "tramp" serve as witnesses to the leaving. They stare as figures in Edvard Munch's paintings stare, pained and hollow-eyed. They are the tramps of Robert Frost and James Wright who, living away, see what happens on the margins, at the moment of transition, the passing over.

The soldiers move out, not through any action of a person, a commander designated by rank or name. *Signals* nod; a *lamp* winks. The mechanism of war is turned by the invisible, anonymous hand of Death. And the poem pulls out, is sent off to its third, broken stanza, as if the form itself was having a hard time holding together. "So secretly, like wrongs hushed-up, they went. / They were not ours: / We never heard to which front these were sent. // Nor there if yet they mock what women meant / Who gave them flowers."

The soldiers are compared to other secrets, other shames, Owen still depicting them generally, in a tone that evokes the two-pointed bayonet of evil and sin, to which all or any guilt can be attached. And then the strong, four-beat, paradoxical statement with its punctuated colon: "They were not ours:" Owen could mean that the soldiers were not this town's men. But, of course, by declaring and yet not claiming these warriors, they do become ours and everyone's. We identify with them through the opposite assumption that these and the other, unnamed men are indeed ours. The closest we get to reading nametags is in the use of the adjective "these." The closest we come to hearing about their fate is in *not* knowing where they were sent, not hearing their specific fear and rage, their grief. At the front, in seeing action, they "mock," strip sentiment from the flowers with which women would send them away or grieve them home.

In the final, unbroken stanza, the speaker/soldier/Owen asks "Shall they return to beatings of great bells / In wild trainloads?" Alliteration and the line break brings us—those who were not sent off, who are waiting—to the simultaneous possibility of glory and grief. "Beatings" is the horrible, right choice here. The bell beating out its meter, the bruisings, and defeat. Or is it a return in victory, unwounded? The soldiers could come back in "wild trainloads," wild with relief and celebration or wild, I imagine, as Owen has written in other poems, with madness. The trains we readers at the turn of the twentieth century see are Europe's trains of 1918 *and* 1939.

But the poem confirms its witness to death and horror. Owen saw action, held dead men in the trenches, and was decorated for it. His war poems are the real medals of grief; they go beyond elegy, as heard in this poem's last three lines. "A few, a few, too few for drums and yells, / May creep back, silent, to still village wells / Up half-known roads." These two-beat phrases are the heart's and Death's beat. The truth is there will not be enough men returning in whole bodies to celebrate. Return, too, is doubly conditional: they "may creep back." If they come back at all, they could be limping, and like the porters and tramp of the second stanza, they could be mute, dulled, and staring. If they come back, it could be to English villages whose wells are stilled by loss, whose roads don't know them, whose roads the soldiers, shocked and disabled, may not, cannot remember.

War is the firefight, the courage and the fear, the aftermath. It is surrounded by soldiers sent off, returning, and returned, by those left and waiting. Owen's "The Send-Off" sees the sending off of his generation of soldiers. As his readers, having seen planes and ships leave for Germany, Japan, Korea, Cuba, Vietnam, Grenada, Panama, Somalia, Kuwait, and Haiti, we see ours sent off, too.

Serving first in England's Artist's Rifles and then in the Lancashire Fusiliers, Owen never crept home. He had been injured and hospitalized after falling into a fifteen-foot shell hole while searching for a soldier overcome by fatigue. He had been shellshocked and treated in Craig-lockhart Hospital. Returning to the front, he was killed attempting to get his men across the Sambre Canal north of Orrs, France, November 4, 1918, one week before the end of his war, the signing of the Armistice.

III

I was never ordered to Southeast Asia. I never flew home to my country's anger and ambivalence those veterans felt and still feel. After three months' active duty in Texas, I was sent home. My name was put on a list to serve in the reserves. In 1973, I trained for two weeks at Fort Drum in Watertown, New York.

One afternoon, setting up a mock medical evacuation, a helicopter landed on our coordinates. The pilot tilted up his helmet shield. It was Willy Sumner, a Vietnam vet, a college friend of mine. He told me to get in. He said, "No snipers here." The dirt swirled below the chopper's blades. We angled up, the cloth we had laid out below forming into its white cross, the higher we rose into the air.

The Send-Off

Down the close, darkening lanes they sang their way
To the siding-shed,
And lined the train with faces grimly gay.

Their breasts were struck all white with wreath and spray
As men's are, dead.

Dull porters watched them, and a casual tramp
Stood staring hard,
Sorry to miss them from the upland camp.
Then, unmoved, signals nodded, and a lamp
Winked to the guard.

So secretly, like wrongs hushed-up, they went.
They were not ours:
We never heard to which front these were sent.

Nor there if yet they mock what women meant
Who gave them flowers.

Shall they return to beatings of great bells
In wild trainloads?
A few, a few, too few for drums and yells,
May creep back, silent, to still village wells
Up half-known roads.

                                        Wilfred Owen

Hart Crane's "O Carib Isle!":
"Clenched Beaks Coughing
for the Surge Again"

U ndoubtedly every poet has experienced it and most have written of the experience: a dry time, when words refuse to yield themselves, a time when everything seems dust. Hopkins, in the last months of his life, calling on God to send his roots rain; Yeats, nearing the end, cataloguing the myths that had sustained his poetry for fifty years, only to have to watch as his circus animals—his high subject matter and his themes—one by one began deserting him; Williams, having suffered a debilitating stroke, wondering if the shadowy deathlike figure curled up on the international bridge between Texas and Mexico—"interjurisdictional"—wasn't after all the mirror image of his present self.

So, too, with Hart Crane, in his powerful lyric, "O Carib Isle!" standing before a graveyard on the Isle of Pines (off the southern coast of Cuba) in the late summer of 1926, having just turned twenty-seven, and wondering—as Whitman sixty years before him had in "As I Ebb'd with the Ocean of Time"—whether the whole project of poetry—including his long project, *The Bridge*, envisioned as the positive to T. S. Eliot's despairing vision in *The Waste Land*—would after all amount to anything more than a futile exhalation of air.

Like so many of Crane's poems, "O Carib Isle!" is a self-conscious poem about poetry, a reflex questioning of the efficacy of language itself and, by extension, the efficacy of metaphor to transform the quotidian bread of existence into something more. And so the poem begins by questioning Emerson's idea of a correspondence between nature and meaning, including the very notion of meaning itself. In the first line we see and hear an indifferent, in fact hostile, nature dominating the landscape with its own sounds:

> The tarantula rattling at the lily's foot
> Across the feet of the dead, laid in white sand
> Near the coral beach

These opening lines have the shadow of blank verse behind them, but they are more irregular, flatter, even dissonant. That lily may be there to remember the resurrection of the dead, but it is the tarantula after all that dominates the scene. It and the white sand and the coral beach made up of the remains of millions on millions of once-living creatures reduced now to this white scene of death.

There are also fiddler crabs to contend with, which likewise seem out to subvert the poet's attempts to create an order out of words. Instead, they merely leave illegible markings in the sand as they "side-stilt" across the beach. More, they actually seem intent to "shift, subvert / And anagrammatize" Crane's name, and with it, his very identity. These fiddler crabs mock Crane's endeavors to order the world, rewriting his script, in the process mocking his attempts at order, which he has traditionally accomplished by calling things by their living names. Crane has even gone so far as to reshuffle his name here, anagrammatizing "Crane" several lines later into "Nacre"—mother-of-pearl. By providing us with the adjectival form of "nacre" in the ninth line—"nacreous frames of tropic death"—he at once suggests that in this world not only is all life eventually metamorphosed into a kind of white death—limestone, coral, bone, the "Brutal necklaces of shells" that frame and mock these graves—but he also provides a despairing image of poetry's ultimate entropy, a frame whereby life itself must at last surrender itself to one or another of the chalklike frames of death. Poetry does, after all, come down—as his first book of poems, published that fall, reminds us—to an aggregate of white buildings: "nacreous frames of tropic death."

Nothing mourns the passing of life here in the tropics, Crane knows, and there is also the undifferentiating sea always somewhere near, ready to swallow one. In Crane's negative Mallarmean syntax, "neither" is actually the unspoken first word of the poem, the stripped syntax reading, "Neither the tarantula . . . nor the zigzag crabs . . . mourn." Nothing mourns the passing of life here, nothing "Below the palsy that one eucalyptus lifts / In wrinkled shadows." And even the eucalyptus seems whitened by ague and fever, as it shimmers in the intense noonday heat, itself an image of hell (hell, we might remind ourselves, is backformed on the Greek, *kalyptos*: something hidden, concealed, like crypt, *kryptos*, later in the poem).

Against nature's gargantuan pressure to white out all human meaning and human feeling, Crane has no recourse but to either surrender to or to answer that pressure with the pressure of the human imagination, by ordering, by naming. Like Adam in the Garden making the world in his own image, Crane too will name, though to be sure he no longer has Adam's assurance that there is any correspondence between the things he names and the names and music he has at his disposal. The human tongue, he has been warned by the philosophers (Oswald

Spengler—whom he has just read—among them), has become an utter stranger to the world outside. And yet to name—to utter "Tree names, flower names" deliberately, in the teeth of indifferent nature—is all the poet can do to "gainsay" for a little while "death's brittle crypt," which is also "death's brittle script."

Crypt, kryptos: something hidden, something concealed. It is a key concept for Crane, as for all the Romantics. Bodies hidden, meanings concealed. The dead tell no secrets, Crane knows, though—as he had iterated earlier in "At Melville's Tomb"—they maddingly intimate them, much as seashells, washed up on the beach, give us intimations of the secrets of the great sea and so of our origins and of our destinies. Against our feeble utterances, our little namings, our tiny exhalations of clicking syllables, our beating of the gums, Crane places a version of the vast Sublime in "The wind that knots itself in one great death— / Coils and withdraws."

A great wind coiling itself like a snake, ready to strike, then striking, then withdrawing for a time. Ananke (fate, necessity). Hurricane season in the tropics. When Crane began writing this poem in late August the hurricane that would render unlivable the house where he was staying was still two months away. But when the cataclysm struck, Crane spent the night under the bed with "Aunt Sally" Simpson, the elderly caretaker of the estate, along with Aunt Sally's parrot, Attaboy, while above them ceiling plaster buckled and caved, the roof screamed as it was peeled loose, and two-by-fours were wind-hammered six feet into the ground at a single stroke. Next morning Crane would watch horrified as a donkey, near death, staggered blindly out of the jungle and collapsed. That night was enough to remind Crane of what nature could reduce even the strongest to. It was a natural force not unlike the vast and terrifying aurora borealis in Stevens's late "Auroras of Autumn," or the eruption of Mt. Pelée that, Williams recalled in his poem, "Catastrophic Birth," wiped out his mother's French relatives in a single night.

Indeed, Crane's hurricane doubles in the closing lines of his poem in its metaphoric force *as* a volcano, leaving the poet and his words mere shells cast up in the aftermath of its demonic passing:

> Slagged of the hurricane—I, cast within its flow,
> Congeal by afternoons here, satin and vacant.
> You have given me the shell, Satan,—carbonic amulet
> Sere of the sun exploded in the sea.

But if these are the poem's final words, at least the poet is a living witness to nature's violent passing, and in the process he has managed to hear—and even to record—something of the glory of the Sublime. True, he seems forced to admit by time's evidence, there seems to be no "Captain," no God, no ordering principle of "this doubloon isle / Without a turnstile"; there is no way in, and no possibility of a way to a deeper understanding. This carib isle belongs not to him but to the "catchword crabs" scuttling about in the underbrush, repeating their same, unvarying sounds ad nauseam, until the crabs themselves become anagrammatizations for the experience of the place itself. In this world vision seems impossible, he is ready to admit, his senses "ambushed," his ideas of order, shaped by images of Ohio and New York, all rendered void here in the tropics, where his eyes have been first "webbed" then "baked."

And yet, having admitted to the overwhelming difficulties of transcribing the transcendence he has tasted, something in Crane continues to cry out. "Let fiery blossoms clot the light," he prays now, and "render my ghost" (the phrase is suggestive, and means not only melting down, transforming, but also delivering one's spirit over; it seems to call to mind Christ's final agonizing cry from the cross to be delivered into the Father's hands), the spirit "Sieved upwards. . . . Until it meets the blue's comedian host." In spite of the absence of any Captain or any other God he can name, Crane's prayer—the cry of this prisoner in his "black and white" uniform in a black and white world—strikes us perhaps all the more with its force and vulnerability. We want that cry of utter destitution, I think, to be answered. And, almost miraculously, it is.

For now, suddenly, Crane gives utterance to five of the most powerful lines in all of modern poetry. These lines—four of which rhyme on a single note—are the cry of the pilgrim, a prayer, a petition, a striving for eloquence, a desire to hear the mighty strain of the Sublime again. Longer than blank verse, these epic lines are six and seven stresses, interlaced with stately spondees, Marlovian lines perhaps, as Crane sees himself like those sea turtles, pulled up from their hidden world to be bound, spiked, eviscerated—crucified—along the wharves of the world's marketplace each morning, their eyes, caked by bitter salt, reminding them of their lost world.

"Such thunder in their strain," Crane nevertheless marvels as these strange visionaries strain, like Crane himself, to sing something of the otherworldly strain of what they have seen and lost, their "clenched beaks coughing for the surge again!" Though they cannot tell us what they have seen, Crane makes us feel something of the unearthly music these creatures have heard and that they manifest in their stifled cries. It is something of what we, too, must feel here, in the majestic music that Crane has managed to (yes) render here in these lines, in the slow evisceration of their speaker, in the trembling, electric surge and majesty of the vision towards which the poem, made up of clenched words, can only point. It is a shadow music, then, of the unheard music Crane somehow heard, this "nacreous frame" of words that somehow—and it is Crane's signature—could net such "thunder in their strain."

CHARLES MARTIN

Herself Regather'd: On Jonathan Swift's "A Beautiful Young Nymph Going to Bed"

Although Jonathan Swift has long been regarded as the author of several masterpieces of our prose, his poetry has had a much more difficult time finding acceptance. The nineteenth century dropped him completely: Sir Arthur Quiller-Couch, that dependable bellwether of late Victorian taste, admitted nothing of Swift's to his *Oxford Book of English Verse*, published in 1900. As recently as 1962, Padraic Colum, Irish and sympathetic, began his introduction to a selection of Swift's poems by wondering whether they could be properly spoken of as poems at all. He decided they could, but only if the reader is willing to settle for sound workmanship, memorable statement, and vigorous form. If one requires more—and Colum does—Swift must inevitably disappoint: "For us, *poem* means a regularly rhythmical piece that is charged with emotion, that reaches beyond the rational into the imaginative, that transports us from the here and now." It may be that Swift's verse has been for so long the victim of its own bad reputation that even his admirers feel some sort of ritual obligation to discredit the work; nevertheless, it seems to me that in his best poems, including "A Beautiful Young Nymph Going to Bed" the qualities that obtain are precisely those that Colum mentions.

In that poem, Swift follows the nymph Corinna, an impecunious prostitute, who has come back alone to her garret after an unsuccessful evening on the streets. As Corinna undresses for bed, the reader discovers that her apparent charms have all been supplied by artifice:

> Then, seated on a three-legg'd Chair,
> Takes off her artificial Hair:
> Now, picking out a Crystal Eye,
> She wipes it clean, and lays it by.
> Her Eye-Brows from a Mouse's Hyde,

Stuck on with Art on either Side,
Pulls off with Care, and first displays 'em,
Then in a Play-Book smoothly lays 'em.
Now dextrously her Plumpers draws,
That serve to fill her hollow Jaws.
Untwists a wire; and from her Gums
A Set of Teeth completely comes

Worse is yet to be, for Swift will spare us—or rather Corinna—nothing at all in the way of degradation, as an impromptu vaginal examination reveals the signs of venereal disease:

With gentlest Touch, she next explores
Her Shankers, Issues, running Sores,
Effects of many a sad Disaster;
And then to each applies a Plaster.

Needless to say, Swift's poem would not have been let into any proper Victorian parlor; one might very well argue that parlors were invented in order to keep this sort of thing out. Nevertheless, it is difficult to imagine the poem finding a warm welcome in our own times. It goes against the contemporary grain in a number of important ways, not the least of which is the fact of its metrical virtuosity and the deliberate, in-your-face syncretism of its diction: this is a poem written in the vernacular of an uncommonly erudite poet. And while ours is an age that gives lip service to the notion that a poem can be written about any subject at all, the contents of the magazines that publish poetry these days suggest that we are most comfortable with poems of sensibility that explore chiefly the question of what, if anything, is going on in the poet's own head. Relationships go on in poets' heads, and readers of contemporary poetry like to have clear answers to certain kinds of questions: What kind of feeling does Swift have for Corinna? What is the nature of their relationship? The poem offers no obvious answers to either question, and Swift's distance from his subject, his apparent detachment from Corinna's predicament, as well as the pleasure that he appears to be taking in it, makes this poem appear suspect to a contemporary reader. The modern reader of Swift's poem is apt to feel that what is most likely going on in Swift's head is a condition with a Greek name—scopophilia, for instance—and a secure place in the psychiatrist's Diagnostic Manual.

Our age also places a very high value on the therapeutic function of poetry: it ought to make us feel better about ourselves; at the very least, like a competent physician, it ought to do no harm. Here, too, we have a problem, for, far from being detached from Corinna's predicament, Swift is in fact its creator, instigator, and only true begetter, skillfully marshalling his octosyllabic couplets in a display of heartless virtuosity and gusto, driven by what might very well be a pathological fear and hatred of women and the need to see them degraded and humiliated.

Given the sensibilities of our age, that seems to me one likely way in which the poem might be read today. Swift's attitude toward women was varied and complex, too much so to be treated responsibly in an essay as brief as this. But his attitude toward the victims of political and economic oppression was clear and straightforward, though irony was the most often used weapon in his armory. And as Swift presents her, Corinna is—no mistake about it—a victim of economic and social oppression. Swift's description is indeed cruel, but the cruelty isn't Swift's. Or does anyone suppose that the author of the tract that we call "A Modest Proposal" seriously intended to raise Irish children in commercial quantities for the tables of the well-to-do? Is it not possible that the cruelty of Swift's description of Corinna is somehow necessary for us to be able to see her in a sympathetic fashion?

Nevertheless, one must admit that there is something unsettling about the writer who can entertain, even speculatively, the "Modest Proposal," or who can describe Corinna's sordid disrobing with such evident gusto. But this is a poem that is meant to be unsettling, meant to move the reader from the comfortable assurance of moral and aesthetic certainties into an awareness of the fact that unimaginable horrors can be spoken of in the most reasonable of tones, that physical and moral degradation can be presented in a chillingly funny way; our laughter is the admission of our complicity. The technique is various in its applications, but its effect can be summed up in a single sentence from Swift's "Tale of a Tub": "Last week I saw a woman flayed, and you will hardly believe how much it altered her person for the worse."

At this point in the poem, Corinna, too, is very much worse for the wear. Between her sleep and her waking, however, comes a passage that is central to the way in which I believe the poem should be read:

> Or if she chance to close her Eyes,
> Of *Bridewell* and the *Compter* dreams,
> And feels the Lash, and faintly screams;
> Or by a faithless Bully drawn,
> At some Hedge-Tavern lies in Pawn;
> Or to *Jamaica* seems transported,
> Alone, and by no Planter courted;
> Or, near *Fleet-Ditch's* oozy Brinks,
> Surrounded with a Hundred Stinks,
> Belated seems on watch to lye,
> And snap some Cully passing by;
> Or, struck with Fear, her Fancy runs
> On Watchmen, Constables and Duns

From whom she meets with frequent Rubs;
But never from Religious Clubs,
Whose Favour she is sure to find
Because she pays them all in Kind.

One unsettling revelation, that of Corinna's physical reality, the abscesses and absences underneath the disguises and arrangements that make her socially presentable, if not socially acceptable, leads into a second revelation: Corinna's dream, in which Swift reveals his vision of the underside of the respectable society that rejects Corinna, and whose institutions oppress and torment her; Bridewell and the Compter were debtors' prisons, where a Corinna would very likely have wound up. Jamaica stands for Britain's expanding empire, with special reference, of course, to the slave trade; though the couplet is ambiguous, Corinna seems to have been transported there not in order to serve the lusts of some plantation owner, but to service his slaves or their overseers; that is to say, her economic condition is even lower than theirs. And of course, the Religious Clubs are meant to stand for the established Church, which lent its moral authority to both the debtors' prisons and the slave trade.

Corinna's undressing and her dream both offer revelations; in both she is reduced to nothing: a syphilitic hole, an economic cipher. Worse is yet to come: she awakens to find herself amid the "Ruins of the Night":

A wicked Rat her Plaster stole,
Half-eat and dragg'd it to his Hole.
The Crystal Eye, alas was miss't;
And *Puss* had on her Plumpers pisst.
A Pigeon picked her Issue-Peas;
And *Shock* her Tresses fill'd with Fleas.

What remains of Corinna, the various signs of her arts and artifices, has been ruined, lost, or carried away. Swift manages to achieve a delicate balance between the horrors of the grave and the horrors of the ludicrous. What follows is something of a miracle, as the torn nymph heals herself:

The Nymph, tho' in this mangled Plight,
Must ev'ry Morn her Limbs unite.
But how shall I describe her Arts
To recollect the scatter'd Parts?
Or shew the Anguish, Toil and Pain,
Of gath'ring up herself again?
The bashful Muse will never bear
In such a Scene to interfere.
Corinna in the Morning dizen'd,
Who sees will spew; who smells, be poison'd.

Until this point in the poem, the poet has made no comment in his own voice on Corinna's physical humiliation or on the moral degradation that we might be tempted to infer from it: we know only her behavior, not her character. The poet is an observing *eye* rather than an intrusive, judgemental *I*. It is significant, then, that when he breaks the frame of authorial separation from his character, he does so at the point where Corinna is heroically putting herself together again. Swift asks rhetorically how he might find words capable of expressing her art and her suffering. It is, as he admits, beyond the limitations of the "bashful Muse," who cannot bring herself to confront such a scene; this is likewise a revelation that commonplace morality will find unedifying, indeed, sickening.

And yet of course, bashful Muse or no, Swift does confront the scene and confronts us with it: what are we to make of this? Swift cannot admit to his sympathies for Corinna in her victimization and in her heroic struggle against the social and economic juggernaut: that would be just like having the author of "A Modest Proposal" come out at the end and admit that he really wasn't serious after all about raising those babies for food: it just wouldn't do. Our humanity must be tested right up to the end, and so Swift ends his poem where he must in order to make us feel the weight of the moral challenge it poses.

On Byron's *Don Juan*

"Hail, Muse! *et cetera.*"
So Byron jauntily begins Canto III of *Don Juan*. Later he offers his Muse these guarded instructions:

> March, my Muse! If you cannot fly, yet flutter;
> And when you may not be sublime, be arch,
> Or starch, as are the edicts statesmen utter.
> We surely shall find something worth research:
> Columbus found a new world in a cutter,
> Or brigantine, or pink, of no great tonnage,
> While yet America was in her non-age.
>
> (XV, 210–16)

The comparison of the poem's progress to a voyage of discovery is of course mockingly grandiloquent—surely the central tone of the poem. Byron means to subvert the grandiosity of the epic and to associate its conventionally lofty rhetoric with the banalities of statesmen, but he also means to discover something new—a tone in which a long poem can be written that is resolutely up-to-date and yet can share in the epic's prestige. (He even calls his own poem "this Epic Satire" [XIV, 790].)

Of the classical poets, Byron cites Horace most frequently: this should remind us what urbanity of tone and range of moral authority he aspires to. Indeed, Byron is so eager to be Horatian that he attributes to Horace a swatch from Ovid: "In short, the maxim for this amorous tribe is / Horatian, "Medio tu tutissimis ibis" (VI, 135–36). "You'll fare best on the middle path," Ovid wrote, in *Metamorphoses*, II, 137. And it is indeed a middle path—between the length and grandiosity of the epic and the pointed compression of satire—that Byron has set himself on. Thus Horace is Byron's honorary guide.

And yet Martial is also vitally important to Byron's project. He first appears in Canto I, where Byron is detailing Juan's education.

> And then what proper person can be partial
> To all those nauseous epigrams of Martial?
>
> Juan was taught from out the best edition,
>   Expurgated by learned men, who place,
> Judiciously, from out the schoolboy's vision,
>   The grosser parts; but fearful to deface
> Too much their modest bard by this omission,
>   And pitying sore his mutilated case,
> They only add them all in an appendix,
> Which saves, in fact, the trouble of an index;
>
> For there we have them all at one fell swoop,
>   Instead of being scatter'd through the pages;
> They stand forth marshall'd in a handsome troop,
>   To meet the ingenuous youth of future ages,
> Till some less rigid editor shall stoop
>   To call them back into their separate cages,
> Instead of standing staring altogether,
> Like garden gods—and not so decent either.
>
> (I, 343–60)

The garden gods Byron refers to were statues (usually wooden) of Priapus with exaggerated erections. Much of the diction of this passage ("less rigid," "stand forth," "grosser parts," "modest bard," "mutilated") has been pointedly anticipating this phallic conclusion. For those of Byron's readers who knew what he meant by "garden gods," the last couplet brings to the surface an underground river of snickers. The effect is rather like that of so many Latin sentences in which the verb is deferred to the very end and organizes both the syntax and the sense of the sentence like a tightened drawstring.

As for the edition Byron has Juan taught from, Byron's commentary on his own poem reads: "Fact. There is, or was, such an edition, with all the obnoxious epigrams of Martial placed by themselves at the end." Outside literature and the scholarly presentation of it, the sordid and the noble are inextricably braided together.

Two lines of *Don Juan* consist of a Martial epigram quoted whole and Byron's commentary on it. The italics are Byron's.

> Omnia vult *belle* Matho dicere—dic aliquando
>   Et *bene*, dic *neutrum*, dic aliquando *male*.
> The first is rather more than mortal can do;
>   The second may be sadly done or gaily:
> The third is still more difficult to stand to:
>   The fourth we hear, and see, and say too, daily:

The whole together is what I would wish
To serve in this conundrum of a dish.
(XIV, 161–68)

Byron doesn't translate Martial's epigram for his readers, just as he didn't tell them what he meant by "garden gods." Martial's epigram is X, xlvi. I've translated it as follows:

Whatever you say, Matho, it's got to be smart.
There's nothing good, or dull, or evil in your heart?

The stanza could serve as a motto for the whole poem. Byron's complaint about the great epics is their unmixed tones. Grandeur follows on grandeur. Virgil is never not *belle*, which means in Latin (as in modern Italian) not only beautiful but stylishly so, elegant. Likewise "smart" in modern English points both to modishness and intelligence.

"The first," Byron says, meaning *belle*, "is rather more than mortal can do." Byron has used "mortal" very seriously here. The "mortals" in Homer and Virgil are great heroes. Every male character in *The Iliad* except Thersites is a prince or a king. The gods, of course, can't die, which is why they're finally trivial, except for their power, and why "mortals" like Achilles are at their most foolish when they're most godlike.

The great epics Byron is both honoring and satirizing are not about mortals, in the ordinary sense of the word, but *Don Juan* is. Mortals are not all *belle*, but good, so-so, and evil all muddled together. To be good, *bene*, provides no unmixed sense of moral victory; it "may be sadly done or gaily." Or, by implication, both at once, with very mixed feelings. *Neutrum*, or so-so, or dull, "is still more difficult to stand to," Byron tells us. How so? The translation "dull" suggests why: we're bored by it. *Male* is at least dramatic, which may be why we quickly assent to Byron's observation that "we hear, and see, and say [it] too, daily." The rhyme of "gaily" and "daily" is one of the wonders of this stanza. The erosion of the "daily" eats away at the peak-experience sense of life implicit in "gaily." And daily life is Byron's subject. His characters exist in time, in contrast to the heroes of the great epics, suspended forever in mythological timelessness.

The ottava rima stanza that Byron chose for his satiric epic provides a loping pace congenial to both his narrative impulses and to his love of digression and commentary:

I meant to make this poem very short,
But now I can't tell where it may not run.
(XV, 171–72)

Byron here is being cheerfully disingenuous. He always intended a very long poem.

> I've finished now
> Two hundred and odd stanzas as before,
> That being about the number I'll allow
> Each canto of the twelve, or twenty-four
> (II, 1722–25)

Virgil's poem has twelve books; Homer's two poems have twenty-four each. Byron's aim was always to match the epic in scale but to modernize it, to satirize it, to make it about mortals and their daily behavior rather than about heroes and their legendary behavior. He wanted also a tone that represented not just the *belle*, but the mixed feelings and motives of mortals under stress and in confusion, and he wanted a form that allowed, even demanded, an element of commentary and concision to counterbalance the expansive, digressive, and learned baggage of his authorial journey. So the rhymed couplet that concludes each ottava rima stanza is an opportunity for Byron's epigrammatic instincts, for a series of contractions that counter the expansive chatter of the long, apparently meandering poem.

See what happens in the concluding couplet of the stanza Byron devotes to Martial's epigram.

> The whole together is what I would wish
> To serve in this conundrum of a dish.
> (XV, 167–68)

The idea of a stew (or "mess," to look back to the Biblical meaning of "mess of pottage," which survives into our military diction as mess hall) with a little bit of everything in it derives very exactly from Byron's rejection of the *belle* for the more inclusive range of effects and tones necessary to depict the daily emotional lives of mortals. The muse here is no glowing hologram, but kitchen help with gravy stains on her apron.

But if "dish" serves to deflate a certain literary pretension Byron associates with the great epics, "conundrum" serves to elevate "dish" to one of the mysteries and thus to compare it to the mess, the *missa* (as the Mass, that ceremonial meal at which the celebrants eat the body and drink the blood of a god, is called in Latin).

The major strategy of Byron's poem is packed tightly into his stanza on Martial's epigram. I will invite, he seems to be reminding himself, comparison with the great epics. I will differentiate my satirical epic from those great poems by insisting on a complication of tone necessary to display the full range of daily mortal emotion. The resulting mess will be humbler than Homer or Virgil (or Dante or Milton, models less important to Byron's contrast but by no means ignored by him), but by being humbler, it will be more accurate about the great human mysteries, which happen to ourselves, not to our heroes. And accuracy is Byron's goal.

> But if a writer should be quite consistent,
> How could he possibly show things existent?
> (XV, 695–96)

Pope: A Love Letter

The older I get and the more I have read, the less do masterpieces appeal to me. The Great Books are an ideal school curriculum and in old age may be a refuge from the vanities of the world, but they are not a companionable pleasure of my middle years. I recommend those books and remember them and refer to them, but they are no longer on my night table. For the same reason that I now prefer Vuillard to Michelangelo, or Mendelssohn to Beethoven, so, too, do I prefer the sly lyric to the rigorous epic, the poem that amuses or touches to the one that scowls and stirs. I prefer the poem scaled to a human dimension, one that engages my own memories and desires. Even among the works of a very great poet like Alexander Pope—one of the half-dozen true masters of the art—I want now to single out a smaller, more tender, enchanting, and ultimately sad poem for special regard.

His "Epistle to Miss Blount, on her leaving the Town, after the Coronation" was written in 1714, and published three years later in his *Works*. When we pause to consider that in 1717 Pope was just 29, it may seem presumptuous of him to have issued a collected edition of his work, until we realize that the book includes such poems as his "Essay on Criticism," written when he was 23, the sublime "Rape of the Lock," written at a mere 26, and "Eloisa to Abelard," written at age 28. If he never quite lisped in numbers as he claimed, he remains undoubtedly the most astonishing prodigy of English poetry.

As a child, pampered by doting parents whose Catholicism and wealth he inherited, he showed—in Dr. Johnson's words—"remarkable gentleness and sweetness of disposition." Those qualities did not outlive childhood. As an adult, Pope seems to have been vain, petty, secretive, parsimonious, snobbish, greedy, and irascible. I wonder how much of this "bad character"—the very opposite of the sensible, modest, loyal persona of his poems—was the result of an unconscious self-hatred. He once described his own life as a "long disease." Literally, it was tuberculosis of the spine, resulting in a double curvature. It rendered him helpless, hunchbacked, and repulsive. He was four foot six, "the little Alexander whom the women laugh at." In his life of Pope, Dr. Johnson describes him as

so weak as to stand in perpetual need of female attendance; extremely sensible of cold, so that he wore a kind of fur doublet under a shirt of a very coarse linen with fine sleeves. When he rose, he was invested in a bodice made of stiff canvas, being scarce able to hold himself erect till they were laced, and he then put on a flannel waistcoat. One side was contracted. His legs were so slender, that he enlarged their bulk with three pair of stockings, which were drawn on and off by the maid; for he was not able to dress or undress himself, and neither went to bed nor rose without help. His weakness made it very difficult for him to be clean.

That, by this account, the poet was dependent on women, even as his weakness and deformity were exposed to them, has a haunting analogy in his emotional life. As a young man, Pope had met the Blount sisters, Teresa and Martha, daughters of a woman who had once been a neighbor of Pope's parents. He was infatuated with both the dark, sultry, sensuous Teresa and with her younger, blonde, shy, serious sister. He waited on them, lived to amuse them, Teresa especially. He settled annuities and a legacy on them and eventually paid Teresa the compliment of writing one of his greatest poems for her, the "Epistle to a Lady." But it was all for nothing; they treated him like a pet monkey. In one wrenching letter to Teresa—written in 1717, the same year his "Epistle to Miss Blount" appeared in print—he confessed his romantic frustrations: "Let me open my whole heart to you," he writes.

I have some times found myself inclined to be in love with you: and as I have reason to know from your Temper & Conduct how miserably I should be used in that circumstance, it is worth my while to avoid it: It is enough to be Disagreeable, without adding Fool to it, by constant Slavery. I have heard indeed of Women that have had a kindness for Men of my Make; but it has been after Enjoyment, never before; and I know to my Cost you have had no Taste of that Talent in me, which most Ladies would not only Like better, but Understand better, than any other I have.

Of his first suggestion—that attractive women pursue gifted but ugly men—there is ample evidence; Chateaubriand, whom Princess Lieven called a hunchback without the hump, comes to mind. Even so, women flocked to him, and the greatest beauty of her age, Madame Récamier, was his devoted mistress. Of Pope's second suggestion—that Teresa has ignored not just his person but the very genius that, beneath the body's disguise, is his true self—there is also melancholy evidence. A little after this letter, he sent Teresa a morocco-bound copy of his 1717 *Works*. He inscribed it with these lines:

> This Book, which, like its Author, You
> By the bare Outside only knew,
> (Whatever was in either Good,
> Not look'd in, or, not understood)
> Comes, as the Writer did too long,
> To be about you, right or wrong;
> Neglected on your Chair to lie,
> Nor raise a Thought, nor draw an Eye;
> In peevish Fits to have you say,
> *See there! you're always in my Way!*

But all this sadness lay ahead. In 1714, when Pope wrote his poem to Teresa, he was still a sort of suitor, a man living in and for his hopes. Let us turn back now to the poem itself. In a letter to Pope, Jonathan Swift once noted that "you have been a writer of Letters almost from your infancy, and by your own confession had Schemes even then of Epistolary fame." The letters that brought him fame, of course, are his many verse epistles. His early "Epistle to Miss Blount" is the forerunner of those moral poems about friendship and virtue, modeled on Horace, that constitute his greatest achievement. So different in tone and address from the essay—or a poem such as, say, his "Essay on Man"—the letter allows an intimacy and spontaneity that only help, by casually disguising them, to affirm its serious intentions. Most of us think our letters reveal more about us, because they plumb deeper, than conversation does. Dr. Johnson is less easily convinced:

Very few can boast of hearts which they dare lay open to themselves . . . and, certainly, what we hide from ourselves we do not show to our friends. There is, indeed, no transaction which offers stronger temptations to fallacy and sophistication than epistolary intercourse. In the eagerness of conversation the first emotions of the mind often burst out before they are considered; in the tumult of business, interest and passion have their genuine effect; but a friendly letter is a calm and deliberate performance, in the cool of leisure, in the stillness of solitude, and surely no man sits down to depreciate by design his own character.

And what of Pope's poem? It has the tone of a letter, and is everywhere what Johnson calls a calm and deliberate performance. It is meant not to rush upon Teresa Blount's feelings but to describe them in such a way that he may identify with them. It may also reveal more about Pope himself than he may have intended.

The poem poses as a letter from the poet-in-town to his lady-in-the-country, but its real setting is the "dear, idle time" of a daydream. He imagines her to "hum half a tune," and he clearly means himself, in the poem's last line, to be humming the other half. This is a poem about harmony, the vexations of life yielding to an imaginative sympathy. Each is separated from what the poet would like to think of as the other's true desire. In his poem, each overlaps the other, and the two are joined. It is our thoughts, our "tunes," that unite us. Art may complete what life disrupts. This had been, all along, Pope's bittersweet self-delusion about Teresa Blount, and in this poem his effort to pretend that his ability to imagine will be crowned with success seems—since we know what humiliation ensued—almost unbearably poignant.

The poem's opening stanza is comprised of a single sentence, a single simile. (Its initial "As" finds an echo in the final stanza's "So"—a stanza also made of a single ten-line sentence.) The stanza swoons with barely repressed—or just awakening—sexuality. When Pope says of Zephalinda's friends and admirers that "their pleasures caus'd her discontent," he is referring not just to her envy but to her restlessness. (By extension, of course, Pope is describing his own feelings as well.) The next stanza, with its marvelous description of her routine in the country, is itself virtually a purling brook of words that signal repression: *plain, dull, cold, exact, godly*. Pope's exquisite satirical touch here must be what attracted T. S. Eliot to try the Popean couplets Ezra Pound excised from *The Waste Land*, though the tone remains, along with the image of trifling over cold coffee with one's spoon, in Eliot's best poem, "The Love Song of J. Alfred Prufrock." Poor Zephalinda's rural life here is just the opposite of Belinda's languid, exciting, treacherous life in "The Rape of the Lock," a poem written (or at least revised) in the same year. The bumptious Squire who replaces the city spark in her company is also, with his cry "No words!" the antitype of the poet. He loves you, says Pope to Teresa, "best of all things—but his horse." If you hear, as I do, "he's hoarse" there, then the echo implies that her oafish suitor cannot offer what Pope would like to think she most wants: the language of true seduction, the embodiment of love, the art of poetry. *Words* and distance make Pope more attractive than the awkward Squire who "makes love with nods, and knees beneath a table." By describing her desolate conditions, he suggests that he alone understands what her heart desires—wit, society, charm: everything, in short, that Pope, or his poetic voice, can provide. His muse of fire is its own sort of "spark." The three most seductive words in the language, undoubtedly, have always been not "I love you" but "I understand you."

Since Teresa cannot triumph in the rural shade, Pope imagines that in the rural shade she dreams of triumphs. Her daydream brings her memories to a more vivid life than her very surroundings. She teases them into thought only to dismiss them with a "flirt," or flick of her fan. Pope's allusion to Prospero's dissolving pageant seems an intentional reference to the theatrical nature of the scene, and to Zephalinda's magical power.

But of course the power is Pope's, and he next uses it gently. He puts himself in her circumstances: plagu'd and wanting and abstracted. What business seems to preoccupy him merely distracts him from his dreams of Zephalinda; his fancy has become his reality, and their interruption mirrors what happens to Zephalinda in the rural shade. His friend John Gay disturbs Pope's daydream, whereas Zephalinda wantonly makes her own vision fly. Perhaps Pope means to make Teresa seem the more willful. He had reason to. The poem's final rhyme itself contains Pope's own repressed anxiety. "As you may now" is a phrase that combines wishful thinking and uncertainty; he rhymes it with "I knit my brow."

"He used almost always the same fabric of verse," said Johnson. Indeed, Pope may be said to have perfected the heroic couplet. Yet isn't that very perfection a sort of limitation? It tends to lend the same tone and weight to everything. It concentrates, but narrows. It creates the vertiginous effects of balance and contrast, but is always pushing the lines toward irony. It creates expectations that can be cleverly satisfied or upended, but tends to finesse the same tricks over and over. I say all this not to criticize Pope's technique—though I would acknowledge the drawbacks—but to praise his constant invention and flexibility, that astonishing way he has of making a line, or a set of lines, so expressive. My mind's ear links him in this regard to a poet most readers would wrongly think his opposite: Walt Whitman, who perfected the free-verse line. Both poets make remarkable use of detail—Whitman, to contract and shape his line, which is always bulging outward; Pope, to expand and vary his, whose instinct is to turn back in on itself. Whitman could make a scene, and sometimes a short story, out of each line in any of his catalogues:

> The pure contralto sings in the organ loft,
> The carpenter dresses his plank, the tongue of his foreplane whistles its
>   wild ascending lisp,
> The married and unmarried children ride home to their Thanksgiving
>   dinner,
> The pilot seizes the king-pin, he heaves down with a strong arm,
> The mate stands braced in the whale-boat, lance and harpoon are ready,
> The duck-shooter walks by silent and cautious stretches,
> The deacons are ordain'd with cross'd hands at the altar,
> The spinning-girl retreats and advances to the hum of the big wheel

In his "Epistle to Miss Blount," Pope too lavishes detail; some lines have as much as any chapter in a Fielding novel. His descriptive and narrative genius is self-evident in this poem, but note, too, his dramatic panache. "From the dear man unwilling she must sever"—that phrase "dear man" resides in Zephalinda's own account of him to another lady; "And dine exact at noon"—the dull aunt's pinched reminder; "And loves you best of all things—but his horse"—Pope's mocking quotation.

What continually draws me to this poem is less its consummate art, its canny observations, its elegant stratagems, than that all this art—each layer applied with the most delicate touch—failed. That failure only adds to the poem's melancholy pavane of crossed desires. Even without bringing a little biography to bear on the poem, we can read a larger perspective into it. I return to my earlier observation about avoiding the grandiose. The mighty themes can be treated so deftly in miniature. Isn't Pope's poem, after all, its own ironic *Paradise Lost*? In her Edenic garden world, Zephalinda innocently thinks she has lost the fallen world of town life, its gaiety, its dashing beaux, and glamorous power. In his hellish city, plagued with headaches and noise and confusion, the poet knows he has lost his heart and fears he has lost its mistress, the beautiful girl. Both are unconsciously mourning their youth. That dull aunt and coarse Squire stand in as parodies of what the fair Zephalinda and the witty Pope will become. Perhaps Pope's genius in part lies in his having written a poem that, while hiding his heart from himself, has laid it open to us.

Epistle To Miss Blount, on her leaving the Town, after the Coronation

As some fond virgin, whom her mother's care
Drags from the town to wholsom country air,
Just when she learns to roll a melting eye,
And hear a spark, yet think no danger nigh;
From the dear man unwilling she must sever,
Yet takes one kiss before she parts for ever:
Thus from the world fair *Zephalinda* flew,
Saw others happy, and with sighs withdrew;
Not that their pleasures caus'd her discontent,
She sigh'd not that They stay'd, but that She went.
    She went, to plain-work, and to purling brooks,
Old-fashion'd halls, dull aunts, and croaking rooks,
She went from Op'ra, park, assembly, play,
To morning walks, and pray'rs three hours a day;
To pass her time 'twixt reading and Bohea,
To muse, and spill her solitary Tea,
Or o'er cold coffee trifle with the spoon,

Count the slow clock, and dine exact at noon;
Divert her eyes with pictures in the fire,
Hum half a tune, tell stories to the squire;
Up to her godly garret after sev'n,
There starve and pray, for that's the way to heav'n.
    Some Squire, perhaps, you take a delight to rack;
Whose game is Whisk, whose treat a toast in sack,
Who visits with a gun, presents you birds,
Then gives a smacking buss, and cries—No words!
Or with his hound comes hollowing from the stable,
Makes love with nods, and knees beneath a table;
Whose laughs are hearty, tho' his jests are coarse,
And loves you best of all things—but his horse.
    In some fair evening, on your elbow laid,
You dream of triumphs in the rural shade;
In pensive thought recall the fancy'd scene,
See Coronations rise on ev'ry green;
Before you pass th' imaginary sights
Of Lords, and Earls, and Dukes, and garter'd Knights;
While the spread Fan o'ershades your closing eyes;
Then give one flirt, and all the vision flies.
Thus vanish sceptres, coronets, and balls,
And leave you in lone woods, or empty walls.
    So when your slave, at some dear, idle time,
(Not plagu'd with headachs, or the want of rhime)
Stands in the streets, abstracted from the crew,
And while he seems to study, thinks of you:
Just when his fancy points your sprightly eyes,
Or sees the blush of soft *Parthenia* rise,
Gay pats my shoulder, and you vanish quite;
Streets, chairs, and coxcombs rush upon my sight;
Vext to be still in town, I knit my brow,
Look sow'r, and hum a tune—as you may now.

Alexander Pope

SHEILA McGRORY-KLYZA

To Claim a Voice

Sonnets from the Portuguese, Elizabeth Barrett Browning's sonnet sequence composed during her 1845–1846 courtship with Robert Browning, represents the first time in the sonnet tradition that the "I" as a woman and the "I" as a poet were joined. The poems defy the poetic and social conventions of Victorian England and signify Barrett Browning's claiming of her poetic voice. The most unconventional of the sequence, I believe, is Sonnet Twenty-two: it is also the most finely crafted and emotionally complex sonnet, challenging not only the assumptions of Victorian England, but of the contemporary reader as well.

The lovers in Sonnet Twenty-two are equal partners in their love relationship. Immediately in the first two lines the speaker confidently claims this relationship, asserting that she and her lover "stand up erect and strong / Face to face, silent, drawing nigh and nigher." The lovers wear none of the masks of the hierarchical roles of courtship, but instead view each other honestly, "Face to face." This image expresses, too, the intuitive ("silent") communication between the two lovers and their ever-stronger ("drawing nigh and nigher") bond. That is, their equality does not drive them apart, but strengthens their union. They do not suppress their passion: instead it "break[s] into fire," fueled by their mutual respect and admiration for the various dimensions of each other's being: spiritual, physical, and intellectual.

The poem gains its structure from a discussion of these three kinds of love. Emotional love, usually the most commonly cited type of love and stereotypically associated with women's poetry, is not overtly included in the construct of this sonnet. Granted, the sonnet form itself is considered a vehicle for emotional expression, but any direct reference to emotional love is conspicuously absent from this one. In the first line of the poem the speaker establishes the lovers as "two souls," a spiritual identity that is maintained throughout the poem. The two souls, though, exist on earth, a place of ambiguity ("silence"), of the unknowable ("darkness"), and of mutability ("the death-hour"). But "what bitter wrong / Can the earth do to us, that we should not long / Be here contented?" the speaker asks, voicing the central conflict of the poem. The "bitter wrong" is soon revealed, as is the speaker's lack of faith in an extended earthly contentment. Still, the "pure spirits" of the lovers prefer earth to heaven, which threatens with a "golden orb of perfect song." This image recalls the sun, mythologically associated with the masculine sun god. The musical perfection exerted by the sun implies clearly defined hierarchical roles that operate harmoniously, or without objection.

Physical love is expressed overtly through the images Barrett Browning uses to describe the lovers, an eroticism not typically found in the poetry of Victorian women. Not only does she violate decorum by expressing female desire, but the eroticism of the two lovers is conveyed through androgynous imagery: the two souls "stand up erect and strong" (a masculine sexual image); their "wings break into fire / At either curvèd point" (suggestive of the female body, passionate, on fire).

The lovers, however, in their passionate, equal exchange, are threatened by another force: "In mounting higher, / The angels would press on us," for it is the angels who have the power to drop the "golden orb." In the nineteenth century, angels were associated with females: thus, external societal forces, this time feminine, may have impelled Barrett Browning to lead a more conventional life (denying her poetic talent, perhaps) or assume a more traditional position in her love relationship. Equally conceivable is the threat from what Barrett Browning perceives to be the feminine (with all of its nineteenth-century associations) within herself, squelching her intellectual and artistic aspirations and her desire for an equal partnership with her lover. Either way, the speaker recognizes that the lovers' attempts to ascend to heights beyond what they know on earth are certain to be defeated.

Elizabeth Barrett Browning emphasizes the intellectual love relationship she found with Robert Browning, evidenced by their esteem for each other's poetry: "Think," she plainly writes. Throughout the poem the tone is assertive, but it is here that the speaker addresses her lover most confidently. Significantly, the word is central to the line and nearly central to the poem's structure. What follows is the weighing of what would be gained and lost by aspiring to free themselves from the earthly world. The speaker appeals to her lover's intellect, not his emotions, in arguing for the "deep, dear silence," the isolation, and the brevity (but "for a day") of earthly love.

Although the rhyme scheme of this particular Petrarchan sonnet does not demonstrate the originality of Barrett Browning's off-rhymes (for example, "reassure" and "fewer" in Sonnet Twenty-four and "counterfeit" and "commemorate" in Sonnet Thirty-seven), for which she was criticized in her day, it does display her unconventional variations with the use of meter. The poem begins with a line of standard iambic pentameter: "When our two souls stand up erect and strong"; she frequently deviates from this pattern, however, sometimes in extreme ways for a poet of her time. The lines "Into our deep, dear silence. Let us stay" and "With darkness and the death-hour rounding it," each possessing three accented syllables in a row, inventively anticipate Gerard Manley Hopkins's theory of sprung rhythm. Barrett Browning's refusal to constrain her unorthodox artistry demonstrates her determination to find her own poetic voice within the masculine tradition; however, it must be added that she composed these sonnets with the intention that they be kept private, between Robert Browning and herself, presumably liberating her voice.

In the other forty-three sonnets of this sequence, Barrett Browning uses the first-person singular, poetic "I" to address her lover, thus inverting the traditional speaker of a Petrarchan sonnet: the adoring male lover. She is both the poet and the subject of her sonnets, as opposed to the traditionally objectified woman. In Sonnet Twenty-two, however, she goes one step further and uses the first person plural throughout, asserting repeatedly the equality of the two lovers: *our, us, we, us, our, us*. This assertion is a bolder one, I believe, for not only is it more difficult to trivialize and dismiss as a romantic fantasy, but in depicting a world without hierarchy altogether it calls for a more complete abandonment of a power-based society. Thus, Barrett Browning is envisioning a highly radical change in the prevailing social structure.

The speaker recognizes the resistance the couple inevitably would meet in living as equal partners. But even as the speaker acknowledges the isolation that would result from such a "pure" union, she chooses to remain on earth, accepting the "unfit / Contrarious moods of men [who would] recoil away" from them. She reasserts the forthrightness of the two souls in line 1 by repeating *stand*, followed closely by her first use of *love*, which by this point in the poem has taken on new meaning. But the difficulty of maintaining such equality in love she quickly recognizes: she hopes only "for a day" that has "darkness and the death-hour" at its end. Perhaps the speaker is recognizing the inevitability of their own deaths, or she is commenting on the mutability of love itself, for the darkness does contrast with the passionate "fire" of line 3. Perhaps. I think, rather, that she is voicing the impossibility of maintaining an egalitarian love relationship in Victorian England. Is this an acceptance, then, of the patriarchy? Clearly not, for the totality of the sonnet, indeed the sonnet sequence by which she takes her place, unconventionally, in the tradition, demonstrates a complete rejection of the current hierarchical norm.

Barrett Browning's poems have been criticized, even ridiculed, by contemporary readers for not being universal, for being too personal, too intimate. Whereas male poets could present their experiences as representative of modern man (for example, George Meredith's *Modern Love*), female poets could not. As Barrett Browning knew, readers would not accept a woman exemplifying humanity, or a poet exemplifying a woman.

As a woman poet writing one hundred and fifty years later, in the post–sexual revolution United States, I find myself struggling with the same overly "personal" issue: how to claim my voice as a woman and a poet. In a society where gender hierarchies still exist, I am trying to reconcile in my own marriage all the pressures (external and internal) that threaten to defeat the equality for which we strive. Elizabeth Barrett Browning's courageous expression of her ideas and emotions and her innovative manipulation of poetic conventions remain a source of inspiration to "stand up erect and strong."

Sonnet Twenty-two

When our two souls stand up erect and strong,
Face to face, silent, drawing nigh and nigher,
Until the lengthening wings break into fire
At either curvèd point,—what bitter wrong
Can the earth do to us, that we should not long
Be here contented? Think. In mounting higher,
The angels would press on us and aspire
To drop some golden orb of perfect song
Into our deep, dear silence. Let us stay
Rather on earth, Belovèd,—where the unfit
Contrarious moods of men recoil away
And isolate pure spirits, and permit
A place to stand and love in for a day,
With darkness and the death-hour rounding it.

Elizabeth Barrett Browning

Sir Thomas Wyatt: Strange Fashion

The poet's province is an unmapped territory lying just beyond the known, a world discovered in acts of inspiration and imagination, privileged moments in which glimpses of the past, present, and future are revealed in language at once original and exciting. "The whole of world poetry, which [knows] no bounds of time and space," is what Nadezhda Mandelstam named the commonwealth to which her husband, Osip, was called. "It does not matter what place a poet has in it," she insisted, "however small it may be. The very smallest place—just a couple of successful lines, one good poem, a single well-said word—entitles him to enter the fellowship of poets, to be one of 'us,' to partake of the feast." Sir Thomas Wyatt the Elder (1503–1542) has a distinguished seat at that banquet, which resembles a blank space on a map only to those who do not attempt to cross the border into the land of the marvelous.

Wyatt's biography is rich with incident: diplomatic missions to France, Italy, and Spain; a love affair with Anne Boleyn, who later married King Henry VIII; imprisonment—twice—in the Tower of London, where on his second stay he may have watched the execution of his former lover. A courtier and statesman in a tumultuous time, he traveled extensively, survived scandals and internal exile, killed at least one man, was rumored to have plotted against another (the powerful Cardinal Pole), and witnessed in silence the beheading of his friend and patron, Thomas Cromwell, who was the administrative force behind the Reformation, the signal event of the sixteenth century.

Which is to say: Wyatt lived and wrote during a period of extraordinary change, not unlike our own. The Reformation, ostensibly a return to pure Christianity, destroyed the hegemony of Western Christendom, while the Act of Supremacy, which made Henry VIII head of the Church of England, laid the groundwork for the rise of English nationalism—

the first expression of a sentiment that over the centuries has come to dominate political discourse. This was, indeed, one of those rare historical moments in which the political organization of the world was turned upside down. And Wyatt was in the middle of it all.

Although he died before his fortieth birthday, he left behind a full range of poetry: rondeaux, sonnets, epigrams, canzoni, songs, ballads, epistolary satires, and even paraphrases of the Penitential Psalms. Like John Donne, he understood the intimate connection between erotic and religious poetry, the ways in which the beloved, who in the deepest sense must remain unknowable, may become a figure for the mystery of God. And his flexible, intuitive grasp of meter, which allowed him to explore a bewildering variety of subjects and emotional states, still tunes our ears to rhythmic possibilities. His best poems, W. S. Merwin notes, "vibrate with mixed feelings—desire, anger, mortification, mockery, bitterness, even tenderness." In short, his is a complex poetic vision, as befits a man of his wide experience.

He wrote about the eternal verities: the inconstancy of love, the certainty of loss, the challenges of the court. ("I, cannot, I! No, no, it will not be!" he cried, explaining why he would not endorse tyranny at the court.) And his language of choice was English, not Latin; his vibrant use of the vernacular only heightened the national feelings of his countrymen, who in his lifetime read the first English translation of the Bible and learned to associate their religious faith with their new-fashioned patriotism. "My King my Country alone for whom I lyve," Wyatt exclaimed—a nationalist line hitherto impossible to imagine anyone writing. (No doubt he had occasion to question it himself when he was locked up in the Tower.)

Perhaps it is in times of upheaval that navigating the waters between the political and poetic is most difficult—and most crucial. Wyatt charted a course predicated on the wildness of his conceits, imagery, and music. Notwithstanding the machinations of his first publisher, Richard Tottel, who "smoothed out" Wyatt's verse, and the criticism of subsequent readers unable to appreciate the passionate music of his lines, the poet was in control of his material. He could compose pentameters at will, and the roughness of his meters owes more to his determination to honor the truth of his perceptions, which deepened syllable by syllable, than to any supposed defect of his ear. What he caught in his bold variations from an iambic norm was the sound of the future—a century in which new organizing principles would take shape in the political sphere, lasting, in one way or another, until the present.

Consider the dazzling opening to Sonnet XI, Wyatt's adaptation of Petrarch's *Rime* 190—"Whoso list to hunt, I know where is an hind." The statesman who introduced the sonnet into English was quick to translate the Italian form into an indigenous expression, hence the alliteration and echo of the Anglo-Saxon hemistich, the ghostly four-beat measure haunting the pentameter. In fact, it is not until the second line ("But as for me, alas, I may no more") that we may be entirely certain of Wyatt's metrical orientation. By then his conceit—the beloved as a hind-hunter's prize—has begun to take a strange turn, the poet having lost all hope:

> The vain travail hath wearied me so sore,
> I am of them that furthest cometh behind.
> Yet may I by no means my wearied mind
> Draw from the deer, but as she fleeth afore
> Fainting I follow; I leave off therefore,
> Since in a net I seek to hold the wind.

Trapped in a futile chase, far behind and in a faint, he gives up in order to catch the wind in the net of form, a poet's favorite occupation. The hunt is futile, or so he advises other suitors and his King: "Who list her hunt, I put him out of doubt, / As well as I, may spend his time in vain." Yet the poet holds the wind, if only for a moment, in the spirited meters of his conclusion, the most daring of which are found in the final rhyming couplet, one of his—and England's—contributions to the development of the sonnet:

> And graven with diamonds in letters plain,
> There is written her fair neck round about,
> "*Noli me tangere*, for Caesar's I am,
> And wild for to hold, though I seem tame."

The hind belongs to Caesar, as Anne Boleyn was now the mistress of Henry VIII; appearances aside, she had a wild spirit, like poetry. It may come as no surprise to learn that the Queen met an untimely end; accused of adultery (with Wyatt, among others) and incest, the woman behind the King of England's break with Rome was hunted down and beheaded. This, then, is not only a heart-rending love poem but an indirect expression of political reality. And this intersection of poetry and politics cannot fail to interest contemporary writers perplexed by the speed with which our world is changing: at the time of its composition Wyatt's allegory was true in an artistic sense and prophetic on the political level; today it transcends its allegorical imperative to offer a timeless vision of the end of an affair.

The conceit of comparing his beloved to a wild animal is likewise central to Wyatt's most famous ballad, "They Flee from Me." Written in Chaucer's stanza, the popular seven-line ballad stanza that employs a rhyme royal scheme (named after King James I of Scotland, who used it in *The Kingis Quair*) and what Robert Frost might call "loose iambics," this poem has baffled strict prosodists for centuries. How to scan the second line, for example, or the fifth, without resorting to complicated metrical schemes bearing little relation to normal speech patterns is the problem facing the student of prosody. (One possible solution:

> With naked foot stalking in my chamber
> That sometime they put themselves in danger)

To explain such departures from normal practice, one of his editors suggests that Wyatt "regards precision, clarity, or concentration of meaning as of primary importance." But it is more than that: such precision has its own music, which hearkens back to the stress-based prosody of Anglo-Saxon verse; that is, Wyatt is happy to sacrifice a syllable here or there in favor of rhythms buried in our ancestral memory. What better tune for the oldest subject in poetry, the lover's grief at the beloved's indifference?

In like manner, Wyatt has no fear of pulling readers up short, literally speaking, offering four-beat lines (foreshadowed in lines two and five?) when he wants to draw attention to the consequences of his loss. The emotional logic of this poem resides in moments of metrical uncertainty—"That now are wild, and do not remember," for example, or "And I have leave to go, of her goodness"—juxtaposed with the rhythmic certainty of, say, the run of pleasing pentameters in the second stanza. Here the poet celebrates one glorious night, culminating in a four-beat line—"Therewithall sweetly did me kiss"—as if to suggest the flee(t)ing nature of love: we expect to hear another beat, in the same way that the poet may have imagined he would have more nights with his beloved.

To reinforce his point, Wyatt begins the final stanza with another four-beat line: "It was no dream, I lay broad waking" is an intimate revelation, as if the poet has no choice but to confide, in the plainest tones, the nature of his loss, his sorrow. What he reveals is his bitter knowledge that nothing will ever be the same, for fortune has abandoned him. And his "strange fashion of forsaking"? This is how he bids farewell to a woman and a world. What he mourns is the loss of the certainty by which he once lived, which was embodied in the love of one woman— Anne Boleyn?—who "softly said, 'Dear heart, how like you this?'"

"Uncertainty," according to Joseph Brodsky, "is the mother of beauty, one of whose definitions is that it's something which isn't yours." And what was more uncertain in Renaissance England than the courtier's life? Wyatt's properties were confiscated in 1541, at which point only a pardon from the King spared him the loss of his head. More, he lived through a revolution in thinking, which began with a rival's love for his mistress and ended in the Reformation of the English Church. What makes "They Flee from Me" so poignant is that while the poet says good-bye to a woman, an age, and a world, there is such "passionate intensity" in his verse that one cannot help feeling he was in his way also greeting the new order.

"The pass to poetry," Nadezhda Mandelstam affirmed, "is granted only by faith in its sacramental character and a sense of responsibility for everything that happens in the world." Sir Thomas Wyatt the Elder was a poet responsible for his time and ours, which is why we may yet learn lessons from him vital to our own period of change, when the world is once again reorganizing itself day by day, stanza by stanza.

They Flee from Me

They flee from me that sometime did me seek
    With naked foot stalking in my chamber.
I have seen them gentle, tame, and meek
    That now are wild, and do not remember
    That sometime they put themselves in danger
To take bread at my hand; and now they range
Busily seeking with a continual change.

Thanked be fortune it hath been otherwise
    Twenty times better, but once in special,
In thin array after a pleasant guise,
    When her loose gown from her shoulders did fall
    And she me caught in her arms long and small,
Therewithal sweetly did me kiss
And softly said, "Dear heart, how like you this?

It was no dream: I lay broad waking.
    But all is turned thorough my gentleness
Into a strange fashion of forsaking.
    And I have leave to go, of her goodness,
    And she also to use newfangleness.
But since that I so kindly am served,
I would fain know what she hath deserved.

                Sir Thomas Wyatt the Elder

George Herbert, "The Pearl": Poetry as Plain Saying

One's favorite poems change, not only from year to year but sometimes from day to day, or even from mood to mood. My durable favorites over many years have been the "Cántico Espiritual" of San Juan de la Cruz and "Le Cimetière Marin" of Paul Valéry, though two poems more different in spirit could hardly be imagined: San Juan with his vision of dizzy bliss, the fulfillment of love in an exotic mountain hideaway, with pomegranate wine, the song of the nightingale from a luxuriant grove, and the peace of an ecstatic night that nothing can ever disturb; and Valéry with his astringent scorn for all that:

> Le beau mensonge et la pieuse ruse!
> Qui non connaît, et qui ne les refuse,
> Ce crâne vide et ce rire éternel!

Poetry has room for both visions, but I do not have room here for either of these long poems and must settle for a shorter one. As Pope said, "Beauty draws us with a single hair," and sometimes a poem can draw us into itself with a single line. That happened to me with Valéry's poem; reading it for the first time, I came on his line about a burial ground, "L'argile rouge a bu la blanche espèce," and that became a favorite poem ever since. Something like that happened with George Herbert's much shorter "The Pearl." About halfway through it, I came on his lines about the pleasure of physical love:

> I know the wayes of Pleasure, the sweet strains,
> The lullings and the relishes of it

"The lullings and the relishes of it" caught me and has held me ever since. How languorous and alluring the excitement of those two nouns, and how their two accents alone dominate and glorify the pentameter. Here is what I learned from later readings of the poem:

Herbert's title is explained by his reference to Matthew 13:45. After several related parables, we read, "Again, the kingdom of heaven is like unto a merchant man, seeking goodly pearls: who, when he had found one pearl of great price, went and sold all that he had, and bought it."

The first three stanzas of the poem inventory what the speaker means to sell to gain the pearl that stands for that kingdom. He emphasizes that he is not moved by blind superstition; all three stanzas have the logical pattern "I know . . . yet . . ." He knows very well what he is giving up. First, there are "the wayes of Learning," in quest of which he had spent all those years at the University. Secondly, there are "the wayes of Honour," the ways of worldly position and prestige, the savoir faire of the aristocratic world he is born to and was at home in. Thirdly, there are "the wayes of Pleasure," especially that of love and love making, presented in terms of the music he was passionately fond of and excelled in.

Had it come from the mouth of a humble country pastor, this poem would not have meant what it meant coming from George Herbert. At least in youth he had been proud of the fact that he came from one of the great families of England. Several Herberts had been among its most illustrious military leaders. His brother was Lord Herbert of Cherbury, ambassador to France. His mother was the beautiful Magdalen Herbert, to whom John Donne was devoted and for whom he wrote "The Autumnall":

> No *Spring*, nor *Summer* Beauty hath such grace,
> As I have seen in one *Autumnall* face

At Cambridge Herbert enjoyed a brilliant career as student, teacher of rhetoric, and Public Orator, a post that has been compared to that of being official spokesman and public-relations director, though it involved duties and privileges of more consequence than those, including correspondence with the court itself and the preparation of ceremonial speeches in English and Latin for great occasions. Each of his two predecessors in the post had become Secretary of State; Herbert himself had his eye on that office and seemed destined for it. Most of his life had been spent in the world of the learned, the famous, and the powerful, although increasingly he had been torn between that life and one devoted to the service of God. But it was not until 1630, when he was 37, that he was ordained as an Anglican priest. The year before, he had fallen in love and within weeks ("the propositions of hot blood"?) married the young woman he was to live quietly and happily with in the little country rectory at Bemerton—though, never of sturdy health, he died only three years later, just short of his fortieth birthday.

Plain as his language is in "The Pearl," paraphrase may enrich the poem for some of today's readers. The imagery of the opening lines suggests a wine press, an olive press, and of course a printing press. If we would like "head / And pipes" to have a more specific reference, it could be an allusion to the university and to its men of learning who disseminate knowledge. The rest of the stanza lists some of the kinds of knowledge he knows the ways of: natural science, legal and political theory, astrology, the alchemists' researches, geographical explorations. (His "new-found seas" might remind us of his friend John Donne's very different invocation to a mistress: "Oh my America, my new found lande.")

The second stanza assures us that he knows the ways of the world, its etiquette, its politics, knows how to play the game of giving and receiving favors; how, when ambition "swells the heart," to use speech and body language to impress; how to giftwrap the world itself as if in a pretty package for a lover, and how to carry the package where opportunity suggests. The "drammes of spirit" is interesting: does it just mean that he knows how to calibrate his courage and ardor to the advantage of friends and the discomfiture of enemies? Or has it, as some think, a more down-to-earth meaning: that he knows how to hold his liquor, how to drink diplomatically, never so much as to start blabbing secrets that might betray his friends or himself? Twice in Parliament, it seems he could handle himself amid maneuvering.

The third stanza—third as the climax of the best that earth could offer?—admits he knows about earthly love, its delight, its impulsiveness and intrigue ("hot blood and brains"), its reveling, its centuries-old history since the amorous writings of such ever-young ancients as Anacreon, Ovid, and Catullus. He himself wrote poems, including Anacreontics and Ovid's elegiac couplets, in Greek and Latin. Modern readers would catch his first allusion to love in terms of music; his "sweet strains" would recall the lovesick Duke in *Twelfth Night*, with his "That strain again! It had a dying fall." But we might not know that "lullings" had not only its modern meaning but that of "soothing music": Trevisa in the fourteenth century had written about how nurses "singe lullynges and other cradel songis." "Relishes," besides its zesty modern meaning, meant melodic embellishments or ornamentation. If we think we know what "propositions" meant to him, we are probably half right, but meant also the statement of a theme to be developed musically, as in a fugue. He knew, too, the world of the very wealthy, and how a bottomless purse ("unbridled store") could help lovers indulge their wildest fantasies. "My stuffe is flesh," he bluntly confesses, his one rational soul outnumbered by his five physical senses, which "grumble" at being curbed.

The last stanza sums up what he knows, has experienced, and could possess. His eyes are not sewn shut, like those of a young hawk in training. (The variant spelling "seeled," a technical term in falconry, occurs in one early manuscript.) He knew precisely what he was selling, precisely what he would get for it ("the commodities"). He uses "Yet" in a different sense at the start of his last sentence than he did three times before in the refrain. Knowing the world and choosing to trade it for a better one is not enough; he needs divine help, needs a cord of twisted silk dropped from heaven to conduct him "through these labyrinths" and then be his means of climbing to heaven. Is the metaphor somewhat mixed here, with the "silk twist" serving both as a guide (like the thread Ariadne gave Theseus to get him out of the minotaur's labyrinth) and then as a rope strong enough to climb? An Old Testament source has been proposed, the "scarlet thread" of Joshua 2:18. But Herbert's use of "labyrinth" suggests that in this instance he is Christianizing the pagan mythology he used more freely in his Greek and Latin poems.

What kind of poetry could we expect a teacher of rhetoric at Cambridge to write in the age of Donne and the metaphysicals, especially one who had composed, in the original meters, poetry in Greek and Latin? Whatever we might expect, it is far from what we find in "The Pearl," in which the language is as plain and down-to-earth as it has ever been in poetry in English. One of our "peasant poets" could hardly have been less literary. It is as if Herbert had deliberately given up more flowery possibilities, as if he were saying, as in his "The Forerunners":

> Farewell sweet phrases, lovely metaphors . . .
> Lovely enchanting language, sugar-cane,
> Hony of roses . . .

We might notice first how monosyllabic the language is, in key phrases like "My stuffe is flesh, not brasse," and in lines like:

> I know all these, and have them in my hand
> . . . .
> And at what rate and price I have thy love.

In the climactic last three lines of the poem, only one of the twenty-three words is longer than a monosyllable, and that is the ordinary word "conduct." ("Heav'n" was a monosyllable in Herbert's time.) These lines are all the starker in contrast with the lavish line preceding them, "Yet through these labyrinths, not my groveling wit," in which the diction is unusual, but functionally so: the two polysyllables and the two ampler anapests—instead of the usual iambs of the pentameter—help to mime the groveling through labyrinths. That Greek derivative is the most exotic word in the poem. "Groveling" would have had more graphic connotations than it has today; "groof" was an old word for "face," so that "groveling" is almost "face in the dirt." Exceptional words for an exceptional effect; generally when Herbert uses longer words they are ordinary ones, like the "discoveries," "expressions," and "circumstances" of this poem.

Not only are his words common, but they seem deliberately demotic, avoiding the traditionally "poetic" or "devotional." We do not find even an expression like "divine grace" at the end of the poem, where it might be expected. His manner of speech prefers terms like "stock and surplus," "rate and price," "main sale and the commodities." This no-nonsense, straight-from-the-shoulder tone is that of a man of practical affairs. Loving God is good business procedure, or, as Pascal thought, odds well worth betting on.

Everywhere the language is terse and spare. There are few adjectives, which are often a sign of "fat" writing, and what ones we do find are necessary to the sense: "willing nature," "hot bloud." However carefully we go through the poem, we find few words, if any, that could be omitted without detriment to the sense. Herbert probably came closest to indulgence, almost carried away by thoughts of love and music, when he added *sweet*, that most conventional of adjectives, to "strains." But only a reader more rigidly Puritanical than Herbert (who was not sympathetic to Calvinist excess) might wish it deleted. Even in talking about love he prefers to have his independent nouns unchaperoned (as Pound put it) by adjectives: "lullings," "relishes," "propositions," "mirth," "music," "love," "wit."

Made out of stuff so wiry, it is not surprising that his sentences are the disciplined and athletic performers that they are. "Now we go a-sentencing," Frost would say of poetry. This forty-line poem has four stanzas, its four sentences neatly measured one to a stanza, like the work of a graceful skater doing her compulsories. In the ten-line twirls and leaps of each stanza, he meets in every line the requirements of a rhyme, and every time he "nails" it without wavering. Check the rhymes and see if any other word could be more natural! An interesting rhyming word is "wit," used in one sense in stanzas two and three, in a very different sense in the last stanza.

Herbert rarely dazzles us, as Donne and Crashaw often do. The regular architecture of his stanzas reminds us less of fanciful Gothic or Baroque than of the sturdy Norman Romanesque of his warrior ancestors. "Is all good structure in a winding stair?" he asks, in "Jordan (I)," a poem that objects to ornately artificial stanzas. His preference is for those that "plainly say" what they mean. "The Pearl" seems to me one of his best and most enduring examples of plain saying.

The Pearl. Matth. 13. 45.

I know the wayes of Learning; both the head
And pipes that feed the presse, and make it runne;
What reason hath from nature borrowèd,
Or of it self, like a good huswife, spunne
In laws and policie; what the starres conspire,
What willing nature speaks, what forc'd by fire;
Both th' old discoveries, and the new-found seas,
The stock and surplus, cause and historie:
All these stand open, or I have the keyes:
          Yet I love thee.

I know the wayes of Honour, what maintains
The quick returns of courtesie and wit:
In vies of favours whether partie gains,
When glorie swells the heart, and moldeth it
To all expressions both of hand and eye,
Which on the world a true-love-knot may tie,
And bear the bundle, wheresoe're it goes:
How many drammes of spirit there must be
To sell my life unto my friends or foes:
          Yet I love thee.

I know the wayes of Pleasure, the sweet strains,
The lullings and the relishes of it;
The propositions of hot bloud and brains;
What mirth and musick mean; what love and wit
Have done these twentie hundred yeares, and more:
I know the projects of unbridled store:
My stuffe is flesh, not brasse; my senses live,
And grumble oft, that they have more in me
Then he that curbs them, being but one to five:
          Yet I love thee.

I know all these, and have them in my hand:
Therefore not sealèd, but with open eyes
I flie to thee, and fully understand
Both the main sale, and the commodities;
And at what rate and price I have thy love;
With all the circumstances that may move:

Yet through these labyrinths, not my groveling wit,
But thy silk twist let down from heav'n to me,
Did both conduct and teach me, how by it
　　　　　To climbe to thee.
　　　　　　　　　　　　　　George Herbert

Edna St. Vincent Millay:
Heroes She Begot

The Edna St. Vincent Millay poem that first moved me as a fifteen-year-old high-school student was "Renascence," a poem she composed at the age of only nineteen. Submitted to *The Lyric Year*'s poetry contest under the name "Mr. E. Vincent Millay," it won the judges' attention but not the prize, and prompted the prizewinner himself, Orrick Johns, to declare his "an unmerited award" (Norman A. Brittin, *Edna St. Vincent Millay*).

In that same high-school English class in New York City, my teacher Mr. Rogoff also had us read some Millay sonnets that I avidly committed to memory. Love that was not all, lips my lips had kissed, and rain full of ghosts were images that accompanied me through and well past my adolescent loves. For decades since, Millay has remained interned in those same anthologies where I first encountered her. While enjoying a wide popular audience, Millay became the target for "critical" volleys such as John Crowe Ransom's:

She is an artist. She is also a woman. No poet ever registered herself more deliberately in that light. She therefore fascinates the male reviewer but at the same time horrifies him a little too. He will probably swing between attachment and antipathy, which may be the very attitudes provoked in him by generic woman in the flesh. . . . Miss Millay is rarely and barely very intellectual, and I think everybody knows it.   "The Poet as Woman," *The World's Body*

This tone toward Millay is echoed by Louis Untermeyer in his introduction to her poems in my college textbook: "She is not a thinker, though she tries hard to be one; she is intuitive, not intellectual." At the close of his commentary, Untermeyer concedes that Millay "has not yet received final appraisal. . . . Critics of the future will be quick to discern the exaggeration, unevenness, and variety of Miss Millay's gifts; they will not fail to find, beyond the literary aptitude, the notes of authority" (*Modern American and British Poetry*, 458–59). *Aptitude?* Weren't those the tests we took in the same high schools and colleges to determine which careers to pursue? Consider that this language described a Pulitzer Prize–winning poet of the day.

In a provocative reassessment of Millay's poetry ("The Unwarranted Discourse: Sentimental Community, Modernist Women, and the Case of Millay"), Suzanne Clark examined Ransom's remark in terms of the Modernist horror of the sentimental, incorporating the historicity of the term that links it to a literary type dominated by women. Clark also quotes Bogan on Millay: "It is a dangerous lot, that of the charming, romantic public poet, especially if it falls to a woman." The more clearly and successfully women poets appealed to shared feelings of a popular community (other women), the less seriously they were taken as writers—by male, as well as some female, critics. I find that criticism reexamining Millay now begins to articulate and explore more fully the achievements of her work and its sometimes uneasy place in the canon.

Having sniffed around the edges of literary and cultural context, I come to Sonnet cxxvi (from *Huntsman, What Quarry?*, 1939) with a renewed admiration for Millay's poetry. The *Collected Poems* evince a range and variety far more complex than the beloved poems of my youth would have suggested, though even if there had been no others those still conferred substantial gifts. I see now in her work expressions, too, of the political passions of her life; her biography details the singularity of her connection to the world in life as in art. I also see enacted in Millay some of the perennial struggles and challenges of the female artist—to me a most compelling quest.

In the sonnet "Thou famished grave, I will not fill thee yet" I find some characteristic Millay maneuvers and tones as well as some points of departure. First and most significant perhaps from a woman poet chastised by critics for being too much a woman in her art, in this poem we hear at once the archaic, elevated, and intimate address of *Thou*, establishing an immediate connection with particular literary conventions associated with male deployers of the sonnet in English, most notably Shakespeare. The first line of this nonetheless Petrarchan sonnet personifies the "famished grave" as an adversary against whom the speaker immediately assumes a challenger's stance: "I will not fill thee yet." The tone of defiance is as characteristic in Millay's poems as the lyrical one to which it often provides a countervailing tension. If the opponent to the vital speaker, the grave, is personified in the opening line, it becomes more beast in the next two lines with *Roar* and *Gnaw*. But fierce as this hungry grave may be, the intrepid speaker balances against its power his own happiness and fearlessness (ll. 2–3), his determination to live, to not feed the grave (ll. 4–5). My use of the male pronoun is deliberate: until line 5, "I have heroes to beget," we have no gender identification for the speaker. We now know that Millay has assumed a male persona as well as the archaic pronouns of a Shakespearean sonnet—a strategic move for the poet who in life was called Vincent by her mother and sisters, and who lived intensely as a female in part by claiming the unfettered sexuality typically reserved for males. One reason this *I* of the sonnet is set on living is that he wants to father not just children, but *heroes*. I take these heroes to be poems, in life the ones that Millay did both beget and deliver. And in the process of defying his adversary, the speaker develops his own roar: from the neatly halved and end-stopped first three lines with their seesawing opponents separated by caesuras, to the enjambments and accelerations of lines 3–6, halted again at the end of line 7 with a semicolon, and reaching a first full stop at the close of the octave with the pithy line that could almost form a motto stitched across a jouster's banner—or a sampler. Aiming "not to be eat" (pronounced *et*, as the rhyme and Renaissance convention would require) linguistically asserts the speaker's power to act, not be acted upon. The words *be . . . not to be* recall inescapably Shakespeare's Hamlet, with the ironic difference that this speaker has no doubts about the merits of one state versus the other, resisting the grave rather than contemplating a choice to occupy it.

True to the volta of the Petrarchan sonnet form, in line 9, the opening of the sestet, the poem takes both tonal and rhetorical turns as the speaker acknowledges his limitations. Though he's just declared that he will not be "eat" by the grave until he's old and has completed his own projects, now he concedes "I cannot starve thee out: I am thy prey / And thou shalt have me." Any apparent capitulation is provisional, however, intensifying an ultimate, exquisite defiance. The struggle assumes a dimension of argument with the self as the *I* dominates these lines. Now the speaker is the "prey"—suggesting animal, too, like the roaring, gnawing grave. "And thou shalt have me" plays on the sexual connotation of *have* and echoes Shakespeare's "little death." Millay works a crucial interplay between "starve" and "stave," the one impossible, the other not. The word *stave* demands closer examination: both a violent gesture—to break a hole in, to smash or crush inward—and, more importantly, a set of verses. Millay's (speaker's) weapons against the grave are poems, just as the heroes/poems the speaker has to beget will constitute her/his posterity.

In the sestet of the sonnet, the speaker who has dared to oppose the grave from line 1 invokes the word *dare* twice, not only to reinforce his stance but to assert inherent self-knowledge, with the felicity of form that *stave* and *say* occur in the same line. Now as the poem winds up for

its final burst of daring, I linger on the words *defend, force,* and *spend.*
Defend in line 10 denotes first "to contest," as a claim; from the very
act of contesting derives the second meaning here, "protect." The para-
dox is that one achieves power by spending it. The speaker wins the
struggle with mortality by living till he or she is, triumphantly, "but
bones and jewels"—all flesh having been spent in the service of life. To
me the dazzling image directly introduces a woman first: female bones
adorned with jewels. Then I hear Shakespeare's Ariel singing "Those
are pearls that were his eyes," the figure resurfacing much later in Eliot.
But Millay's speaker is worlds from both the drowned father and the
arid twentieth century. The final line of her sonnet recapitulates the
challenge of the opening, with additional irony in the word *leave* ap-
plied to the hungry grave. The speaker must leave life on that day in the
imagined future, but having lived so fully, she won't be hungry when
she does. Thus her triumph is permanent: never will the speaker fill the
grave's hunger.

In looking over the language of the sonnet, I am struck by the number
of words referring to time and distance, suitable for a poem challenging
mortality. *Yet, here, fast on* (indicating continuing time), *before, anear,
year, till, out, off, on that day,* and *in the end* are examples; the alter-
nations of present and future tense throughout the poem also signal
its central preoccupations. But mortality isn't all that Millay challenges
here, as she declared at the outset through her choices of form and per-
sona. Finally, Millay appropriates the male role as both biological and
poetic initiator of creation in order to stake her claims as a poet, and the
sonnet form thoroughly suits the argument and emotions of this poem.
A form that consumes itself in its own service, containing no extrane-
ous elements, the sonnet reinforces the exhaustiveness that the poem
advocates. Millay presses the form harder when she uses not the seven
rhymes demanded by the Shakespearean sonnet, nor the possible five
rhymes of the Petrarchan, but a mere four—two in the octave, two in
the sestet—which the poem consumes entirely.

Another Millay poem that relates directly to the sonnet "Thou fam-
ished grave" in terms of its attitude toward the flesh is "The Fitting" (also
from *Huntsman, What Quarry?*). The woman being fitted for dresses
says "Tant mieux"—so much the better—when the dressmaker com-
ments on her weight loss. Alongside the sonnet, in which weight is
spent, not lost, this woman's feelings and situation read as ominous, for
she contains and denies the flesh, rather than using it to be "happy here."

I also like reading this sonnet by Millay beside a poem such as "Con-
scientious Objector" (from *Wine from These Grapes,* 1934) which is ani-
mated by the same defiant tone and rejection of death, but seen in terms
of a specific historical context of warfare and betrayal in the Balkans, in

Cuba. (A reference to not telling death "the whereabouts of my friends nor of my enemies either" at the end of the poem propels me ahead to the '50s and America's hunt for subversives, led by Senator Joseph McCarthy.) This poem, along with "Justice Denied in Massachusetts" and the last sonnets from *Mine the Harvest* register Millay's political activism: antiwar, "Come home, victorious wounded!" (Sonnet clxix), retrospective and questioning man's place on earth, "Read history: so learn your place in time" (Sonnet clxx) and "Read history: thus learn how small a space" (Sonnet clxxi). This last poem resonates especially with contemporary ecological concerns. Together these poems represent an essential aspect of Millay's life and work, one which my high-school text overlooked.

Journeying again to the Millay I knew and meeting other Millays has only made me want to go back and back to the poems—the voice that promises to consume itself with living, and the voice that calls me to "Look what I have!—And these are all for you."

Renascence

Thou famished grave, I will not fill thee yet,
Roar though thou dost, I am too happy here;
Gnaw thine own sides, fast on; I have no fear
Of thy dark project, but my heart is set
On living—I have heroes to beget
Before I die; I will not come anear
Thy dismal jaws for many a splendid year;
Till I be old, I aim not to be eat.
I cannot starve thee out: I am thy prey
And thou shalt have me; but I dare defend
That I can stave thee off; and I dare say,
What with the life I lead, the force I spend,
I'll be but bones and jewels on that day,
And leave thee hungry even in the end.

                                  Edna St. Vincent Millay

ROBERT PACK

Origins and Endings in Hardy's "Channel Firing"

In his essay "Thoughts for the Times on War and Death," written at the beginning of World War I when Thomas Hardy wrote "Channel Firing," Sigmund Freud states:

> The warring state permits itself every such misdeed, every such act of violence, as would disgrace the individual man. . . . It tramples in blind fury on all that comes into its way, as though there were to be no future and no goodwill among men after it passed.

How can a poet deal with a theme as monstrous as war without being dwarfed by it? Adjectives such as "bloody" or "cruel" seem trivial and inadequate in the face of national aggression, and the problem of writing truthful poetry is further complicated by the fact that war vastly increases mendacity. As Freud says, "The warring state . . . practices not only the accepted stratagems, but also deliberate lying and deception." Thus Hardy attempts to deal with his awesome theme elliptically, either through the shock of radical understatement, as when one character exclaims, "How quaint and curious war is," or through satire and irony on a scale unequaled by any other modern poet.

In Hardy's "Channel Firing," the speaker, who has been awakened by the noise of "great guns," is a skeleton lying in a cemetery beside a church. The word *great* is immediately unsettling since it is unclear whether it suggests some kind of unacknowledged approval of the machinery of war. The skeleton first thinks that "Judgment-day" has arrived, and he sits "upright" in his coffin to converse with his fellow skeletons. Meanwhile, inside the church, the "mouse let[s] fall the altar-crumb," as if interrupted in the act of communion. The image of the worms drawing back, either in shock or disapproval, and the flat phrase, "The glebe cow drooled," evoking extreme stupidity, indicate that Hardy wishes to establish an atmosphere of farce and a tone of blasphemy.

To assuage the skeletons' fears, God tells them that it is only "gunnery practice out at sea," not Judgment Day, and that the conditions of the world have not changed: as usual, men are preparing for war. This situation is grounded in Hardy's sense of the absurd, and the irony of God's supposedly consoling assurance extends this dark humor into theological comedy. Hardy offers his readers a parody of divine grace when God includes the gunners in his ironic consolation by saying that it would be a "blessed thing" to be merely dead, for if the gunners were resurrected on Judgment Day, surely they would be given the demeaning punishment of having to "scour / Hell's floor." God's diabolical "Ha, ha" underscores the joke He has made at the expense of both the gunners and the befuddled skeletons.

This malicious laugh may be read as the iconoclastic Hardy's parody of God's apparent indifference to human suffering. But since Hardy did not believe in God, the parodic figure in this poem must be read as Hardy's projection of human indifference onto God. God's laughter here is the ironic equivalent of its opposite—God's creative laughter, as seen in the Book of Job, when God projects His own spirit onto the image of the horse that He has made: "He saith among the trumpets, Ha, ha! and He smelleth the battle afar off." If we assume, moreover, that God's laughter in this poem denotes the absence of a biblical God, then Hardy's creation of a fictive God who does not exist can be seen as a projection of Hardy's own defeated longing for a protecting God, and also as protection against that longing. Because he cannot bring himself to believe in the traditional Hebrew or Christian God, and because he cannot find another belief to replace Christianity, Hardy can only defend himself through perversely defiant laughter that makes ironic the very God in whom he cannot believe but to whom he wishes he could pray.

God's sardonic "Ha, ha" is followed by His further taunting of the skeletons, suggesting capriciously that He may decide not to bring about the apocalypse and the day of resurrection: "It will be warmer when / I blow the trumpet (if indeed / I ever do; for you are men, / And rest eternal sorely need)." "Rest eternal" is not the consoling phrase it appears to be; rather, it means simply that the skeletons will have to continue being dead, though even their restfulness is questionable since we witness them sitting up in their coffins. The psychological effect of Hardy's humor, projected and twisted into God's laughter and joking, is to hold in check Hardy's despair as he confronts the human condition—warfare, mendacity, self-deception, and cosmic meaninglessness—as if there is no basis in human psychology, as Freud points out, for good will to emerge and redeem the fortunes of humankind.

The response of the skeletons to God's ironic jesting is chillingly bland as one wonders, "Will the world ever saner be?" and another, revealing the empty morality in his regrets about his career as a parson, replies, "I wish I had stuck to pipes and beer." No doubt he had been named Parson Thirdly to describe his hypocritical rhetorical style throughout his lifetime of sermonizing, just as Thucydides had pointed out in *History of the Pelopennesian War* that in a time of war "words, too, had to change their usual meanings." Freud also emphasized this point when he claimed that the debasement of language, "deliberate lying," was one of the paramount casualties brought by war. Such casualties to language and meaning are not unusual, Hardy suggests, evoking the implications of the word *indifferent*. The twentieth century is "indifferent" in the sense that people are indifferent to each other's suffering and in that it appears to be no different from the centuries that preceded it. Human nature, unhappily, remains the same.

The tone of the poem, however, changes dramatically in the last stanza: there is a radical transformation from comic parody and theological farce to something that might be described as mystical awe, in which the poem's angry and defiant laughter dissolves into allusion and impersonal wonder. The attentive reader realizes that the voice that speaks the poem's last stanza is not the original voice of the skeleton, but the voice of a distant consciousness that seems to have borne witness to human suffering and strife throughout history: "Again the guns disturbed the hour, / Roaring their readiness to avenge." The pattern of stressed alliteration in "again" and "guns" and in "Roaring" and "readiness" has a mesmerizing and oracular effect. Such disturbance, it seems, has always been the inclination, the "readiness," of human nature to act aggressively, and yet by this late date in human history the original source of human violence—some primal act that evoked the passion for revenge—has been forgotten or repressed. The speaker of this final stanza cannot name what needs to be avenged. Vengeance has ceased to be a response to a specific affront; it has become a condition of the human mind, a cause of further vengeance. In Thucydides's words, "Revenge was more important than self-preservation." If what has been repressed in our human origins could be recovered, this poem suggests, that recovery might bring about the abatement of violence.

The final two lines of the poem are even more mysterious as they plunge us back into mythic-historical time to evoke a sense of origins and perhaps also of destiny: "As far inland as Stourton Tower, / And Camelot, and starlit Stonehenge." The heavy alliteration of the "st" and "t" sounds sharpens the speaker's breath as it rushes from the teeth to become the blunt, highly stressed final phrases. The word, "inland" (like Wordsworth's "though inland far we be"), suggests that early civilization has come from the sea where life first emerged and that some originating force continues to drive its course. Stourton Tower refers to Alfred the Great, who fought the Vikings and unified England in the ninth century, while Camelot evokes the myth of order and chivalry associated with King Arthur. Stonehenge is a 350-foot-wide circle that was built about four thousand years ago on England's Salisbury Plain, no one knows how, as an astronomical calendar that perhaps enabled the ancient priests to make human sacrifices or calculate eclipses and other heavenly events. One cannot say with certainty what Hardy intends to imply with these images and references to the deep past, but surely they evoke a sense of wonder and a sense that the human future may have been contained in our very origins.

What might these priests have witnessed in the configurations of the stars in "starlit Stonehenge"? Might they have seen disaster—the inevitability of human destructiveness—or might they have seen the possibility of human order and civilization? Likewise, does Camelot suggest the potential for an ordered and graceful society, a society of what Freud calls "goodwill among men," or the inevitable collapse of attempts for order and grace, since war and blind vengeance, as Thucydides asserts, seem to usurp even the wish for self-preservation? Does Stourton Tower offer a model in King Alfred, an early champion of Christianity, of social cohesion and purpose, or does it reveal the inevitability of lying and contending forces? Are these images of hope or are they images of despair? Hardy raises these questions only to leave them deliberately unresolved, to shock the reader into speculating about the inevitability of war—human nature being what it is—and pondering the enigma of human origins and endings. The final form that Hardy's laughter takes is openness of thought in the face of our worst fears; his laughter expresses a detachment so profound that it becomes its own kind of passion, as if one could say "Ha, ha" even to a universe in which God is only a fiction to whom no appeal for peace or what elsewhere Hardy calls "The Spirit of Pity" can be made. This is a poem that is dreadful to contemplate and equally dreadful to avoid.

Channel Firing

That night your great guns, unawares,
Shook all our coffins as we lay,
And broke the chancel window-squares,
We thought it was the Judgment-day

And sat upright. While drearisome
Arose the howl of wakened hounds:

The mouse let fall the altar-crumb,
The worms drew back into the mounds,

The glebe cow drooled. Till God called, 'No;
It's gunnery practice out at sea
Just as before you went below;
The world is as it used to be:

'All nations striving strong to make
Red war yet redder. Mad as hatters
They do no more for Christés sake
Than you who are helpless in such matters.

'That this is not the judgment-hour
For some of them's a blessed thing,
For if it were they'd have to scour
Hell's floor for so much threatening. . . .

'Ha, ha. It will be warmer when
I blow the trumpet (if indeed
I ever do; for you are men,
And rest eternal sorely need).'

So down we lay again. 'I wonder,
Will the world ever saner be,'
Said one, 'than when He sent us under
In our indifferent century!'

And many a skeleton shook his head.
'Instead of preaching forty year,'
My neighbour Parson Thirdly said,
'I wish I had stuck to pipes and beer.'

Again the guns disturbed the hour,
Roaring their readiness to avenge,
As far inland as Stourton Tower,
And Camelot, and starlit Stonehenge.

Thomas Hardy

JAY PARINI

On Browning's "Love in a Life"

More so than Tennyson, his great contemporary, Robert Browning has always struck me as the first of the genuinely modern poets. Ezra Pound, of course, noted this, and paid homage to Browning in several poems and essays. What is "modern" about Browning, I think, is his almost shocking refusal to write in a manner that his readers would have recognized as "poetic." He refused to succumb to the self-consciously elevated, even inflated, rhetoric of most Victorian poets. By contrast, his poetry adheres steadfastly to the rhythms of ordinary speech. It is dramatic, too—a language that addresses a specific human situation, even what may be called a predicament. It looks forward to the rough-hewn monologues and dramatic lyrics of Hardy, to the mad chatter of Pound in the *Cantos*, to the situational rhetoric of Eliot's "Love Song of J. Alfred Prufock." In so many ways, Browning is our contemporary.

A poem such as "Love in a Life" might have been written yesterday. It has always been, for me, a marker of sorts, a poem that poets must read and absorb to understand fully what Thomas Campion meant when he defined poetry as "a system of linked sounds." "Room after room, / I hunt the house through / We inhabit together," the poem begins. Although it does conform to a makeshift rhythmical pattern and, in an offhand way, rhyme, the verse seems extraordinarily free. Browning does not write to the tick of the metronome; instead, he lets the speech of his lyric narrator unfold, as normal speech does; the rhythms we hear are those of ordinary conversation, ever so slightly heightened. Rhythm becomes pulse, recurrence; rhyme becomes echo.

The plot of the poem is straightforward: the poet-narrator is searching for his beloved, looking for her throughout the house. The house is, as it must be, literal; indeed, the poem is full of domestic imagery: curtains, couches, a cornice-wreath, a looking glass. The house is substantial, with wings extending from a center. But the literal house gives way, invisibly, to the emblem of a house, the house of memory. Freud once suggested that whenever one dreams of a house one is dreaming of one's own soul. Browning's lover in this poem may be searching his own soul, hoping to find his lover there. He ransacks his memory, trying perhaps to raise from the dead the ghost of one who can save him.

In the first stanza, Browning maintains (and very nearly satirizes) a typical Victorian attitude of optimism: "Heart, fear nothing, for, heart, thou shalt find her." But he will not find her, we fear. The rooms of this apparently vast house reek of her absence; she has brushed through these well-appointed quarters and left nothing but traces, such as the scent of perfume that still clings to the couch where she presumably once sat. The looking glass, that perfect and obsessive late-nineteenth-century symbol for the thin membrane that separates life from death, reality from the imagination, wake from sleeping, is conjured with a certain melancholy: "Yon looking-glass gleamed at the wave of her feather." It does no more.

The second, final stanza is almost Kafkaesque—another aspect of its modernity. The narrator wanders the endless rooms of his life, of his soul, of his memory, and grows wearier with each step that does not bring him closer to his beloved as "door succeeds door." This house rapidly becomes a nightmarish dwelling, with too many rooms and corridors; the speaker pushes doors open that lead to rooms with more doors. The house becomes a maze as the speaker is forced to "range the wide house from the wing to the centre." *Where is she?* he wonders. Chance does not seem to be helping him at all, for as he enters one room, she seems to leave it: "she goes out as I enter."

He suggests, enigmatically, toward the end of the poem, that he would happily spend the whole day looking for her, but "'tis twilight." This may suggest that the life of this couple is close to the end; perhaps the woman is already dead, and the poet-narrator is at the end of his own life as well. On the most literal level, a man is searching at sundown for a woman whom he loves, and he is growing panicky because there seem to be "such suites to explore, / Such closets to search, such alcoves to importune!" His hope of finding her recedes as the poem ends rather abruptly. Browning will not offer us a soft option, an easy way out. The poem refuses to conclude.

Browning called his poem "Love in a Life" with a strange bravura. It might well have been called "Lost in a Life" or "Where Is Love in a Life?" The title takes on a melancholy twang in the context of the poem itself, lingering as we read, adding to our anxiety as we become, during the course of the reading, the speaker. If there is love in a life, it is always just beyond the door. One pushes into a room, and it is empty; one's love seems always to have slipped, once again, into the next room, where she lingers only long enough to tempt us toward her again. When she hears us coming, she absconds to the next room. One is lured through rooms that are like Chinese boxes, opening into themselves. Hopeful signs are everywhere: traces, like marks on a page, odors that draw us forward. But we never arrive at the point we desperately seek. The poem is cruel in its way, and subtly ironic. It is true and deep in the way of all real poems.

Love in a Life

Room after room,
I hunt the house through
We inhabit together.
Heart, fear nothing, for, heart, thou shalt find her—
Next time, herself!—not the trouble behind her
Left in the curtain, the couch's perfume!
As she brushed it, the cornice-wreath blossomed anew:
Yon looking-glass gleamed at the wave of her feather.

Yet the day wears,
And door succeeds door;
I try the fresh fortune—
Range the wide house from the wing to the centre.
Still the same chance! she goes out as I enter.
Spend my whole day in the quest,—who cares?
But 'tis twilight, you see,—with such suites to explore,
Such closets to search, such alcoves to importune!

Robert Browning

On "The World as Meditation" by Wallace Stevens

From the time in fourth grade when *The Odyssey* was narrated to us in weekly installments by a teacher who seemed to be making the story up as he went along, I have been half in love with Penelope. I say half in love because another part of me loved Ulysses and wanted to be the hero, not the heroine, the one to have adventures out in the world, not the one who remained at home, watching at a window or pacing a widow's walk. But coming of age as I did in the '50s, it seemed to me that as a woman of my times I was destined to be Penelope. I started writing poems in her voice early on and still do so, sometimes in frustration or anger, sometimes in true satisfaction, happy to wrap myself in my own weavings.

I have also looked for Penelope in the poems of other people, and it is not as ironic as it may seem that my favorite Penelope poem was written by a man. Wallace Stevens didn't venture much farther out into the world than I did, not much farther than the streets of Hartford, Connecticut, and the insurance-company offices where he worked for so many years. But in his poem "The World as Meditation," there is no need to travel in the sense that a Ulysses traveled, for it is the point of this poem, as of so many of his others, that real journeys take place in the imagination, particularly for the artist. As Enesco puts it in the stanza that serves as epigraph for this poem, too much time can be spent in voyaging. Meditation is the permanent and essential dream.

"The World as Meditation" grows out of two very specific passages in *The Odyssey*. Telemachus, speaking to Athena in book 1, says of his father: "that sun has long gone down." And in book 19 Penelope, also speaking of Ulysses, asks: "Or did I dream him?" The action of the poem takes off from these two places and is simple: Penelope waits, dreaming of Ulysses, and as the sun warms her pillow she thinks she sees him approaching in the distance—or is it simply the sun she is seeing? By his placement of two interrogatives, one at the very beginning of the poem and one near the end, Stevens involves the reader actively in this question. But in fact it hardly matters whether it is Ulysses or the sun, reality or a dream, that approaches, for in a typical Stevens paradox it is both and neither. This poem, then, is not only about the centrality of the imagination but about the imagination as an ongoing process, and thus it is a poem about process itself. It is about "constantly coming so near," not about arriving. For it is in her very quest for Ulysses that Penelope finds herself. ("She has composed so long a self with which to welcome him.") It is her own imagination, her own "savage" presence, that wakens the sun. And the word *savage* here prepares us for the word *barbarous* in line 21, which is also an adjective modifying the imagination, whose strength is primal and not to be domesticated.

For me this poem has many other pleasures, large and small. The cadences remind me of the cadences of the Odyssey itself, particularly as translated by Fitzgerald, though the muscularity of the vocabulary may be more reminiscent of the Lattimore version.

And there are the small sensual delights, particularly effective in such a cerebral poem: Penelope combing her hair and talking to herself; Ulysses' arms as her "necklace" and her "belt," how much closer to the skin can anything be? There is the repetition of the word *beating* in "The thought kept beating in her like her heart. / The two kept beating together." What a frisson, as of wings, the sound of that repetition evokes. Even the way the syllables of Ulysses' name are described as "patient," an adjective usually linked to the name of Penelope, reinforces the physical bond between them.

There are also the details that create a palpable landscape for us, the "mended" trees, for instance; the metaphoric and real winter that has been "washed away"; the winds (or their absence) "like dogs."

And, despite the seriousness of the subject, there is a kind of sly humor to be enjoyed, as when Ulysses is called the "interminable" adventurer. What wife has read the Odyssey without secretly wanting to shake Ulysses, to send him directly home, with no more loitering allowed on Circe's island or anywhere else.

There is even, as so often in Stevens, a touch of the idiosyncratic, represented for me here by that unexpected word "cretonnes"—an unglazed cotton, printed on both sides and produced in Normandy, France —a kind of sublime linen.

So, garbed in anachronistic cretonnes and in a trance of language, Penelope sits dreaming. She is not only an instrument of her own imagination but of Stevens's and ultimately, of course, of ours.

ROBERT PINSKY

Donne's "A Valediction:
Forbidding Mourning"

"It's just a flesh wound," says Sid Caesar to his comrades, with the arrow going through his chest and protruding six inches from his back—a valiant contradiction.

And if it were a real arrow instead of a trick prop, a real war, real pain, real death? We would recognize the same joke then, too: it would be a gallant piece of kidding somewhere between heroism and terminal foolishness—a convention of its own, as when the heroes of adventure movies joke about their wounds, even mortal ones. Implausibly, against our better judgment but aligned with our childish desires, those graceful sufferers reassure their comrades and us that all calamities can be endured with all our humanity intact. History and experience tell us otherwise, but we love to be kidded by this kidding.

John Donne is kidding. His poem stirs echoes in the hallways of suffering lovers—haunting archival echoes of the exaggerated tear floods of Petrarch and the courtiers of Provencal, the hyperbolic sigh tempests of Shakespeare, Sidney, and Greville—just as the flesh-wound gag awakens the conventions of suffering warriors. If, as Izaak Walton says, "Valediction: Forbidding Mourning" was written for Donne's wife on the occasion of the poet's leaving for France, the poem was a brilliant gift, a bright garland of counterentwined jokes and anxieties, comedy and endearment.

The preposterously farfetched opening simile of the dying man, for example, makes a formidable comic scene: the comparison, funny in itself, culminates a death joke, the masterful timing of that blunt, one-syllable word that closes the stanza: "Whilst some of their sad friends do say / The breath goes now, and some say, No." This quite funny moment has both a surface barb and a buried one. On the surface, any death joke has to be a reminder that journeys are risky; just under the surface is a still crueler little hook: if the parting of body and soul is like the parting of the couple, then which is like the soul, man or wife? And which is like the body?

The poem, written to cheer up the loved partner, with its parody of the traditionally hyperbolic tears and sighs of love poetry, touches awkward doubts and queries in its gentle, kidding way. Protesting that the couple's bonds are so spiritual that they are barely made of matter at all, the poem pauses to catalogue the flesh in detail—more monosyllables, short words with a bodily force that deflates the pretty, polysyllabic blimps of "profanation" and "trepidation" and "sublunary" and "Interassurèd of the mind" by reminding the lovers of what they will surely miss: "eyes, lips, and hands."

It is pretty to think of love expanding with distance, like gold hammered into finer and finer leaf, but there is an undertow of fear in the image, too, the fragility and unlikeliness of that all-but-matterless, unsupported expanse of brightness. Both "airy" and "beat" emphasize the nervous comedy of that glittery trope.

In the airport, at curbside or dockside, at the door or gate, at all departures, people characteristically joke and worry. That there is something to worry about and that there is something funny are the dual opposed propositions of valediction. The last, departure-lounge embrace is sexual, but also more than sexual in its meaning and less than sexual in its formality; Donne's amusing, poignant poem catches this quality with amazing precision, the words miming the dance of laughter and fear.

The fear, too, is sexual: to name concerns about "firmness" and just circles is to confess anxieties about unfaithfulness. There is something wrong—in the sense of a meaningful logical defect—in each of the poem's famous images and formulas, and this is most strikingly true of the stiff twin compasses. Why is it the female part that "grows erect"? Why raise the question of ending where one begins at the very last moment? The poem moves with the awkward grace of an improvised, heuristic joking, rooted in the need to amuse and to be reassured. He's only kidding when he says how sure they are of the spirit: the spirit feels the wound of separation in the flesh. The medicine of matchless wit can only soothe the wound, not heal it—the grief of separation is real. It hurts, it kindles fear. By registering that limit, too, Donne achieves a tender, glorious, delicate clowning that mocks even the limitations of clowning.

A Valediction: Forbidding Mourning

As virtuous men pass mildly away,
  And whisper to their souls to go,
Whilst some of their sad friends do say
  The breath goes now, and some say, No;

So let us melt, and make no noise,
  No tear-floods, nor sigh-tempests move,
'Twere profanation of our joys
  To tell the laity of our love.

Moving of th' earth brings harms and fears,
  Men reckon what it did and meant;
But trepidation of the spheres,
  Though greater far, is innocent.

Dull sublunary lovers' love
  (Whose soul is sense) cannot admit
Absence, because it doth remove
  Those things which elemented it.

But we by a love so much refined
  That our selves know not what it is,
Inter-assuréd of the mind,
  Care less, eyes, lips, and hands to miss.

Our two souls therefore, which are one,
  Though I must go, endure not yet
A breach, but an expansion,
  Like gold to airy thinness beat.

If they be two, they are two so
  As stiff twin compasses are two;
Thy soul, the fixed foot, makes no show
  To move, but doth, if th' other do.

And though it in the center sit,
  Yet when the other far doth roam,
It leans and hearkens after it,
  And grows erect, as that comes home.

Such wilt thou be to me, who must
   Like th' other foot, obliquely run;
Thy firmness makes my circle just,
   And makes me end where I begun.

Wordsworth's "Elegiac Stanzas"

Along with the sonnet and the ode, the elegy has traditionally been one of the essential emotional and formal occasions for a poem. In "Elegiac Stanzas, Suggested by a Picture of Peele Castle, in a Storm, Painted by Sir George Beaumont," William Wordsworth combines occasions and enlarges the ambition of his fraternal elegy into the philosophic scope of an ode. The emotional distance required to move from the immediacy of grief to the perspective of reflection is at the heart of his elegiac stanzas. And just as grief is recollected within the tranquility of the classic quatrain, the overall methodology of the poem—the logic of its development—acquires its meaning by indirection. Had Wordsworth tried to address the subject of his brother John's death relative to the time of the event he would have probably failed, and the fact that he did not try is the evidence. He needed space and the indirect object of the Beaumont painting in order to arrive at his point of departure, at the place of his subject, which for a poet committed to direct experience was somewhat difficult. The direct experience here is neither nature nor natural—not, at least, in any obvious way—but artificial, an artifice of nature. Even the inspiration is based on what is suggested.

Wordsworth's method, therefore, is almost completely roundabout, particularly as the source of his elegizing is never named nor addressed, and is deferred, as a reference, until the last third of the poem. If these stanzas were ultimately about his brother they might, in the strictest sense, constitute an elegy, but they are about a larger and more spiritual issue outside the circle of the family romance. These stanzas try to come to terms with a crisis of faith in which "A power is gone, which nothing can restore." Whether the passing power is funded in transcendence or transformation—nature or art—is to be decided in due course. In the year between the brother's death and the encounter with the storm in the painting more than a loved one, it seems, has been lost. (The painting, in what it suggests and states, is both the reminder of the past and, finally, the agency of change.) The potency of Wordsworth's crisis and his need for some kind of reconciliation account for why he takes his time getting to the point. The removals not only help to build and confirm the "new control" he has submitted to, they give him room to reconcile with the loss of the old, illusory control. Hence the late acknowledgment that "A deep distress hath humanised my Soul," an acknowledgment delayed—as if its truth were being discovered—until halfway through the poem.

On February 5, 1805, John Wordsworth drowned at sea in a shipwreck, just off the coast of England, on his way to China. As captain he went down with his ship in one of the worst disasters in British maritime history (232 souls lost). When the Wordsworths received the news they were inconsolable. "Grief will . . . and must, have its course," wrote Wordsworth to Robert Southey. His comments to his close friend George Beaumont show how deeply his grief ran for a brother who was "as noble a spirit as ever breathed":

my departed Brother . . . walked all his life pure among the impure. . . . In prudence, in meekness, in self-denial, in fortitude, in just desires, and elegant and refined enjoyments, with an entire simplicity of manners, life and habit, he was all that could be wished-for in a man.

In the year following John's death Wordsworth dealt with it in letters, using only the eulogizing language of his words to Beaumont. At the Royal Academy Exhibition in 1806, there was some concern that Beaumont's depiction of a ship threatened in an angry sea, especially of a setting—Peele Castle—that Wordsworth was personally familiar with, might be problematic. When Beaumont, at the exhibition's opening, tried to steer Wordsworth's attention away from the picture, the poet assured him that perhaps now was the time to look at disaster in perspective. Wordsworth must have taken a long look. The poem was published a year later.

"Elegiac Stanzas" actually renders three pictures of Peele Castle: the one Wordsworth remembers from a month-long visit nearby in 1794; the one he would have painted in the idealized light of the "Poet's dream"; and the one, of course, in the painting—an active picture of a lightning-split sky and broiling sea. The implication is that Beaumont has seen with eyes that Wordsworth himself can only now see with, having passed through grief. The structure of the poem more or less follows the plot of these three "visions," plus a little more. The argument, at least at the outset, seems simple enough. In remembering his summer weeks as a "neighbour" of the castle, which like many Celtic castles is set out strategically on a small, close-in island, Wordsworth calls to mind an image of serenity and purity. ("Thy Form was sleeping on a glassy sea. // So pure the sky, so quiet was the air!") The memory is so serene, in fact, that the impressionable Wordsworth hyperbolizes, rather like a Biblical author, and sees the water as a "mighty Deep . . . the gentlest of all gentle Things." This grand summer memory is enhanced by the poet's added vision: had he been the painter then of the hoary, rugged Pile before him now he would have "planted thee . . . Amid a world how different from this!" That different world comprises, in its lining out, description, and qualification, a full five stanzas, the longest stretch in the poem. Wordsworth is determined to abuse his own failed fantasy.

In the presence of Beaumont's dramatic sea-storm, he is determined to exploit the former "fond illusion of my heart." He pushes the gleaming distortions of light and "Elysian quiet" about as far as he can. He would have created, he tells us, an enchanted painting of an enchanting subject, "without toil or strife." Worse, he would have seen in his fanciful handiwork "the soul of truth in every part / A stedfast peace that might not be betrayed." This is a vision of insistence, and to a very large extent Wordsworth's purpose is to inflate the innocent vision in order to give greater gravity to his vision of Beaumont's vision of experience. It is as if Wordsworth were judging the basis of happiness, differentiating between innocent, attractive memory and true, autobiographic experience, while negotiating a way to resolve the results of the difference. This is another reason for the roundabout argument of his poem, since he must set himself up so that he can work out a rescue.

The rescue begins, in line 33, when, by his own admission, he has found a new power in lieu of the power that is gone. Yet it is almost no power at all, but rather a kind of humiliating self-knowledge. Beaumont's painting, with its passion and honesty and wisdom, is the vehicle of insight, a picture to confirm the process of an imagination coming to terms. Against the theatrical noise and chaos implicit in the seascape he is looking at, Wordsworth understands that "The feeling of my loss will ne'er be old," but he also knows that this understanding is possible only in a "mind serene." He places his new serenity against the anger of Beaumont's sea—a serenity of reality in the present tense, not a serenity of fantasy from nostalgia. In these long mediative seconds he realizes that "Not for a moment could I now . . . be what I have been." In recognizing the at once evolutionary and epiphanic change from dreamer to mourner to stoic, he recognizes that *serene* is now no longer what he wants to see but is instead the peace and acceptance of what he, after a year's passage, feels. It is a complete imaginative transfer and transformation. Leaving his vision of illusion, he can turn, at last, from addressing the painting to addressing the painter himself, with the further strategy of finally admitting his dead brother into the poem.

> Then, Beaumont, Friend! who would have been the Friend,
> If he had lived, of Him whom I deplore,
> This work of thine I blame not, but commend;
> This sea in anger, and that dismal shore.

Here, in a celebration of fortitude, it is a pleasure to watch Wordsworth anticipate attaching himself and absorbing the castle's stoical qualities as part of his new self-control. The castle becomes the model of "nobility of soul at odds with circumstance," to quote Theodore Roethke. It towers sublimely above "That Hulk which labours in the deadly swell," under "This rueful sky, this pageantry of fear!" He goes so far as to imply a kind of envy of the castle's cold strength, "Cased in the unfeeling armour of old time." (Such cold strength will be required of Wordsworth soon enough, as eventually three of his children pass away and his sister Dorothy suffers a breakdown.) The details of the virtues of the Pile and the castle against the angry assailant storm dominate this section of the poem, just as the earlier illusory visions of both memory and the would-be painting displace the entire first half. The personal source of Wordsworth's motive is masked in the false-serenity-cum-true-storm sequence of the poem's action. Wordsworth both needs to and can afford—at this distant juncture—to disguise his dead brother in a pronoun. He both needs and can afford to reduce his tragic role. John may be the figure lost to his family, but he is also a figure lost at sea in the enormity of the subject of the painting, caught among "The lightning, the fierce wind, and trampling waves." After a year of being grieved he has become a figure of emotional scale, in what is by now Wordsworth's vision of Beaumont's work.

The close of this magnificent poem extends as much as it solves. The circuitry of Wordsworth's meditative method has matched the way his mind has processed the experience of being confronted by a picture of what before could only be imagined, distorted, or dismissed. John died in a storm in the coldest month of the year, wrecked against the Shambles off Portland Bill. The actual tragedy must have, at the least, resembled the vivid suggestion of Beaumont's picture, a powerful and painful reminder, by a friend, of a ship at the edge of disaster. The final two stanzas—as Wordsworth says of the insight of the painting—are "well chosen" for "the spirit that is here." And it is in this spirit of acceptance and reconciliation that the mourner poet is able to "welcome fortitude, and patient cheer." But before he can accept he must reject something and bid farewell to the pale happiness of the poet's blind dream and to the hermetic isolation of the "heart that lives alone, / Housed" in such a dream. In addition, as is his habit from "Tintern Abbey" to *The Prelude*, he must say farewell to yet another hyped vision of tranquility and bliss ("tranquil land, beneath a sky of bliss"). Much of the logic of "Elegiac Stanzas" is framed to make a case for what nature is as opposed to what Wordsworth wished it to be. The land-mass of the sea is potentially the most deluding surface on the face of "natural things." Throughout Wordsworth's career nature has been stationed on a Westmoreland hillside or Cumberland lake—steady, cyclical places, with spots-in-time surprises. The surprises often become epiphanies, discoveries of memory and patience. Wordsworth, in fact, is the great waiter-outer in English literature. "Elegiac Stanzas" has tested that patience and found that in this profound instance—the death of his favorite brother at sea—the poet of photographic memory remembers his vision to be blurred. Perhaps it was the sun shining off the surface of that memory sea; perhaps it was his own deluding innocence at Rampside in 1794 that led him to believe that by painting with a light that never was, on sea or land, he could show "the soul of truth in every part." His brother's death opened his eyes as well as humanized his soul. So farewell to the pitifully blind happiness of experience without sufficient depth and weight of loss, and welcome to the lightning, fierce wind, and trampling wave.

In the company of his friend and within the community of his kind, Wordsworth can welcome what is strongest in himself, a granite stoicism. It is interesting how Wordsworth's stoicism—no matter how cold —depends on those close and near to him, whether it is Dorothy, Coleridge, or Beaumont, or the circle of friends who make up his correspondence. The event of these elegiac stanzas—a meditation in front a murderous sea—takes place at a public exhibition, among those for whom "Such sights, or worse, as are before me here" are probably no more than excitement and high drama—nothing personal. Yet Wordsworth is able to focus, with clarifying intensity and simultaneity, on the reality both in and of the picture. The social context this occurs in contributes to his ability to accept the terms of the painting against the terms of his feelings. Hence his negative emphasis on the heart that lives alone, at distance from its kind. Life goes on, moment by moment, in spite of the memory of loss. And life must be lived in the moment, amid other lives. The social theme of the necessity for the individual to find a way to return to the fold against the backdrop of the temptations of solitude and the risks of nature is a constant in Wordsworth—it underscores the growth of the mind in passage after passage in *The Prelude*. Here it becomes a central fact of his living experience: how to acknowledge what he has learned in the passage of a year; how to accept that the difference between the illusion of the picture he would have painted and the reality of the picture he is seeing through new eyes is the difficult grief he has passed through. It helps to have Beaumont, "who would have been the Friend, / If he had lived, of Him whom I deplore," and the painter of the real picture, at his side.

The uses of memory and the sources of art are issues Wordsworth was the first great poet to claim. The elegy, as such, cannot in this hard instance hold all that is on his mind and in his heart; as a formal occasion it is too direct and focused for the size of a loss that is more than the death of a brother but a loss of faith in the vision that makes meaning of memory. For the sake of the crucial memory of his brother he must conceal in order to reveal his subject, choose indirection over direction. He must circle a subject that transcends its underlying emotional source by transforming itself into an essay on art. In true art lies the hope for which we suffer and mourn; in true art lies the community of our experience; in true art lies the healing of the fragment and the broken piece. That Wordsworth is willing, at the close, to allow the pragmatism of his conversion to teach us a lesson is his faith that his method by indirection has worked. "Such sights . . . as are before me here" could only get worse if we were in fact witnessing or participating in the actual disaster, in which case we would make our report as survivors, living witnesses. Wordsworth's power in this poem is that he writes like a survivor, that his empathies have admitted him into the near-shipwreck in the Beaumont painting while his sympathies have kept him far enough away to create. It is a work of art that has forced him to remember what before he could at best, or worst, imagine. And in the course of his fifteen elegiac stanzas he has remembered a good deal and tested and answered with his art his fond illusions and grievous memory.

Elegiac Stanzas

Suggested by a Picture of Peele Castle, in a Storm, Painted by Sir George Beaumont

I was thy neighbour once, thou rugged Pile!
Four summer weeks I dwelt in sight of thee:
I saw thee every day; and all the while
Thy Form was sleeping on a glassy sea.

So pure the sky, so quiet was the air!
So like, so very like, was day to day!
Whene'er I looked, thy Image still was there;
It trembled, but it never passed away.

How perfect was the calm! it seemed no sleep;
No mood, which season takes away, or brings:
I could have fancied that the mighty Deep
Was even the gentlest of all gentle Things.

Ah! THEN, if mine had been the Painter's hand,
To express what then I saw; and add the gleam,
The light that never was, on sea or land,
The consecration, and the Poet's dream;

I would have planted thee, thou hoary Pile
Amid a world how different from this!
Beside a sea that could not cease to smile;
On tranquil land, beneath a sky of bliss.

Thou shouldst have seemed a treasure-house divine
Of peaceful years; a chronicle of heaven;—
Of all the sunbeams that did ever shine
The very sweetest had to thee been given.

A Picture had it been of lasting ease,
Elysian quiet, without toil or strife;
No motion but the moving tide, a breeze,
Or merely silent Nature's breathing life.

Such, in the fond illusion of my heart,
Such Picture would I at that time have made:
And seen the soul of truth in every part,
A stedfast peace that might not be betrayed.

So once it would have been,—'tis so no more;
I have submitted to a new control:
A power is gone, which nothing can restore;
A deep distress hath humanised my Soul.

Not for a moment could I now behold
A smiling sea, and be what I have been:

The feeling of my loss will ne'er be old;
This, which I know, I speak with mind serene.

Then, Beaumont, Friend! who would have been the Friend,
If he had lived, of Him whom I deplore,
This work of thine I blame not, but commend;
This sea in anger, and that dismal shore.

O 'tis a passionate Work!—yet wise and well,
Well chosen is the spirit that is here;
That Hulk which labours in the deadly swell,
This rueful sky, this pageantry of fear!

And this huge Castle, standing here sublime,
I love to see the look with which it braves,
Cased in the unfeeling armour of old time,
The lightning, the fierce wind, and trampling waves.

Farewell, farewell the heart that lives alone,
Housed in a dream, at distance from the Kind!
Such happiness, wherever it be known,
Is to be pitied; for 'tis surely blind.

But welcome fortitude, and patient cheer,
And frequent sights of what is to be borne!
Such sights, or worse, as are before me here.—
Not without hope we suffer and we mourn.

William Wordsworth

W. H. Auden: Limestone
and Granite

W. H. Auden's "In Praise of Limestone" unfolds a debate that Auden pursues through two controlling figures, limestone and granite. Limestone represents one understanding of the world and our place in it, and granite represents another. The first stone is organically based and malleable; the second is crystalline-based and by comparison obdurate. Auden's limestone-sense of the world is that it is responsive; his granite understanding is that the world is nonanthropomorphic and intractable. Auden's approach to his subject is to achieve didactic ends by thinking figuratively. His complex debate is carried out in terms of simple objects. Positions are presented in terms of vegetation, streams, fields, and, encircling all of these, two kinds of "landscape," limestone and granite.

The idea of landscape is a human invention, of course, as is the pastoral tradition behind Auden's poem. In the poem there are two pastoral extremes, but only limestone lends itself to human concerns. Chief among these are free will and right choice, great subjects for a poet-didact such as Auden. At its conclusion, the poem addresses someone—Auden begins his final sentence with, "Dear, I know nothing of / Either." That, along with the poem's conversational tone created by its long leisurely lines, concludes Auden's didactic stroll through his subject.

Auden's limestone and granite are figures for creation and accident. The poem offers no promises for either, but at the conclusion it opts for a "limestone landscape." The scape Auden chooses is an area where we can act, rather than "the granite wastes" where we cannot. Because life is denied by "wastes," despair is the logical response to them. They teach a lack of faith in any tie or relationship.

In the recorded reading of "In Praise of Limestone," Auden stumbles at one point. Toward the end of the poem, he almost says, "faithless," rather than "faultless." Having debated the possibilities of redemption and an afterlife, the poem reads, "Dear, I know nothing of / Either, but when I try to imagine a faultless love / Or the life to come, what I hear is the murmur / Of underground streams, what I see is a limestone landscape." This slip carries the telling implication that there is a correlation between faith and fault and that limestone somehow accommodates both. In Auden's mind, this correlation is figured by limestone, which unlike granite is subject to erosion and, like the "us" and "we" Auden is so fond of invoking, comes from former sealife and is subject to change.

Auden's error at the end of his reading of the poem brings back the poem's opening lines, "If it form the one landscape that we, the inconstant ones, / Are consistently homesick for, this is chiefly / Because it dissolves in water." That is, part of the virtue of the home Auden's limestone landscape represents is physical change, that it "dissolves" just as we are "dissolve[d]," absolved, resolved by our mortality and, on a moral level, just as we are "inconstant" as the water Auden includes in his description. Water, a symbol for life here, is the faultless/faithless force that brings about change in both the landscape and its inhabitants. Its movement above and below ground parallels our fall into time and the way "we, the inconstant ones," meet what we are "consistently homesick for."

"In Praise of Limestone" is further organized along lines that are both rhetorical and figurative. There are the commands to "Mark," "hear," "examine," and "Watch," plus the invitations made by "the granite wastes," "the clays and gravels," and finally "the oceanic whisper." Taken in the aggregate, these appeals provide the reader with a complex picture of the human will, which may be "inconstant" but is continuous. Or, to return to the idea of erosion, the water that cuts new paths through limestone and the limestone itself are like ourselves. We erode and are eroded. We change ourselves, each other, and our surroundings just as water erodes and changes the limestone landscape whose "caves and conduits" nevertheless direct its way.

Auden's landscape, a description of the human condition he sees, begins with the "fragrance of thyme," moves to "springs" that "chuckle," next "short distances and definite places," then settles momentarily on a "band of rivals" on a field who are "never, thank God, in step." The human world figured by this varied landscape ranges from its initial beauty and ability to surprise to "rivals" capable of going "to the bad." But the rhetoric that unfolds the figures of this world does not end with just "bad" individuals.

Beyond the limestone area Auden introduces, there is another region characterized by granite. It is a place of "Immoderate soils" where many, "The best and worst," wind up—"Saints-to-be" who "slip away sighing" and "Intendant Caesars" who storm out at the suggestion that they are "soft as the earth" and like the earth "Need to be altered." For the "Intendant Caesars," these "modifications of matter" go first with tilling the "soft . . . earth," while on a second level "altered" means castrating any "Caesars" on hand, including, one imagines, fascist dictators of the 1930s.

Auden's "Immoderate" area is a place where "the beauty [is] not so external." Ultimately it is a place where things human, even the concept of beauty itself, are lost. Again, it is here the reader encounters three appeals to the will, couched in its negative form, which is oblivion. Invitations to despair, the three appeals are spoken by "the granite wastes," "the clays and gravels," and "the oceanic whisper." What before made the allusions to "thyme" (both flower and the auditory pun, time) and "springs / That spurt out everywhere with a chuckle" possible was the "limestone landscape" underneath, something that Auden now contrasts with the three voices of oblivion, beginning with "granite wastes." This contrast is the center of the poem's argument, and is sustained by the particulars Auden draws from his two controlling figures—limestone and granite.

If limestone can be modified by Auden's symbolic water (by erosion on one level and by human effort on another), granite, in contrast, seems out of time and beyond human modification. A limestone landscape supports culture, whether by tillable soil, marble statues, or "tiled colonnade[s]," whereas granite neither supports life nor erodes, gives way, as limestone does, producing underground streams and "springs" that "chuckle." More characteristically, granite is the raw stuff for Auden's idea of meaninglessness, ground where nothing grows and the view is that of someone lost. One might quarry tombstones here but find little other purpose.

What Auden has to "Praise" is a landscape that is changeable, a place where one can move "from a wild to a formal vineyard." And it is important to note that all the implications of garden imagery are echoed by Auden's allusion to a "vineyard," although before anything else, of course, the shift Auden has in mind is our progress from raw to cultivated nature. Beyond that, however, there is the implied owner of the vineyard, the typology of the vine, and the vineyard worker's reward at end of day. All of these are related to redemption and the concept of an afterlife mentioned at the end of the poem. Auden maintains he "know[s] nothing of / Either," leaving faith as an option, knowledge and belief being different modes of understanding.

Along with its capacity for change, however, Auden's "limestone landscape" has its share of enduring faults, physical and otherwise. It is a habitat subject to erosion the way we are subject to aging and death. In human terms, the virtuous limit of the scape Auden praises is that over time it is changed by a culture that ranges from agriculture to sculpture to the other arts. We are "homesick" for this landscape because we have inherited it; it is the place of our origin and the grounding of our perspective about who we are. But we are its place also, to the degree that, like "a stone that responds," the landscape responds to the work we perform upon it. We inhabit a "region" (a realm, kingdom, division of inanimate creation, particular part of the universe, geographical area, subdivision of the body) that is constantly modified by both natural laws and human success and failure, as Auden's *faultless* / *faithless* slip reminds us.

Contrasting limestone and granite the way he does, it is hard to imagine that Auden did not also have in mind opposites such as the marble statuary of a Greek democracy and the granite architecture of a 1930s fascist state. Such a contrast raises the issue of the right displacement of the will. There is the promise of life, which caught in time must erode its own ground and be lost, and there is the "oceanic whisper" that promises its gray freedom from restraint, saying, "There is no love; / There are only the various envies." Measurable, possibly accountable, erosion is at one extreme, the openness of some nonanthropomorphic freedom at the other. One knows which choice "Intendant Caesars" prefer. Doors slam. (We hear them regularly, as in "the granite wastes.") There is the promise of power squeezed from the denial of life. That is, the last desperate gesture here is a negative. Saying "no" seems free, while being told "no" does not. One coin's two different sides. The human limitations implicit in the "wastes," "clays and gravels," and "the oceanic whisper" are adopted by the "really reckless," but Auden's final position is more judicious than that.

Auden is not reckless but guardedly optimistic. He does not deny the existence of "granite wastes" any more than he overlooks Yahweh viewed "Through the lattice-work of" an Old Testament "nomad's comb." What the nomad sees is "a god whose temper-tantrums are moral / And not to be pacified by a clever line / Or a good lay" but instead are capable of becoming "a crater whose blazing fury [cannot] be fixed." Auden is left with two choices—pure possibility that cannot be realized on the one hand and human ability and limitation on the other. Auden simply makes one choice rather than another. He opts for "a limestone landscape" subject to time and full of imperfections, including "underground streams" that "murmur" in a way that seems to echo the unconscious mind.

Auden accepts his "region / Of short distances and definite places" as a human habitat where life can be sustained and meaning made possible. The freedom promised by the "oceanic whisper" is beyond the boundary of human habitation and thus, despite its promise of solitary power, actually destroys all that is human. Auden knows this much, and beyond that he believes that the limits that make life possible and meaningful in this world, the "short distances and definite places" of "a limestone landscape," suggest how life may be made possible in the next world. This is a view that carries obvious moral implications. The figures of limestone and granite enable Auden to debate and finally instruct us on the everyday ways we choose between living and dying.

Robert Frost's "Mending Wall"

Robert Frost once said that "Mending Wall" was a poem that was spoiled by being applied. What did he mean by "applied"? Any poem is damaged by being misunderstood, but that's the risk all poems run. What Frost objects to, I think, is a reduction and distortion of the poem through practical use. When President John F. Kennedy inspected the Berlin Wall he quoted the poem's first line: "Something there is that doesn't love a wall." His audience knew what he meant and how the quotation applied. And on the other side of that particular wall, we can find another example of how the poem has been used. Returning from a visit to Russia late in his life, Frost said, "The Russians reprinted 'Mending Wall' over there, and left that first line off." He added wryly, "I don't see how they got the poem started." What the Russians needed, and so took, was the poem's other detachable statement: "Good fences make good neighbors." They applied what they wanted. "I could've done better for them, probably," Frost said, "for the generality, by saying:

> Something there is that doesn't love a wall,
> Something there is that does.

"Why didn't I say that?" Frost asked rhetorically. "I didn't mean that. I meant to leave that until later in the poem. I left it there."

"Mending Wall" famously contains these two apparently conflicting statements. One begins the poem, the other ends it, and both are repeated twice. Which are we supposed to believe? What does Frost mean? "The secret of what it means I keep," he said. Of course he was being cagey, but not without reason.

At a reading given at the Library of Congress in 1962 Frost told this anecdote:

In England, two or three years ago, Graham Greene said to me, "The most difficult thing I find in recent literature is your having said that good fences make good neighbors."

And I said, "I wish you knew more about it, without my helping you."

We laughed, and I left it that way.

Why doesn't Frost want to say what he meant? When asked, he'd reply, "What do you want me to do, say it again in different and less good words?" "You get more credit for thinking," Frost wrote in a letter, "if you restate formulae or cite cases that fall in easily under formulae, but all the fun is outside: saying things that suggest formulae that won't formulate—that almost but don't quite formulate." The formula is the easy answer that turns out to be, if right or wrong in general, certainly inadequate in particular. The formula, like a paraphrase of the poem itself, is made of those "less good words" the poet has tried to resist.

"Mending Wall" seems to present us with a problem, and appears to urge us to choose up sides. I suspect most readers are eager to ally themselves with the speaker, to consider the neighbor dim-witted, blockheaded, and generally dull. Such a reading is nicely represented by the following passage from a booklet on Robert Frost put out by Monarch Notes:

By the end of the poem [the wall] has become a symbol, and the two farmers have turned into allegorical figures representing opposing views of freedom and confinement, reason and rigidity of mind, tolerance and violence, civilization and savagery. . . . There is no mistaking the poet's meaning, or his attitude toward what the wall represents . . . it stands for . . . the barrier between human contact and understanding. It is erected by all that is primitive, fearful, irrational and hostile [in the neighbor]. It is opposed by a higher "something" that Frost recognizes as in himself . . . the desire not to be alone, walled in, but to be one with the rest of the world.

There is no mistaking what the authors of the Monarch Notes want to believe, and on which side of the wall they stand. And of course it's pleasant—even comforting—to believe that the poem encourages us to be "one with the rest of the world." But is that what the poem actually says?

"Mending Wall" opens with a riddle: "Something there is . . ." And a riddle, after all, is a series of hints calculated to make us imagine and then name its hidden subject. The poem doesn't begin, "I hate walls," Or even, "Something dislikes a wall." Its first gesture is one of elaborate and playful concealment, a calculated withholding of meaning. Notice also that it is the speaker himself who repairs the wall after the hunters have broken it. And it is the speaker each year who notifies his neighbor when the time has come to meet and mend the wall. Then can we safely claim that the speaker views the wall simply as a barrier between human contact and understanding?

Speaker and neighbor work together and equally. Although the job is tedious and hard, the speaker considers it "just another kind of outdoor game / One on a side." He acknowledges that his whimsical spell— "'Stay where you are until our backs are turned!'"—is useless, and that the result is impermanent and perhaps less important than something else. For all practical purposes this particular wall is not needed. But the project of mending it has taken on significance: "Spring is the mischief in me, and I wonder / If I could put a notion in his head . . ."

The speaker's mischievous impulse is to plant an idea. He does not say that he wants to change his neighbor's mind, to make him believe what he himself believes. He wants to nudge the neighbor's imagination, just as a teacher might wish to challenge a student. So he asks questions: "'*Why* do they make good neighbors? Isn't it / Where there are cows? But here there are no cows.'" But the neighbor is unwilling to play this game of teacher and student. He won't answer the questions, or consider the riddle. The speaker could suggest "Elves" but "it's not elves exactly," and of course it's not elves at all. The speaker's frustration is beginning to get the better of him. He wants to be fanciful—he wants to talk—and his neighbor does not. More importantly, and again like a good teacher, "I'd rather / He said it for himself."

"I wish you knew more about it," Frost says he told Graham Greene, "without my helping you." This is the poem's essential challenge, which the neighbor will not accept. But the challenge is ours as well—our work, our play. The relationship between speaker and neighbor is like the relationship between poem and reader, another kind of indoor game, one on a side.

But this is a relationship between poem and reader, not poet and reader. Frost, I want to believe, is not the speaker *exactly*. He is behind the whole poem, rather than narrowly inside it. We need to be at least a little skeptical of the speaker and not associate him automatically with the side upholding freedom, reason, and tolerance. At the end, because the neighbor won't play his game, the speaker imagines him as "an old-stone savage," a harsh judgment to apply even to the most recalcitrant student. Because the neighbor will only repeat what he remembers his father having said, he seems to "move in darkness . . . Not of woods only and the shade of trees." But of what else? We should say it for ourselves. His ignorance? Confinement, violence, and savagery, as the Monarch authors have it? Not exactly. It's his refusal to be playful and imaginative that irks the speaker, and his unwillingness to consider work as anything more than a job to be accomplished. The speaker, after all, does not ask the neighbor to give up his father's notion. He wants him to "go behind" it. If, as I want to suggest, the poem is about education, this distinction is important. The poem does not merely advocate one position over another. It asks neither for advocacy nor for application, but for investigation. It is not a statement but a performance. It enacts its meanings.

Who, finally, is right about the wall? The poem does not answer that question exactly, swerving off into deeper and more interesting territory. It *uses* that problem to engage us and demand that we think, which is the poem's pleasure, and its strategy. Sometimes good fences do indeed make good neighbors, and we might recall that the phrase "mending fences" means to restore communication and neighborliness. Equally true is the notion that something doesn't love a wall. The riddle isn't a difficult one. We know that natural forces disturb those boulders, that the frozen groundswell is frost. But not, for all the play of the pun, "Robert Frost." "All the fun's in how you say a thing," says a character in another Frost poem. But fun can be serious, just as work can be turned into play.

The wall in the poem is not "the barrier between human contact and understanding." Certainly a wall may be just that, but it can also serve precisely the opposite function.

> I let my neighbor know beyond the hill;
> And on a day we meet to walk the line
> And set the wall between us once again.
> We keep the wall between us as we go.

The repetition of *between* should give us pause and remind us of its two equally common meanings: *between* as separation, as in "something's come between us," and *between* as what might be shared and held in common, as in "a secret between two people" or "a bond between friends." The wall divides but it also connects, if you look at it that way. All the meaning is in how you look at it—how the poem encourages you to think about it.

Frost once wrote about his experience as a teacher, "I was determined to have it out with my youngers and betters as to what thinking really was. We reached an agreement that most of what they had regarded as thinking, their own and other peoples', was nothing but voting—taking sides on an issue they had nothing to do with laying down." "Mending Wall" is a poem that lures the unwary reader into believing that thinking is merely voting, choosing up sides, taking out of the poem what most fits our own preconceived ideas. It adopts this subversive tactic because its ultimate purpose is to challenge us to go behind what we might find initially appealing in the formulas that lie on its surface. "We ask people to think," Frost says, "and we don't show them what thinking is." "Mending Wall" is less a poem about what to think than it is a poem about what thinking is, and where it might lead.

In his essay, "Education by Poetry," Frost writes,

Poetry provides the one permissible way of saying one thing and meaning another. People say, 'Why don't you say what you mean?' We never do that, do we, being all of us too much poets. We like to talk in parables and in hints and in indirections—whether from diffidence or some other instinct.

Perhaps we are, all of us, so much poets, or might be; but Frost, who certainly was, doesn't really answer his question. Surely diffidence is not the reason why writers are drawn to the indirections of figurative language. What might that "other instinct" be? One answer is the instinct of the teacher who speaks in hints, in questions, and in challenges, who refrains from saying what he means because he wants his students to discover it for themselves. Similarly, the apparent meaning of a poem remains merely a formula unless the reader has understood how the poem came to articulate and embody that meaning. The speaker of "Mending Wall" fails in his attempt to become a successful poet/teacher. Each year, it seems, he fails at the same task. Frost's poem, of course, depends upon and survives this failure, recreating a similar moment each time it is encountered.

Mending Wall

Something there is that doesn't love a wall,
That sends the frozen-ground-swell under it
And spills the upper boulders in the sun,
And makes gaps even two can pass abreast.
The work of hunters is another thing:
I have come after them and made repair
Where they have left not one stone on a stone,
But they would have the rabbit out of hiding,
To please the yelping dogs. The gaps I mean,
No one has seen them made or heard them made,
But at spring mending-time we find them there.
I let my neighbor know beyond the hill;
And on a day we meet to walk the line
And set the wall between us once again.
We keep the wall between us as we go.
To each the boulders that have fallen to each.

And some are loaves and some so nearly balls
We have to use a spell to make them balance:
"Stay where you are until our backs are turned!"
We wear our fingers rough with handling them.
Oh, just another kind of outdoor game,
One on a side. It comes to little more:
There where it is we do not need the wall:
He is all pine and I am apple orchard.
My apple trees will never get across
And eat the cones under his pines, I tell him.
He only says, "Good fences make good neighbors."
Spring is the mischief in me, and I wonder
If I could put a notion in his head:
"*Why* do they make good neighbors? Isn't it
Where there are cows? But here there are no cows.
Before I built a wall I'd ask to know
What I was walling in or walling out,
And to whom I was like to give offense.
Something there is that doesn't love a wall,
That wants it down." I could say "Elves" to him,
But it's not elves exactly, and I'd rather
He said it for himself. I see him there,
Bringing a stone grasped firmly by the top
In each hand, like an old-stone savage armed.
He moves in darkness as it seems to me,
Not of woods only and the shade of trees.
He will not go behind his father's saying,
And he likes having thought of it so well
He says again, "Good fences make good neighbors."

Robert Frost

Ben Jonson's "On My First Sonne"

For two decades Ben Jonson's assertion that the fruit of his loins was of equal, or perhaps superior, value to the outpourings of his imagination has given me leave to pursue my obsessions as both poet and parent. No high-school English text in Rochester, New York—my hometown—was without Jonson's great elegy, "On My First Sonne."

I was raised and formally educated to understand the charge given Jewish women of my generation: study, marry, be fruitful and multiply, and learn to cook along the way. It was the work of the body that was to be my life's occupation, after a brief flurry of intellectual activity sustained just long enough to engage the interest of a worthy mate. For me, a worthy mate would have the mind's work to do: he'd be a professor, as he was (the first time around) and as our son is now. That I also would be a professor never occurred to me. Pregnant, nursing, cooking, I took time to read the several biographies of Queen Elizabeth Tudor that were popular during the sixties, and I took time then to reread the work and some of the lives of her men: Sir Philip Sidney, Shakespeare, Sir Walter Raleigh, among others, and, of course, Ben Jonson. As I read, each took on family, politics, context. But my understanding "On My First Sonne" never was challenged: one of Elizabeth Tudor's greatest courtiers cherished the body and its good work.

Ben Jonson is remembered by his nickname rather than his full first name, perhaps a sign of affection. By all reports Jonson was likable, brilliant, and contentious. He hated the bricklaying skills his stepfather taught him, and he joined the army as a young man to avoid practicing. During his lifetime he killed two men, one in single combat when like the young David he challenged a member of the enemy army and won the fight; the second he killed in a tavern. In penalty he was branded on his thumb. Married in his early twenties he was father to three children, none of whom survived him. He spent time in a coffeehouse with lively friends who called themselves "sons of Ben"; this group included Shakespeare. An actor and playwright who came to triumph when he was twenty, Jonson remained an influential man of letters until his death at sixty-five—a very long life for the time. A portly man, he suffered a stroke in his middle fifties, my age now, and thereafter was confined to bed. He was born in poverty; his father died before or shortly after his birth. A brilliant satirist in an age of brilliant courtiers, he was partially self-taught, though as a child he studied with a major historian, William Camden. ("Camden," he wrote in 1616 when he was forty-four, "to whom I owe / all that I am in arts, all that I know / (How nothing's that!) . . . What name, what skill, what faith hast thou in things!" I note what Jonson noted about Camden, that he loved the *things* of the world.) Afterward he taught himself, so when his library burned he must have been disconsolate. At the height of his fame he was unable or chose not to write for many years. He hung out with great and rich men. His works include the first poem written to a specific place—"To Penshurst," the country home of Sir Philip Sidney's family. He was tutor to Sir Walter Raleigh's son. His affection for and deep understanding of Latin verse, which he translated and published, changed the taste in English poetry from fussy to hard-edged, and the reason for his popularity during my school days had more to do with the formal elegance of his poetry than affection for his satiric plays. He was a master of formal prosody. Among his remembered poems are two simple elegies of twelve lines each, "On My First Daughter" and "On My First Sonne," poems with interesting differences.

A recent browse in Barnes and Noble lit on Jonson's poems, always available in new collections of "most popular poems in English." They are examples of a cultural ideal we students learned to call—from E.M.W. Tillyard's book of the same name—*The Great Chain of Being*. That little book, not much more than 150 pages, stresses the importance of cultural context in literature. In England, and especially at court, all parts of creation were thought to have an assigned place, order, and value. So long as society perpetuates this just order, God remains in His heaven, the king or queen on the throne, the master at the head of the table, his firstborn son at his right hand, his wife at the foot, and all creatures from the most highly developed through the most primitive (from the mighty oak down through John Donne's flea), each in their proscribed place, each available for the sustenance and continuance of those higher on the list.

An old preface to Jonson's "To Penshurst" notes "how the description rises through the scale of creatures, from vegetables to animals to pretty girls—who carry emblems of themselves in the form of ripe fruit—to the lord of the manor, and finally to the king himself. Each person is in his place, each is in harmony with general nature, all things are ordered according to an architecture of full proportion; so that a kind of heroic image of the just society rises out of a simple description of a country house" (*The Norton Anthology of English Literature Revised*, ed. M. H. Abrams, New York: W. W. Norton, 1968).

What Jonson's fluency, erudition, and wit made of his society's ideas I note here and now. I am a middle-aged professor, a woman, who sits at the head of my own table. Having come so far from my first reading of "On My First Sonne," I now cherish a briefcase filled with books and papers—evidence of the work of the imagination—as well as the photos and mementoes of my own daughter and son. Still Jonson's poem rises fresh for me.

"On My First Sonne" is written in couplets. Six pairs of rhyming iambic-pentameter lines packed syntactically to express a parent's grief. This son, named after his father Benjamin, "child of the right hand" in translation from the Hebrew, died on his seventh birthday. The first son is always the inheritor, always sits at table on the right hand of the father, always is possessed of good fortune thereby. His father bends his head to him, conversing. Pass the salt.

With the death of his first-born children, Jonson packed couplets with the muscular arm of the young soldier/brawler. Mary died at six months and is remembered in twelve lines of four beats each. Benjamin died at seven years, on his birthday. How to set right that event? In twelve metered lines of iambic pentameter, five beats each line, the first part soft, the second hard, five times like breathing: "Farewell, thou child of my right hand, and joy." Why did he die? "*My* sinne was too much hope of thee, lov'd boy, / Seven yeeres tho' wert lent to me, and I thee pay, / Exacted by thy fate, on the just day" (my emphasis). Our children must die, as we must. Do we give them death as we give them life? Jonson tells us each has a separate fate, but the loan of children must be paid. "O, could I loose all father, now! For why / Will man lament the state he should envie? / To have so soone scap'd worlds, and fleshes rage, / And, if no other miserie, yet age?" Life exacts such harsh payment for its pleasures: illness—I am still recovering from cancer—anger, libraries burnt, loss of love and the body's delights, and silence, the worst. Why then should we mourn so bitterly the deaths of children, even to the extent of begging to be spared the title *father*? Dying young, aren't children saved the miseries of age and the grief we suffer? (Too young even to enjoy the pleasures of the flesh or the mind, or the embodiments of each, or their losses.) Ah, were we not parents we would not mourn the death of ourselves in our children. Were he able to "loose all father now" still he would lament the deaths of children. But so keenly? The world is imperfect, as we are.

The poem ends with the famous couplet, a spoken injunction to his young son: "Rest in soft peace, and, ask'd, say here doth lye / BEN. JONSON his best piece of *poetrie*." Soft peace surely with the dissolution of body into earth, the grave silence. And if you are asked, child, by the angels or their master—or by readers four hundred years later—to say who you are, say then you are both your father, his identical name and self, who dies here as he was before your birth, and yourself, the particular seven-year-old Benjamin who was, in human form, this master poet's "best piece of *poetrie*." The poem's coda is the completion of the prayer: "For whose sake, hence-forth, all his vowes be such, / As what he loves may never like too much." These couplets have been much worried for meaning, but I like to suppose the father swears to the child that for his sake, from now on, whomever he may come to love in a future bereft of his first son, he will not care for them so much as to invoke the repayment of the loan. Nor will the future child be so like himself, nor can he be, since Benjamin, his namesake, is dead.

A square flagstone in the Poet's Corner of Westminster Abbey marks a grave with this inscription: "O Rare Ben Jonson!" We ought to visit.

On My First Sonne

Farewell, thou child of my right hand, and joy;
    My sinne was too much hope of thee, lov'd boy,
Seven yeeres tho'wert lent to me, and I thee pay,
    Exacted by thy fate, on the just day.
O, could I loose all father, now. For why
    Will man lament the state he should envie?
To have so soone scap'd worlds, and fleshes rage,

    And, if no other miserie, yet age?
Rest in soft peace, and, ask'd, say here doth lye
    BEN. JONSON his best piece of *poetrie*.
For whose sake, hence-forth, all his vowes be such,
    As what he loves may never like too much.

Ben Jonson

PETER SACKS

Yeats's Heart: A Reading of "The Circus Animals' Desertion"

It's not coincidental that Yeats's most thoroughly valedictory poem, completed in 1938, the year before his death, should end with the same object as the lyric in which he claimed to have first discovered his own music fifty years before. Indeed, it seems unavoidable, for that object forms the center of all his poetry. By an almost physiological destiny, from the deep core of "The Lake Isle of Innisfree" to the foul rag-and-bone shop of "The Circus Animals' Desertion," at the heart of Yeats's poetry lies the image of the poet's heart. If that seems too constant a center for such diversity, it would take just a few crucial poems to reveal how radically Yeats revises what he feels or means regarding his heart, and how fully he understands, yet also masks, the degree to which the heart is not merely some entity taken for granted, but rather what we make, break, and remake of it—poetry being a prime instrument if not the motive of that labor.

"The Circus Animals' Desertion" has been among the most misread of Yeats's lyrics because readers have been persuaded that the poem replaces artificial "emblems" with bluntly antipoetic "things," such as the mortal heart itself. And yet despite Yeats's contrast between emblem and thing, or between poetic artifact and old bare heart, these are not to be so clearly distinguished. Not least of the poem's triumphs is its concealing of relentless poesis and self-fabrication in the disguise of a concession to ugly facts. Far from conceding anything except his age, Yeats ended his career by demonstrating once again that "facts," especially including the heart—as apprehended and forged within poems— are objects of human making. As he had written in "The Tower," "Death and life were not / Till man made up the whole."

We can begin to gauge the high degree of artful making in this poem simply by noticing the virtuosic ottava rima, a form well suited for displaying traditional craft. The inherited stanza, derived from Italian epic romances, retains the marks of that genre, sometimes crossed in English with a current of rueful irony—traceable through Byron all the way to Wyatt's version of the so-called penitential psalms. Depending on the semantic content of the rhymes, if the antiphonal *ababab* pentameters make a nicely terraced wall of lines, the *cc* couplet can either cap the wall or challenge its foundation—as in the near-dismissal of the first stanza's "burnished chariot" by "the Lord knows what," a rhyming sound that will be strengthened with unironic effect at the end of the poem.

From his working drafts, we know that Yeats chose ottava rima while sketching in phrases for the first stanza, and that the formal armature then governed whatever followed throughout the poem. So often viewed in terms of abandonment and tearing down, this poem is thus rigged carefully in alignment with Yeats's own masterpieces in this form (many of them evoking actual buildings such as a gallery, schoolroom, or country house—"Great works constructed there in nature's spite"). The poem is itself a means of erecting what will after all be the newly asserted structure—no less than a shop, however derelict—of the heart.

"The Circus Animals' Desertion," which transforms a threatened dead end into a starting place, and which Yeats meant to serve as the penultimate but last substantial lyric of his collected poems, begins by looking back over its shoulder to review an experience of failure: "I sought a theme and sought for it in vain." By the initiatory act of review, that failure—dramatized by the immediately preceding poem, "Man and the Echo"—is now remade into a foundational rather than terminal event, as it begins a poem that refashions the very premises of the poet's concluding art. And it is exactly this kind of action that provides one of the most far-reaching means of interpreting the poem at large. For even as we read "The Circus Animals' Desertion" as a brave bow to the fate of the body, what the poem actually transforms that biographical necessity into is a performance that has as much to do with the poet's relation to his own practice, as with his wrestling with age or death. Admittedly he lies down in the heart, but the force of the poem is to make both the act and the site into something not only vital but regenerative.

As by poetic reflex, the very first mention of the heart brings on the word *although*. This shunting juxtaposition (coupled around the first piece of midline punctuation in the poem), creates a jolt like that of an emergency resuscitation—one that signals the entire poem's way of reinvigorating the heart, or at least of outweighing any confessions of its organic helplessness. We could subtitle the poem, "I must be satisfied with my heart, although," and I would suggest that one way to come to grips with much of Yeats's poetry is to study what it makes happen on the far side of that conjunction. Indeed, the *although* here ushers in a review of the career's past fabrications. With the opening and closing eight lines of the poem as frame, the reader shouldn't lose sight of how those two outside stanzas are outnumbered by what the retiring circus-master makes revolve in the center ring for his farewell. Nor should we fail to see how much his closing gesture of prostration renews rather than terminates his recirculatory powers.

I haven't space here to comment fully on the three figures of Yeats's retrospect: the young-then-suddenly-superannuated questor Oisin, the Countess Cathleen, and Cuchulain. Each is meant to display the poet's life-evading obsession with an emblematic fiction, the manifest "dream itself" rather than the dream's supposedly hidden promptings. In his own summary, "Players and painted stage took all my love / And not those things that they were emblems of." Enumerating the first two themes, the poet tags them with confessional analyses. While driving his legendary Oisin "Through three enchanted islands, allegorical dreams," he had lusted bitterly after Oisin's paramour Niamh—the bitterness etched more expressively now into a phrase such as "led by the nose," which not only tugs at the circus-beast aspect of the questor, but also stresses the passive, physically demeaning nature of what once had seemed so elevated a pursuit. By then referring to his own desire as a form of starving, Yeats keeps the bodily insistence at the fore, even as he binds this stanza to the next one's focus on a play about famine.

The overt hinge between stanzas, however, is that of "countertruth," alerting us to Yeats's Blakean view of his career as a progression by contraries and undergirding the poem's own dialectical impulse. Whereas Oisin had remained bound by his choice of heroic damnation, Cathleen (who had sold her soul to the devil to save her starving subjects) was saved by divine intervention. Perhaps Yeats meant us merely to infer that these opposed scenarios of spiritual judgment pressed again on his mind, but I want to stress the term "masterful Heaven," for the epithet recurs in an odd, revealing way. As for his commentary, the poet acknowledges that by dramatizing the social sympathies of the Countess, he had displaced his agonizing over Cathleen's living prototype, Maud Gonne, whose activism he had in fact regarded as spiritually corrupting, not just erotically frustrating: "I thought my dear must her own soul destroy / So did fanaticism and hate enslave it, / And this brought forth a dream and soon enough / This dream itself had all my thought and love."

The animal trainer provides no interpretation for the third creature, Cuchulain. "Heart mysteries there," is all he offers, as if to block further inquiry. My hunch is that of the three figures, this Cuchulain of

On Baile's Strand is now the closest to the old poet, whose deathbed work was "Cuchulain Comforted"; the poet's near-identification with the maddened, son-slaying warrior could not yet bear too much self-analysis. No less interesting is the foregrounding of the Fool and Blind Man who stole the bread in the play. They represent the kind of anti-heroic foraging that will end this poem as well, but they also mark both the crude materialism and the clairvoyant poetic knowledge of common folk—we might recall the Fool's songs in *On Baile's Strand*, and that it was the Blind Man alone who knew the identity of Cuchulain's son before the duel. By a compounding that is fundamental to most of Yeats's late poems, the allegedly anti-idealistic, antipoetic gropings of the crazy, foolish, and blind thus embody a surviving poetic craftiness and vigor of their own; it is this "ungovernable" kind of poesis—from the bottom up, or from the core outwards—that will dominate the close of the poem.

"Those masterful images because complete / Grew out of pure mind but out of what began?" Even as Yeats dismisses his half-dismantled images, he calls them "masterful," hence linking them with the saving powers of "masterful Heaven." Or does the association now imply that Heaven itself was yet another image, its mastery designed and conferred by a prior, still more masterful act of image making? Either way, we need to register how this stubborn emphasis on mastery shifts from divine to human dominion as it is borne downward to the climactic staging of desolation.

There is another contrariety at work as Yeats makes his final crossing. He values completeness, as of "the finished man" or perfected work, but more pressingly he seeks the ragged incompleteness of a self-renewing vitality. If "pure mind" completes an image, Yeats turns instead toward the previously obscured (*poetically* obscured) source of images themselves. And by a form of recycling—like that of the living heart, whose revolvings after all make up a kind of circus—he is drawn precisely to the kinds of origin that lie among endings or leavings. As the previous, fictional creatures are sent off, they are replaced by different recruits, bristling with the presence of actual things, whose claims to actuality depend on their age and degradation.

Despite their recalcitrant trashiness, these succeeding items behave in beguilingly ordered ways. For at this moment of supposed disen-chantment and abandonment, the poet moves into the most enchanting, musically compelling passage of the poem. I hear the rhythmic crack of his whip as he lines up his "Old kettles, old bottles, and a broken can, / Old iron, old bones, old rags, that raving slut / Who keeps the till." If the former creatures went out in a procession, their replacements enter with an almost jostling gusto, a marching rigor that renews as much as it parodies the procession of a renaissance triumph. And a look at the early drafts shows what actual selections governed the seeming capitulation to what is merely found: in the act of composition, the poet discards "bits of old newspaper . . . dirt, orange peel . . . whiskey bottles." That such choices are made partly for sound and stress underscores the degree to which the poet remains in charge of his material, or at least in service to an art that powerfully picks and chooses what it will construct in the face of ruin and impotence.

There is more than musical fitting and turning here. Since no poetic image ever began out of actual kettles, rags, or bottles themselves but only out of the site or faculty that these may figuratively represent, the confession about poetic beginnings is counterfactual unless read metaphorically. Neatly in step with the marching anaphora, the jumble of sweepings thus turns out, like the former procession, to be made up of emblems for something else, namely the heart or the place where images begin. Notwithstanding the clatter of junk, and despite the former lines about the now supposedly remote "allegorical dreams" of Oisin, Yeats is up to his old tricks of near-Spenserian allegory. (An early version of this section had "From rag and bone, that raving slut / Called Heart and Company.")

If we doubt that Yeats's bric-a-brac makes up a parade of emblems in the guise of things or harsh facts, we need only follow where these lead. If we don't wish to admit that things and facts, especially as presented in poetic language, are objects of gathering and making (the very words *thing* and *fact* preserve a reference to such actions), we might at least notice that all of Yeats's items bear traces of human labor, whether obviously in the case of kettles, bottles, cans, rags, and iron, or less markedly in the case of moundings, sweepings, or the gathering of bones. In addition, while they may have been old things in themselves, nonetheless within and by means of the poem as poetic entities they are startlingly new. And as we start to observe them, we find they are manipulated yet further.

Yeats now conjures the things that had previously lain around, using them to build and furnish the higher-order construction (still posing as a low-level, indeed ladderless finding) of the shop. On the level of rhetoric and craft alone, the disjoined, metonymic "old bones, old rags" become the unitary, metaphoric "rag-and-bone shop of the heart," the chiasmus acting like combinatory mortar to erect the shop, just as the rhyme words *street, slut,* and *start,* with their residue of *chariot* and *what,* go to compose and determine the sound we hear, and therefore the sense we make, of the word *heart.*

Before exploring the heart, it is worth scouting out the shop a little further. Apparently it, too, functions emblematically, despite the actual existence of rag-and-bone shops in the nineteenth century and after. And as with the wares in stock, the shop itself—even as a word—has its cellar door open to a long history of makings. Well before the age of modern commerce that Yeats so loathed, shops were places of artisanal work, the work Yeats would have associated with his own poetic forgings or heartwork. Moreover, for a poet obsessed with the deep ancestry of his art, the word *shop* might have resonated with *scop*, etymologically related as they are to each other and to the work of creation. If the ladders of image making begin in the shop of the heart, they are set firmly upon a carefully laid ground of prior makings where the poet may lie in more ways than one. We may recall the couplet from "Byzantium," "Those images that yet / Fresh images beget," and my sense is that those flood-breaking smithies of the Emperor would have known their way around Yeats's shop.

Of the heart. As in his earlier "themes of the embittered heart," Yeats's genitive works in two ways. The foul shop describes the heart, yet also belongs to it and is even generated by it as both the passive object of description and as a source, agent, or proprietor of self-descriptions—perhaps even to the raving slut with which the word nearly rhymes. The heart, then—if it is something more than the fist-size muscle in the chest—is what we make of it, but we do that by making something of the heart's own makings. If he had "made" his soul in "The Tower," Yeats's achievement in this poem is to have re-started the heart's capacity for self-remaking and to have done so under the combined stresses of age and of his own intensifying need for poetic yet credible products that he could still sell to and from his own heart—the kind of things that others in an increasingly skeptical age will still want to buy, beg, borrow, or steal.

In closing, I need to address an obvious puzzle that may not have an obvious answer. Since we've come to recognize the high degree of artifice that has made and remade "the heart," shouldn't we challenge Yeats's contrasting of heart and mind? Just as we've found emblem and thing to be less separable than he proposes, so, too, by a related entangling, the elements of mind and heart seem hard to untie. Far from being a self-constituting natural organ, Yeats represents the heart as already framed and compounded by a slew of prior mental imagings, most of which come from before or outside any mortal individual. I think of the paradox at the end of Sidney's sonnet (which Yeats's poem very closely resembles): "Fool," said my Muse to me, "look in thy heart and write." Look in thy heart, yes, but it is the Muse who tells him so, the Muse who also exists outside of his heart and has instructed others before him, others from whose oft-turned leaves and studied inventions Sidney had first come to hear of Her. The heart in which Sidney and Yeats need to lie down in order to make a new start or an end must then be an archive or shop in which old acts of mind have been absorbed until they are possessed by the heart that they in turn possess. Thus, mixed into the "fury and the mire of human veins," mental acts recircle through that larger mound of artisanal shopwork that feels closer to a bodily resource than to a region of "pure mind." We still speak of memorizing words by heart; perhaps the heart is partly what we memorize by words.

In a poem about our skeletal remains, Wallace Stevens wrote that "what we said of it became / A part of what it is." And in "A Prayer for Old Age," Yeats had chosen the anonymously sedimented form of the ballad, in which to write, "God guard me from those thoughts men think / In the mind alone. // He that sings a lasting song / Thinks in a marrow-bone."

Walt Whitman's "The Sleepers"

Walt Whitman is one of our most maddening poets: simultaneously ambitious and grandiose, programmatic and contradictory, on the one hand a great defender of democracy and the union, on the other a racist and imperialist (in "Passage to India," the metaphor of the railroad far exceeds its spiritual and temporal connections). He lectures pompously on equality while declaring visionary superiority; a moralist who proclaims the virtues of immorality, he combats censorship while disguising his homosexuality; like many depressed people, he's willfully optimistic; he's our first confessional poet, yet he's also deathly afraid of intimacy; he's a shameless, narcissistic self-promoter, but his poems display an obviously empathic and generous heart.

When Whitman's poems cohere he creates a dazzling dialectical symbolic universe out of these contraries, but I'm more interested in his wilder, ambivalent, dramatic narratives and metaphors that overrun his idealized Transcendentalism and polemical Eastern spiritual legislation. In Whitman's uncharacteristically dark, prescient, and surreal poem, "The Sleepers," the poet inhabits instead of intellectualizes his essential conflicts: here, the ecstatic who longs to sexually, spiritually, and artistically merge with the other also deeply fears that arousal: he's terrified of being consumed, of losing his identity as a male and an artist, and of experiencing separation, the terrifying loss of love. He wrestles with how much his art, which he views as timeless imagination, can transform these struggles.

The poem mediates its godlike quest for justice and coherence with the speaker's longing to join the rest of humanity, who resist neither closeness nor death: the sleepers. The poem's project, then, is to approach what Conrad's Kurtz called, "the horror," to accept, even embrace, the chaotic amorality of the metaphorical world of the dream, the unconscious, and death. In a series of unprecedented surreal dream-narratives and reveries, "The Sleepers," portrays the artist in the midst of a conflict so overwhelming that his intellectual resolution in the poem's last two sections cannot relieve his tormented ambivalence.

The poem begins with the artist lost in Dantean restlessness, "wander(ing) all night in my vision," a vision that imprisons the speaker in solitude but offers the hope of salvation, of comprehending the thickly coded universe. Throughout the poem the speaker aspires to the phallic power of the Lacanian gaze, but he's both envious and fearful of the vulnerable sleepers who have suffered in their waking lives but now rest fitfully. His "piercing" the darkness expresses his erotic connection with the night and the dream but also his desire to break its "infolding" code. Imagination becomes the vehicle for union. "I dream in my dream all the dreams of the other dreamers, / And I become the other dreamers."

The content of the manic dream in the first section, though, is infantile: the speaker sees specters and becomes a pirate ("onward we move, a gay gang of blackguards"). The night becomes a confusing erotic fantasy, and by the end of the section, in one of Whitman's Shakespearean imitations, the speaker doubts the substance of what he has seen and felt ("I thought my lover had gone, else darkness and he are one") and the closure "fades" with a loss of power and fear of insubstantiality.

In the second dream the speaker, by becoming an old woman, tries to imagine the process of dying. His fear of becoming a shroud, of becoming blank ("reason" or no), leads him to retreat from the vision ("it seems to me that every thing in the light and air ought to be happy"). Provisionally, death is so fearful and empty here that life becomes all the more precious. The causality does not suffice, however, and this stance is soon enough dismantled in section three, when life is replete with unjustifiable suffering at the hands of the chaotic, omnivorous, and maternal sea.

Whitman's attraction to—and combat with—the maternal is essential to "The Sleepers." The regressive dream fantasies all engage the mythic female: after the speaker chooses the persona of an old woman, the metaphor of the all-encompassing and consuming sea (explicitly connected with the mother in the last line of the poem) controls sections three and four; in the poem's most crucial reconstructed reverie, section six, the speaker revisits a childhood scene virtually from the point of view of his mother. The fantasies are probes: in each of the quests the hope for justification or transcendence is undone: the Promethean male swimmer is destroyed, the erotic figure of the exoticized Native American woman (here Whitman's homosexuality is transposed and transfigured with his connection to his mother) brings only unredeemable loss;

those who nobly do battle die (an emasculated Washington serves as a helplessly nurturing mother saying goodbye to his children). Whitman's biographical attachment to his mother is of less interest here than his attempt to negotiate conflicting needs: irrevocably drawn to the feminine, Whitman also needs protection; he distances himself from the dangers of merging (love, intimacy, and the unconscious) by dwelling in the Apollonian sun of male reasoning. The visionary speaker wants to acquire power and control over desire and over the phallic mother he fears. But he also literally and metaphorically wants to close his eyes, to wed the dark, to return to the womb. Since Whitman always conflates eros with death and the loss of self, he must retreat (into daylight and the intellectual catalogue) from the dark almost as soon as he enters it.

In the third section the artist, the powerless risk-taker, is heartlessly destroyed by that maternal sea ("Will you kill the courageous giant? Will you kill him in the prime of his middle age?"). In a flourish of alliterative language, Whitman concludes the section tragically with "His beautiful body is borne in the circling eddies, it is continually bruised on the rocks." The rescue mission narrative of section four also offers a flurry of confusion: diction like "helplessly," "floundering," "howls of dismay," "fainter and fainter," cue the reader to the speaker's spiraling uncertainty. The more he probes, the less the speaker finds justice or meaning. Just as urgently, he is incapable of transforming, imaginatively or otherwise, the unbearable suffering of others.

The symbolic father of the country in section five who sends troops to war to die cannot save nor repress his tears. Sections three through five confront inexplicable suffering and pain as rigorously as any poem of Whitman's (though they are infused with the same amalgam of death and love as his great Civil War poems), but the recollection in the sixth section offers the most intimate reverie, culminating in a tragic vision of unfulfilled love, of the heartbreaking loss of the love object that pains the speaker more than death itself. The Native American woman, here idealized and sexualized ("My mother looked in delight and amazement at the stranger"), is "free and elastic," "profuse," "black," "at one with the night" and her own sexuality: she is a true sleeper, and as the plot unfolds we hope she can provide the speaker with the experiential model that will transform the suffering of the first five sections. But Whitman simultaneously desires her qualities and needs to suppress them, to ward them off. Despite his protests, "I turn but do not withdraw," Whitman's fears of intimacy and his own sexuality lead him to end the episode abruptly without poetic or sexual gratification. Nothing happens in the reverie between mother and squaw ("she gave her remembrance and fondness") though "mother was lothe to have her leave." In this astonishing section, Whitman witnesses simultaneously the sensual joy life provides while being forced to comprehend that any attempt to control attachment is tragically impossible.

In Whitman's best work the linguistic and narrative process—the dramatic evidence of the poems—leads the speaker to its inevitable culminating wisdom. In "Crossing Brooklyn Ferry," readers experience the spatial and temporal bridges the speaker convincingly crosses. In "The Sleepers," though, the tragic evidence, coupled with Whitman's strategy to regress, to move backwards (in the fashion of psychoanalysis) in order to discover the truth, leads only to the clichéd and inadequate wisdom that death is the great equalizer. "I swear they are averaged now—one is no better than the other, / the night and sleep have liken'd them and restored them." In section seven, death and sleep provide the comfort of the backward glance (imagination restores meaning to the past, but not the past itself), through the womblike "voyages home" and "returns" of the Irishman and the sailor. In this section people are saved or healed only by negating or erasing their adult historical experience in a pointless and regressive search for origin.

In the last section Whitman seems to realize that the conflict has not been completely resolved. The speaker is indecisive, unable to choose the forces of day or night (to choose is to commit oneself to either passionate engagement or clarifying repression). In these wish-fulfillment fantasies, the speakers' anxieties are eased when "the father holds his grown or ungrown son in his arms with measureless love," when the "Asiatic and African are hand in hand." This utopian vision of death and dream does not issue forth from the first six sections of the poem; indeed, "the wrong is (never) made right." The speaker must "pass from the night," and in spite of his protestations concerning his willingness to return and love the night, the poem ends inconclusively with doubt. "I know not how I came of you and I know not where I go with you, but I know I came well and shall go well." The speaker concludes the poem by glossing it in the coordinate clause, "O my mother," thereby acknowledging the connection between the maternal forces of flux, the sea, and death. But even then he is unable to choose: he merely resolves in the future (a future the poem turns away from) to "duly pass the day, O my mother, and duly return to you." Whitman chooses the regressive fantasy of union with the mother, but experience (the cumulative wisdom of the dream sections) excludes this possibility. The poem ends on a willful note of hope, but the choice to return to the mother is more fearful than hopeful.

I love the open-ended closure of "The Sleepers" because I find a poet's probing emotional investigation more engaging and satisfying than any single illumination. Illuminations are commodities, the distant objects of philosophy, but poems are dramatic processes engaging conflicts and anxieties from which a writer cannot escape, difficult struggles he or she must face in order to find fulfillment and happiness. Said more simply, I'm more interested in participating in the writer's journey than listening to his conclusions culled from those experiences. I'm certain, too, that the confluence of personal histories draws me to "The Sleepers." As a man who is equally drawn to the feminine—few poets aren't—but has also experienced a close and conflicted relationship with his mother, I'm probably moved by this poem more than readers with different histories. While that makes the poem neither greater nor lesser, those connections always spark attachments to poems and present the opportunity for self-knowledge. I confess, too, to loving poems where the stakes are high: in "The Sleepers," the skeptic Whitman does battle with the dreamy mystic and is prepared to go to war over the question of a just universe and the restorative power of art or love. If he doesn't resolve the irresolvable, so much the better. Finally what draws me to this Whitman poem and what draws me to most poems I love is its capacity to surprise, to change its mind, to qualify, deepen and transform, to take the reader some place the writer has seen with a particularity and linguistic density no one has given syntax to before. The best Whitman keeps my ambitions high, keeps my heart open, and affirms the shifting dynamic between the intimate and sensual and the spiritual and metaphysical. This is the poetry of a rich and wide-ranging emotional life, reminding us why we still need poetry so much.

Shelley in Ruins: The Appeal

of "Ozymandias"

Popular opinion of Percy Bysshe Shelley's mysterious sonnet "Ozymandias" periodically undergoes a sea change. Newman Ivey White's definitive, two-volume, fourteen hundred-page biography (1940), for instance, never even mentions the poem once, though it was included in Palgrave's *Golden Treasury* (1861), and today it is generally considered one of Shelley's finest lyric achievements—the only one of his sonnets, according to Desmond King-Hele (1960), that "can bear comparison with Shakespeare's." The reason for this is both more and less baffling than might first appear, for the rise and fall of this poem's individual reputation seems inversely correspondent to the rise and fall of the overall reputation of Shelley's work. To put it more bluntly, those who are drawn to this poem appear to admire it, not because it's quintessential Shelley, but because it's so out of keeping with Shelley's style. Likewise, those who dislike or ignore it appear to do so for the very same reason. Where Shelley is normally oracular, extravagant, intuitional, and transportive, here he is detached, ironic, skeptical, and cool—as though the Orphean lute had been traded in for the slide rule of the metaphysical poet.

So who was Ozymandias anyway? At one level we know that this was the Greek name for Rameses II, and that inscribed on an Egyptian temple, as recorded by Diodorus Siculus, is the sentence "I am Ozymandias, king of kings." In the autumn of 1817, around the time of the poem's composition, things Egyptian were making quite a stir in England, and the British Museum had just taken in a collection of pieces from the empire of the Rameses—pieces including the Rosetta Stone and a large-scale figure of Rameses II. Following a visit to the museum with Horace Smith (the stockbroker poet who served as Shelley's London financial agent), Shelley proposed that they each compose a sonnet on the subject, and that "Ozymandias" is the wholly unimaginable result of that seemingly offhand proposal. But that information is circumstantial at best, and as such it only leads us back to itself. The more telling story lies elsewhere.

The son of a member of Parliament, Shelley was a poet who in his youth—and since he lived to be only twenty-nine, I use that term in a relative sense—believed passionately in the role of the poet as world reformer, political activist, agent of justice, and enemy of commerce, royalty, and religion. This was the poet who at eighteen sent copies of his pamphlet *The Necessity of Atheism* to all the faculty and administrators at Oxford (where he was a student at the time) and to all the bishops in the United Kingdom—a quixotic gesture for which he was duly and promptly expelled. This was the same poet who, months later in Dublin, attempted to organize the Irish into "the society of peace and love," and then, having failed at that, resettled in Wales where he sent out into the waiting world yet another hopeful pamphlet, *A Declaration of Rights*, which he launched into the air in bright balloons and onto the sea in toy boats and corked bottles. By then he was nineteen and midway through the writing of his first significant poem, *Queen Mab*, a long verse narrative studded with lectures on politics, religion, and society. In an 1812 letter to the philosopher William Godwin, he described that period of his life this way: "I could not descend to common life: the sublime interest of poetry, lofty and exalted achievements, the proselytism of the world, the equalization of its inhabitants, were to me the soul of my soul."

"Ozymandias," I think, needs to be read in light of that early, and apparently boundless, moral fervor, and in light of that age-old, ongoing, back-and-forth struggle—as germane today as then—between the social and aesthetic demands of an art. For though Shelley was only twenty-five at the time of its composition, his illimitable earlier claims on the world and his role as crusader within it, had been tested seriously by events in his life: the abandonment of his children and wife, Harriet Westbrook, to elope with Mary Godwin; the suicide of Mary's half-sister, for which Shelley felt partially responsible; the death and possible suicide of Harriet; the scandal surrounding Mary's stepsister, Claire Clairmont, pregnant by Byron though assumed by many to be pregnant by Shelley; the court's denial of custody of his children by Harriet, and his fear that he'd eventually lose custody of his children by Mary as well. The list goes on. His own small "society of peace and love" had proven to be anything but. His political aspirations had likewise come to nought. And his poetry was now generally received with a resounding public indifference. So the magnitude of his disillusionment—matched only by the vastness of his early ambitions—suffuse "Ozymandias" with a sobering retrospective self-contempt.

For though "Ozymandias" characteristically assumes Shelley's life-long disdain for despots and kings—that "sneer of cold command"—and though the poem can be (and normally is) read as a political tract to express that disdain, it is also tempting to see the poem as a moment when Shelley steps back from himself. When, through the eyes of posterity, he observes that hopelessly failed persona—that venerated, long-suffering, super-sensitive "*Me*," as he described it in "Julian and Maddalo," "who am as a nerve o'er which do creep / The else unfelt oppressions of this earth."

It is tempting in fact to see "Ozymandias" as an instance of the poem revising the poet, abruptly caught out in that (sometimes) painfully clarifying light that poetry and dreams will cast. It may be that there is more of Shelley in that "shattered visage" than we first perceive. For are the grand delusions of a tyrant who could boast "Look on my works, ye Mighty, and despair!" all that different from those of a poet who had once aspired to "lofty and exalted achievements, the proselytism of the world, the equalization of its inhabitants"? Perhaps pressing into being through the features of that disintegrated stone is a self Shelley now finds betrayed by destiny and lying in the rubble of his own exuberant idealism.

Yet oddly enough—and herein lies the poem's unspoken promise to the poet—within that bitter self-negation resides a deeper, more enduring affirmation. For out of "the decay / Of that colossal wreck," the world reformer will discover at last a more truly self-centering (hence, as he'd hoped, self-transcending) relationship to his art. As true for Shelley as it was for Keats, the death of the self was a prerequisite for the birth of the poet. By the time he'd write the *Defense of Poetry*—composed the year before his death, four years after "Ozymandias"—Shelley would finally come around to claim that a poet "would do ill to embody his own conceptions of right and wrong, which are usually those of his place and time, in his poetical creations, which participate in neither."

But let's go back to the beginning.

That eerie sense of detachment that distinguishes "Ozymandias" from others in the Shelley canon—and which determines for some its value as a poem—is established through a complex layering of voices, and an equally complex layering of historical times. In a prototypical modernist vein, the poem unfolds as a story within a story within a story. We have, first off, what might be called the poem's "frame," a tale recounted by the poem's anonymous narrator, who, to whatever degree, might be seen as the poet himself. His story holds a second story, as told by a "traveler from an antique land," a story before which the original narrator quickly disappears. In some faraway and long ago place, the traveler is reported to say, exists a desert in which he'd found "Two vast and trunkless legs of stone" and, nearby, "a shattered visage." And that was all, "Nothing beside remains." No trace of those achievements about which an inscription on the pedestal proudly claims, "Look on my works, ye Mighty, and despair!"

But the time the traveler refers us to points back to another time, to yet another story within *his* story, a time preceding the pedestal and the trunkless legs, a time from which a message was launched, as in a toy boat or corked bottle, onto a sea of random connections that have brought it here today. That message appears to have something to do with "those passions . . . / Which yet survive," though the artist who "mocked them" (*mocked* here means copied, not ridiculed) and the king whose heart they fed are both now reduced to "lifeless things." The message appears to exist somewhere in that pointed juxtaposition of what survives and what is swallowed up by the inexorable movement of time.

A curious thing has happened here, for the role of the artist, while linked by those passions to the role of the sovereign, is also implicitly distinguished from it. What survives of the ruler—or, in my reading, of the youthful idealist Shelley—is not, as the inscription claims, "my works," but a subordinate and reducible disposition. What survives of the artist, while reducible to neither the work nor the disposition, still of necessity contains them both (the "sneer" is inseparable from the stone on which it is carved). More significantly, the artist's making has somehow managed to outstrip time. For this reason one might assume safely that the poem has less to do with Ozymandias as an emblem of those absolute rulers Shelley deplored—after all, whether tyrant or benevolent leader, the fate of Ozymandias would remain the same—and more to do with that carefully nuanced chain of connections that has accurately "read," skillfully "mocked," and successfully kept alive "those passions."

That process, of course, only begins with the sculptor. Had it ended with him, his works, like those of Ozymandias, would have been equally lost to time. For in order to keep those passions alive, there is a second artist (whose art is telling) who has had to read and record their movement: that mysterious "traveler from an antique land," without whose story we'd know nothing of this. And then, as well, as we circle back through the layers of the poem, we are reminded of a crucial tertiary link: the poet himself, who composed the poem "Ozymandias," which contains and keeps alive both the traveler's story and the sculptor's stone.

Oddly enough, the poet proves the least present of all the figures in the poem. He ostensibly speaks only the first ten words of the sonnet, and those are directed away from himself: "I met a traveler from an antique land / Who said: . . . ." So where is he, this poet who, after a visit to the British Museum, proposed to a friend that they each attempt a sonnet on the subject? The poet who, through a mysterious confluence of events in his life, sat down to write a poem unlike anything he'd written before? It's appealing to imagine—and for some it may be instructive as well—that for the moment anyway there was no poet, that the poem was composed in that stupefying silence ("boundless and bare") between the death of one self and the birth of another; or that the poet who would be had not yet come into being, while the poet who was turned to rubble. It's appealing to imagine that at most there existed a consciousness, the faintest whisper of a consciousness, gazing back over the ruined prospect of its own past life. And what did this consciousness see? To borrow the words addressed to yet another famously uprooted statue—the great stone statue of General Du Puy in Stevens's *Notes Toward a Supreme Fiction*—"There never had been, never could be, such / A man."

The drama of this poem as anomaly—or more accurately as poem *donnée*—demands that we read it against the lavish backdrop of Shelley's earlier work, not as the negation or ratification of that work, but as an unwitting, and perhaps even unwanted, revelation of a spirit that had, until then, fueled that work—and would thereafter be called upon to transfigure it. "Ozymandias" serves as a cautionary tale—told by the poem to the poet midway in his writing life—about the futilities of worldly ambition and the transience of fame. But it's a poem with a darker interior as well, for at the heart of its revelation lies nothing less than a harrowing encounter with the desolate experience of self-extinction: "Round the decay / Of that colossal wreck, boundless and bare / The lone and level sands stretch far away." The shock of that experience accounts for the almost posthumous tone that attends its lines, and the effect of those lines remains one of the more urgent and unsettling and unmediated moments in Shelley's work.

Ozymandias

I met a traveler from an antique land
Who said: Two vast and trunkless legs of stone
Stand in the desert . . . Near them, on the sand,
Half sunk, a shattered visage lies, whose frown,
And wrinkled lip, and sneer of cold command,
Tell that its sculptor well those passions read

Which yet survive, stamped on these lifeless things,
The hand that mocked them, and the heart that fed:
And on the pedestal these words appear:
"My name is Ozymandias, king of kings:
Look on my works, ye Mighty, and despair!"
Nothing beside remains. Round the decay
Of that colossal wreck, boundless and bare
The lone and level sands stretch far away.

Percy Bysshe Shelley

PETER SCHMITT

Sad Heart at the Supermarket:
Randall Jarrell's "Next Day"

One of the challenges for any poet, just as for a playwright or novelist, is to write convincingly in the voice of the other sex. If Randall Jarrell's dramatic monologue, or persona poem "Next Day" succeeds in this endeavor, it must do so by persuading us that this modern suburban woman's voice is entirely credible. For the poem to transcend the mere impersonation of the other gender, it must speak for humanity in general—clearly the larger of the poet's tasks.

"Next Day" begins at the supermarket, specifically in the detergent aisle: "Moving from Cheer to Joy, from Joy to All." The ironies are many in this opening line: the impossibly upbeat names on the boxes, contrasting with the speaker's own disillusionment; she is in some way trying to cleanse her life, but can't get further than her laundry; she has bypassed happiness (Cheer, Joy) for the myth of having it All, as much a fantasy today as in the prefeminist sixties when Jarrell's housewife could conceive of little in her role beyond the traditional cooking and cleaning. For her, of course, "All" turns out to be a box of soap. And ever since the rice thrown at her wedding, what remains for her that is "wild," unruly, undomesticated? Certainly not "my Cornish game hens," bred for nothing more than consumption. Her counterparts in the market, in their frisky suburban wear, are just as deprived ("slacked or shorted") despite the abundance in their carts, and one hears "basket cases" in the remainder of the fourth line. But these other women, faceless as chickens in a coop, "Are selves I overlook," the speaker claims, at least outside of the poem's relentless self-scrutiny. It's a habit she's learned from William James, this knowing when to turn away. Is Jarrell attempting to lend his poem a little academic weight, or would a long-married homemaker really know William James? It's possible, particularly if she were college educated, and if the other wives lack such a sophisticated frame of reference it only tends to make her situation rather more depressing. The internal rhyme of "selves" and "shelves" suggests that her life has indeed been "shelved" intellectually, emotionally, physically.

As the bagboy brings the groceries out to her station wagon, that comfortably suburban vehicle of domesticity, marking her "station" in life, there is at least one self she can't "overlook." Out, briefly, in the open air, her comparisons are no longer to the clucking marketgoers but to the larger world, and "What I've become / Troubles me even if I shut my eyes." Squeezing those eyes shut conjures an earlier self, "When I was young and miserable and pretty / And poor." So much for youth as a carefree time! The speaker acknowledges the conventionality of her youthful desires: "to have a husband, / A house and children" (in the usual order of attainment). "Now that I'm old," and having realized those familiar ambitions, her wish is no less conventional: "That the boy putting groceries in my car // See me." To be favored again by youth itself. The enjambment of "See me" at the beginning of the new stanza, and its repetition at the other end of the line, force us indeed to see the phrase in all its imperative urgency: *See me!* But the bagboy, alas, does not.

It puzzles her, his lack of interest, when "For so many years / I was good enough to eat": a tasty grocery herself, the object of men's desires, when men *were* the "world" that "looked at me / And its mouth watered." (Now she looks at the world, and her *eyes* water.) Once, the eyes of others, "strangers," undressed her, like a stuffed game hen. These undressings are relegated now to the past, as are the allusions in the following lines: "holding their flesh within my flesh, their vile // Imaginings within my imagining, / I too have taken / The chance of life." If we take this passage with at least some literalism (as we should for every line), do we assume Jarrell means her single days, sleeping with virtual strangers? Note the breath taken at the stanza break after "vile": how the "imaginings," which she herself shares, are somehow more daunting than the very acts themselves. Or has she only undressed the others with her own eyes? Taking "The chance of life" would hint otherwise— that actual, physical liaisons with others, even relative strangers, are what one must sometimes risk to gain something greater, something Jarrell quietly terms "life." It is as if she insists, *I, too, have lived, I have known desire*—if in the past.

Now, however, the speaker would settle for attracting not even men, but, from her middle-aged outlook, a "boy," who instead of giving her the eye, "pats my dog." "Now I am good," she says, if not "good enough to eat." Safe, leashed, beyond the lusts of strangers, she thinks back to "The last mistaken, / Ecstatic, accidental bliss," not necessarily sexual at all, but a "blind // Happiness"—a filmy bubble of contentment, perhaps illusory—"that, bursting, leaves upon the palm / Some soap and water"—the detergent with which the poem began, the residue on one's hands after marriage and at least three children, now nearly grown. "It was so long ago," she reflects, "back in some Gay / Twenties"—*her* twenties?—"Nineties, I don't know." Possibly her confusion is meant to call back an imagined simpler time.

"Today," instead of an almost unlooked-for happiness, what she has is painfully felt absence, especially of her loved ones—daughter and sons away at school, husband at work—everything she once wished for and acquired, and yet she still feels alone and wishes for them still, even wishes on their behalf. The delight and pride she can take in her "accomplishments," so to speak, is limited; her daughter is "lovely," but still away from her. With only the dog and maid for company, she "go[es] through the sure unvarying days / At home in them." Home here means only routine, and yet it is precisely that safe, orderly predictability or constancy she most fears losing: "As I look at my life, / I am afraid / Only that it will change, as I am changing." What she fears, of course, is getting older and facing death.

The speaker's language is direct and exposed to the very degree that she feels exposed and vulnerable and would like to turn away but can't. "I am afraid," she repeats, "this morning, of my face." What one has known intimately all one's life now seems virtually dissociated, disembodied from the self: "It looks at me / From the rear-view mirror" just as she reviews her life. Aspects of her appearance—her eyes and smile—that have always bothered her are now, she tells us point-blank, features "I hate," even, ironically, as she smiles bravely and ruefully at her reflection. That face holds no surprises for her anymore, whatever is to be found there is "plain, lined . . . gray," bearing only one message that it repeats: "You're old." And she repeats it to herself, and for us: "That's all, I'm old." Everyone ages; how is my problem different from anyone else's? With this momentary, offhand deflection, we are all implicated in the poem.

And yet what age brings is not solely, if at all, the comforting wisdom of perspective, the wisdom of a William James. What it brings instead is a palpable fear, as the speaker repeats for the third time, "I'm afraid"; and only now do we grasp the import of the poem's title, "as I was at the funeral / I went to yesterday." We realize that the poem has been set not in the morning-after of a gratifying sexual rendezvous, but the at least as sobering *mourning* after, more frequent with age, of going to a funeral. And what frightened her so was seeing herself in the guise of her late friend, most likely another prosperous, middle-aged housewife.

"My friend's cold made-up face," rouged by morticians, is also unreal in the same way hers seems to be from that rearview mirror as she drives home. She replays touching the dead woman's face, and finding it "granite among its flowers"—that jarring juxtaposition—just as our speaker is hardened amid whatever mitigating influences her life may offer—her children, say, her house, her husband. "Her undressed, operated-on, dressed body" brings back with what one might call an almost surgical irony the earlier line, "How often they have undressed me," and the speaker spells both her lost youth and her waiting future in looking at her dead friend and conceding that what she gazed on "Were my face and body." Now it is the dead she identifies with, this self she cannot overlook. In this harsh light of mortality, even her youthful passionate encounters now dull in memory to clinical probings, mechanical exploratories that prepare us for the desolation of the poem's closing lines.

"As I think of her I hear her telling me // How young I seem"—a voice that reaches the speaker from memory, a remembered conversation, or through imagination, out of the grave—though the stanza break's white space communicates the span of the gulf in either case. She wants to be reassured, and alongside the dead it isn't difficult to feel relatively young. And she experiences, as she has more than once in the poem, momentary relief and gratification: "I *am* exceptional; / I think of all I have." But investing the dead with the authority she herself cannot summon proves just as futile as any attempt at self-assurance: despite her seeming youth and blessings, "really no one is exceptional" (that last word repeated to dull its distinctiveness), and she continues, bleakly: "No one has anything." She rejects the worth of material advantages, or even human bonds, in the face of death, and her identification with humanity's mortal condition is now complete: "I'm anybody." Jarrell's choice of *body* over *one* emphasizes both her physical decline and refutes any claims to individuality. In fact, in this final stanza's fourth line the one indefinite pronoun that seems to be missing is *anyone* (though shadowed by the "No one"), and the speaker's terrible sense of aloneness, and not just of a momentary nature, comes fully across.

At this point in the poem we remember that she has been driving back from the supermarket, her thoughts darkening along the way, and when she says in the penultimate line, "I stand beside my grave," we know at last she has arrived home. It isn't far, the poem would seem to say, from the detergent where we began to the boxes of house and coffin. Her home, she realizes, is her grave, it's what her life, so outwardly comfortable, has come to, and little wonder it is "Confused with my life," just as she wonders how all this time her home could so completely have become her life. What Jarrell mourns here is the virtual loss of an inner life—call it intellectual, or emotional, even spiritual—when it has been so thoroughly taken over by domestic routine. But if our housewife is confused by how her life can be both "commonplace and solitary" (just like the grave), how her life has become a living death, the poem offers little consolation to us as readers, because nowhere does it suggest that our fates—however we avoid the ensnarements of routine and tedium—should be any different from hers ("I'm anybody") in its desolation and bewilderment. No matter if William James is but a solitary entry in her commonplace book, it's enough to tell us that cultivating rich interior lives brings us no closer to what the woman who has everything is missing.

With its unobtrusive rhyme scheme and midlevel diction, "Next Day" has done nothing to distract us from the voice of the speaker in all her emotional directness. Jarrell has created a persuasive woman's voice by delivering throughout a convincing *human* voice. He has somehow managed for his 1960s suburban homemaker to speak for all of us, male and female, who at one time or another find our lives more empty than complete, and so offers us the possibility that our differences as men and women may yet prove secondary to our likenesses.

TOM SLEIGH

Raleigh's Ride

Sir Walter Raleigh the saturnine skeptic, whose South American voyages of plunder and exploration would earn him the nickname, "Butcher of Guiana," resists the balladeer of "Walsinghame," his Neoplatonic, thoroughly heartbroken lament. What tentative consolation the final stanza offers, the "durable fire" of true love echoing painfully off "dureless content" two stanzas back. Even the flame of love "In the mind ever burning; / Never sick, never old, never dead, / From itself never turning," hints at a fiery ether of self-contained isolation. Forever unreachable by the hard give-and-take of human affection, this love's timeless immunity to sickness, age, and death sorrowfully underscores the human limits that the triumphant stoicism almost overturns. Yet the voice's poise and supernatural calm as it reaches for the casual, unemphatic feminine rhyme hovers above the quiet anguish like the quaver of an overtone.

Perfectly achieved, effortless, above all *spoken*, this naturalness of diction recalls Yvor Winters's statement about poetry

which is perhaps the hardest to compose and the last to be recognized . . . a poetry . . . not striking or original in rhetorical procedure . . . but which permits itself originality . . . only in the most restrained and refined of subtleties in diction and in cadence, but which by virtue of those subtleties inspires its universals with their full value as experience.

By universals, Winters means something like the poem's general truths, though these are realized in us only because of the poet's complex intonations. And though the speakers in this poem clearly never strain after Browningesque "personality," nevertheless the skeletal narrative supplies the aura of individual circumstance. The disillusioned universals in the last four stanzas possess not only philosophical detachment but a hard edge of personal rancor. When the speaker lapses into the cliché of the fickle mistress in the penultimate stanza ("Of womenkind such indeed is the love"), his self-pity is undercut by the next line's tough-minded recovery of perspective ("Or the word love abused")—though without relinquishing totally the sense of personal injury that keeps the final stanza rooted in the complexity of our conflicting feelings toward others. The speaker's display of temperament keeps the final stanza from seeming like easy eloquence: beneath the masterful sublimity lurks the troubled reminder of our darker impulses.

Less than Neoplatonic cool also marks the speaker when earlier in the poem, in what seems like a highly conventional gesture, he says of his mistress "There is none hath a form so divine / In the earth or the air." Since Chaucer, carnal obsession on a pilgrimage is a commonplace, but the other pilgrim's enraptured acquiescence to the lover's obsession, claiming "Such an one did I meet, good Sir, / Such an angelic face, / Who like a queen, like a nymph did appear / By her gait, by her grace," effectively collapses the sacred and the sexual. Neither speaker seems worried about, or even cognizant of, this conflation of a pilgrimage to a shrine dedicated to the Virgin Mary with the lover's quest to find news of his mistress. But the eager, self-conscious, smutty zest with which a religious poet like John Donne would have treated such a paradox is alien to this poem's grave, utterly transparent style. Perhaps this simplicity of address coupled with a lack of Christian self-consciousness explains in part the poem's great attraction to a contemporary reader: the pilgrim/lover speaks to our half-ashamed, half-conscious fears of abandonment, of waning sexual attractiveness, and of a consolation not dependent on a changeable, sectarian God but located, "ever burning," in the alchemical fastness of the mind.

Here I am driven to ask how many champions of rhetorical ingenuity can begin to match the subtleties of the poem's formal resources? Of course Mallarmé or Hart Crane, even at their most ornate, are, like Raleigh, emotionally clear. High style, plain speech can both be life-lines or blind doodlings. For me, the poetic texture of "Walsinghame" is almost overwhelmingly complex: the songlike call and response between the lover and the other pilgrim that creates a charged dialectic between past joy and present pain; the syntactic parallelisms that drive home the speaker's moral judgments with irrevocable finality ("He is blind, he is deaf when he list"); the many repetitions, through which echolalia creates a haunted, obsessive sense of sorrow ("She hath left me here all alone, / All alone as unknown") while tonal shifts in pivotal phrases grow progressively more ironic, more heartbroken ("Met you not with my true love," "How shall I know your true love," "But true love is a durable fire"); the frequent loosening of ballad meter to accommodate the colloquial diction and to keep the rhymes from becoming overly insistent, both features that appeal to contemporary ears ("What's the cause that she leaves you alone / And a new way doth take, / Who loved you once as her own / And her joy did you make?"); all these subtleties help bring home what Winters called "the truth of a truism." At the same time, the poem's unselfconscious indifference to either Christian guilt or consolation, its secular frankness about the fading of sexual vitality, makes "Walsinghame" a quietly radical love poem.

In how many other poems in English does a male speaker acknowledge "Love likes not the falling fruit / From the withered tree"? Even his moment of misogynistic bitterness ("Of womenkind such indeed is the love") opens up to a less partial, if no less saturnine vision of lovers' relations: the jilted lover's sour grapes, his attempt at philosophical detachment, the dispassionate calm with which the rest of the stanza chastens his loss of cool—these complexities both embrace and ward off the final stanza's bleak grandeur.

In this quatrain, the self-constancy of the fire, "from itself never turning," stands quietly but fiercely indifferent to Mary's intercession or Christ's bounty. Still, it is tempting to envision Raleigh riding a horse in the shade of tall chestnut trees that grow together on either side of the muddy or dusty path trod by pilgrims on their way to the shrine. Skeptic that he is, Raleigh would want to see for himself the Madonna's expressionless face that, expressing nothing, expresses God. But, of course, the shrine was destroyed fourteen years before Raleigh was born. Perhaps the poet who wrote this poem was a phantom, the collective voice of anonymous balladeers, which my version of Raleigh overhears as his horse clops along between hedgerows nervous with insect rant and hum.

Meanwhile, the historical Raleigh, who, in exchange for his freedom from thirteen years of imprisonment in the Tower, had promised to enrich James's bankrupt England, was beheaded on October 29, 1618, for his failure to bring back nonexistent gold from Guiana. But as my phantom poet rides through fields and woods, the words, whether composed by "Raleigh" or the singers of the hedgerows, continue to ripen with the force of philosophical revelation: our three ineluctable negatives— sickness, age, death—drive the lover past complaint to the heights of speech.

Walsinghame

"As you came from the holy land
    Of Walsinghame,
Met you not with my true love
    By the way as you came?

"How shall I know your true love,
    That have met many one
As I went to the holy land,
    That have come, that have gone?"

"She is neither white nor brown,
    But as the heavens fair,
There is none hath a form so divine
    In the earth or the air."

"Such an one did I meet, good Sir,
    Such an angelic face,
Who like a queen, like a nymph did appear
    By her gait, by her grace."

"She hath left me here all alone,
    All alone as unknown,
Who sometimes did me lead with herself
    And me loved as her own."

"What's the cause that she leaves you alone
    And a new way doth take,
Who loved you once as her own
    And her joy did you make?"

"I have loved her all my youth,
    But now old as you see,
Love likes not the falling fruit
    From the withered tree.

"Know that Love is a careless child
    And forgets promise past;
He is blind, he is deaf when he list
    And in faith never fast.

"His desire is a dureless content
    And a trustless joy;
He is won with a world of despair
    And is lost with a toy.

"Of womenkind such indeed is the love
    Or the word love abused,
Under which many childish desires
    And conceits are excused.

But true love is a durable fire
    In the mind ever burning;
Never sick, never old, never dead,
    From itself never turning."

Sir Walter Raleigh

John Crowe Ransom and
Captain Carpenter

In 1977 I was asked by a courtly gentleman at Kenyon College to read my poetry there. I accepted. In the course of arrangements, he inquired if there was not something he might do in advance to make my visit pleasant. I answered that he might produce Mr. Ransom for dinner. A silence followed, then the man replied gravely that Ransom had died in 1974. It was instantly clear this gentleman felt both Ransom's presence and loss so palpably that he could assume I simply hadn't known of the death. But with a lame cleverness, I had asked deliberately for a hero I knew to be dead. John Crowe Ransom's poems are among the most civil and civilizing of our age. It is a black irony that the man who taught Allen Tate, Robert Penn Warren, Cleanth Brooks, Randall Jarrell, Anthony Hecht, and James Wright remains, however absent, vividly present in American poetry.

Ransom was many things. He came out of Tennessee, the son of a Methodist minister. He was, as Andrew Lytle has written, recipient of a sense of wholeness in man, meaning an awareness of a community of folk whose relationship defined him, whose values he absorbed as what Tate called "his culture." But Ransom, who set out to be a teacher in the dawning of Vanderbilt University's new hope for the South, went to France as an infantry lieutenant, serving in the most individually violent war Americans have experienced, with the possible exception of the War Between the States (many of whose veterans were still robust men when Ransom shipped over). In the tides of intellectual change then sweeping Europe, of which that war was an expedient, Ransom got a hard baptism. It reinforced the image of society adrift he had discovered as a Rhodes Scholar at Oxford.

The result was a man shriven by the specters driving Modernism through European life. It made the innocently pastoral outlook of the

Tennessee hills seem heavy baggage for Ransom's dualistic nature. His lifelong struggle was to accommodate a conservative spirit with a forward-looking intellect, and in poetry it would yield a style so individual "an imitator would have made a fool of himself," as Tate said of it. But Ransom's poetry was the man: genteel, meditative, courteous, eclectic, smart, cautious. Such a personality seems designed for an attitude of irony, that much-deployed marching order of the twentieth century.

Ransom's irony looks now unavoidable, the tongue inside everything he has to say. Ransom was a man of intense feeling, as his many poems about lovers' fortunes reveal, but he was courtly, private, so that he did not permit centering himself in a poem; nor would he pander to what might seem scandalous. His was what Robert Penn Warren called a "responsible self." To Ransom it meant putting distance from the subjectivity of human experience sufficient to give the poem dignity, grace, memorability, a sonic order that might endure the roughest human actions. The range of Ransom's irony includes wit, eggheaded puns, learned allusions, imitations, satire, and more—all keeping the poet enshadowed, as he might have said, so that the reader may be worked upon by words, not a rhetoric of personalism. The late Howard Nemerov thought this made for "elegance" and nicely defined this as:

a means to precision of statement, more especially a means to control of tone: it implies manners, or style—the general code, that is, by which particular choices are made, by which objects are arranged in one order rather than another. At a deeper level the quality insists even abstractly and generally that order and choice always matter, whether the world is reasonable or not.

It is not hard to imagine a man like Ransom, impelled by the new century's change, writing poetry to make moral, political, and cultural statements. Certainly his young disciples, the Vanderbilt Fugitives, had their tendencies in didactic directions. But his ironic stance reveals an inability to abide the didactic poem. He wanted the accurate portrayal of people and actions in the fluidity and contradictory pressures of actual life, in style often local and naturalistic. He fixed his vision, by definition destructive of the monistic view of his heritage, in language molded from archaic vocabulary and colloquial phrase, mixed diction, and overt, if customized verse forms. Minor in scope and miniature in structure, Ransom's poems nevertheless blister us with a yearning for tranquility and final harmony that is ever beset by the erosive way of the world. He might have dealt in the psychology of obligation, responsibility, and blame so common to engaged poets of our period, but he did not. He chose to dramatize by fable, reserving himself and his authority.

Ransom's fastidious reservations and ironic absence mean he has not the engagement with public issues found in Eliot, Crane, and Robinson. He hasn't the brio of sophistication in Stevens and little of the personal walk in the world of Williams. He came to regard the poetry of his student Warren as unnecessarily crude. He did not write about hunger, homelessness, or Americans at war. He makes no mention of black citizens of the South, many of whom were living ex-slaves in Ransom's lifetime. Except by implication, one finds no description of waves of southerners migrating to Detroit, Chicago, and elsewhere because the South seemed poor. There is scant presence of the failure of southern farms, the brutality of southern mills, the hopeless schools, the lack of hospitals, roads, what we now call "infrastructure." There is no clear sex, no drugs, alcohol, or new insidiousness. Ransom's world cannot be easily set beside Faulkner or Erskine Caldwell because it isn't really a world at all; it is a style, and Ransom's style invites us away from the worst. His poetry can seem the fiddly preoccupations of a tame old man.

In fact, Ransom's style hides the toughness of a mind that knows final and irrefutable vulnerability, violence, and death. He might have said, as Flannery O'Connor did, that violence was one way people have of getting to Heaven, if he had not been disabused of Heaven. Randall Jarrell argued "Ransom's poems are produced by the classical, or at worst semi-classical, treatment of Romantic subjects." Jarrell called Ransom's poetry a war "of Feeling and Power" and noted his ironic strategy was an armor with which a campaigner might survive in an uncivil world. Yet Ransom loves man's potential most, hence the Romanticism Jarrell attaches to him. Most poets believe, however bad the world undeniably is, the heart remains a wondrous, unpredictable, and instructive organ. Abuses to love constitute the primary plot of Ransom's great tale. Love's enemy, death, is his favorite character, the actor who literally plucks out the heart in my favorite Ransom poem, "Captain Carpenter," which Jarrell argues is the fabular equivalent of Kafka's "Metamorphosis."

If Ransom is as local as Thomas Hardy or Robert Frost, there is in him also, formidably, James Joyce's nightmare. Kafka's Gregor Samsa is the crawling image of nightmarish change, but Ransom's farcical psychodrama in "Captain Carpenter" makes a mean historical jest. Published by the thirty-six-year-old Ransom in the third issue of *The Fugitive* (1924) and included in his finest volume *Chills and Fever*, the poem is a study in brutality. If filmed for television, it would be censored despite the lullaby of its saying.

Ransom regarded the Captain as "an old hero who dies with his boots on" and declined to see an image of doomed Southern warriors. Captain Carpenter is no one we know. A midlevel officer of an unnamed army, modern to his pistols and archaic on horseback, the man takes his military duty so lightly he is distracted, if not waylaid by "ladies in a rout" among whom one, with a sword, "twined him of his nose for evermore." The Inspector Clouseau of his organization, the Captain seems by destiny bound to encounter bad opposition. Barely three stanzas into the sixteen-stanza poem, he meets a "rogue that looked unchristian" and he attacks. Both of his legs are broken.

Captain Carpenter is a screwup with good intentions. His defeats create amusement for us, but they could be most costly; worse, they are continuous. They are campaigns against mysterious forces such as "the wife of Satan" who "bit off his arms at the elbows," a "black devil" that took his ears, and another who got his "sweet blue eyes." Miss O'Connor might have said, at such a point, he was now ready to fight. He broadcasts his challenge:

> To any adversity it is fame
> If he risk to be wounded by my tongue
> Or burnt in two beneath my red heart's flame
> Such are the perils he is cast among.

Ransom must have delighted in his warrior's near-malapropism with that echo of *heartburn*. What he surely most loved, however, was the Captain becoming, finally, pissed off after "threescore and ten years." Ransom would not permit us to identify the old warrior with himself, yet for both this is an act of temporary settling up with the nettlesome and, alas, invincible otherworld. Drawing on the Anglo-Saxon tradition of epic heroes from Beowulf to Galahad to Davy Crockett, caging them in the commonest lyric stanza, Ransom ends his lines with ascending rhythms of childish pleasure. Whiffs of song send his man to battle the biggest, baddest Bluto yet:

> It was the neatest knave that ever was seen
> Stepping in perfume from his lady's bower
> Who at this word put in his merry mein
> and fell on Captain Carpenter like a tower.

The mincing, delicate footwork of the stanza's first three lines, dominantly iambic, archaic in diction, idiomatic in tone, magically set up the vaudevillian tumble and thump of the last line. You can hear the drum in the pit. But as Yogi Berra said, "it ain't over till it's over." Knocked to the dirt, the seventy-year-old battler still has "the old heart in his bust / And a blade shook between rotten teeth alack." Indeed.

For readers who insist upon the Romantic triumphs of good souls afforded by escapist entertainments, Ransom is not the man. His Captain's combat for life ends when a villainous little knave simply "pierced him and produced the Captain's heart." The poem proceeds three stanzas on to allow the narrator, never identified, never a participant, to declare an overt curse upon the undefeated opponents of this determinedly brave, if ineffectual man.

> The curse of hell upon the sleek upstart
> That got the Captain finally on his back
> And took the red vitals of his heart
> And made the kites to whet their beaks clack clack.

The whole poem is transparently fabular, comic, a cartoon built of off-the-shelf conventions exaggerated ludicrously to satirize violences we give in the name of whatever cause. Ransom keeps the gore squarely before us. No offstage Greek blood for him. What, then, is our proper response to such an evil world? Are we to imagine the Captain should have held his challenge? Been prudent? Was he only inept? Maybe Ransom values whatever motivates man to persist in principled, if misguided action. Americans have fought for self-defense as well as self-deception. Wars have been fought for glands as well as love; for freed lives as well as for lippy jingoism. Ransom has defeated his Captain as handily as did his opponents, but Ransom makes solidarity with that man, who is none other than himself, padded by the cooly deflective, suasive costuming effects of his entertainment, itself sent up in that last double-beat, wryly belligerent, "clack clack."

Among the expressions of "Captain Carpenter" nothing is more softly, grimly put than the inevitable end of things. The hero, Captain Carpenter, links in one active image athletes, soldiers, frontiersman, all who strive mightily in our steads, even Jesus the carpenter. But the Captain is willy-nilly reduced to a heap of rubble. And isn't it a pity, though sweet the saying of that pity. Ransom doesn't tell us to emulate great ones but to know they stand as diced and dicey in the world as we do. All he offers is pleasure in a way of saying, the beauty of words memorable and fresh with the experience of being alive. "Captain Carpenter" refuses to make moral even as it makes lesson. Its joke depends on a veneration of manhood, virtue, and artistic striving.

Ransom's was a deeply powerful imagination trying to yoke the good past to a weak present in the language of heroes. He made of language a grail, of the poet a necessary hero. He taught that to greater talents like Warren, who, mocking Milton in "Folly on Royal Street Before the Raw Face of God," asks "For what is man without magnificence?" and answers "Delusion, delusion!" But perhaps he has spoken too quickly, for Warren leaves unclear whether he thinks magnificence is what deludes or man's ambition to know. Almost immediately, then, he adds "Passion / is all. Even / The Sleaziest." It doesn't finally matter whether

Ransom gave Warren to know that, as I suspect he did. What matters is that it is so, and "Captain Carpenter" continues to shudder with all the passion a poet can get into a lyric. I am certain this is why I sometimes think I did meet the dead, surely heroic, and hardly absent poet in Ohio.

Louis MacNeice: "House on a Cliff"

Louis MacNeice (1907–1963) was almost universally beloved by his peers among the English poets, though he was an Irishman from Ulster who fits into none of the categories retrospectively conferred upon his generation. His clergyman father, with roots in the west of Ireland, rose in the Protestant Church of Ireland to become a bishop. Louis was educated in classics at two famous English public schools, adopting at an early age the pose of an atheistic, rather coolly aesthetic bohemian. At Oxford, MacNeice relished the role of a maverick eccentric. He knew, but was junior to, Auden and Spender, and although he later associated with the pro-Communist, pro-Republican intellectuals of the thirties—on two occasions visiting Spain—an unfinished autobiography published after his death (*The Strings Are False*) shows him to have been, on the whole, a modern stoic, skeptically detached from politics and wittily scornful of simplistic dogma.

As is true of many poets, public and private personas were dissociated in MacNeice, the one built up fancifully, one supposes, to protect the other. Tom Paulin, in an interesting essay, describes him as an Irishman "from no part," drawing attention to the "anguished sense of displacement that is so fundamental to his imagination." It was not that MacNeice was socially rejected or disliked. Manifestly, he could at will charm his way into any group that attracted him. It was more (or so I apprehend) that his loneliness was intensely personal, perhaps even self-induced, and that his sharp intelligence restrained him from adopting wholesale ideologies to staunch some incurable yet poetically indispensible wound.

"House on a Cliff," written in 1955, may, as Paulin suggests, metaphorically indicate Ireland, or the ambiguous role that divided nation played in the poet's private history. The poem speaks to me, however, almost entirely of a divided sense of being. Notice, though, how often the words *indoors* and *outdoors* appear in the same line, suggesting that they are extremes of the same spectrum. The "house," more symbol than actuality, is nonetheless a real house where a man has to live, confronted "indoors" and "outdoors" with his lonely condition in an indifferent cosmos.

The first three lines call attention to all five senses: the "tang" of the oil lamp, both smelled and tasted; the visible "winking signal" at sea; then the sound of the wind indoors as compared to the feel or touch of the wind outside. This emphasis on immediate sensation is brought about by a syntactical, surely deliberate, omission of verbs; indeed, no copulative verb appears anywhere in the poem. The nouns succeed each other disjointedly, arhythmically, here and there colored by a lopped participle. In the arresting fourth line, two participial phrases, "locked heart" and "lost key" signal an abrupt drop into another register. The lonely house becomes metaphorically the soul, and the two images together throw their long shadows forward, as it were, over a tightening panic.

Though house and sea still preside in the second stanza, the word *siren* (ambiguously warning and enticing) introduces an urban scream, a wail of urgency juxtaposed with the ticking of the "blind clock" (a characteristic MacNeicean image) suggestive both of blind mechanical time and the helpless aging of a human heart. Again, a jagged enjambment— "Outdoors" at the end of the third line—leads to a renewed image of the sea, ruled by the contrastingly "silent" and timeless moon. Surprisingly (or maybe not) the moon in this mechanical universe remains female: "the garrulous tides she rules." Both personifications may appear inappropriate to the ahuman emptiness of "outdoors"—unless the she-ness of the moon represents a threat to the he-ness of the speaker. One doesn't know how conscious or unconscious MacNeice was of this.

MacNeice was surely conscious, though, of the explicit nihilism that "outdoors" brings to the final stanza: "the empty (Godless) bowl of heaven, the empty deep." In the face of which the "purposeful (intellectual) man," caught helplessly in the "ancestral curse-cum-blessing" of his inheritance, "talks at cross / Purposes, to himself, in a broken sleep." The repercussions of that *cross* at the end of the penultimate line are extraordinarily resonant. *Cross* suggests anger, of course, and impotence (crossed wires that defeat attempts at communication with others) while at the same time symbolizing the Christian cross (which MacNeice had abandoned, not without guilt) together with all the other implications that being "crossed" or importantly frustrated bring to mind. There is also a sense in which the entire poem is a cross between the stressed meters of English and the quantitative meters of Greek and Latin, a cross that makes for restlessness and rhythmic tension in nearly all MacNeice's work.

This seemingly simple English lyric, sealed in traditional stanzas and rhymes, is in fact a work of mysterious, dreamlike profundity. *The Strings Are False* records a number of MacNeice's dreams, and "House on a Cliff" may well be oneiric in origin. Yet the surrealism of its imagery, like the "nihilism" of its message, is so brilliantly confounded by the compressed passion and *puissance* of its form, that a reader is drawn into the spell before he begins to search for meanings.

I should add that I'm personally drawn to this lyric because some six or seven years ago, unaware that "House on a Cliff" existed, I found myself writing a poem I called "The Other House." My house was, quite by accident, of the same archetypal construction, though forty years on from MacNeice's time it may be easier to accept that men and women are not the measure of all things, and that living in a "purposeless" universe does not have to detract from the preciousness of life.

> Beneath me, infinitely deep,
> solidity dissolves.
> Above me, infinitely wide,
> galactic winter sprawls.
> That house of the utterly outside
>   became my home.
>
> In it, the house of childhood
> safeguards my mother's face.
> A lifted eyebrow's 'Yes, and so?'
> latches the rooms in place.
> I tell my children all I know
>   of the word 'gone'.

From Eternity to Here: Traherne's "The Salutation"

Thomas Traherne's "The Salutation" begins with questions that we might, in the last decade of the twentieth century, reflexively try to answer from a psychological perspective. It is almost as if, we might imaginatively project, the poem's speaker is looking at a photograph of himself, wondering why he hasn't been able to uncover, hidden in his childhood, the unconscious sources of his present problems. The questions the speaker asks imply repression, the reasons for which one would seek, along with the repressed content itself, to reveal. Speech is crucial here, hidden in a formidable depth. We might conjecture that his infancy (literally, the inability to speak) has extended into adulthood and long silence now pressures him to articulate hitherto unknown or unconfronted emotions.

A seventeenth-century expectation of what this opening stanza might lead to, however, would probably have been quite different. The son of a cobbler, Traherne lived only thirty-seven years (1637–1674), the last thirteen of them as rector of Credenhill in Herefordshire, England, although he resided in London and Middlesex from 1667 until his death, working as chaplain for a nobleman, and as vicar at Teddington. One might have anticipated, then, a poem unfolding from this greeting stanza to present a theological answer to the questions it raises; its tone of welcome discovery might be a prelude for thanksgiving to God who has revealed a long-kept secret. One might expect the image of the obscuring curtain to grow into a trope involving God as playwright and director, whose purposes, hidden for part of his actor's life, are revealed when the right time comes. Or, perhaps, the Lord, who was in the beginning word, would reach down into the awful abyss of silence that has so long afflicted the speaker and raise him to speech, in all likelihood praise for the hoisting.

One would, of course, by taking the latter course be closer to what Traherne actually does. But even then, I think, we find him departing radically from the expected norm, eccentric in the literal sense of the term.

The first rather stunning turn is his immediate specification of "so long." Traherne doesn't limit the phrase to a lifetime, or part of one. At first it covers instead "so many thousand thousand years," a period considerably preceding his birth. It is an imaginative conception comparable to the one underlying the question in the old hymn—"Will there be any stars in my crown?"—where in the asking the singer becomes a constellation. In Traherne's poem the source he seeks, the span of time in which his question resides, is eventually nothing short of eternity. He has been hidden from himself not since his childhood, but since he lay "in a chaos" "beneath the dust." The repetition of "so long" in stanza three is incremental, but hugely so; it is "from eternity" that he has been "nothing." Even with the rhetorical question (lines 7–11) that tempers the speaker's expectations of himself, this evocation of the timelessness before (and after) time is a monumental inflation of that initially manageable, homey "so long."

Traherne's speaker—or, one imagines from the evidence of *The Centuries* (Traherne's collected poetic meditations), Traherne—has recovered, or met for the first time, himself, newly created from dust, from chaos, which had been directed toward his creation from eternity. The focus for twenty lines is on the bodily aspect of this being ("limbs," "rosy cheeks," etc.), with implications of emotional life ("smiles," "tears"), including the joys of speaking and listening. At almost the precise center of the poem (line 21) Traherne adds the soul. One might notice in the accumulation of a "definition" of man in these four stanzas that the mind, unlike the soul, is excluded—and there is no scholastic nostalgia for a distinction among the various kinds of soul Traherne might be referring to. His poem is emotional, celebratory, playful, not concerned with pedantic calisthenics, or, particularly, wit, another characteristic highly valued in the verse of the period.

It is also, in Traherne's exemplary way, an unabashedly self-centered poem. This is perhaps its most surprising aspect, given its subject. Traherne does write, after all, a poem praising God for his creation, but with a decidedly immodest twist.

> A God preparing did this glorious store,
> This world for me adorn.

He becomes implicitly Adam, the end of God's creation. There is no qualification of this, no equivocation about it, no argument considered against it. On the contrary, the discovery is jubilant and self-radiant.

It may be appropriate to mention here a few of the many passages from *The Centuries* that complement the focuses of "The Salutation." In *The First Century*, #55, for instance, Traherne writes for Mrs. Hopton, that

the contemplation of Eternity maketh the Soul immortal. Whose glory it is, that it can see before and after its existence into endless spaces. Its Sight is its presence. And therefore is the presence of the understanding endless, because its Sight is so. O what glorious creatures should we be could we be present in spirit with all Eternity.

Much of *The Third Century* approximates an "account" of Traherne's mystical love of childhood. The following scraps from the first three sections suggest the richness and delicacy of his intoxication.

Will you see the infancy of this sublime and celestial greatness? Those pure and virgin apprehensions I had from the womb, and that divine light wherewith I was born are the best unto this day, wherein I can see the Universe. By the gift of God they attended me into the world, and by His special favour I remember them till now.

All appeared new, and strange at first, inexpressibly rare and delightful and beautiful. I was a little stranger, which at my entrance into the world was saluted and surrounded with innumerable joys. . . . Is it not strange, that an infant should be heir of the whole World, and see those mysteries which the books of the learned never unfold?

Eternity was manifest in the Light of the Day, and something infinite behind everything appeared: which talked with my expectation and moved my desire. . . . The skies were mine, and so were the sun and moon and stars, and all the World was mine; and I the only spectator and enjoyer of it.

To return to the poem itself: among the joys he cites, the one that touches me most immediately concludes stanza three: "such feet, / Beneath the skies, on such a ground to meet." I set this meeting of human feet with earth against G. M. Hopkins's famous "have trod, have trod, have trod," and, not surprisingly, prefer Traherne's delight to the other cleric's lament. One poet is, of course, blessing the dawn of things, the other is overcome with their decline, and perhaps because of the toil he includes in "God's Grandeur" Hopkins's eventual image of the Holy Ghost as a brooding bird may be said to be harder earned. But that's the point: Traherne's subject is the glorious gift of the world, and his joy in the fundamental act of walking on it. He finds, in fact, that the human body is itself worth more than the world it inhabits, containing in its young, articulated limbs and circulatory system "More wealth . . . than all the world contains."

Were it not for the tone of childlike ecstasy Traherne has managed to extend unbroken through the poem, one might be tempted to call this response to the personal self as creation's aim an example of the root sin of pride and seek ways to discredit the poem's attitude. But as I read these stanzas, and almost all of Traherne's work, the tone is seamless, and the sense of wide-eyed (but no longer "infant") joy genuine.

There is more, however, to the exclusion of pride than tone. Traherne sets a condition on God's "gift" to him of "these brighter regions." "The earth, the seas, the light, the day, the skies, / The sun and stars are mine: *if those I prize*" (my emphasis). For his ownership to transpire, he must value at its innate worth the created universe that his existence crowns. Similarly, he is awed at poem's end by what he has become "son and heir" to. Amid the multitude of strange things and glories and treasures he (himself "A stranger here") meets, the strangest of all is that he, "who nothing was," is the inheritor of such extraordinary creation.

Traherne's poem, then, characteristic of his general attitude throughout his *Centuries*, is a far cry from either the psychological structures we might take those opening lines to imply, or the conventional praise of God for his creation we might expect from a less individual poet of the period. The simultaneous self- and God-centered understanding that arises from the speaker's perspective joy makes him unique among a galaxy of contemporaries. This may recall a condition that is alien to many mid to late twentieth-century sensibilities: a shared literary tradition with its concomitant conventional expectations and a mutual dispensation of mental, religious, and social habits, produces highly individualized voices so sharply differentiated from one another. We haven't seen its like since, I think, in terms of disparate jewels in one crown. Traherne's shines as brightly as any. He had to wait, as we say, for this to occur, however. As he was hidden so long from himself in the course of his creation in "The Salutation," so was his work hidden from readers for some two hundred years before Bertram Dobell's lucky discovery of it in a London bookstore. So dust gathers for its inscrutable purposes.

The Salutation

I

These little limbs,
These eyes and hands which here I find,
These rosy cheeks wherewith my life begins,
Where have ye been? Behind
What curtain were ye from me hid so long!
Where was, in what abyss, my speaking tongue?

When silent I,
So many thousand thousand years,
Beneath the dust did in a chaos lie,
How could I smiles or tears,
Or lips or hands or eyes or ears perceive?
Welcome ye treasures which I now receive.

I that so long
Was nothing from eternity,
Did little think such joys as ear or tongue,
To celebrate or see:
Such sounds to hear, such hands to feel, such feet,
Beneath the skies, on such a ground to meet.

New burnisht joys!
Which yellow gold and pearl excell!
Such sacred treasures are the limbs in boys,
In which a soul doth dwell;
Their organized joints, and azure veins
More wealth include, than all the world contains.

From dust I rise,
And out of nothing now awake,
These brighter regions which salute mine eyes,
A gift from God I take
The earth, the seas, the light, the day, the skies,
The sun and stars are mine; if those I prize.

Long time before
I in my mother's womb was born,
A God preparing did this glorious store,
The world for me adorn.

Into this Eden so divine and fair,
So wide and bright, I come his son and heir.

7

A stranger here
Strange things doth meet, strange glories see;
Strange treasures lodged in this fair world appear,
Strange all, and new to me.
But that they mine should be, who nothing was,
That strangest is of all, yet brought to pass.

Thomas Traherne

T. S. Eliot's "Love Song of J. Alfred Prufrock"

In 1952, sailing to Korea as a U.S. Navy librarian for Landing Ship Tank 914, I read T. S. Eliot's *The Love Song of J. Alfred Prufrock*. Ill-educated, a product of Chicago's public-school system, I was nineteen years old and, awakened by Whitman, Eliot, and Williams, had just begun writing poetry. I was also reading all the books I could get my hands on.

Eliot had won the Nobel Prize in 1948 and, curious, I was trying to make sense of poems like *Prufrock* and *The Waste Land*.

"What do you know about T. S. Eliot?" I asked a young officer who'd been to college and studied English literature. I knew from earlier conversations that we shared an interest in what he called "modern poetry." A yeoman third class, two weeks at sea and bored, I longed for someone to talk to. "T. S. Eliot was born in St. Louis, Missouri, but he lives now in England and is studying to become an Englishman," the officer said, tapping tobacco into his pipe. "The 'T. S.' stands for 'tough shit.' You read Eliot's *Love Song of J. Alfred Prufrock*, what one English prof called 'the first poem of the modern movement,' and if you don't understand it, 'tough shit.' All I can say is that's some love song."

An anthology of poetry open before us, we were sitting in the ship's all-metal, eight by eight-foot library eating bologna sandwiches and drinking coffee. Fortunately, the captain kept out of sight and life on the slow-moving (eight to ten knots), flat-bottomed amphibious ship was unhurried and anything but formal.

"Then why does Eliot bother calling it a love song?" I asked, as the ship rolled and the coffee sloshed onto a steel table. The tight metal room smelled like a cross between a diesel engine and a New York deli.

"Eliot's being ironic, sailor. *Prufrock* is the love song of a sexually repressed and horny man who has no one but himself to sing to." Drawing on his pipe, the officer scratched his head. "Like you and I, Mr. Prufrock is a lonely man on his way to a war zone. We're sailing to Korea and we know the truth, don't we? We may never make it back. Prufrock marches like a brave soldier to a British drawing room that, he tells us, may be the death of him. He's a mock heroic figure who sings of mermaids and peaches and drowning."

Pointing to lines 129–31, the officer read aloud:

> We have lingered in the chambers of the sea
> By sea-girls wreathed with seaweed red and brown
> Till human voices wake us and we drown.

"Prufrock is also singing because he's a poet. Prufrock *is* T. S. Eliot and, the truth is, Eliot is so much like Prufrock that he has to distance himself from his creation. That's why he gives the man that pompous name. Did you know 'Tough Shit,' as a young man, sometimes signed himself 'T. Stearns Eliot?' You have to see the humor—the irony—in *Prufrock* to understand the poem."

"I read it, I hear it in my head, but I still don't get it," I confessed. "What is *Prufrock* about?"

" 'Birth, death and copulation, that's all there is.' That's what Eliot himself says. Of course the poem also touches on aging, social status, and fashion."

"Aging and fashion?" I asked.

The officer threw back his head and recited:

> (They will say: "How his hair is growing thin!")
> My morning coat, my collar mounting firmly to the chin,
> My necktie rich and modest, but asserted by a simple pin.

He paused, then went on:

> I grow old . . . I grow old . . .
> I shall wear the bottoms of my trousers rolled.

"At the time the poem was written it was fashionable for young men to roll their trousers. In lines 120–21, Thomas Stearns Prufrock is laughing at himself for being middle-aged and vain.

"Anyway, *The Love Song of J. Alfred Prufrock* is an interior monologue," said the officer, finishing his bologna sandwich and washing it down with dark rum. Wiping mustard from his mouth, he continued. "The whole thing takes place in J. Alfred Prufrock's head. That's clear, isn't it?"

I had read Browning's *My Last Duchess* and understood about interior monologues.

"Listen, sailor: Prufrock thinks about drawing rooms, but he never actually sets foot in one. Am I right?"

"Yeah," I said after rereading the first ten lines. "I think so."

"The poem is about what goes through Prufrock's mind on his way to some upper-class drawing room. It's a foggy evening in October, and what Mr. Prufrock really needs is a drink. He's a tightass Victorian, a lonely teetotaling intellectual. Anyone else would forget the toast and marmalade and step into a pub and ask for a pint of beer."

Setting down his pipe, the naval officer opened the flask and refilled our coffee mugs.

"Every time I think I know what *Prufrock* means it turns out to mean something else," I said. "Eliot uses too many symbols. Why doesn't he just say what he means?"

"The city—'the lonely men in shirt-sleeves' and the 'one-night cheap hotels'—are masculine," said the officer. "That's what cities are like, aren't they: ugly and oppressive. What's symbolic—or should I say, what's obscure—about that?"

"Nothing," I said. "That's the easy part—Prufrock walking along like that."

"Okay," said the officer. "And in contrast to city streets, you've got the oppressive drawing room that, in Prufrock's mind, is feminine—'Arms that are braceleted and white and bare' and 'the marmalade, the tea, / Among the porcelain, among some talk of you and me'." Using a pencil, the officer underlined those images in the paperback anthology.

"You ever been to a tea party, Sward?"

"No, sir, I haven't. Not like Prufrock's."

"Well," said the officer, "I have and I have a theory about that 'overwhelming question' Prufrock wants to ask in line 10—and again in line 93. Twice in the poem we hear about an 'overwhelming question.' sailor?"

"Prufrock wants to ask the women what they're doing with their lives, but he's afraid they'll laugh at him," I said.

"Guess again, Sward," he said leaning back in his chair, stretching his arms.

"What's your theory, sir?"

"Sex," said the officer. "On the one hand, it's true, he wants to fit in and play the game because, after all, he's privileged. He belongs in the drawing room with the clever Englishwomen. At the same time he fantasizes. If he could, I think he'd like to shock them. Prufrock longs to put down his dainty porcelain teacup and shout, 'I am Lazarus, come from the dead, / Come back to tell you all, I shall tell you all.'"

"Why doesn't he do it?" I asked.

"Because Prufrock is convinced no matter what he says he won't reach them. He feels the English gentlewomen he's dealing with are unreachable. He believes his situation is as hopeless as theirs. He's dead and they're dead, too. That's why the poem begins with an image of sickness, 'a patient etherized upon a table,' and ends with people drowning. Prufrock is tough shit, man."

"You said you think there's a connection between Eliot the poet and J. Alfred Prufrock," I said.

"Of course there's a connection. Tommy Eliot from St. Louis, Missouri," said the officer. "Try as he will, he doesn't fit in. His English friends call him 'The American' and laugh. Tom Eliot the outsider with his rolled umbrella. T. S. Eliot is a self-conscious, make-believe Englishman and you have to understand that to understand *Prufrock*.

"The poem is dark and funny at the same time. It's filled with humor and Prufrock is capable of laughing at himself. Just read those lines, 'Is it perfume from a dress / That makes me so digress?'"

"You were talking about Prufrock being sexually attracted to the women. How could that be if he is, as you say, 'dead.'" I asked.

"By 'dead' I mean desolate, inwardly barren, godforsaken. Inwardly, spiritually, Prufrock is a desolate creature. He's a moral man, he's a civilized man, but he's also hollow. But there's hope for him. In spite of himself, Prufrock is drawn to women.

"Look at line 64. He's attracted and repelled. Prufrock attends these teas, notices the women's arms 'downed with light brown hair!' and it scares the hell out of him because what he longs to do is to get them onto a drawing-room floor or a beach somewhere and bury his face in that same wonderfully tantalizing 'light brown hair.' What do you think of that, sailor?"

"I think you're right, sir."

"Then tell me this, Mr. Sward: Why doesn't he ask the overwhelming question? Hell, man, maybe it's not sexual. Maybe I'm wrong. Maybe what he wants to do is to ask some question like what you yourself suggested: 'What's the point in going on living when, in some sense, we're all already dead?'"

"I think he doesn't ask the question because he's so repressed, sir. He longs for physical contact, like you say, but he also wants another kind of intimacy, and he's afraid to ask for it and it's making him crazy."

"That's right, sailor. He's afraid. Eliot wrote the poem in 1911 when women were beginning to break free."

"Break free of what?" I asked.

"Of the prim and proper Victorian ideal. Suffragettes, feminists they called themselves. At the time Eliot wrote *Prufrock*, women in England and America were catching on to the fact that they were disfranchised and had begun fighting for the right to vote, among other things, and for liberation, equality with men.

"Of course Prufrock is more prim and proper than the bored, over-civilized women in the poem. And it's ironic, isn't it, that he doesn't understand that the women are one step ahead of him. What you have in Prufrock is a man who tries to reconcile the image of real women with 'light brown hair' on their arms with some ideal, women who are a cross between the goddess Juno and a sweet Victorian maiden."

"Prufrock seems to know pretty well what he's feeling," I said. "He's not a liar and he's not a coward. To be honest, sir, I identify with Prufrock. He may try on one mask or another, but he ends up removing the mask and exposing himself."

"Now, about interior monologues: to understand *Prufrock* you have to understand that most poems have one or more speakers and an audience, implied or otherwise. Let's go back to line 1. Who is this "you and I" Eliot writes about?"

"Prufrock is talking to both his inner self and the reader," I said.

"How do you interpret the first ten lines?" the officer asked, pointing with his pencil.

" 'Let us go then, you and I,' he's saying, let us stroll, somnolent and numb as a sedated patient, through these seedy 'half-deserted streets, / The muttering retreats / Of restless nights in one-night cheap hotels.' "

"That's it, sailor. And while one might argue that Prufrock 'wakes' at the end of the poem, he is for the most part a ghostly inhabitant of a world that is, for him, a sort of hell. He is like the speaker in the Italian epigraph from Dante's *Inferno*, who says, essentially, 'Like you, reader, I'm in purgatory and there is no way out. Nobody ever escapes from this pit and, for that reason, I can speak the truth without fear of ill fame.'

"Despairing and sick of heart, Prufrock is a prisoner. Trapped in himself and trapped in society, he attends another and another in an endless series of effete, decorous teas.

> In the room the women come and go
> Talking of Michelangelo.

"Do you get it now? Do you see what I mean when I say 'tough shit'?" said the officer.

"Yeah, I'm beginning to," I said.

"T. S. Eliot's *Prufrock* has become so much a part of the English language that people who have never read the poem are familiar with phrases like 'I have measured out my life with coffee spoons' and 'I grow old . . . I grow old . . . / I shall wear the bottoms of my trousers rolled' and 'Do I dare to eat a peach?' and 'In the room the women come and go.'

"Do you get it now? Eliot's irregularly rhymed, 131-line interior monologue has become part of the monologue all of us carry on in our heads. We are all of us, whether we know it or not, love-hungry, sex-crazed soldiers and sailors, brave, bored and lonely. At some level in our hearts, we are all J. Alfred Prufrock, every one of us, and we are all sailing into a war zone from which, as the last line of the poem implies, we may never return."

THOMAS SWISS

John Skelton and "A Ballade of the

Scottysshe Kynge"

It's not surprising that in some of John Skelton's poems there is a kind of narrow nationalism. A professional man of letters, Skelton (1460–1529) was by most accounts a conservative in a conservative age. As tutor to the young prince Henry VIII, and later as both church rector and royal orator, Skelton was a true believer; he saw himself as responsible in part for the preservation of the English state. But if Skelton's political attitudes don't surprise us, if they reflect too well the orthodoxies of his late medieval times, many of his poems still manage to charm us. His metrical skill, his excited descriptions of historical events, his capacity for high drama combined with caricature, and, above all, his quick wit distinguish Skelton's poems from his contemporaries. More than five hundred years after his birth, Skelton still has something to teach us about the purposes and pleasures of poetry.

Skelton's poems aren't particularly complicated, but new readers need guidance. There's the fact of Skelton's middle English, of course, but beyond that there are the references, allusions, the quirky music. Skelton is a famously uneven writer: even his best poems have weak passages or sections. But when he's writing with all engines on, he's terrific. In poems such as "Colin Clout" and "Speak Parrot," in his long satires and lyric poems, Skelton employs and mixes in delightful ways what was then the high and common styles of speaking. Vigorous and inventive, his meter, too, has a natural ease. Many of his poems use what has come to be known as a "skeltonic" meter: rapid two- or three-stress lines (though some lines have as many as five stresses) with frequent alliteration and a single-rhyme pattern repeated for as long as the poet pleases. In "The Garland of Laurel," a dream allegory, Skelton uses his meter to address Mistress Margaret Hussey:

Merry Margaret,
As midsummer flower:
Gentle as falcon
Or hawk of the tower.
With solace and gladness,
Much mirth and no madness,
All good and no badness,
So joyously,
So maidenly,
So womanly . . .

This rhythm to our contemporary ears may be a bit too whimsical, reminding us of a nursery rhyme or a jazz lyric by Cole Porter or even a more recent rap-inspired lyric. But the fact is that Skelton was there first. As critics have noted, there really wasn't any English verse quite like Skelton's until Skelton. In poems like "The Tunning of Elinor Rumming" and "Philip Sparrow"—a mock-heroic poem that immortalizes the pet bird of a young neighbor—Skelton's robust rhythms create a pacing that borders on the frantic. But Skelton's not a once-around-the-track kind of writer; he's not a sprinter. His best poems, most of them, are over five hundred lines long, and many are over a thousand.

"A Ballad of the Scottish King," written in early September of 1513, is one of Skelton's shorter poems, a tidy seventy-five lines. But a revised and augmented version of the poem, "Against the Scots," runs more than twice as long. While neither poem is among Skelton's most reprinted, "A Ballad of the Scottish King" is representative of Skelton in ways that bear thinking about. Fiercely nationalistic, hectoring, sarcastic, the "Ballad" dispenses with the aureate style of the times that signaled a kind of detachment; the "Ballad" is a poem of involvement, and like many of Skelton's poems, its subjects are topical and historically specific.

In 1513, Henry VIII went to France to try his hand at war for the first time. Like many English kings before him, Henry believed it was his duty to unite the two countries under a single crown—his own. What Henry didn't know was that even as he was preparing to conquer France, the Scottish king, James IV, was preparing to invade England. Having earlier signed a treaty with the French, James sent a message to Henry, demanding that Henry not go to France. But by the time Henry got the message, he had already embarked on his mission, and luckless, impatient James had invaded England and been killed near Norham Castle.

Skelton must have intended the "Ballad" to serve a number of functions, some of them unfamiliar to readers in the late twentieth century. Poetry as the vehicle for news? That the "Ballad" was turned out anonymously, in hundreds of copies only days after James had been defeated, suggests that the poem was indeed a way of circulating information in timely fashion. Of course, then as now, political news is never neutral. Thus while the poem is concerned with "Jamy"'s undeniably inept challenge to the English king, the "Ballad" serves other purposes as well. For as royal orator, Skelton was necessarily a sometime propagandist—a "spin doctor" in today's parlance—and a number of his poems, whatever their many virtues, represented a kind of official correspondence meant to elicit support for the king and his policies.

Skelton is well known for heaping abuse on his enemies; his most famous target was the arrogant, powerful Cardinal Wolsey. And as in the poems attacking Wolsey ("Colin Clout" and the less artful "Why Come Ye Not to Courte?"), the "Ballad" pulls out the stops. Skelton, after all, was not yet certain at the time he wrote the "Ballad" whether James had been killed or was merely a prisoner:

> Gyve up your game, ye playe chek mate;
> For to the castell of Norham
> I understonde to soone ye cam,
> For a prysoner therenow ye be
> Eyther to the devyll or the trinite.

Skelton is characteristically merciless in his mocking of James. The "Ballad" alternately questions his judgment ("Knowe ye not salte and suger asonder?"), insults him ("Your wyll renne before your wytte"), and admonishes ("Before the Frensshe kynge, Danes and other / Ye ought to honour your lorde and brother"), all in exaggerated ways. The skeltonic meter offers a linguistic freedom and simplicity that make the poem both more powerful and more memorable than it might have been otherwise. And yet, readers will note, in most ways the poem is extraordinarily conventional.

It is difficult to fault Skelton for taking his contemporaneous commonplaces seriously—even if, as is sometimes true, his positions are incompatible with our own sensibilities. For instance, the notion that political dissent is the same as heresy drives the "Ballad" and other Skelton poems; it's one of the ways, according to Skelton, that the here and now is linked intimately to the hereafter. Could Skelton be a verbal bully? Certainly. Did he sometimes proclaim instead of question? Yes. Did he moralize? Sure. Still, Skelton more often than not found a way to complicate things for himself (and his audience) as he explored the world of his time. About the faults of both the church and court life, he could sometimes be unsparingly frank. In his elegy to Henry VII, Skelton asks: "Why were you shocked that you had accumulated great riches?" At other moments, however, he could only bluster.

Aware of the disparity between what he sees and what he wishes, between what happens and what he believes should happen, Skelton rails, complains, and cries out. In the epigraph to "Against the Scots," he asks in Latin: "If I am telling the truth, why don't you believe me?" A defender of the faith, a late medievalist aware of corruption but not especially receptive to the changes the coming Renaissance would bring, Skelton saw in the events of history a way of considering God's power.

> Thanked by sanynte Gorge, our ladyes knythe,
> Your pryd is paste, adwe, good nycht.
> Ye have determyned to make a fraye,
> Our kynge than beynge out of the waye;
> But by the power and myght of God
> Ye were beten weth your owne rod.
> By your wanton wyll, syr, at a worde,
> Ye have loste spores, cote armure and sworde.

Other poems by Skelton may be richer in their dramatizations and less narrow in their approach, but "A Ballad of the Scottish King" finds Skelton as he often must have found himself: a poet at the end of an age. Caught in an enormous seachange, fixed between feudalism and the coming reformation, Skelton was left clinging to poetry itself as his hope for salvation.

A Ballade of the Scottysshe Kynge

> Kynge Jamy, Jomy your joye is all go.
> Ye summoned our kynge. Why dyde ye so?
> To you no thyng it dyde accorde
> To sommom our kynge your soverayne lorde.
> A kynge a sommer it is wonder;
> Knowe ye not salte and suger asonder?
> In your somnynage ye were to malaperte,
> and your harolde no thynge experte;
> Ye thought ye dyde it full valyauntolye,
> But not worth thre skyppes of a pye.
> Syr squyer-galyarde ye were to swyfte;
> Your wyll renne before your wytte.
> To be so scornefull to your alye
> Your counseyle was not worth a flye.
> Before the Frensshe kynge, Danes and other
> Ye ought to honour your lorde and brother.
> Trowe ye, Syr James, his noble grace
> For you and your Scottes wolde tourne his face?
> Now ye proude Scottes of Gelawaye

For your kynge may synge welawaye.
Now must ye knowe our kynge for your regent,
Your soverayne lorde and presedent.
In hym is figured Melchisedeche,
And ye be desolate as Armeleche.
He is our noble champyon,
A kynge anoynted, an ye be non.
Thrugh your counseyle your fader was slayne;
Wherfore I fere ye wyll suffre payne.
And ye proude Scottes of Dunbar,
Parde ye be his homager
And suters to his paylyment.
Ye dyde not your dewty therin,
Wyerfore ye may it now repent.
Ye bere yourselfe somwhat to bolde,
Therfore ye have lost your copyholde.
Ye be bounde tenauntes to his estate;
Gyve up your game, ye playe chek mate;
For to the castell of Norham
I understonde to soone ye cam,
For a prysoner therenow ye be
Eyther to the devyll or the trinite.
Thanked be saynte Gorge, our ladyes knythe,
Your pryd is paste, adwe, good nycht,
Ye have determyned to make a fraye,
Our kynge than beynge out of the waye;
But by the power and myght of God
Ye were beten weth your owne rod.
By your wanton wyll, syr, at a worde,
Ye have loste spores, cote armure and sworde.
Ye had be better to have busked to Huntley Bankes,
Than in Englonde to playe ony suche prankes;
But ye had some wyld sede to sowe,
Therefore ye be layde now full lowe.
Your power coude no lenger attayne
Warre with our kynge to meyntayne.
Of the kynge of Naverne ye may take hede
How unfortunately he doth now spede;
In double walles now he dooth dreme.
That is a kynge without a realme.
At hym example ye wolde none take;
Experyence hath brought you in the same brake.
Of the out yles ye rough foted Scottes

We have well eased you of the bottes.
Ye rowe ranke Scottes and dronken Danes
Of our Englysshe bowes ye have fette your banes.
It is not syttynge in tour nor towne
A sumner to were a kynges crowne.
That noble erle, the Whyte Lyon,
Your pompe and pryde hath layde a downe.
His sone the lorde admyrall is full good,
His swerde hath bathed in the Scottes blode.
God save kynge Henry and his lordes all
And sende the Frensshe kynge suche another fall.

Amen, for saynt charyte and God save noble
Kynge Henry the viij.

John Skelton

Lines 2–9. The meeting in France between the Scottish herald and Henry VIII. Skelton may also have had in mind the stigma attached to the name of a summoner in Chaucer's *The Canterbury Tales*.

Lines 6, 10, 12, and 14. The lines are proverbial.

Line 19. Gelawaye: Galloway.

Lines 23–24. Melchizedek was the priestly king of Salem with whom Skelton in another poem compared Henry VIII. The Amalekites were enemies of Israel with whom Skelton identifies the enemies of England. Both references come from *Genesis*.

Lines 38–41. These lines suggest that at the time the poem was written, Skelton did not yet know for certain that James IV had died in the Battle of Flodden.

Line 50. Huntley Bank: a hill where the English army was defeated by the Scots in 1314.

Line 62. "ye rough foted Scottes": "rough footed" because they wore shoes of undressed deerskin with the fur outwards.

Lines 68–70. The "Whyte Lyon" was the badge of the Earl of Surrey, commander of the English forces who defeated James at Flodden; his son was made "lorde admyrall."

Frederick Goddard Tuckerman's "The Cricket"

I have come to love the poems of Frederick Goddard Tuckerman for their grief and their intelligence. The grief is inconsolable, alert, relentless: a condition of the universe, not a function of style or of psychological grievance. The intelligence is flexible, encompassing, a wind that blows across the water: strong enough to raise waves but not enough to turn the tide. Finally, the processes and contingent conclusions of consciousness do not suffice for Tuckerman, but he makes this accession while honoring and exercising human intelligence. His best poems, the sonnets and the ode "The Cricket," record the sequence by which he searches for consolation and comprehension—in the physical world, in knowledge, in theories of evolution and of mythic repetition—but discovers, again and again, the intractability of loss.

Raised in Boston, educated at Harvard, and trained as a lawyer, Tuckerman moved to western Massachusetts (eighteen miles from Emily Dickinson, whom he never met), in 1847. His wife Hannah, to whom he had been married for ten years, died shortly after giving birth to their third child in 1857. Tuckerman had never been an ambitious, social, or peripatetic man (though he went to England, where he met Tennyson, and he travelled occasionally to Cambridge, Massachusetts, to visit the Harvard astronomical observatory), but after his wife's death Tuckerman chose an even more radical isolation; until his death in 1873 he lived an almost hermetic life in his house in rural Greenfield, Massachusetts, living "apart from friends, remote in misery." There he wrote five sets of sonnets addressing his grief at the loss of his beloved wife. Only one small book, a set of sonnets, was published during his life.

At the same time, Tuckerman's solitude—less quirky than Dickinson's, less rhetorical than Emerson's—grounded him in the physical environment of the Connecticut Valley. He collected plants, built herbaria, studied geology and the stars—not so much as hobbies, but as approaches toward an understanding of the formative energies of the world in their stern particularity. Tuckerman's poems reflect these interests, both in precise descriptions of physical phenomena and in macroformulations of the possible consolations of positivist science, evolution, and glacial time. He can detail the "wasted red" of fallen pitch-pine needles, and "shattered on the roof like fallen snow / The tiny petals of the mountain ash." He can also record, with muscular physicality, patterns of physical science as a set of universalizing metaphors that enclose human emotions as well:

> As when down some broad river dropping, we
> Day after day behold the assuming shores
> Sink and grow dim, as the great watercourse
> Pushes his banks apart and sees the sea

Romanticism arrived late in North America, but it quickly locked into American concepts of self-reliance and democratic individuation. Still, both Tuckerman and Dickinson sometimes seem to be working *past* the terms of Continental High Romanticism even as the Transcendentalists in Concord are enthusiastically adapting those terms for American use. Tuckerman comes closer to Victorian questions of faith and responsibility than to Emersonian mystical veneration of nature. His sonnets about his enduring grief for his wife sound close to Tennyson's *In Memoriam* (1853): both series are elegiac lyric sequences, both are interested in Darwinian progress as substitutes for personal faith, both work through odd tonal conjunctions of lyrical beauty and informed scientific specificity. Even when he does seem to share central concerns with the American Romantics, Tuckerman's differences are as profound as those similarities. If he shares with other Americans a sense of privileged solitude, it is not the self-reliance of the early Emerson, nor the aggressive self-celebration of Whitman, nor the "home-cosmography" of Thoreau at Walden, nor even the lament of the Sentimentalist novelists that modern social circumstances alienate individuals from one another. Rather, Tuckerman's solitude is unmeliorable, unregenerate, and always analytically intelligent, not mystical. Tuckerman does not seek his solitude, but it seems to seek him; it does not generate his meditations and his work, but at times endangers them, questioning the possibility of the poem even as the poem evolves.

> Sometimes, when winding slow by brook and bower,
> Beating the idle grass,—of what avail,
> I ask, are these dim fancies, cares and fears?
> What though from every bank I drew a flower,—
> Bloodroot, king orchis, or the pearlwort pale,—

And set it in my verse with thoughtful tears?
What would it count though I should sing my death
And muse and mourn with as poetic breath
As in damp garden walks the autumn gale
Sighs o'er the fallen floriage? What avail
Is the swan's voice if all the hearers fail?
Or his great flight that no eye gathereth
In the blending blue? And yet depending so,
God were not God, whom knowledge cannot know.

series I, sonnet 1

Sometimes Tuckerman's conclusions seem to resemble conclusions his more traditionally Romantic American contemporaries would more famously draw, but Tuckerman's poems are more "Modern" in their textual nuances, more emotionally conflicted, even more formally self-canceling, than theirs. I love line 5 of that sonnet: "Bloodroot, king orchis, or the pearlwort pale." Look how specific that line is, as Tuckerman includes the ordinary names for plants native to his place and to his local idiom. Whitman would have been proud to have written that line—proud of its spondaic inclusiveness, of his involvement with the experiential truth, of the line's idiom and specificity, its folk names in a list. But look again at the use to which Tuckerman puts his knowledge: the line occurs as the clinching proof of an argument about the limitations of human consciousness and knowledge. He lists these particular names even as he is asking: of what use is this knowledge of the world's lives and names? Toward what can it build if not an understanding of the limitations of knowledge in the face of life's mystery and sadness? That is, he makes the Whitmanesque technique of enumeration serve a very different rhetorical function than Whitman does. Clearly, in this poem Tuckerman is not espousing a conventional Romantic idealism, a belief in the power of scientific or intuitive knowledge, nor a hope for an ecstatic poetic recognition of correspondences. But neither is he simply dismissing those possibilities. Rather, the force of this sonnet springs from Tuckerman's raising of those conventional Romantic issues and from his use of the conventional strategy, in order to criticize those empowering Romantic beliefs from within the form they empowered. More simply, Tuckerman turns the Romantic technique against Romantic beliefs. He explodes Romantic sentimentality from within its dominant forms, appropriating the technique to make it ironically serve his own, radically different, purposes.

Those purposes are even clearer in Tuckerman's most famous poem, "The Cricket" (which Yvor Winters called "the greatest poem written in English of the [nineteenth] century.") In that poem Tuckerman once again appropriates traditional Romantic verbal gestures and images into an argument markedly different from their original contexts. Here is the complete first section:

> The humming bee purrs softly o'er his flower;
>   From lawn and thicket
> The dogday locust singeth in the sun
>   From hour to hour:
> Each has his bard, and thou, ere day be done,
>   Shalt have no wrong.
> So bright that murmur mid the insect crowd,
> Muffled and lost in bottom-grass, or loud
>   By pale and picket:
> Shall I not take to help me in my song
>   A little cooing cricket?

Behind this deceptively mild voice I hear several Romantic concepts and voices, raised in order to be challenged. Keats is primary, of course, in the observation "Each has his bard"; that particular yet general song of the cricket seems at first to resemble the medley of individual songs at the end of "To Autumn." In that poem, Keats addresses the personification of autumn ("thou hast thy music, too") and then enumerates the "songs" the creatures of the world offer in the decline of the year, which marks their own mortality: gnats choir, lambs bleat, hedge-crickets sing, the redbreast whistles, the gathering swallows twitter in the skies. But in the Keats poem such songs are the compensatory, sacrificial songs that rise from the earth as it prepares to die; they are songs of loss without mourning, almost objective songs of the victims, recognition of continuity in the face of the greater law, loss. The singing in "To Autumn" forms an unselfconscious song of harvest—not a humanly chosen emblem of mortality like the song of Tuckerman's cricket ("Shall I not take to help me. . . ?") For Tuckerman to summon that Keatsian association at the start of his own poem is a tricky maneuver; in the course of "The Cricket" that little cooing song will come to seem as mortally tolling as the songs of "To Autumn," but without Keats's mellowing affirmations.

I hear Keats not only in the song but in the cricket itself. When in "On the Grasshopper and the Cricket" Keats insists "The poetry of earth is never dead," and "The poetry of earth is ceasing never," he uses the cricket to embody exactly the opposite argument that Tuckerman is suggesting throughout his ode. According to that early Keats poem, human memory, association, and imagination participate in a cyclical vitality of the earth; the listener who heard a grasshopper in the spring (in the octet of the sonnet) recalls that spring song when a cricket sings in winter (in the sestet). Tuckerman plays this association against its controlling assumptions, however. In section two of "The Cricket," the sound of the cricket rouses human memory, but not toward the vernal, vitalistic associations of Keats' poem. Eventually the vast collective song of masses of crickets sounds in the poem like the sea—universalizing, cyclical, but fatal to the individual. By section three the insects' song draws the individual listener into personal reverie and memory ("edged remembrances of joy and pain"), but those memories are tangled, willful, and mortal—hardly the large affirmations that Keats suggests, but searing in Tuckerman's personal registry of absence as a condition, a force of the universe.

> Thou bringest too, dim accents from the grave
> To him who walketh when the day is dim,
> Dreaming of those who dream no more of him,
> With edged remembrances of joy and pain;
> And heyday looks and laughter come again;
> Forms that in happy sunshine lie and leap,
> With faces where but now a gap must be,
> Renunciations, and partitions deep
> And perfect tears, and crowning vacancy!

Tuckerman's poem hears cycles in the sounds of the crickets, but they are cycles that generalize the personal loss into an image of universal diminishment and disappointment, hauntings; thus the poem ironically pictures the disappointments that come from the ruin of high Romantic hopes. If he hadn't been tempted to consider natural phenomena as signs of spiritual truths, the poem argues implicitly, the speaker might never have learned to recognize these general truths of disillusionment, disappointment, and loss. Because Emerson and Whitman and Keats (and Coleridge and Shelley) had idealized the mortal song of the earth, in its tendency to lead us toward a generalizing merger or oversoul, we are even more disappointed when our experience fails to achieve that intensity, that blessed generality. We find, instead, that the objective world continues regardless of the projective significance we attach to it, even to the songs of little insects in the bottom-grass. Thus the ending of Tuckerman's poem—"Rejoice or mourn, and let the world swing on / Unmoved by cricket song of thee or me"—sounds to me both stoically harsh and tonically jubilant. It is not High Romantic celebration; in fact, its tone resembles that of Rilke in the early *Duino Elegies*, or the Stevens of "Sunday Morning." Tuckerman isn't advocating jubilation because of the fact of cyclical mortality and continuity. In any case, the physical world will swing on "unmoved" (note the pun, with its flavor of Thomas Aquinas) by the metaphorical significance the human imagination may project onto earthly particulars. In the face of such blunt moral factuality, however, Tuckerman does advocate an arbitrary and willful assertion of joy, a will toward a "Supreme Fiction" of meaning, which can overcome the tendency of the human mind to make spiritual symbols from the unregenerate facts of physical life.

I think Tuckerman invites these contextual associations—Whitman, Emerson, Keats—and then explodes them from within. He asks us to read his poems from within—and at the same time beyond—that context. His ironic use of his antecedents most nearly resembles Emily Dickinson's. Think of the ways in which Dickinson uses the rhythms of the hymnal, the 7-7-7-7 or 7-5-7-5 syllabics, for instance, to score her own skeptical, angry hymns that quietly attack God on his own terms. We can sing those Dickinson poems to music because they are her own ironic counterhymns. More formally, Tuckerman reminds me of Thomas Hardy, with his deliberate fracturing of verse forms from within, to indicate that traditional forms are no longer appropriate to embody modern emotions. As Delmore Schwartz wrote of Hardy's poem "A Drizzling Easter Morning": "both the belief and the disbelief are necessary; the belief is necessary to the disbelief . . . the belief and disbelief operate upon the particular *datum* of the poem to give it a metaphysical significance it would not otherwise have." For Dickinson or Hardy, the received ideology and imagery are chiefly derived from Christianity, or evolutionary meliorism; in Tuckerman's case, the temptations of Christianity never seem so compelling, but the temptations of Romanticism, residual just beneath the rough surfaces of his poems, are still strong enough to give the poems an undercurrent, a resistance.

I don't mean that I love Tuckerman as a derivative or parodic poet, or that my admiration is academic and historical. But when he adapts traditional images from high Romanticism, Tuckerman does so to intensify the grief with the disillusion of failed consolations. He subverts the ideology that the image traditionally embodies, and so he makes his grief seem even more intense because of its stubborn, ironic recuperations, its longevity and intensity. The Romantic ideal may still be possible, but not here, not now, not for this grief under the pressure of this intelligence. The poem suggests the possibility of intuitive, mystical peace, and yet it also portrays its improbability and the pain of loss that hope provokes. These details are not the stage properties of received Romantic beliefs, I think. Rather, the power of Tuckerman's poem "The Cricket," like that of his best other work, consists in his poignant, reluctant repudiations of Romantic hope and grace. In Tuckerman's poems, "the belief is necessary to the disbelief." That's why he speaks to me, in the strength his grief has to resist intellect and its consolations, as consciousness faces "the crowning vacancy."

The Cricket

I

The humming bee purrs softly o'er his flower;
  From lawn and thicket
The dogday locust singeth in the sun
  From hour to hour:
Each has his bard, and thou, ere day be done,
  Shalt have no wrong.
So bright that murmur mid the insect crowd,
Muffled and lost in bottom-grass, or loud
  By pale and picket:
Shall I not take to help me in my song
  A little cooing cricket?

II

The afternoon is sleepy; let us lie
Beneath these branches whilst the burdened brook,
Muttering and moaning to himself, goes by;
And mark our minstrel's carol whilst we look
Toward the faint horizon swooning blue.
  Or in a garden bower,
Trellised and trammeled with deep drapery
  Of hanging green,
  Light glimmering through—
There let the dull hop be,
Let bloom, with poppy's dark refreshing flower:
Let the dead fragrance round our temples beat,
Stunning the sense to slumber, whilst between
The falling water and fluttering wind
  Mingle and meet,
  Murmur and mix,
No few faint pipings from the glades behind,
  Or alder-thicks:
But louder as the day declines,
From tingling tassel, blade, and sheath,
Rising from nets of river vines,
  Winrows and ricks,
  Above, beneath,

At every breath,
At hand, around, illimitably
Rising and falling like the sea,
    Acres of cricks!

III

Dear to the child who hears thy rustling voice
Cease at his footstep, though he hears thee still,
Cease and resume with vibrance crisp and shrill,
Thou sittest in the sunshine to rejoice.
Night lover too; bringer of all things dark
And rest and silence; yet thou bringest to me
Always that burthen of the unresting Sea,
The moaning cliffs, the low rocks blackly stark;
These upland inland fields no more I view,
But the long flat seaside beach, the wild seamew,
    And the overturning wave!
Thou bringest too, dim accents from the grave
To him who walketh when the day is dim,
Dreaming of those who dream no more of him,
With edged remembrances of joy and pain;
And heyday looks and laughter come again:
Forms that in happy sunshine lie and leap,
With faces where but now a gap must be,
Renunciations, and partitions deep
And perfect tears, and crowning vacancy!
And to thy poet at the twilight's hush,
No chirping touch of lips with laugh and blush,
But wringing arms, hearts wild with love and woe,
Closed eyes, and kisses that would not let go!

IV

So wert thou loved in that old graceful time
    When Greece was fair,
While god and hero hearkened to thy chime;
    Softly astir
Where the long grasses fringed Caÿster's lip;
Long-drawn, with glimmering sails of swan and ship,
    And ship and swan;
    Or where

Reedy Eurotas ran.
Did that low warble teach thy tender flute
    Xenaphyle?
Its breathings mild? say! did the grasshopper
Sit golden in thy purple hair
    O Psammathe?
    Or wert thou mute,
Grieving for Pan amid the alders there?
And by the water and along the hill
That thirsty tinkle in the herbage still,
Though the lost forest wailed to horns of Arcady?

v

Like the Enchanter old—
Who sought mid the dead water's weeds and scum
For evil growths beneath the moonbeam cold,
    Or mandrake or dorcynium;
And touched the leaf that opened both his ears,
So that articulate voices now he hears
In cry of beast, or bird, or insect's hum,—
Might I but find thy knowledge in thy song!
    That twittering tongue,
Ancient as light, returning like the years.
    So might I be,
Unwise to sing, thy true interpreter
Through denser stillness and in sounder dark,
Than ere thy notes have pierced to harrow me.
    So might I stir
    The world to hark
    To thee my lord and lawgiver,
    And cease my quest:
Content to bring thy wisdom to the world;
Content to gain at last some low applause,
    Now low, now lost
Like thine from mossy stone, amid the stems and straws,
    Or garden gravemound tricked and dressed—
    Powdered and pearled
    By stealing frost—
In dusky rainbow beauty of euphorbias!
For larger would be less indeed, and like
The ceaseless simmer in the summer grass
To him who toileth in the windy field,

Or where the sunbeams strike,
Naught in innumerable numerousness.
　So might I much possess,
　So much must yield;
But failing this, the dell and grassy dike,
The water and the waste shall still be dear,
And all the pleasant plots and places
　Where thou hast sung, and I have hung
　To ignorantly hear.
Then Cricket, sing thy song! or answer mine!
Thine whispers blame, but mine has naught but praises.
It matters not. Behold! the autumn goes,
　The shadow grows,
The moments take hold of eternity;
Even while we stop to wrangle or repine
　Our lives are gone—
　Like thinnest mist,
Like yon escaping color in the tree;
Rejoice! rejoice! whilst yet the hours exist—
Rejoice or mourn, and let the world swing on
Unmoved by cricket song of thee or me.

Frederick Goddard Tuckerman

SUE ELLEN THOMPSON

Edward Thomas: The Wild Rain

I spent the summer of 1978 sleeping in the room of a stranger, a young Englishman who had decorated it with midnight blue wallpaper and heavy mahogany furniture. Outside the leaded glass window of my sitting room lay The Grove—the most secluded and, to my way of thinking, the loveliest of the three quads that comprised Lincoln College. I would study modern British poetry and then, at the summer's end, return to the States to fashion a new life for myself as a free-lance writer and poet.

My bedroom at Lincoln College was narrow and poorly lit. Its only window overlooked the slate roof of the kitchen, on which the cook routinely scattered the remains of our most recent meal for the pigeons: wet slate strewn with soggy, half-dissolved bread; wet slate splattered with trifle or scrambled egg. I usually kept the drapes drawn, which cast the room in a bluish dusk on even the rare sunny day. Most nights I fell asleep to the drumming of rain on hard surfaces—slate, stone, asphalt, glass.

Taped to the wall above my bed was a copy of the poem "Rain" by Edward Thomas, who had been a student at Lincoln College in the closing years of the nineteenth century. His career as a poet was brief: he wrote his entire oeuvre of over two hundred poems between 1915 and 1917, and was killed at the age of thirty-nine during the Battle of Arras. Up to that point he had been a prose writer, turning out thirty books on travel and literary history as well as countless reviews of books on nature and modern poetry as he struggled to support his growing family. It was Robert Frost, whom Thomas had met in London in 1913, who encouraged him to turn to poetry, pointing out that many of the passages in his prose books had all the elements of poetry running through them. And it was Thomas, in his capacity as a book reviewer, who saw to it that Frost received the recognition in England that had so far eluded him in the United States. The two men, in their thirties at the time, had much in common. Both were melancholic and occasionally suicidal, haunted by their failures as husbands, fathers, and writers. Their friendship reached its apogee in August 1914, when the two men and their families spent an idyllic month's vacation as neighbors in Little Iddens, Gloucestershire. Frost and Thomas took walks there together every day. In fact, it was Thomas's tendency to regret choices even after they were made, according to Frost, that inspired "The Road Not Taken."

As an eager student of poetry and apprentice poet, I loved "Rain" not only for the way it captured the prevailing rhythm of the English climate and the gloom that descended frequently upon me that summer in Oxford as I approached my thirtieth birthday without having yet launched my writing career, but for what it taught me about how poems are made. Acting on Frost's advice, Thomas had distilled his poem from an earlier prose passage in *The Icknield Way*, one of his English travelogues. I read the prose passage repeatedly, trying to discern the path that Thomas had followed as he culled from it the language for his poem:

I lay awake listening to the rain, and at first it was as pleasant to my ear and my mind as it had long been desired; but before I fell asleep it had become a majestic and finally a terrible thing, instead of a sweet sound and symbol. It was accusing and trying me and passing judgment. Long I lay still under the sentence, listening to the rain, and then at last listening to words which seemed to be spoken by a ghostly double beside me. He was muttering: The all-night rain puts out summer like a torch. In the heavy, black rain falling straight from invisible, dark sky to invisible, dark earth the heat of summer is annihilated, the splendour is dead, the summer is gone. The midnight rain buries it away where it has buried all sound but its own. I am alone in the dark still night, and my ear listens to the rain piping in the gutters and roaring softly in the trees of the world. Even so will the rain fall darkly upon the grass over the grave when my ears can hear it no more. . . . I put my face to the window. There is nothing out there but the blackness and sound of rain. Neither when I shut my eyes can I see anything. I am alone. Once I heard through the rain a bird's questioning watery cry—once only and suddenly. It seemed content, and the solitary note brought up against me the order of nature, its beauty, exuberance, and everlastingness like an accusation. I am not a part of nature. I am alone. There is nothing else in my world but my dead heart and brain within me and the rain without. . . . Now there is neither life nor death, but only the rain. Sleep as all things, past, present, and future, lie still and sleep, except the rain, the heavy, black rain falling straight through the air that was once a sea of life. That was a dream only. The truth is that the rain falls for ever and I am melting into it. Black and monotonously sounding is the midnight and solitude of the rain. In a little while or in an age—for it is all one—I shall know the full truth of the words I used to love, I knew not why, in my days of nature, in the days before the rain: "Blessed are the dead that the rain rains on."

While the original prose passage, abridged in the interests of space above, rambled on for four pages, the poem is only eighteen lines long. Stripped of the self-indulgence and overwriting that frequently characterized Thomas's travel books, it manages not only to maintain but to intensify the sense of isolation and disconnectedness brought on by the rain and the poet's sense of his own impending death.

Although the prose piece describes the speaker's response to the rain as he lies half-asleep in his bed at a country inn after a day's journey, the poem, written three years later while Thomas was in boot camp, is set in an army hut. Despair, which Thomas unsuccessfully attempts to keep at arm's length in the prose passage by giving it the form of a "ghostly double," is a clear and immediate presence in the poem, embodied by the speaker. The prose passage always struck me as sounding like the journals I kept throughout my twenties. But the poem—ah! that was a different story. What could I learn from it? How could I take the debris strewn throughout my journals and turn it into something as compelling as "Rain"?

While the prose passage portrays a man abandoning himself gradually to the sound of the rain and the morbid thoughts it provokes, it is the rain that dominates the poem from the very first line, with its downpour of stressed syllables and triple repetition, to the murky realm of the ending, where the poet's thoughts are awash in negatives and uncertainties:

> Like me who have *no love* which this wild rain
> *Has not dissolved* except the love of death,
> *If love it be* for what is perfect and
> *Cannot*, the tempest tells me, disappoint. (my emphasis)
> (ll. 15–18)

The rain washes the speaker "cleaner than [he has] been" at the beginning of the poem and that "dissolve[s]" all sense of human connection at the close. As can be seen from the gradual disappearance of "me" and "I" over the course of the poem, the rain is its most enduring character and driving force. In the prose passage, it is little more than an objective correlative for the speaker's diminishing sense of self.

Lying there in my narrow bed at Lincoln College reading Thomas's poem, I learned a great deal about the power of repetition. Although the prose passage also relies heavily on repeated words—*rain/rains*, *dark/darkly*, *black/blackness*, and *death/deathly* make numerous appearances—the overall effect is more cumulative than evocative. The word *rain* appears eight times in the eighteen-line poem. But woven throughout the larger pattern established by the sustained repetition of *rain* are other, less obvious patterns of repetition, overlapping and occasionally yielding to each other. Consider the progress of the word "die" in line 3, which shifts to "dead" in line 7, "dying" in line 9, "dead" again at the end of line 12, only to reappear as "death" in line 16 ("the love of death"), at which point it is overtaken by the repetition of "love" in lines 15, 16, and 17. Even repeating a word or phrase once ("solitude" in lines 2 and 6, "broken reeds" in lines 13 and 14) provides another stitch in the poem's already densely textured surface, as do internal rhymes ("Is dying tonight or lying still awake"; "listening to the rain / Either in pain or thus is sympathy") and partial consonance ("solitude" . . . "dead" . . . "loved" . . . "cold" . . . "reeds" . . . "dissolved"). The overall effect of this subtle and skillful use of repetition is not unlike that of a heavy rainfall: the louder it gets, the less one hears from the outside world, until eventually that world ceases to exist.

While it is certainly not difficult to see the spirit of the poem dispersed throughout the passage from *The Icknield Way*, it is interesting to note some of the choices Thomas made in creating one from the other. The quotation that appears so prominently at the end of the prose passage—"Blessed are the dead that the rain rains on"—is shifted to the center of the poem. It must have been a line for which he had great affection—something, perhaps, that he remembered from the less troubled days of his childhood, "in the days before the rain." Ending the poem with this line must have been a temptation, but instead Thomas chose to move it to the pivotal point at which he breaks free of his self-absorption and despair to display concern for other human relationships:

> But here I pray that none whom once I loved
> Is dying tonight or lying still awake
> Solitary, listening to the rain,
> Either in pain or thus in sympathy
> Helpless among the living and the dead
> (ll. 8–12)

Surely Thomas was aware of the danger in ending his poem with someone else's words, especially when they might not carry the same weight and meaning for the reader. Rather than relying on them to support all that has gone before, he wisely takes them out of quotation marks and puts them where the authority implicit in the language will do the job in a more subtle manner.

It is instructive, too, to note what in the prose passage Thomas might have included in his poem but chose to leave out:

Once I heard through the rain a bird's questioning watery cry—once only and suddenly. It seemed content, and the solitary note brought up against me the order of nature, its beauty, exuberance, and everlastingness like an accusation.

The prose passage's only flicker of hope, quickly dashed against the speaker's relentless sense of isolation and despair, is absent from the poem, in whose constricted space there is no room for "beauty, exuberance, and everlastingness," and where such thoughts would undoubtedly have struck a false note. In its place, Thomas uses the image of "a cold water among broken reeds." By employing the indefinite article, he contains that water; it becomes a *body* of water and an apt image for human existence in times of war, when life flows inexorably around the dead and the dying, the "Myriads of broken reeds all still and stiff," while remaining curiously untouched.

The poem's only simile performs another crucial function. If in the first six lines the speaker is preoccupied with his own isolation and thoughts of death, in the next six lines he moves out of this emotional morass to pray that his friends and fellow soldiers are spared the same fate. But then, with the introduction of "a cold water among broken reeds" in lines 13 and 14, he moves seamlessly back into his own thoughts—"Like me who have no love which this wild rain / Has not dissolved." The image of his life as "a cold water," a force diminished in its capacity to feel, flowing among the "broken reeds" of failed human relationships at home in England as well as the corpses that litter the battlefields of France, not only completes the circular movement of the poem's consciousness but returns the reader to the element that is both the subject and the setting of the poem as a whole.

There are other things I learned from reading Thomas on those sodden summer nights. I learned about the strength and sinuosity of the sentence and the importance of line breaks and pacing. "Rain" consists of only two sentences. The second, beginning with "Blessed are the dead," pushes outward from the colon and continues for twelve lines. Just at the point where the flow of the sentence runs up against a logjam of qualifying phrases ("Solitary, listening to the rain, / Either in pain or thus in sympathy / Helpless among the living and the dead"), Thomas introduces the image he has been saving for just this purpose ("Like a cold water among broken reeds") and the rest of the sentence suddenly spills over and runs swiftly to its conclusion:

> Like me who have no love which this wild rain
> Has not dissolved except the love of death,
> If love it be for what is perfect and
> Cannot, the tempest tells me, disappoint.
>
> (ll. 15–18)

Note the enjambment of the penultimate line. It is the one point in the poem where the reader cannot possibly catch a breath before continuing; it is a final quickening of the pace, which has been slowed by so many end-stopped lines preceding it. But like any good ending, it raises more questions than it answers. "If love it be . . ."—well, is it or isn't it? And the long pause between "Cannot" and "disappoint" throws the reader into further doubt. Is "the tempest," after all, a reliable source of information? By the time the poem has ended, our grasp on it—in fact, our grasp on exactly what constitutes "love"—has begun to dissolve as well.

I was a late bloomer who came to poetry with little in the way of formal instruction. What I learned, I learned from reading poems that I loved. I learned slowly, pondering a line or passage for months until its secrets revealed themselves to me. That I chose a poem by Edward Thomas to guard my sleep that summer in Oxford, that he turned out to be a former student at Lincoln College and a confidante of Robert Frost, in whose immense shadow I had been raised, is not so much co-incidence as evidence of how we choose our friends, both in literature and in life.

Rain

Rain, midnight rain, nothing but the wild rain
On this bleak hut, and solitude, and me
Remembering again that I shall die
And neither hear the rain nor give it thanks
For washing me cleaner than I have been
Since I was born into this solitude.
Blessed are the dead that the rain rains upon:
But here I pray that none whom once I loved
Is dying tonight or lying still awake
Solitary, listening to the rain,
Either in pain or thus in sympathy
Helpless among the living and the dead,
Like a cold water among broken reeds,
Myriads of broken reeds all still and stiff,
Like me who have no love which this wild rain
Has not dissolved except the love of death,
If love it be for what is perfect and
Cannot, the tempest tells me, disappoint.

Edward Thomas

The Virtue of Arnold's "Dover Beach"

While generally conceded to be a great, as well as canonical poem, Matthew Arnold's "Dover Beach" has not been without its detractors. Some criticisms, such as Edith Sitwell's general estimate that readers who like Arnold's poetry are precisely those who do not like poetry, amount to little more than the posturing of a minor poet with a major agenda. Other negative judgments are to be taken more seriously, being made by writers who, if they are finally led astray by a mistaken emphasis, have a genuine commitment to poetry. Examples of such critical judgments are those of Donald Hall in his essay "Ah, Love, Let Us Be True" (1959), and Douglas Bush in his *Matthew Arnold* (1971).

My own judgment is that two qualities above all stand out in Matthew Arnold's poems, of which "Dover Beach" is among the finest and most representative. One, a characteristic noted by generations of sympathetic readers, is Arnold's sustained, elegiac tone evoking loneliness and isolation, a sense, which one encounters more frequently in twentieth-century writers, of lostness in a hostile world seemingly devoid of authentic moral value. The central issue of Arnold's poems is the problem of modernity—as he phrases it in "The Scholar Gypsy," "This strange disease of modern life, / With its sick hurry, its divided aims, / It's heads o'ertaxed, its palsied hearts." The other characteristic, which has perhaps commended itself less to our own age, is Arnold's determination to resist despair and its facsimile, specious affirmation. He wrote poems hospitable to ideas, poems informed by genuinely complex thought, that were adequate representations of the pain and dislocations of modern existence, but that refused to succumb to nihilism. The difficulty he faced was how to do this without assenting to creeds outworn or fostering illusions about the human prospect. Implicitly or explicitly, Arnold's poems raise the question that he said Wordsworth had asked with "profound genuineness" in his writing; the Socratic question of how to live. "It is important, therefore, to hold fast to this," Arnold wrote in his essay on Wordsworth, "that poetry is at bottom a criticism of life; that the greatness of a poet lies in his powerful and beautiful application of ideas to life—to the question: How to live." It is a question, whatever the literary fashion of the moment, that is unlikely ever to disappear entirely from poetry.

"Dover Beach," like Wordsworth's "Lines composed a Few Miles Above Tintern Abbey," is a meditative monologue in which the character of the meditation arises organically out of the topographical situation. In the opening lines of "Dover Beach" the scene is sketched in conventionally picturesque terms. The elements of the setting are "calm," "full," "fair," "tranquil," "sweet." The lovers in the poem might be tourists at a resort hotel (Arnold and his wife spent a night at Dover on their honeymoon). But there is something more in the scene than the merely picturesque. Midway through the first stanza, the speaker begins a new sentence with an ominous "only":

> Only, from the lone line of spray
> Where the sea meets the moon-blanch'd sand,
> Listen! you hear the grating roar
> Of pebbles which the waves draw back, and fling,
> At their return, up the high strand,
> Begin, and cease, and then again begin,
> With tremulous cadence slow, and bring
> The eternal note of sadness in.

The passage constitutes a crucial turn in the poem, introducing in a single hauntingly cadenced sentence a new, unsettling sound of waveborne pebbles that the lovers hear "Begin, and cease, and then again begin." The onomatopoeia here imitates the movement of successive waves breaking on the shore. And "the grating roar" made by the pebbles being drawn back across the rocky shingle suggests to the speaker "The eternal note of sadness," a phrase that echoes, with a distinctive qualification, Wordsworth's "Still, sad music of humanity, / Nor harsh nor grating, though of ample power / To chasten and subdue." The cadence of Arnold's language, miming the motion of the water, is a rhythmic imitation of human sorrow repeating itself throughout the generations.

The allusion to Sophocles in the next stanza functions in several ways. By alluding to the lines in *Antigone* that use the sound of the sea as a figure for human misery, Arnold establishes a genealogy for his perception and connects the present with the distant past. The note of sadness is eternal. I think, however, that Arnold had something more in mind. Sophocles occupied a position in antiquity analogous to Arnold's in the nineteenth century; he was a poet with a profoundly religious sensibility, articulating a religious view of life in an age when Greek religion, the traditional forms of belief, were losing their power to compel assent. Similarly, though Arnold was at odds with Victorian orthodoxy, at the same time that he was attacking superstition, idolatry, and dogma, he was arguing for a religious, essentially poetic, mode of consciousness and fighting the debunking positivism of much contemporary liberal thought. Arnold saw in Sophocles a tragic sense of life very like his own, a sense of human isolation in a world without any sustaining code of value. The centuries of Christian consolation between Sophocles and Arnold may have given humans hope and help in bearing the inevitable, but for Arnold, the tide of faith had turned and, like the speaker in "Dover Beach," he can hear only "Its melancholy, long, withdrawing roar, / Retreating, to the breath / Of the night-wind, down the vast edges drear / And naked shingles of the world." The plangent lyricism here is characteristic of Arnold's best poems, as is the bleak evocation of an existence bereft of belief's sustaining power.

The desolation in these lines is the lowest point of the poem and gives rise to the illumination that follows. The speaker's despair before the retreat of the tide of religious faith, a retreat that weakens the bonds of community established by belief, can only be countered by an appeal to another kind of community, one based on a demythologized commitment to others, the emblem of which is the relationship between two people, grounded in love or friendship, and supported by the virtue of fidelity. Without fidelity, men and women are left in a universe emptied of ethical content to contend against one another in meaningless violence. The insight in "Dover Beach" arrives at the poem's nadir, as if to remind us, as Wallace Stevens put it in "No Possum, No Sop, No Taters," "It is only here, in this bad, that we reach / The last purity of the knowledge of good." The retreating tide of faith leaves bare in the moonlight the naked shingles of the world. The speaker, with the insight engendered by his historical situation, laments that

> the world, which *seems*
> To lie before us like a land of dreams,
> So various, so beautiful, so new,
> Hath really neither joy, nor love, nor light,
> Nor certitude, nor peace, nor help for pain [my emphasis]

The world is not a benevolent, meaningful seascape but a "darkling plain / Swept with confused alarms of struggle and flight, / Where ignorant armies clash by night." These are the last lines of the poem, clinching it in a couplet—one of only three in the poem—as if Arnold wished to leave the reader with a strong enough image of a nihilistic universe to persuade him to accept the appeal to human solidarity presented earlier.

The poet Donald Hall, writing at the end of the 1950s and seeking to correct what he sees as a fault among his contemporaries, presented a reading of "Dover Beach" significantly different from mine. Both Hall and Douglas Bush, writing a decade later than Hall, read the poem as a turning away from the threatening violence of the public realm to find refuge in the private sphere of domesticity. Says Bush, "Here, as in other poems, salvation, a very limited salvation, comes through feeling, not reason, although love is only a desperate refuge." And Hall pronounces categorically, "Like so many Victorian poems, its negation is beautiful and its affirmation repulsive." Hall finds the affirmation in "Dover Beach" repulsive because he sees it as an irresponsible appeal to the safe haven of domesticity—and for him, during this period at least, "domesticity is the real enemy." "I see a pattern among us," he writes, "of provinciality and evasion, which results in a reliance on the domestic at the expense of the historical." And again, "The evasion of history by domesticity is a fault both moral and technical."

The animus of Hall's reading is evinced succinctly in his reduction of what I take to be Arnold's serious affirmation to the dismissable kitsch of popular culture: "The [contemporary] poet says with Hollywood, 'In this mixed-up world, all we have is each other' or with Matthew Arnold, 'Oh, love, let us be true / to one another.'" Hall's strategy is to establish an implicit context in which the words of Arnold's poem take on an invidious significance. Another context might be suggested by thinking of Arnold's words in the ambience of his essays on culture and religion, or by reading "Dover Beach" in the light of work by our own contemporaries that addresses similar concerns. For example, a more useful comparison than Hall's might be between Arnold's position, as intimated in the offending line, and that of the poet and cultural critic Wendell Berry. Berry, interrogating the large claims of ideological commitment rooted in historical interpretation, argues in favor of the unassuming discipline of personal and domestic integrity rooted in love. Of the efficacy of public protest, for example, Berry has this to say: "History simply affords too little evidence that anyone's individual protest is of any use. Protest that endures, I think, is moved by a hope far more modest than that of public success: namely, the hope of preserving qualities in one's own heart and spirit that would be destroyed by acquiescence" ("A Poem of Difficult Hope," 1990). Of "the planetary versions—the heroic versions—of our problems," Berry agrees that they "have attracted great intelligence," but he points out that too little intelligence has been directed toward these problems "as they are caused and suffered in our lives, our households, and our communities" ("Word and Flesh," 1989). The focus here is on the "domestic" realm that Hall reviles, precisely because Berry believes that concern with history has too often represented an evasion of the importance of local issues rather than the other way around. A longer passage from "Word and Flesh" provides a summation of the matter:

Our understandable wish to preserve the planet must somehow be reduced to the scale of our competence—that is, to the wish to preserve all of its humble households and neighborhoods.
What can accomplish this reduction? I will say again, without overweening hope but with certainty nonetheless, that only love can do it. Only love can bring intelligence out of institutions and organizations, where it aggrandizes itself, into the presence of the work that must be done.
Love is never abstract. It does not adhere to the universe or the planet or the nation or the institution or the profession, but to the singular sparrows of the street, the lilies of the field, "the least of these my brethren."

I find it interesting that other readers have found "Dover Beach" un-satisfactory as what passes conventionally for a love poem. Though this dissatisfaction differs from Hall's or Bush's, it is nevertheless rooted in the same tendency to read the poem with an exclusive emphasis on the word *love*—used but once in the poem and then only as a term of address—with little attention paid to the word *true* and the context (a poem about meaning and value) in which it appears. As I have already suggested, more emphasis ought to fall on the adjuration to fidelity, grounded in love, but understood as an encompassing virtue not limited to the domestic realm. Given this emphasis, the appeal to "be true" is less the enabling mechanism of retreat from history than a counter to the vagaries of value in a secular, increasingly technocratic universe. It seems to me that to read "Ah, love, let us be true / To one another" as merely an appeal to sexual fidelity and domestic conformity, as Hall does, is to impose some of the social concerns of fifties' America on the work of a writer who in all probability would have seen those concerns as driven by philistinism. Hall may be correct about American writing at the close of the 1950s, but I think he is dead wrong in seeing "Dover Beach" as an anticipatory emblem of the fault he finds with it.

Rather than rely "on the domestic at the expense of the historical," "Dover Beach" places both in a context that reveals their appropriate relationship to each other. History is far from being absent in the poem: it is present in several allusions—the one to Sophocles for instance—and in the painful awareness of the consequences of Christianity's decline. Arnold is fully aware of the historical situation in which he offers his appeal to individual commitment rather than to something more "historical" such as "planetary" action. The latter appeal has been made before, as the speaker suggests when he remarks that the light on the French coast "Gleams, and is gone." Where now is the humanistic light that flashed out of revolutionary France, before ideas ossified into ideology and virtue into tyranny? The cliffs of England—the insular England

Arnold indicted for refusing to open itself to Continental thought—stand, glimmering and vast, reflecting the light without absorbing it. France and England confront each other across the channel like ignorant armies.

The figure of the "ignorant armies" is taken from Thucydides' account of the night Battle of Epipolae, which Arnold's father used as a text at Rugby to suggest the intellectual confusion of his own age. The idea recurs in Arnold's work: it appears in his "Empedocles on Etna" as the rival forces of Sophists and believers between whom Empedocles is caught. And it appears in Arnold's essay on Falkland as the Cavaliers and Roundheads between whom Falkland is caught. In Arnold's religious writings, it is the conflict between Roman/Anglo-Catholicism and dissenting Protestantism in which he himself is the man in the middle.

What these examples suggest is Arnold's tragic sense of life to a large extent informed by his commitment to seeking balance, harmony, and wholeness in an historical situation constituted by the fierce contention of partial and opposing forces. Deeply suspicious of ideological reductions, he appeals instead to what he thinks of as the real possibility of an overarching cultural consensus derived from a careful consideration of the best that has been thought and said in the world. Arnold believed that the idea of love, along with the virtues that it called forth and was nurtured by in turn, were central to this consensus. When belief in God has become problematic, and belief in history as the working out of some transcendent aim has begun to fail, what is there to console humankind in the face of a world devoid of values, where there is neither joy, nor love, nor light, nor certitude, nor peace, nor help for pain? The answer, Arnold implies in "Dover Beach" (and makes explicit elsewhere), the only way to confront the dilemma, is through fidelity to an idea of human solidarity, to one another. This is the ground of value from which all else springs. Arnold is not talking in this poem merely of passionate love nor of a sentimentalized code of romance, but rather of something closer to the Greek *agape*, and of fidelity to the idea of serious engagement from the depth of oneself with the inwardness of another.

Such a conclusion, while perhaps hostile to the metaphysics of traditional Christianity, is not alien to its ethos, in which Arnold was steeped. He insisted throughout his career on the necessity of thought, the free play of intellect, wide knowledge, experience, right conduct, the indispensability of what he called "the imaginative reason." But when all is said and done, these things, if uninformed by love, the breath and finer spirit of all doing and thinking, can effect little good. That is why in "Dover Beach" Arnold made a poetic claim for the virtue of fidelity grounded in love. He believed love capable of helping us toward self-knowledge by making us aware of our buried selves, the fullness of our being, and he believed that love was not illusory but a true source of joy and the necessary ground of genuine community.

Dover Beach

The sea is calm to-night.
The tide is full, the moon lies fair
Upon the straits;—on the French coast, the light
Gleams, and is gone; the cliffs of England stand,
Glimmering and vast, out in the tranquil bay.
Come to the window, sweet is the night-air!
Only, from the lone line of spray
Where the sea meets the moon-blanch'd sand,
Listen! you hear the grating roar
Of pebbles which the waves draw back, and fling,
At their return, up the high strand,
Begin, and cease, and then again begin,
With tremulous cadence slow, and bring
The eternal note of sadness in.

Sophocles long ago
Heard it on the Ægæan, and it brought
Into his mind the turbid ebb and flow
Of human misery; we
Find also in the sound a thought,
Hearing it by this distant northern sea.

The Sea of Faith
Was once, too, at the full, and round earth's shore
Lay like the folds of a bright girdle furl'd.
But now I only hear
Its melancholy, long, withdrawing roar,
Retreating, to the breath
Of the night-wind down the vast edges drear
And naked shingles of the world.

Ah, love, let us be true
To one another! for the world, which seems
To lie before us like a land of dreams,
So various, so beautiful, so new,

Hath really neither joy, nor love, nor light,
Nor certitude, nor peace, nor help for pain;
And we are here as on a darkling plain
Swept with confused alarms of struggle and flight,
Where ignorant armies clash by night.

Matthew Arnold

Animal Music (On Dylan Thomas)

When I was about twenty, I bought the complete recorded poetry of Dylan Thomas. It was a Caedmon double album with a picture of the poet on the front, an enlarged, grainy closeup of his face before it was ruined by illness and alcohol. In school I had read and loved several of his poems but knew nothing of his life or larger work. I bought the record, and others, because I was trying to memorize poems, and wanted to hear them in the writers' own voices.

Now, twenty-five years later, I can still play back whole sections of those word songs in my ear, though I no longer have them entirely by heart. They are sung in Thomas's great reckless bass, yet are impeccable in their enunciation, pacing, pitch, and inflection. For a long time I didn't really hear the words. I heard the sense of them first—the voice as instrument, as animal, producing its sounds, its cries and roars and rages. Only later, when I already loved them, did the poems open for me into the intellectually startling works that they are.

"In the White Giant's Thigh" was the first to seduce me in this way. It's a simple poem, really, in which a man walks through a graveyard at night and meditates upon the women buried there, the survival of their sexual presence in the landscape, and his own mortality. This takes sixty long lines, some too long to be printed unbroken. What happens in that space that I have not just repeated in my poor paraphrase? The answer is hard to articulate because the poem speaks to a part of me that it created, able to receive it both as an event—physical, musical, and emotional—that is communicated directly to my nonverbal self, and as words with meaning. The poem dreams up a landscape, scored like a page of music:

> Where barren as boulders women lie longing still
> to labor and love though they lay down long ago.

Eight *l*-notes in two lines. Few of us would sanction that "lack of sub-tlety" in a contemporary poem. Nowadays, music tends to be a sublimi-nal heightener of meaning, subordinate, and not a kind of meaning in itself, as it is in Thomas's work, where it passes sometimes into what I think of as animal music, written in our other native language. In that sense, Thomas asks us to read bilingually, as does Hopkins. But Hop-kins, probably because his music is categorizably religious, has been spared the erosion of reputation that Thomas has suffered: poor bril-liant drunken talker, wild Welshman with a gift for music and not much discipline. (In retrospect, it's pretty obvious that Thomas suffered from an affective disorder—as did Hopkins, incidentally—most likely manic-depressive illness. If his suicidal drinking is seen in that light, and not as self-indulgence that got out of control, and if we are willing to listen with instinctual ears, we can glimpse the extremity of his suffering in the wrenching, impassioned music of his poems. I learned this by listen-ing to him all one lonely adolescent summer, the moonlight falling in the long vowels onto the stony consonents of the "cudgelling, hacked / Hill").

I loved Thomas's emotional bluntness, too, and his sexual forthright-ness:

> Time by, their dust was flesh the swineherd rooted sly,
> Flared in the reek of the wiving sty with the rush
> Light of his thighs, spreadeagle to the dunghill sky,
> Or with their orchard man in the core of the sun's bush
> Rough as cow's tongues and thrashed with brambles their buttermilk
> Manes, under his quenchless summer barbed gold to the bone

"In the White Giant's Thigh" is a poem that seduces us first to bed, and then to the grave. It's one of the saddest, most passionate poems I know, and one of the most egoless. For all his blustering male noise, Thomas is also capable of abandoning himself to the universal, where what looks at first like recklessness or bravado turns out to be courage. I remember when I first realized how this poem works, that the cru-cial moment is when he abruptly stops the catalog of sexual scenarios, and addresses the curlew and then the dead women underfoot and says, "hold me hard." By then, the yearning for this particular knowledge had lodged in my own soul, and I had to turn, with Thomas, and implore the dead to reveal it, because they're the only ones who know:

> Teach me the love that is evergreen after the fall leaved
> Grave, after Belovéd on the grass gulfed cross is scrubbed
> Off by the sun and Daughters no longer grieved
> Save by their long desirers in the fox cubbed
> Streets or hungering in the crumbled wood: to these
> Hale dead and deathless do the women of the hill

Love for ever meridian through the courter's trees

And the daughters of darkness flame like Fawkes fires still.

I don't know in a literal sense, and have never tried to find out, exactly what the white giant's thigh is. The poem says it's a high place overlooking the sea, built of the living tissue of three long, plaintive *l*'s, and blanched with moonlight. It's a sexual place in spite of its buried dead: "And there this night I walk in the white giant's thigh." The pronoun is interesting: *in.* The ghost lovers wander among the crosses, and the poet tries on the grave. The poem is the map of a terrifying moment of emotional and intellectual realization, sung in a fierce, grieving, sexual voice without words.

Tennyson's Voyage of the Mind

Ulysses hears "many voices" in the beckoning deep, and in this complex and celebrated soliloquy there are also many voices—diverse tones, moods, assertions, and echoes that the reader is challenged to hear rightly and to attune to if he can. To be sure, a poem so handsomely written can easily be plundered for simple messages: Robert Kennedy, campaigning for the Presidency, was given to quoting, " 'Tis not too late to seek a newer world"; that phrase and others are dear to commencement speakers, while "Old age hath yet his honor and his toil" has proven useful with more mature audiences. Tennyson himself tells us that "Ulysses" may securely be taken as a heartening poem written at a time of grief and despondency. It was begun a few days after the death of his dearest friend, Arthur Hallam, whom Tennyson (and others) had regarded as a young man of "high speculative endowments," capable of addressing the intellectual and spiritual problems of the age. It was "written under the sense of loss," Tennyson said, "and gave my feeling about the need of going forward, and braving the struggle of life."

Certainly the salient echoes of the first thirty-odd lines support the idea of getting on with it, of rousing oneself to action. The "sleep, and feed" of line 5 have reminded scholars of a soliloquy of Hamlet's:

> How all occasions do inform against me
> And spur my dull revenge! What is a man,
> If the chief good and market of his time
> Be but to sleep and feed? A beast, no more.
> Sure he that made us with such large discourse,
> Looking before and after, gave us not
> That capability and godlike reason
> To fust in us unused.
>
> (IV, iv)

The sound and sense of that last phrase may also have helped to prompt lines 22–23 of "Ulysses":

> How dull it is to pause, to make an end,
> To rust unburnished, not to shine in use!

The same two lines have reminded me and others of Shakespeare's own Ulysses, in *Troilus and Cressida*, urging Achilles not to rest upon his laurels:

> Perseverance, dear my lord,
> Keeps honor bright; to have done, is to hang
> Quite out of fashion, like a rusty mail,
> In monumental mockery.
>
> (III, iii, 150ff.)

In what it says and in what it echoes, the forepart of Tennyson's poem is largely the soliloquy of a heroic spirit bestirring itself to further adventure; we rightly respond to Ulysses' great appetite for life and to such splendid measures as "Far on the ringing plains of windy Troy." And yet the first five lines of the poem, which Tennyson latterly printed as a discrete paragraph, are the musings not of a hero but of a depressed island ruler who is weary of his faithful Penelope, contemptuous of his people, and too bored and lazy to improve the laws that he administers. Such attitudes cannot be appealing in a poem by Tennyson, who by 1833 was already becoming the poet of duty and social responsibility, and they jar as well with the expectations of Ulysses that we derive from Homer's *Odyssey*. But in fact the *Odyssey* is not the main and formative source of "Ulysses," which in many respects is inconsistent with Homer; for instance, if Tiresias prophesies in Homer's Book XI that Ulysses, having regained his home and beloved queen, must set forth on yet another journey, it is an inland journey from which he will return to die "after a rich old age, surrounded by a happy people."

Tennyson's version of Ulysses is chiefly based upon the twenty-sixth canto of Dante's *Inferno*, where Ulysses—the wily deviser of the Trojan horse—is found among those who, by deceit and by counseling others to deceive, have misused the high faculty of reason. Ulysses tells, in a long and beautiful speech, how on leaving Circe's island he exhorted his companions, saying, "Consider what you were born to: you were not made to live like brutes, but to pursue excellence and knowledge"; and how he sailed with them then, in a "foolish flight" (*folle volo*) through the Pillars of Hercules toward a final engulfment in the South Atlantic. "Neither fondness for my son," his narrative begins, "nor piety toward my old father, nor the due love that should have comforted Penelope, could conquer in me the yearning to know the world entire, and the good and evil ways of men."

Tennyson's poem begins also with Ulysses' culpable rejections and forsakings, and then—despite a pompous frequency of *me* and *I* unmatched except by Milton's Satan—becomes more attractive, more positive, more vigorous, more eloquent as the hero recalls his past adventures and consolidates his will to go voyaging again. That the second paragraph is self-persuasive rather than fully resolved, we know by certain negative overtones that seem almost like slips of the tongue. "Yet all experience is an arch wherethrough / Gleams that untraveled world whose margin fades / Forever and forever when I move" is a way of saying that much remains to be seen; yet the weariness of "Forever and forever" seems to grant that the quest for final knowledge is vain, and that (as the voice of despair whispers in "The Two Voices") the aged seeker is doomed to "seem to find, but still to seek." The words "To follow knowledge like a sinking star," however one may parse them, have disastrous implications in a voyage-poem, and make the reader ask whether Ulysses is seeking or fleeing, and whether his goal is renewed life or suicide. The reader must try, I think, to conceive of a troubled, wavering Ulysses of whom all those things might be true.

Up to this halfway point, Ulysses has been expressing disgust with his life in Ithaca or talking himself into a last embarkation; now, as I read the poem, he imagines what he will say to the leading citizens of Ithaca when he abdicates and embarks. His tone grows accordingly politic, measured, and reassuringly colorless. There is none of the gruff dismissiveness of the poem's opening lines; the savage Ithacans, those beastly sleepers and feeders, are now merely "rugged," and Ulysses speaks with some affection of Telemachus, though condescending toward his son's merely "blameless" and "decent" capacities. In a poem responsive to the loss of Arthur Hallam, who had he lived might have been "A life in civic action warm, / A soul on highest mission sent, / A potent voice in Parliament, / A pillar steadfast in the storm," Ulysses' low regard for governance and public service, though understandable in a restless hero of action, is not in itself admirable.

In the closing paragraph of the poem, Ulysses imagines or rehearses what he will say to his mariners—how he will enlist them in a *folle volo* beyond the set limits of the known world. Homer's Odysseus returned alone to Ithaca, having lost all his companions, but Tennyson provides his hero with sailors who are veterans of Troy. Ulysses can thus magnificently appeal to their heroic memories, as he has earlier done to his own, and thereby impress them into his service. At the same time, his inspiring speech is once more peppered with discordant notes.

As Christopher Ricks has brilliantly pointed out, Ulysses' discourse, though urging departure for a "newer world," exhibits a weird and near-total avoidance of the future tense. "Gloom," "dark," moaning waters, swooning rhythms, and the phrase "until I die," hint once again at a morbid wish for death. And a number of phrases, such as "strove with Gods," evoke not only Troy but Milton's war in Heaven and prepare us for a final sinister echo of Satan's "And courage never to submit or yield" (*PL*, I, 108).

It may be that some of the dissonances in "Ulysses" belong not to Tennyson's portrait of his hero but to his own inclination to be sad, slow, and sonorous regardless of the subject. I think, nonetheless, that we can derive from the poem a vivid, intelligible personality who has the vices of his virtues. Ulysses is nobly eloquent, and he is also a crafty spellbinder; he is both great-hearted and egotistical; he loves bracing adventure and is a shirker of "common duties"; he vigorously defies old age and yet is depressed; he loves life and is sick of it; he is fearless but suicidal. We are left, however, with two uncertainties about him. The first is this: how far are we instructed to condemn this Ulysses, seeing as he is based on a damned soul in the *Inferno* and puts us in mind of Satan's rhetoric in Hell? In the second place, though Ulysses is clearly not some globe-trotting retiree, what sort of knowledge is he sailing after, what sort of thought does he share with his shipmates, how will he use the reason that distinguishes him from brute beasts, and what "work of noble note" is he likely to accomplish? The answers to these questions only come, I think, when we change our focus and see "Ulysses" as an allegory of the bereaved Tennyson's resolution to ponder man's place in Nature, God's purpose in the world, our grounds for faith, and our hope of immortality—great questions raised by Hallam's death, which Hallam (had he lived) might have illuminated for his time and society.

This is a poem about thinking—not the sort of thinking that deals in received ideas and concerns itself with "common duties" and "household gods," but the kind that Wordsworth meant when he spoke of Newton as "a mind forever / Voyaging through strange seas of thought, alone." C. G. Jung has said in our century that "all consciousness separates," and Hannah Arendt has written of the riskiness of philosophic thought, which withdraws from the senses, from action, and from the world. But on the whole our day sees little danger in estranging mental adventure, and we have to be reminded that earlier ages were wary of it. Just before he tells of his encounter with the burning shade of Ulysses, Dante says, "I sorrowed then, and sorrow now again, when I direct my memory to what I saw; and more than usually do I rein in my poetic genius, lest it run where Virtue does not guide it." W. H. Auden is right,

I believe, in saying that Dante sees Ulysses, the foolhardy voyager, as succumbing to "the concupiscence of curiosity" and reins in his own mind lest he likewise be tempted to *libido sciendi*.

From Christian tradition, from his own conservative nature, and from a family history full of brooding and aberration, Tennyson would have understood Dante's fear of unbridled thought and enquiry. The poet who had his Tithonus say

> Why should a man desire in any way
> To vary from the kindly race of men,
> Or pass beyond the goal of ordinance
> Where all should pause, as is most meet for all?

was not an enthusiast of overreaching. He would understand the angel Raphael's rebuking Adam for his abstruse questionings of God's order—

> Solicit not thy thoughts with matters hid,
> Leave them to God above, him serve and fear.

—and Adam's enlightened response:

> apt the Mind or Fancy is to rove
> Uncheckt, and of her roving is no end;
> Till warn'd, or by experience taught, she learn
> That not to know at large of things remote
> From use, obscure and subtle, but to know
> That which before us lies in daily life,
> Is the prime Wisdom.
> (*PL*, VIII)

He would further have understood the angel Uriel's saying, in Book III, that there is no excess in searching the works and ways of God, so long as the purpose of such searching is "to glorify / The great Work-Master." Here is but one of many possible quotations in which Tennyson may be seen as agreeing with Dante and Milton:

> Make knowledge circle with the winds;
>   But let her herald, Reverence, fly
> Before her to whatever sky
> Bear seed of men and growth of minds.
> ("Love Thou Thy Land," written 1833-1834)

The reader may also wish to look at the prologue of *In Memoriam*, stanzas 5–8, and section CXIV in toto.

"Ulysses" is a poem that knows that speculative thinking about ultimate things entails some spiritual risk; it is a poem that intends to speculate, come Hell or high water. It shakes off all misgivings and sets out after faraway truth, refusing the bonds and bounds of Virtue,

Wisdom, Reverence. That bold resolve best accounts, I think, for the poem's flavor of defiance, and its occasional whiff of brimstone. These dangerous elements are counterbalanced by lines 63–64—

> It may be we shall touch the Happy Isles,
> And see the great Achilles, whom we knew.

—in which there is an implicit hope that Tennyson's intellectual quest will be justified. The critic John Pettigrew thinks it possible that "the Happy Isles, the dwelling of the virtuous after death, suggest a goal of renewed life in opposition to the gulfs" of line 62; I think that a certainty. It seems safe to identify Achilles with Hallam, as most readers do, and to infer that if Tennyson's mental journey should in some sense attain to Hallam, now a soul in bliss, he would then be acquitted of presumption, preserved from error, and put in possession of higher truths. Under the guise of Achilles, Hallam thus figures as the Beatrice of "Ulysses."

Between 1833 and 1849, Tennyson wrote many lyrics in memory of Arthur Hallam and in search of answers to the large issues raised by his friend's death. Arranged then into a loose unity, and published in 1850 as *In Memoriam A.H.H.*, these poems are his finest accomplishment (though finer in feeling than in thought) and may in retrospect be identified with the "work of noble note" of which "Ulysses" speaks. Section CIII of *In Memoriam* looks back to "Ulysses," both illuminating and revising it. What we have in CIII is a pageant-like dream-vision in which, as the poet himself explained, Tennyson voyages down the river of Life, accompanied by maiden-mariners who symbolize poetic and artistic powers: "all that make life beautiful here, which we hope will pass with us beyond the grave." As they draw near the sea of death and afterlife, the poet and his maidens grow in size, strength, and grace, and soon, upon the deep, they see "A great ship lift her shining sides."

> The man we loved was there on deck,
> But thrice as large as man he bent
> To greet us. Up the side I went,
> And fell in silence on his neck.

The vision obviously affirms the immortality of the soul; Hallam's size expresses Tennyson's view of him as a precursor of "that great race which is to be"—a much improved human species; and, since Tennyson had come to see our spiritual development as continuing in the afterlife, the maidens are asked on board:

> And while the wind began to sweep
> A music out of sheet and shroud
> We steered her toward a crimson cloud
> That landlike slept along the deep.

Section CIII is a happy dream, and has none of the ambiguity of Ulysses'
nature, none of the doubtfulness and defiance of his contemplated jour-
ney. But it may help to confirm our sense of an allegorical dimension in
the earlier poem, letting us see what sort of thought the mariners share,
what sort of knowledge is sought, and how a reunion in the Happy Isles
might vindicate and crown the expedition.

Ulysses

It little profits that an idle king,
By this still hearth, among these barren crags,
Matched with an aged wife, I mete and dole
Unequal laws unto a savage race,
That hoard, and sleep, and feed, and know not me.

I cannot rest from travel; I will drink
Life to the lees. All times I have enjoyed
Greatly, have suffered greatly, both with those
That loved me, and alone; on shore, and when
Through scudding drifts the rainy Hyades
Vexed the dim sea. I am become a name;
For always roaming with a hungry heart
Much have I seen and known—cities of men
And manners, climates, councils, governments,
Myself not least, but honored of them all—
And drunk delight of battle with my peers,
Far on the ringing plains of windy Troy.
I am a part of all that I have met;
Yet all experience is an arch wherethrough
Gleams that untraveled world whose margin fades
Forever and forever when I move.
How dull it is to pause, to make an end,
To rust unburnished, not to shine in use!
As though to breathe were life! Life piled on life
Were all too little, and of one to me
Little remains; but every hour is saved
From that eternal silence, something more,
A bringer of new things; and vile it were
For some three suns to store and hoard myself,
And this gray spirit yearning in desire
To follow knowledge like a sinking star,
Beyond the utmost bound of human thought.

This is my son, mine own Telemachus,
To whom I leave the scepter and the isle—
Well-loved of me, discerning to fulfill
This labor, by slow prudence to make mild
A rugged people, and through soft degrees
Subdue them to the useful and the good.
Most blameless is he, centered in the sphere
Of common duties, decent not to fail
In offices of tenderness, and pay
Meet adoration to my household gods,
When I am gone. He works his work, I mine.

There lies the port; the vessel puffs her sail;
There gloom the dark, broad seas. My mariners,
Souls that have toiled, and wrought, and thought with me—
That ever with a frolic welcome took
The thunder and the sunshine, and opposed
Free hearts, free foreheads—you and I are old;
Old age hath yet his honor and his toil.
Death closes all; but something ere the end,
Some work of noble note, may yet be done,
Not unbecoming men that strove with Gods.
The lights begin to twinkle from the rocks;
The long day wanes; the slow moon climbs; the deep
Moans round with many voices. Come, my friends,
'Tis not too late to seek a newer world.
Push off, and sitting well in order smite
The sounding furrows; for my purpose holds
To sail beyond the sunset, and the baths
Of all the western stars, until I die.
It may be that the gulfs will wash us down;
It may be we shall touch the Happy Isles,
And see the great Achilles, whom we knew.
Though much is taken, much abides; and though
We are not now that strength which in old days
Moved earth and heaven, that which we are, we are—
One equal temper of heroic hearts,
Made weak by time and fate, but strong in will
To strive, to seek, to find, and not to yield.

                                    Alfred, Lord Tennyson

Ding-Dong, Bell:

"Ariel's Song" from *The Tempest*

by William Shakespeare

I grew up near the thumb of a lost mitten floating on the big waters of Lake Michigan and Lake Erie—lost, because only a single mitten remained, the left one. Until I was fifteen I lived my entire life between these two lakes. Summers we lived on the edge of one of the hundreds of small lakes scoured out by the glacier. My father showed me how to recognize fossil coral and the imprint of ancient flowers in the stones that lapped at the shore. The stones were my first science books; they told me that a warm-water sea once covered the entire state.

When my father took a job in Los Alamos, New Mexico, I felt as if we were moving to Mars. I had never seen the desert; the very word tasted like a dead planet. After school let out, my father packed the maps. My mother packed our clothes, sheets, blankets, pots and pans, and the radio. I packed my *Selected Poems of Emily Dickinson* and my *Poems and Songs from the Plays of William Shakespeare*. On the three-day drive from Ann Arbor to Los Alamos, I watched the familiar landscape of trees and cornfields disappear. The roads were so straight and the countryside so bare you could see to the naked rim of the earth.

We unpacked and settled in; my father went off to work every day— he worked in a high security area protected by an impressive fence— and I set myself the task of memorizing three poems a week from the books I'd brought. The first poet on my list was Shakespeare, and the first poem was a song from *The Tempest*, "Full fathom five thy father lies." I went over the poem before I left for my job teaching art to first graders in a summer bible school. The regular teacher had read them the story of Noah's Ark, and my assignment was to help the children produce an illustration for the story. On a long piece of shelf paper I painted the ark, that clumsy vessel of salvation, and the children painted the water and the animals. Purple tigers roamed the sky, dinosaurs gamboled in the bushes, butterflies as big as cows soared over Noah and his family. The teacher was not pleased; she reminded me that the animals had come in two by two, as if she'd personally witnessed the departure. There were no drowned people, no flooded homes, no deaths.

After supper I took out my Shakespeare and found that I had effortlessly memorized every word, as if the song had also been memorizing me. Now, many years later, I still marvel that it has stayed with me, perhaps for the very reason that it is a song, in which shape, sound, and image strike us deeper than the sense.

Sound is the very subject of the last lines:

> Sea-nymphs hourly ring his knell

A knell, of course is the sound of a bell rung slowly to announce a death. Though the phrase "Ding-dong" is only given twice in "the burden" (or refrain), the nymphs must have gone on singing it during the remark that follows: "Hark! Now I hear them." If the words "Ding-Dong" were not written out, the effect might be ominous; the word *burden* derives from an old French word, *bourdon*, which can describe both a humming and the drone of a bagpipe.

This bell is not rung by human hands, however; it is a sound that seems to come from the waves themselves. And the sea-nymphs ringing it do not feel the fear and sympathy that weigh on the minds of earthly mourners; as creatures of magic, they live outside of human mortality. The singer, Ariel, is a spirit of the air and a trickster. In *The Tempest*, Ferdinand, the son who hears the song, believes his father has drowned in the shipwreck that cast them both up on an enchanted island. Ariel knows that Ferdinand's father is not drowned. Does this make the song a lie? No. Father and son have lost something of their civilized selves and have indeed been changed by their encounter with the sea into "something rich and strange."

Because the sound of the bell is spelled out in syllables that echo Mother Goose ("Ding, dong, bell, / Pussy's in the well"), the listener knows this drowning is not the stuff of tragedy but of fairy tales, in which a transformation so often brings about the happy ending. Though the refrain is a death knell, the drowned man is as exquisite as a temple god, newly wrought in coral and set with pearls. He has crossed over into the kingdom of the spirits of air and water, who sing of human tragedies without participating in them.

I loved that song because it reminded me of water in a place where water was precious and of change in a time when I did not yet know what time would make of me. I have forgotten who I was at fifteen, but I have not forgotten the song. It still holds something of who I was, living in the atomic city where I first learned those words. Hark, now I hear them. Ding-dong, bell.

Ariel['s] Song

Full fathom five thy father lies,
    Of his bones are coral made:
Those are pearls that were his eyes:
    Nothing of him that doth fade,
But doth suffer a sea-change
Into something rich and strange.
Sea-nymphs hourly ring his knell:
        Burthen [within]. Ding-dong.
Hark now I hear them—ding-dong bell.
                        William Shakespeare

A Consideration of John Milton's "When I Consider How My Light Is Spent"

Always remembering that much of the art in a poem will be discovered not in what the poem says but in how it goes about saying it, that art will nevertheless be lost to us if we don't know what the poem says. To paraphrase a poem is not to understand it, but a poem will not be understood if it cannot be paraphrased.

Usually this is not a deliberate or even a conscious thing; when we read most poems, we see the dramatic situation readily enough, know who is saying what to whom, and what is happening. Milton's sonnet on his blindness calls for more attention to these matters of fact than many poems do. This is partly because the language itself has undergone some changes over the past three and a half centuries, and partly because of the syntactical structure of the poem.

A reader coming for the first time to this sonnet on Milton's blindness at forty-four is apt to lose track somewhere in the eleven lines of the first sentence, bending as it does around six subordinate clauses, one of which contains a seventh. The sentence is simplified, somewhat, when we realize that the semicolon after "I fondly ask" in line 8 might be a period for a modern writer. If we take these first lines and drop the subordinate clauses for a moment, we are left with their sense:

> When I consider how my light is spent,
> I fondly ask (so he won't scold me)
> if God demands day-labor, light denied.

The omitted clauses elaborate on the opening fact and explain Milton's anguish at being unable to serve God as he could if he could see. This agonizing extends to Milton's comparison of his lot to that of the unhappy servant in the parable of the talents, who was chastened by his returning master. So much goes on in these lines that by the time

Milton asks the question it comes after what seems a prolonged and passionate plea for understanding.

Then the poet's better self—represented by the virtue Patience—realizes the impertinence of his suggestion that God might need either the products of human labor or the means of it, in this case Milton's eyes. You serve your king, Milton chastens himself to remember, by accepting what he lays upon you. It is not doing what we must but in doing what we can that we serve God best.

Milton's words do not become poetry when he sets them in the form of an Italian sonnet, but they take on the sound-play that characterizes the language of poetry, and they move to a pattern of iambic pentameter, a norm against which the poet can play for effect. The iambic movement is regular through the first eight and a half lines, except for the reversed first foot of line 4, where "lodged with" forms a trochee. Then there is a foot reversal in each of lines 9, 10, and 11, with two substitutions in both lines 12 and 13, when a pyrrhic foot and a spondee replace two iambs.

> That murmur, soon replies, "God doth not need
> Either man's work or his own gifts; who best
> Bear his mild yoke, they serve him best. His state
> Is kingly. Thousands at his bidding speed
> And post o'er land and ocean without rest:
> They also serve who only stand and wait.

The effect of this is threefold. It allows the poet to give extraordinary notice to the words *God, either, bear, his bidding,* and *without rest,* all central words in his religious argument—considerably more notice than they would have received if their accents had not broken the established pattern in the poem. Also, it helps to distinguish the voice of Patience from the poet's opening plea and rationalization, because the foot reversals and substitutions make the second voice seem more naturally conversational, less studied, and therefore more sure of itself. Thirdly, the shift away from the stricter iambic movement established in the first eight lines allows Milton to strengthen the sense of closure in the last line by returning to that pattern, one of the most effective means a poet has of saying, It is finished.

Another way in which the manner of saying shapes what is said is seen in the move from those rhetorical circumlocutions of the first sentence through nearly eleven lines of the poem to the simple, unadorned assertion of the second sentence in its four short words: "His state / Is kingly." No argument is made in defense of this assertion because it needs none. The truth of it is made more resounding, though, because of the bluster that precedes it, as the contention, confusion, and fear of the opening cry are made more evident, more moving, as they are set against this firm realization.

A poem has internal, or rhetorical, as well as external, or prosodic, form. The internal form of this sonnet is that of thesis-antithesis-synthesis: the opening complaint is answered with a scolding voice, and these blend into a closing in which the contention is resolved and in which both the tone and concern of each previous presence in the poem are molded.

One cannot discuss a poem—especially one by Milton—without discussing the words themselves. Milton was a man of great learning; he wrote in Latin as comfortably as in English and knew Greek well, which is to say that he knew the histories behind the words he used, knew what various meanings they might carry at the time and what vestigial meanings lay within them. He took advantage, as a poet must, of all that he knew, and a reading of this poem is enriched by that.

"Lodged," in line 4, for example, can mean both "stuck" and "abiding in a humble place"—the poet's own self. "Bent," in the same line, suggests both "inclined" and "humbled." "State," in line 11, means at the same time "God's place in the scheme of things," and the realm over which he rules. "Wait," the last word in the poem, means not only "be still" and "attend," but "defer action until later," a suggestion consistent with and consoling to a Christian sensibility. The sense of unity and the coherence of the poem are enhanced by an almost invisible thread of language running through having to do with bookkeeping, debt, and payment, playing on the vision of a God who keeps a record of our sins and calls us to account. "Consider" means, among other things, "to take into account." "Spent" is not only "used up" but "paid out." A talent was a biblical monetary unit. "Present," in the seventeenth century, carried the sense of "make an offering." "Account," of course, means "financial record" as well as "story" and "report."

Apart from what artful ways the poet worked his deliberate way with the resonance of these words, it's useful also to know that in the seventeenth century "fondly" meant "foolishly" and "prevent" meant "forestall" or "head off," almost the same but somewhat richer in its suggestion than the contemporary meaning of *stop*.

It is interesting to compare this sonnet to an earlier one by Milton, "On His Being Arrived at the Age of Twenty-Three," not only because in both the poet moves through distress to resignation in the will of a demanding God, but to see how much Milton grew as a poet in the intervening twenty-four years, given that he was more accomplished at his craft and art at twenty-three than most ever become.

John Milton's contention with himself as he thought on his blindness was not simply a complaint and a chastening. Clearly he was in anguish not only at his loss of sight but at his inability to serve God as he thought he should, but—like the dying Keats a century later, writing "When I Have Fears that I May Cease to Be"—Milton found through his loss not only the resignation to abide it but the stuff of art, to which he turned his mind with a startling clarity of thought and vision.

It is by such alchemy that all poetry, finally, no matter the situation out of which it comes, is an act of joy and a celebration of what we are.

When I Consider How My Light Is Spent

When I consider how my light is spent
  Ere half my days, in this dark world and wide,
  And that one talent which is death to hide,
  Lodged with me useless, though my soul more bent
To serve therewith my Maker, and present
  My true account, lest he returning chide;
  "Doth God exact day-labor, light denied?"
  I fondly ask; but Patience to prevent
That murmur, soon replies, "God doth not need
  Either man's work or his own gifts; who best
  Bear his mild yoke, they serve him best. His state
Is kingly. Thousands at his bidding speed
  And post o'er land and ocean without rest:
  They also serve who only stand and wait."

John Milton

CLARA YU

A Journey of Enquiry: Reading Anne Sexton's "For John, Who Begs Me Not to Enquire Further"

Often we come upon poetry accidentally. Like running into a stranger and falling in love, we are intrigued, invited to explore, and challenged to understand. In the process, we recognize beauty and affinity, feel twinges of excitement, learn something about the poem and ourselves, and we want to acquaint ourselves further with the poet's art and world. This is how I came to read Anne Sexton.

I like to spend time on weekends at bookstores, browsing and foraging in the aisles. It is a private pleasure that I indulge in from time to time. One Saturday morning late in the fall, I drove forty miles through the most glorious, sun-drenched Vermont pastures and hills to get to my favorite bookshop, not knowing that it was the start of a different, but equally delightful journey. As I walked idly by the poetry section, my eyes came to rest on a copy of *Anne Sexton: The Complete Poems*. Flipping through the pages quickly, I saw a small poem bearing the intriguing title, "The Moss of His Skin." I read on. It is a first-person account of a girl buried alive with her dead father. The calm and casual narrative voice of the poem collides violently with its horrifying subject. When I read the lines "I lay by the moss / of his skin until / it grew strange" and "I hold my daddy / like an old stone tree," I knew I had to buy the book. Back at home I read randomly from the collection, until I came to "For John, Who Begs Me Not to Enquire Further." There I stayed.

In the title of the poem, the poet addresses "John," someone who begs her not to enquire further. On the most obvious level, there is some danger or pain that John wishes to convince the poet to avoid by not probing deeper, not asking more questions. What is this thing that is so terrible to enquire about? What is the nature of this enquiry? What will be the poet's arguments? Will all the answers to these questions be contained in the poem itself, or will we have to look elsewhere? The poem, by its very title, begs the reader to enquire further. The poem is not divided into stanzas, but for ease of discussion, I will divide it into five sections.

The opening sentences drop clues, but just clues, to the nature of the enquiry. The references to the asylum, the cracked mirror, and the "selfish death" combine to achieve the effect of an emotional turbulence under strenuous control, a "sense of order" that is charged with terror and tension. In section 2, the poem plunges deeper into despair, in a conversational tone that subverts the dark subject, proposing that, "the worst of anyone can be, finally, an accident of hope." Nevertheless, up to this point, the reader is led to take the poet's voice as straightforward, ordinary, and sane. The next section, however, tests our composure. The image of the poet tapping her head, an inverted glass bowl, and raging in it, suggests a vacuous frenzy, a passion that has gone mad.

The emotional power of the poet now comes to rattle even the most distant reader in section 4: the bowl, the container of genius and rage, is glass, fragile, and cracked. Because of the cracked surface, however, it shines with brilliance, like stars. In the face of John's rejection, the poet will hold her bowl "like a complicated lie," and give it a new surface. There is something jarring yet fresh in the connection between the cracked cerebral bowl and its possible new skin—the orange, a colorful, fragrant, yet ordinary fruit on the one hand, and the sun, blindingly brilliant, source of light and heat for all, on the other. The tension between the household images and the exuberant flashes of ambition and brilliance is vivid and genuine.

Structurally, section 5 recapitulates the major themes and extends them: the consolation felt in a haven of order; the reiteration of hope, fear and alienation; the distance between the poet and her reader. By tightly knitting these elements together, repeating some lines and altering others, the poet creates an effect that comes close to a refrain, but that is more than just that. The last two lines of the poem lapse into seeming mindlessness, enumerating the familiar in a monotonous chant: "my kitchen, your kitchen, / my face, your face." This exemplifies powerfully Sexton's ability to strike at the center of psychological complexities with astonishing simplicity. The trancelike vacancy that borders derangement makes the poem seem to trail off, yet it strengthens the authenticity of the poet's voice.

A purely textual reading of the poem yields several possible interpretations. The terms of endearment used in the poem make it possible to imagine John as a lover, though the exact nature of the enquiry that John advises against remains somewhat of a mystery. The "it" in the opening sentence, "Not that it was beautiful, / but that, in the end, there was / a certain sense of order there" can be simply interpreted as a physical place, perhaps the asylum. Alternatively, the poem can be read as about the art of poetry and the poet's own mindwork, in context. But what exactly is the context? Who is John? What is the relationship between John and the poet? There are so many questions that cry out for further exploration. An engaged reader is invited to go on finding the pieces that will complete the puzzle.

Anne Sexton did not start writing poetry until 1957, when she was in therapy for depression and was advised by her doctor to take up writing. Yet by the early 1960s she was already widely published in such places as the *Saturday Evening Post, Christian Science Monitor, Harper's, The New Yorker*, and the *Hudson Review*. She had published three collections of poems, *To Bedlam and Part Way Back, All My Pretty Ones*, and *Selected Poems*, by 1965. She was reviewed favorably, even considered a major poet. She was appointed "scholar in poetry" in the Radcliffe Institute for Independent Study, taught poetry writing at Harvard and Radcliffe, and was elected fellow by the Royal Society of Literature of London. Her crowning glory came in 1967 when she was awarded the Pulitzer Prize for *Live or Die*. Nevertheless, Sexton was often labeled as a "confessional" poet, "female" poet, or "housewife turned poet," which muffled critical acclaim. Her bouts with depression, her mental breakdowns, and her treatment of "unconventional" subjects also combined to create a dubious reputation.

Critical interest in Sexton, however, continued to grow after her suicide by carbon monoxide poisoning in October 1974. Diane Wood Middlebrook's thorough and intimate work, *Anne Sexton: A Biography* (Vintage, 1991), and Linda Gray Sexton's recent *Searching for Mercy Street* (Little, Brown, 1994), in which she gives detailed accounts of growing up under the shadow of her raging, terrified, and terrifying mother will no doubt add to Sexton's posthumous fame and notoriety. It will be interesting to see what the judgment of the reading public will be. My enterprise, however, is to see what light one poem can shed on my understanding of the poet and her art.

When Sexton was first advised by a Dr. Orne to try writing, she gathered enough courage to enroll in an evening poetry workshop at the Boston Center for Adult Education, led by John Holmes, a professor of literature at Tufts University. That was 1957. In the ensuing years, Holmes served as a mentor, friend, and critic. While both were in the poetry group meeting rgularly in Holmes's living room, there was nothing to suggest any romantic involvement. Indeed, according to Middlebrook, "Holmes and Sexton were polar opposites in this group. She set his teeth on edge; he disliked almost everything about her conduct."

When Sexton wrote the poem "For John, Who Begs Me Not to Enquire Further," the occasion was not a happy one. Holmes, upon reading the manuscript of Sexton's first collection of poems, *To Bedlam and Part*

Way Back, expressed his views candidly, for the first time. He began by praising Anne's manuscript as well constructed. Then he went on to say, "I distrust the very source and subject of a great many of your poems, namely, all those that describe and dwell on your time in the hospital. . . . It bothers me that you use poetry this way. It's all a release for you, but what is it for anyone else except a spectacle of someone experiencing release?"

Anne was astonished and distraught. What she eventually came up with as a reply was in the form of a poem, but it was also her personal manifesto. When *To Bedlam and Part Way Back* was published in 1960, it included all the poems that were personal in nature, and the poem "For John, Who Begs Me Not to Enquire Further." The volume bore the following epigraph:

It is the courage to make a clean breast of it in face of every question that makes the philosopher. He must be like Sophocles' Oedipus, who, seeking enlightenment concerning his terrible fate, pursues his indefatigable enquiry, even when he divines that appalling horror awaits him in the answer. But most of us carry in our heart the Jocasta who begs Oedipus for God's sake not to inquire further . . .
From a letter of Schopenhauer to Goethe, November 1815

The quest for knowledge and self-knowledge that Schopenhauer affirms as the courage that makes the philosopher, the nature of that horrible knowledge that Sexton experienced in her life and expressed in her art, and the dilemma of affinity versus alienation in the reader's response, however conscious or unconscious, remain at the heart of our understanding and assessment of Sexton as patient, person, poet, and philosopher. In that light, "For John" is not only a significant poem on its own artistic strength, but can be taken as her *Ars poetica*, against which most of her work can be read with additional insight.

With extraordinary tenacity, obsession even, Sexton held on to her own emotional turmoil as a source for her poetry. She stuck to the true and simple and affirmed the relevance of her life's experiences in her art. She wrote them bravely, frankly, powerfully. Many of the images in "For John" can be found in frequent recurrence in her other poems. Remarkably, when I looked in the archives of the special collections department of the Middlebury College library, where a collection of materials by and about Sexton had been acquired recently, I found several unpublished poems, written in 1974 just before her suicide, that echoed in imagery, sentiment, and conviction found in "For John." One of these, "Looking Glass Upon," dated September 13, 1974, starts this way:

No.
A quick brush of the hair—
and then vamoose!

> There is something awful hiding in the eyes
> that needs a long white Mass

and continues in the next stanza:

> If I were to look in the mirror
> more than one half a minute,
> the nose would quickly crack
> and the forehead and chin split—

ending with:

> At the mirror the stars
> smell cold and a long-fingered
> but aging hand rubs the face right off.
> The mirror is blank.

The recurrent images of the cracked mirror, the staring death, and the stars and faces reflected in the mirror are not only symbols of Sexton's psyche, but also her creativity and her purpose. In an interview with Sexton, Barbara Kevles asked, "What do you feel is the purpose of poetry?" To which Sexton answered: "As Kafka said about prose, 'A book should serve as the ax for the frozen sea within us.' And that's what I want from a poem. A poem should serve as the ax for the frozen sea within us."

Sexton leaves her readers with reflections of the brilliance born out of a tortured but deliberately lived life. She has cracked the frozen sea in many a reader. On October 4, 1974, twenty-two days after she finished "Looking Glass Upon," Anne Sexton took her own life in the garage of her home. The stars are cold. The mirror is now blank. The face is wiped off. But her poetry remains with us. In that clear, vibrant voice she has encouraged us to "enquire further," to quest for self-knowledge, to contemplate, acknowledge, and express our fear and perhaps give poetic order to our passion during that journey.

John Clare's "I Am"

I suspect that some readers (Americans particularly) patronize this old poem. They might say it is sentimental and self-suffering, the diction affected, and the wish for God, the concluding image of heaven as a cathedral of nature, might seem intolerable to contemporary eyes and ears. John Clare's poems are still not included in many contemporary anthologies of poetry in English and he is rarely ranked in the same league with his peers, Wordsworth, Coleridge, Blake, Byron, Shelley, Keats, et al.

Louis Untermeyer liked him well enough in the 1950s to include a few of his poems in some of his hall-of-fame anthologies, but he patronized Clare as a kind of literary accident, a man who taught himself to read and thus was able to discover and be influenced by Thomson's "Seasons"—a country oaf who happened to be sensitive and thus suffered greatly in an indifferent world, ultimately spending the last thirty years of his life as a manic-depressive in mental institutions.

But I don't wish to make a cause of this little piece. I would just like to show how and why this poem and many others by Clare, particularly his wonderful and highly personal and detailed evocations of landscape and place, have meant a great deal to me over the years.

I first read "I Am" four decades ago in the Untermeyer anthology, which I bought off a drugstore rack (believe it or not—hosannah for the old days!) in the unlikeliest of places—Las Vegas. I was twenty years old and stationed at Camp Desert Rock, the army base adjacent to the atomic-bomb test grounds at Mercury in the Nevada desert. I won't linger over details, but I was a miserable young man, having failed at school and subsequently been laid off by a strike at the steel mill where I was employed. In the midst of this total disillusionment, my draft notice came and I was swept into the vast brutality of military life.

I was agonizingly young, lonely, and frightened. We were "witnessing" atomic-bomb tests (the news media of the time referred to us as "atomic guinea pigs") from trenches situated not too distant from ground zero, and then were being asked to walk forward toward the mushroom cloud into the nightmare landscape of the blast area—the dead and scourged animals, shredded plant life, the blasted shacks and equipment.

All of this seems very distant from Clare's gentle English countryside, and yet the story connects. To maintain my sanity in that ungodly place, for the first time in my life I discovered that I like to read. And can you imagine—terrified and lonely young man that I was—what it meant to me to come across "I Am?"

There I was, somehow managing to hang on to my young mind and spirit in the midst of Hades by reading an obscure British poet who had lost everything in his life—his home, his love, what little fame he had achieved, and his sanity. It was an unlikely encounter, yet deeply sustaining to me, and I have been grateful ever since.

The poem is carefully made in the British tradition. The rhymes and rhythm are perfect. In some ways it is a distillation of Clare's life, and he wrote it, apparently in a moment of extraordinary resignation and self-realization, toward the end of his seventy-one years.

The first line sets the stage perfectly. Lines 2 through 10 are deeply poignant, about his stifling, overwhelming loneliness, his endurance of the endless days and years of his illness and institutionalization. The records show that he rarely, if ever, had visitors during his three decades in the madhouse—no family, no friends came and he was compelled to "consume" his own woes. There exists a copy of a note he wrote in 1860, the last item in the edition of his letters. It is written to an unknown inquirer from the outside world. It reads:

Dear Sir
I am in a Madhouse & quite forget your Name or who you are You must excuse me for I have nothing to communicate or tell of & why I am shut up I dont know I have nothing to say so I conclude
Yours respectfully
John Clare

The first lines of the poem's second stanza seem to allude at least in part to his career as a poet. He had been a hedgesetter and day laborer, but had taught himself to read and write. Somehow he published four books, the first of which, printed in 1820 when he was twenty-seven, gained him a good deal of instant fame as the "peasant poet." He became the curiosity and toast of one London season, but thereafter his work was almost totally ignored. He was institutionalized in 1837. The last two lines of this stanza restate the agony of his isolation, even from his loved ones.

The very moving final stanza expresses his desire for the peace of heaven—and to him heaven is a place where there are no neglectful or tormenting people. It is a place of deep and ultimate rest in the midst of nature where he can lie "untroubling and untroubled." How very moving those three words, considering the condition of his life!

I first read "I Am" forty years ago and I have continued over the years to reread it and other great poems by Clare. My love of his writing remains an unlikely encounter, but I am abidingly grateful for it. I managed to survive the miserable events and failures of my youth and for some lucky, unfathomable reason, my life has been full and relatively tranquil. I have had good work and faithful, devoted family and friends, wonderful people to love. I have not been abandoned and lonely in my life. Yet I have stayed in touch with John Clare and his poems.

I even retain membership in The John Clare Society, an earnest organization of over six hundred appreciative readers and scholars that is centered in Helpston, England, in the countryside that Clare wrote of all his life. Every several months I receive their newsletter from overseas, full of lively chat about ongoing Clare scholarship, celebrations, conferences, parties, walks, new publications, etc. I read it from cover to cover and am thus reminded to continue my lifelong appreciation of Clare's gentle and deeply felt poems about birds, trees, sky, grass, insects, hedges, animals, the seasons of the countryside, and also his poems of anguished loneliness. It also sometimes causes me to recollect my earliest, wondrous encounter with "I Am," years ago in that surreal landscape of ultimate evil and destruction, and I remain abidingly grateful for his gentle and sustaining art.

I Am

I am: yet what I am none cares or knows,
    My friends forsake me like a memory lost;
I am the self-consumer of my woes,
    They rise and vanish in oblivious host,
Like shades in love and death's oblivion lost;
And yet I am, and live with shadows tost

Into the nothingness of scorn and noise,
    Into the living sea of waking dreams,
Where there is neither sense of life nor joys,

But the vast shipwreck of my life's esteems;
And e'en the dearest—that I loved the best—
Are strange—nay, rather stranger than the rest.
I long for scenes where man has never trod,
    A place where woman never smiled or wept;
There to abide with my Creator, God,
    And sleep as I in childhood sweetly slept:
Untroubling and untroubled where I lie,
The grass below—above the vaulted sky.

John Clare

CONTRIBUTORS

JULIA ALVAREZ teaches at Middlebury College. Her most recent books are *How the Garcia Girls Lost Their Accents* and *In the Time of the Butterflies*.

DAVID BAKER has published several volumes, including *Sweet Home, Saturday Night*, and *Haunts*.

JOHN BALABAN teaches at the University of Florida and has published numerous volumes of poetry.

ANN BARKER has taught at the Milton Academy and at Middlebury College.

MARVIN BELL has taught for many years at the University of Iowa. His numerous books include a recent volume of *Selected Poems* and *The Book of the Dead Man*.

ROSELLEN BROWN recently published *A Rosellen Brown Reader*. She is a prolific poet, novelist, and essayist.

TERESA D. CADER is the author of *Guests* and *Sumerian Symbol for Bird*.

MICHAEL COLLIER is Director of the Bread Loaf Writers' Conference and a professor at the University of Maryland. His third book of poems, *The Neighbor*, was just published.

WILLIAM C. COOK is chair of the English department at Dartmouth College. His books include *Hudson Hornet and Other Poems*.

STEVEN CRAMER is currently teaching at Bennington College.

THOMAS M. DISCH lives in New York City and has published many novels, including *The Doctor*, and several volumes of poetry. He often writes theater reviews for *The Nation*.

STEPHEN DUNN has recently published a volume of selected poems.

JOHN ENGELS teaches at St. Michael's College and has recently published a volume of *New and Selected Poems*.

DONALD FINKEL has published numerous volumes of poetry, including *Selected Shorter Poems*.

CAROL FROST has published several volumes, including *Chimera* and *Day of the Body*.

ANTHONY HECHT has published many well-known books of poetry and, most recently, a study of W. H. Auden called *The Hidden Law*.

DAVID HUDDLE has recently published *A David Huddle Reader*. He teaches at the University of Vermont and was Acting Editor of *New England Review* in 1993–1994.

RICHARD JACKSON has published many books, including *Alive All Day*. He edited *Four Slovene Poets*.

MARK JARMAN teaches at Vanderbilt University and has published, most recently, *The Black Riviera* and *Iris*.

ERICA JONG has most recently published *Fear of Fifty*, a volume of memoirs. She has written numerous volumes of poetry and many novels, including *Any Woman's Blues*.

DONALD JUSTICE recently published *The Sunset Maker* and *A Donald Justice Reader*.

X. J. KENNEDY has published numerous collections, including a volume of *Selected Poems*.

MAXINE KUMIN is the author, most recently, of *Looking for Luck* and *Nurture*. She has published many books of poetry, fiction, and essays.

SYDNEY LEA recently published a volume of essays called *Hunting the Whole Way Home*. *The Blainville Testament*, a book of poems, was published in 1992.

GARY MARGOLIS is a clinical psychologist at Middlebury College and the author, most recently, of *The Day We Still Stand Here* and *Falling Awake*.

PAUL MARIANI teaches at the University of Massachusetts and published, most recently, *Salvage Operations: New and Selected Poems*, and biographies of John Berryman and Robert Lowell.

CHARLES MARTIN has recently published *Steal the Bacon* and *Catullus*.

WILLIAM MATTHEWS is the author of a recent *Selected Poems and Translations* and a volume of essays, *Curiosities*.

J. D. MCCLATCHY edits *The Yale Review*. His most recent collection of poetry is *The Rest of the Way*.

SHEILA MCGRORY-KLYZA teaches creative writing at Middlebury College.

CHRISTOPHER MERRILL is the author of *Workbook* and *Fevers and Tides*.

JOHN FREDERICK NIMS has published numerous books, including *The Six-Cornered Snowflake* and *Zany in Denim*.

CAROL OLES has published several collections of poetry, including *Quarry* and *Nightwatches*.

ROBERT PACK is College Professor at Middlebury College and was, for many years, director of the Bread Loaf Writers' Conference. He most recently published a volume of new and selected poems, *Fathering the Map*.

JAY PARINI teaches at Middlebury College. His recent books include *Bay of Arrows*, a novel, and *John Steinbeck: A Biography*.

LINDA PASTAN has most recently published *The Imperfect Paradise* and *Heroes in Disguise*.

ROBERT PINSKY teaches at Boston University and has recently published *The Want Bone*, a volume of poetry, and a new translation of Dante's *Inferno*.

STANLEY PLUMLY has published many volumes of poetry, including *Out-of-the-Body Travel* and *Celestial Summer*.

WYATT PRUNTY teaches at the University of the South and directs the Sewanee Writers' Conference. His books of poetry include *What Women Know, What Men Believe*.

LAWRENCE RAAB teaches at Williams College. He has published several books of poetry, including *The Collector of Cold Weather* and *What We Don't Know about Each Other*.

HILDA RAZ edits *Prairie Schooner* and has published several volumes of poetry, including *The Bone Dish*.

PETER SACKS teaches at Johns Hopkins University. His books include *The English Elegy* and *Promised Land*.

IRA SADOFF has published, most recently, *An Ira Sadoff Reader* and *Emotional Traffic*.

SHEROD SANTOS has published, most recently, *The City of Women*.

PETER SCHMITT is the author of *Country Airport* and *Hazard Duty*.

TOM SLEIGH teaches at Dartmouth College and is the author of *After One* and *Waking*.

DAVE SMITH edits *The Southern Review*. His numerous books include *Cuba Nights* and *The Roundhouse Voices*.

ANNE STEVENSON lives in Cambridge, England, and has written numerous books of poetry as well as *Bitter Fame*, a biography of Sylvia Plath. Her *Selected Poems* was recently published.

DABNEY STUART has published many collections of poetry, including *Sweet Lucy Wine* and *Narcissus Dreaming*.

ROBERT SWARD teaches at the University of California at Santa Cruz. He recently published a volume of new and selected poems called *Four Incarnations*.

THOMAS SWISS teaches at Drake University and is the author of *Still Measure*.

STEPHEN TAPSCOTT teaches at M.I.T. and has published numerous books of poetry.

SUE ELLEN THOMPSON is the author, most recently, of *This Body of Silk*.

ERIC TRETHEWEY, who teaches at Hollins College, has published several collections of poetry, including *Dreaming of Rivers*.

CHASE TWICHELL has published several volumes of poetry, including *Perdido*.

RICHARD WILBUR was recently the Poet Laureate of the United States. His *Collected Poems* was recently published.

NANCY WILLARD teaches at Vassar College and is the author of *Things Invisible to See* and *A Nancy Willard Reader*.

MILLER WILLIAMS has published many volumes of poetry and edited several volumes as well.

CLARA YU teaches at Middlebury College, where she directs the summer language school. Her recent book of poems is called *To the Interior.*

PAUL ZIMMER directs the University of Iowa Press. He recently published a volume called *Family Reunion: Selected and New Poems.*

POEM SOURCES

Arnold, Matthew. *Poetical Works*. Edited by C. B. Tinker and H. F. Lowry. London and New York: Oxford University Press, 1950.

Auden, W. H. *Collected Poems*. Edited by Edward Mendelson. New York: Random House, 1976.

Bishop, Elizabeth. *The Complete Poems, 1927–1979*. New York: Farrar, Straus, and Giroux, 1983.

Blake, William. *The Complete Poetry and Prose of William Blake*. Edited by David V. Erdman. Berkeley: University of California Press, 1982.

Browning, Elizabeth Barrett. *Elizabeth Barrett Browning's Sonnets from the Portuguese*. Edited by William S. Peterson. Barre, Mass., and New York: Imprint Society, distributed by Crown Publishers, 1977.

Browning, Robert. *The Poetical Works of Robert Browning*. Edited by Ian Jack and Margaret Smith. Oxford: Clarendon Press, Oxford University Press, 1983.

Burns, Robert. *The Poems and Songs of Robert Burns*. Edited by James Kingsley. Oxford: Clarendon Press, 1968.

Byron, Lord. *The Poetical Works of Lord Byron*. London and New York: Oxford University Press, 1945, 1967 printing.

Chaucer, Geoffrey. *The Complete Poetry and Prose of Geoffrey Chaucer*. Edited by John H. Fisher. New York: Holt, Rinehart and Winston, 1977.

Child, Francis James. *The English and Scottish Popular Ballads*. New York: Folklore Press, 1956.

Clare, John. *Selected Poems and Prose*. Edited by Eric Robinson and Geoffrey Summerfield. London and New York: Oxford University Press, 1967.

Crane, Hart. *The Poems of Hart Crane*. Edited by Marc Simon. New York: Liveright, 1986.

cummings, e. e. *Complete Poems, 1904-1962*. Edited by George J. Firmage. New York: Liveright, 1991.

Dickinson, Emily. *The Complete Poems of Emily Dickinson*. Boston: Little, Brown and Company, 1924.

Donne, John. *The Complete Poems of John Donne*. Edited by Roger E. Bennett. New York: Hendrick House—Farrar, Straus, 1949.

Eliot, T. S. *The Complete Poems and Plays*. New York: Harcourt, Brace, 1952.

Emerson, Ralph Waldo. *Centenary Edition: The Complete Works of Ralph Waldo Emerson*. New York: AMS Press, 1979.

Frost, Robert. *Complete Poems of Robert Frost*. New York: Holt, Rinehart and Winston, 1964.

Greville, Fulke. *Selected Poems of Fulke Greville*. Edited by Thom Gunn. Chicago: University of Chicago Press, 1968.

Hardy, Thomas. *The Complete Poetical Works of Thomas Hardy*. Edited by Samuel Hynes. Oxford: Clarendon Press, Oxford University Press, 1982.

Hayden, Robert. *Collected Poems*. Edited by Frederick Glayshen. New York: Liveright, 1985.

Herbert, George. *The Works of George Herbert*. Edited by F. E. Hutchinson. Oxford: Clarendon Press, 1970.

Housman, A. E. *Complete Poems*. New York: Holt, 1959.

Hughes, Langston. *The Collected Poems of Langston Hughes*. Edited by Arnold Rampersad. New York: Knopf, distributed by Random House, 1994.

Jarrell, Randall. *The Complete Poems*. New York: Farrar, Straus, and Giroux, 1969.

Jonson, Ben. *The Complete Poems*. Edited by George Parfitt. New Haven: Yale University Press, 1982.

Keats, John. *The Complete Poems*. Edited by John Barnard. Hammondsworth, New York: Penguin Books, 1988.

Larkin, Philip. *Collected Poems*. Edited by Anthony Thwaite. New York: Farrar, Straus, and Giroux, 1989.

MacNeice, Louis. *Collected Poems*. Edited by E. R. Dodds. New York: Oxford University Press, 1967.

Marvell, Andrew. *Complete Poetry*. Edited by George de Forest Lord. New York: Random House, 1968.

Millay, Edna St. Vincent. *Collected Poems*. Edited by Norma Millay. New York: Harper, 1956.

Milton, John. *Complete Poetical Works*. Edited by Douglas Bush. Boston: Houghton Mifflin, 1965.

Moore, Marianne. *Collected Poems*. New York: Macmillan, 1951.

Owen, Wilfred. *The Complete Poems and Fragments*. Edited by Jon Stallworthy. New York and London: W. W. Norton, 1984.

Pope, Alexander. *Selected Poetry and Prose*. Edited by William K. Wimsatt. New York: Holt, Rinehart and Winston, 1972.

Raleigh, Sir Walter. *Selected Prose and Poetry*. Edited by Agnes M. C. Latham. London: University of London, Athlone Press, 1965.

Ransom, John Crowe. *Selected Poems*. New York: Knopf, 1969, 1991 printing.

Reed, Henry. *Collected Poems*. Edited by Jon Stallworthy. Oxford and New York: Oxford University Press, 1991.

Robinson, Edwin Arlington. *Selected Poems of Edwin Arlington Robinson*. Edited by Morton Dauwen Zabel. New York and London: Macmillan, Collier Macmillan, 1989.

Roethke, Theodore. *The Collected Poems of Theodore Roethke*. Seattle: University of Washington Press, 1982.

Sexton, Anne. *The Complete Poems*. Boston: Houghton Mifflin, 1981.

Shakespeare, William. *William Shakespeare: The Complete Works*. Edited by Stanley Wells and Gary Taylor. Oxford and New York: Clarendon Press, Oxford University Press, 1986.

Shelley, Percy Bysshe. *Poetical Works of Shelley*. Edited by Thomas Hutchinson. London: Oxford University Press, 1970.

Sidney, Sir Philip. *Selected Poems*. Edited by Katherine Duncan-Jones. Oxford: Clarendon Press, 1973.

Skelton, John. *The Complete English Poems*. Edited by John Scattergood. New Haven: Yale University Press, 1983.

Spenser, Edmund. *The Complete Poetical Works of Edmund Spenser*. Edited by R. E. Neil Dodge. Boston and New York: Houghton Mifflin, 1908.

Stevens, Wallace. *The Collected Poems of Wallace Stevens*. New York: Alfred A. Knopf, 1989.

Sweet, Henry. *Sweet's Anglo-Saxon Reader in Prose and Verse*. Oxford: Clarendon Press, 1975.

Swift, Jonathan. *Jonathan Swift: The Complete Poems*. Edited by Pat Rogers. New Haven: Yale University Press, 1983.

Tennyson, Alfred, Lord. *The Poetical Works of Tennyson*. Edited by G. Robert Strange. Boston: Houghton Mifflin, 1974.

Thomas, Dylan. *The Poems of Dylan Thomas*. Edited by Daniel Jones. New York: New Directions Publishing Corporation, 1971.

Thomas, Edward. *The Collected Poems of Edward Thomas*. Edited by R. George Thomas. Oxford: Clarendon Press, 1978.

Traherne, Thomas. *The Poetical Works of Thomas Traherne*. Edited by Gladys I. Wade. London: P. J. and A. E. Dobell, 1932.

Tuckerman, Frederick Goddard. *Complete Poems*. Edited by N. Scott Momaday. New York: Oxford University Press, 1965.

Whitman, Walt. *Complete Poetry and Collected Prose*. New York: Literary Classics of the United States, distributed by Viking Press, 1982.

Wordsworth, William. *The Complete Poetical Works of Wordsworth.* Edited by Andrew T. George. Boston: Houghton Mifflin, 1932.

Wyatt, Sir Thomas. *Sir Thomas Wyatt: The Complete Poems.* Edited by R. A. Rebholz. New Haven: Yale University Press, 1981.

Yeats, William Butler. *Collected Poems.* London: Pan Books, in association with Macmillan, 1990.

UNIVERSITY PRESS OF NEW ENGLAND publishes books under its own imprint and is the publisher for Brandeis University Press, Dartmouth College, Middlebury College Press, University of New Hampshire, University of Rhode Island, Tufts University, University of Vermont, Wesleyan University Press, and Salzburg Seminar.

Library of Congress Cataloging-in-Publication Data

Touchstones : American poets on a favorite poem / edited by Robert Pack, Jay Parini.
p.   cm. — (A Bread Loaf anthology)
ISBN 0-87451-722-2 (cl : alk. paper). — ISBN 0-87451-723-0 (pa : alk. paper)
1. English poetry—History and criticism.   2. American poetry—History and criticism.   3. Books and reading.   4. American poetry.
5. English poetry.   I. Pack, Robert, 1929- .   II. Parini, Jay.
III. Series.
PR503.T68   1995
821.009—dc20   95-32557
∞